Acclaim for Gore Vidal and

THE LAST EMPIRE

GORE VIDAL

THE LAST EMPIRE

Gore Vidal was born in 1925 at the United States Military Academy at West Point. His first novel, *Williwaw*, written when he was nineteen years old and serving in the Army, appeared in the spring of 1946. Since then he has written twenty-three novels, five plays, many screenplays, short stories, well over two hundred essays, and a memoir.

INTERNATIONAL

Also by Gore Vidal

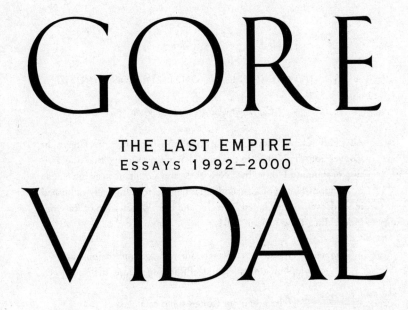

GORE

THE LAST EMPIRE
ESSAYS 1992–2000

VIDAL

VINTAGE INTERNATIONAL
Vintage Books
A Division of Random House, Inc.
New York

FIRST VINTAGE INTERNATIONAL EDITION, JUNE 2002

The Library of Congress has cataloged
the Doubleday edition as follows:
Vidal, Gore, 1925–
The last empire : essays 1992–2000 / Gore Vidal.—1st ed.
p. cm.
I. Title.
PS3543.I26 L37 2001
814'.54—dc21   00-052320
CIP

Vintage ISBN: 0-375-72639-X

Book design by Donna Sinisgalli

www.vintagebooks.com

Printed in the United States of America
10   9   8   7   6

CONTENTS

PART II

PART III

THE LAST EMPIRE

ESSAYS 1992–2000

PART I

EDMUND WILSON:
NINETEENTH-CENTURY MAN

"Old age is a shipwreck." Like many a ground soldier, General de Gaulle was drawn to maritime metaphors. Of course shipwrecks are not like happy families. There is the *Titanic*-swift departure in the presence of a floating mountain of ice, as the orchestra plays the overture from *Tales of Hoffmann*. There is the slow settling to full fathom five as holds fill up with water, giving the soon-to-be-drowned sufficient time to collect his thoughts about eternity and wetness. It was Edmund Wilson's fate to sink slowly from 1960 to June 12, 1972, when he went full fathom five. The last entry in his journal is a bit of doggerel for his wife Elena: "Is that a bird or a leaf? / Good grief! / My eyes are old and dim, / And I am getting deaf, my dear, / Your words are no more clear / And I can hardly swim. / I find this rather grim."

"Rather grim" describes *The Sixties*, Wilson's journals covering his last decade. This volume's editor, Lewis M. Dabney, starts with an epigraph from Yeats's "Sailing to Byzantium," thus striking the valetudinarian note. New Year 1960 finds Wilson at Harvard as Lowell Professor of English. He suffers from angina, arthritis, gout, and hangovers. "*At my age*, I find that I alternate between spells of fatigue and indifference when I am almost ready to give up the struggle, and spells of expanding ambition, when I feel that I can do more than ever before." He is in his sixty-fifth year, a time more usually deciduous than mellowly fruitful. But then he is distracted by the people that he meets and the conversations that he holds, all the while drinking until the words start to come in sharp not always coherent barks; yet the mind is functioning with all its old energy. He is learning Hungarian, as he earlier learned Hebrew and before that Russian, a language whose finer points and arcane nuances he so generously and memorably shared with Vladimir Nabokov, unhinging their friendship in the process.

During his last decade, Wilson published *Apologies to the Iroquois*, a project that he had set himself as, more and more, he came to live in the stone house of his mother's family at Talcottville in upstate New York. Although brought up in New Jersey, Wilson himself was a classic old New York combination of Ulster and Dutch; and so, in a sense, he had come home to die. Also, to work prodigiously. He made his apologies to the Indian tribes that his family, among others, had displaced. In *O, Canada*, he paid belated attention to the large familiar remoteness to the north which he had visited in youth with his father. He wrote book reviews; spent time at Wellfleet where he had a house; visited New York; went abroad to Israel, Hungary.

The decade was made unpleasant by the fact that he had neglected to file an income tax return between the years 1946 and 1955. The Internal Revenue Service moved in. He was allowed a certain amount to live on. The rest went to the Treasury. He was also under a grotesque sort of surveillance. Agents would ask him why he had spent so much money for a dog's cushion. Wilson's response to this mess was a splendid, much ignored polemical book called *The Cold War and the Income Tax*, which he saw as the two sides to the same imperial coin. The American people were kept frightened and obedient by a fear of the Soviet Union, which their government told them was on the march everywhere, as well as by the punitive income tax, which was needed in order to pay for a military machine that alone stood between the cowed people and slavery. It was better, we were warned, to be dead than red—as opposed to just plain in the red.

Maximum income tax in those days was 90 percent. Wilson's anarchic response was later, more slyly, matched by the Reagan backlash; instead of raising money to fight the enemy through taxes, the money was raised through borrowing. The result is that, today, even though we have not only sailed to but made landfall in Byzantium, the economy remains militarized, as Wilson had so untactfully noted. At sixty-eight, his present reviewer's green age, he writes, "I have finally come to feel that this country, whether or not I live in it, is no longer any place for me." Not that he has any other country in view: "I find that I more and more feel a boredom with and scorn for the human race. We have such a long way to go. . . ." He, of course, was a professional signpost, a warning light.

————

Despite boredom and scorn Wilson soldiered on, reading and writing and thinking. He published his most original book, *Patriotic Gore*. He acknowledges a critical biography of him. The book has a preface by a hack of academe who refers to *Patriotic Gore* as a "shapeless hodgepodge." Since remedial reading courses do not exist for the tenured, Wilson can only note that his survey of why North and South fought in the Civil War

> is actually very much organized. . . . I don't think that Moore understands that with such books I am always working with a plan and structure in mind. As a journalist, I sell the various sections to magazines as I can. . . . He is also incorrect in implying, as several other people have, that I studied Hebrew for the purpose of writing on the Dead Sea scrolls. It was the other way around: it was from studying Hebrew that I become curious to find out what was going on in connection with the scrolls.

He ends, nicely, with a list of *errata*, even "though I doubt whether your book will ever get into a second printing."

In the introduction to *Patriotic Gore*, Wilson broods on the self-aggrandizing nature of nation-states, one of which, he is sad to note, is the United States, in all its *un*exceptionalism. Apropos the wars,

> Having myself lived through a couple of world wars, and having read a certain amount of history, I am no longer disposed

to take very seriously the professions of "war aims" that nations make. . . .

We Americans have not yet had to suffer from the worst
of the calamities that have followed on the dictatorships in
Germany and Russia, but we have been going for a long
time now quite steadily in the same direction.

Why did North want to fight South? And why was South willing, so
extravagantly, to die for what Seward had scornfully called their
"mosquito republics"? Through an analysis of the fiction and
rhetoric of the conflict, Wilson presents us with a new view of the
matter while dispensing with received opinion. He also places his
analysis in the full context of the cold war just as it was about to turn
hot in Vietnam. Before anyone knew precisely what our national security state really was, Wilson, thirty years ago, got it right:

The Russians and we produced nuclear weapons to flourish
at one another and played the game of calling bad names
when there had been nothing at issue between us that need
have prevented our living in the same world and when we
were actually, for better or worse, becoming more and more
alike—the Russians emulating America in their frantic in-
dustrialization and we imitating them in our persecution of
non-conformist political opinion, while both, to achieve
their ends, were building up huge governmental bureaucra-
cies in the hands of which the people have seemed helpless.

Predictably, this set off alarm bells. At the Algonquin, May 15, 1962,
Wilson meets Alfred Kazin. "I took Alfred back to a couch and
talked to him about his review of *Patriotic Gore*. He showed a certain indignation over my Introduction: I and my people 'had it
made' and didn't sympathize with the Negroes and people like him,
the son of immigrants, who had found in the United States freedom
and opportunity. He is still full of romantic faith in American ideals
and promises, and it is hard for him to see what we are really doing."

In *Patriotic Gore*, Wilson questioned the central myth of the American republic, which is also, paradoxically, the cornerstone of our subsequent empire—*e pluribus unum*—the ever tightening control from the center to the periphery. Wilson is pre-Lincolnian (or a Lincolnian of 1846). He sees virtue, freedom in a *less* perfect union. Today's centrifugal forces in the former Soviet Union and Yugoslavia he anticipated in *Patriotic Gore* where, through his portraits of various leaders in our Civil War, he shows how people, in order to free themselves of an overcentralized state, are more than willing, and most tragically, to shed patriotic gore.

To be fair, Wilson set off alarm bells in less naive quarters. As one reads reviews of the book by such honorable establishment figures as Henry Steele Commager and Robert Penn Warren one is struck by their defensive misunderstanding not only of his text but of our common state. At times, they sound like apologists for an empire that wants to present itself as not only flawless but uniquely Good. Commager zeroes in on the Darwinian introduction. He notes, as other reviewers do, Justice Holmes's *Realpolitik*: "that it seems to me that every society rests on the death of men." But Commager is troubled that Wilson "does not see fit to quote" the peroration of "The Soldier's Faith," Holmes's memorial address, with its purple "snowy heights of honor" for the Civil War dead. Yet Wilson quotes the crux of Holmes's speech,

> There is one thing that I do not doubt, no man who lives
> in the world with most of us can doubt, and that is that the
> faith is true and adorable which leads a soldier to throw
> away his life in obedience to a blindly accepted duty, in a
> cause which he little understands, in a plan of campaign
> of which he has no notion, under tactics of which he little
> understands.

Surely, that is quite enough patriotic tears for spilled gore.

In 1963, as *pontifex maximus* of the old American republic,

Wilson is speaking out with a Roman hardness and clarity, and sadness at what has been lost since the Union's victory at Appomattox. Our eighteenth-century *res publicus* had been replaced by a hard-boiled soft-minded imperium, ever eager to use that terrible swift sword, presumably for ever, unless, of course, we are struck down by the current great Satan who threatens our lives and sacred honor in the high lands of Somalia. Wilson has no great sentimentality about the Indian-killing, slave-holding founders but he is concerned by the absolute loss of any moral idea other than Holmes's bleakly reductive "every society rests on the death of men." It is not this sad truth that Wilson is challenging, thus causing distress to the apologists of empire; rather it is their clumsy ongoing falsifications of motives, their misleading rhetoric all "snowy heights of honor" (try that one on a Vietnam veteran), their deep complicity in an empire that is now based not only on understandable greed but far worse on a mindless vanity to seem invincible abroad and in full control of all the folks at home. Just as the empire was about to play out its last act in Southeast Asia, Wilson's meditation on the Civil War and war and the nature of our state was published and: "There is shock after shock," as Penn Warren put it, "to our official versions and received opinions." But, surely, shock is what writers are meant to apply when the patient has lost touch with reality. Unhappily, many others are in place to act as shock-absorbers. They also shroud the martyred Lincoln with his disingenuous funeral address at Gettysburg in order to distract attention from the uncomfortable paradox that his dictatorship—forbidden word in a free country—preserved the Union by destroying its soul.

Commager was also dismayed by Wilson's "odd interpretation of World War I—that we were seduced into it by British propaganda, and the assertion that had we but stayed out we could have 'shortened the war and left Europe less shattered and more stable.' Or the astonishing statements that we 'were gradually and *furtively*' brought into World War II by President Roosevelt who 'had been . . . *pretending* . . . that he had not committed himself' [italics mine]." I happen to agree with Wilson but I acknowledge that others hold defensible contrary views. But, surely, Commager might have refrained from *pretending* (italics mine) to be "astonished," even in innocent 1962, at hearing Wilson state views that many others have held about our wars; but then we must recall that both historians were writing not so many months after we had all been assured, most attractively, on a snowy day at the Capitol, that we would bear any burden to make sure that something or other would prevail somehow somewhere and in this process each of us might have the opportunity to become truly adorable.

In these last years Wilson returns to Jerusalem for an update on the Dead Sea Scrolls; he leaves the city on the day before the 1967 war starts. Meanwhile, he revises and reissues earlier books, writes regularly for *The New Yorker* and *The New York Review of Books*; he settles with the IRS largely, one suspects, because he was quirkily honored by President Kennedy at the White House in 1963 with a Freedom Medal. In *Upstate*, Wilson writes that the bureaucracy objected: "When Kennedy saw the man who remonstrated, he said, 'This is not an award for good conduct but for literary merit.'" When Kennedy asked Wilson what *Patriotic Gore* was about, Wilson told him to go read it.

> I have sometimes lately had the impression that my appearance and personality have almost entirely disappeared and that there is little but my books marching through me, the Indian book, the Civil War. They live, I am ceasing to live—But this is partly due to too much drinking, reading and thinking at night. . . .

That he could do all three suggests an oxlike physical structure. Throughout this period as friends die off and new people tend to blur, certain figures keep recurring. There is quite a lot of Auden in and out. Also, Robert Lowell; also, an unlikely but intense friendship with Mike Nichols and Elaine May, who were then enjoying a success with their comic sketches and improvisations in a series of smoky Manhattan caves. Wilson is plainly smitten by Elaine May: "It is a good thing I am too old to fall in love with her. I've always been such easy game for beautiful, gifted women and she is the most so since Mary McCarthy in the thirties. I imagine that she, too, would be rough going."

Anaïs Nin, muse to Henry Miller, Olive Oyl to his Popeye, returns, hustling her jams and jellies. In the forties Wilson had praised her in *The New Yorker*. He had an endearing—to some—habit of falling in love with the work of a woman writer whom he would later want to meet and seduce. Like Montaigne, he thought that a mind and talent of the first order, associated for Montaigne, and, perhaps, for Wilson, only with men, should it be combined with a woman's beauty might produce the perfect other half of Plato's whole, to be desired and pursued with ardor. Sometimes this longing had comic results. Wilson once praised a novel by what he took to be a young woman of the highest sensibility, Isabel Bolton. In due course he contrived to meet her. Bolton was indeed intellectually everything that he had ever desired in a woman. She was also a serene dowager of seventy, disinclined to dalliance.

Ms. Nin was of sterner stuff. In her diaries she is kittenish about Wilson and herself. In life she told me that they had never had an affair, which—in Nin-speak—meant that they did. But he did not do enough for her work and so she wrote bitterly about him in the diaries that she was now preparing for publication. Since the publishers had insisted that she get a written release from each person mentioned, she writes Wilson, who sees her; finds her enchanting. In the next room, her long-suffering husband, Hugo Guiler, is editing a film. "What about?" asks Wilson. "Me," she replies. Then

> she leaned down and put her cheek against mine. She told me that she would send me the first volume of the diary—in which, I believe, I don't appear. . . . I don't know how much her reconciliation and the favorable picture of me may have been due to an eye to publicity on the publication of the diary. . . . She gave me a copy of her last book, *Col-*

lages, and told me it was her first "funny" book. It is actually not much different from her others: stories about exquisite women told by an exquisite woman.

Later Wilson reads her account of him: "she found me aggressive, arrogant, authoritative, like a Dutch burgher in a Dutch painting, and with shoes that were too big. She had become frightened of me and had had to escape. . . . I made her correct a few details about Mary [McCarthy] and a few characteristic inaccuracies. She had said that I had given her a set of Emily Brontë—as if there could be such a thing, actually it was Jane Austen—and she had been offended and sent it back—which was not true, she had kept it."

The relationship between Wilson and Elena, his wife, is occasionally stormy: she prefers her Wellfleet garden and Manhattan to rough Talcottville. Wilson's description of a dinner at the Kennedy White House shows him at his journalistic best and Elena, his handsome German-Russian fourth wife, at her most grand. Wilson's cold eye analyzes her, too. "I had never before been with her anywhere remotely resembling a court, and wasn't prepared for her stiffening attitude. The first sign of this was her 'squeamishness,' as she calls it—this Russian groping for *brezglivost* . . . in the presence of Tennessee Williams—after all he had been in our house at Wellfleet," but, as they stood in line behind Williams, Elena tells Wilson in Russian that she "feels such physical repulsion that she . . . cannot stand to be near him." One would like to think that this was due to his drunkenness.

James Baldwin, as writer and as a black, appeals to both of them. He makes a successful visit to Talcottville. Wilson thought him "one of the best writers that we have," though "when Elena left the table to go into the kitchen, he turned on his adjectival 'fucking' like the people in his novel. . . . I have been wondering whether ordinary people really talked to one another in that way now. I reflected, after seeing later in New York Albee's play *Who's Afraid of Virginia Woolf?*, whether most of the dirty language in fiction and on stage didn't occur in the work of homosexuals? Albee, Tennessee Williams, Isherwood, Baldwin, Genet, and the beatniks Ginsberg and Burroughs." Actually, this is off-the-wall. A degree of candor about same-sexuality is the most that these writers have in common. Four-letter words seldom occur in Tennessee's "poetic" dialogue, nor do they in Isherwood or even in Genet except when he is rendering underworld argot where such words are a normal part of speech. Actually "fuck" entered the general language as ubiquitous epithet thanks to World War II, in which 13 million Americans served. If Wilson had bothered to read *The Naked and the Dead* or *From Here to Eternity* he would have noted the sea-change in language from Hemingway and Dos Passos to our time. But then he liked to say that he himself was a man of the nineteenth century.

Wilson writes apropos Elena's "theory that Jews are bitterly jealous of the attention that Baldwin and others are directing towards the Negroes":

> I did not take this seriously at first, but I now think there's something in it: Podhoretz's article in *Commentary* about his having been persecuted in his childhood by the Negroes, Lillian Hellman's play with its white boy who champions the Negroes, then is robbed by the Negro to whom he has been making an impassioned speech. Elena's conversation . . . with the young Jewish Greek teacher from Brandeis—when Elena asked this young man if he had heard Baldwin's lecture at Brandeis, he had answered certainly not: he had been to school with Baldwin. The Negroes were inferior, they had never produced anything. Why associate with them, or bother about them? They were making capital out of their sufferings, but the Jews had suffered much more. One does get the impression that the Jews regard themselves as having a monopoly on suffering, and do not want the Negroes to muscle in.

Wilson's eye is not only on the great of the world but on those who attract him as well, like Mary Pcolar, who lives in the Talcottville region; she is married with two children and holds various jobs that he describes with Balzacian precision. He is sexually drawn to her but notes his debility in these matters; nothing much happens but then, unlike in the early journals with their sexual graphicness, Wilson seems unable to perform the act to which he had devoted so much time in the past—not to mention so many words; yet, every now and then, oddly there will be a description of a sudden lust for Elena which ends in a successful coupling despite "half-mast" erections.

I suspect that future literary chronicles will find it odd that the generation of Wilson and Miller and Williams and McCarthy—names more or less taken at random—should have felt duty-bound to tell us at length exactly what they did or tried to do in bed. The effect is sometimes bracing, like reading a good description of applied physics, say, but it is never erotic. The thought of Wilson in the act is profoundly depressing. D. H. Lawrence—first in this field?— is not much better in his fictive renderings. On the other hand James Boswell delights us with his drunken swoops on complaisant chambermaids, and his poxy member takes on a plangent life of its own: one responds to its rises and falls as one never does to the clinical Wilson's plumbing.

Wilson enjoys Auden's company; Auden's unremitting pedantry matches his own. When they met it was to exchange lectures until, with alcohol, Wilson would start barking and Auden mumbling and wheezing.

Wystan tends nowadays to plug with me that we both belong to the professional middle class, who are the pillars of civilization. There was, he thought, no distinction [in the United States] between professional people and those in trade. . . . I said that when I was in college, there *had* been a marked distinction and this surprised him. He asked me whether it wasn't true that I never felt myself inferior to anybody. I told him that in my youth I had rather resented the millionaires. I think that he himself had actually resented

being looked down upon as a doctor's son. . . . He said that
he *had* regretted not having been sent to Eton.

Auden complains to Wilson that critics never note his mastery of the
technicalities of verse.

> For example, nobody had mentioned in writing about his
> last book that it contained a poem in stanzas. I said that
> I thought William Carlos Williams had ruined American
> poetry by leading most of the poets to give up verse
> altogether and lapse into "shredded prose." He said he
> didn't care about the early Williams but that he had learned
> something from the later Williams. I said I couldn't see
> any influence. "It's there." "What do you mean?" "Techni-
> cally." "How?" "Length of lines." I still don't know what he
> meant.

Glumly Wilson notes, "The last lusts gutter out." He concludes
man-woman sex is nothing to fuss about. "Yet homosexuals don't
seem to have flowered and borne fruit, don't seem to have fully matured. Auden with his appetite for Tolkien." Surely, Auden's poetry
is . . . well, one of the fine mature fruits of this century while a liking for Tolkien can be philological as well as infantile.

What Wilson maintains to the end is a clear eye for what is in
front of him, whether a text or a person. Great critics do not expli-
cate a text; they describe it and then report on what they have described, if the description itself is not the criticism. Some of his
reports—or even asides—make sense where most readers make none
or nonsense. A friend

> had just read Tolstoy's *Death of Ivan Ilyich*, which had made
> a great impression on him. I do not care for this story as
> much as many people do. I don't believe that a man like
> Ivan Ilyich could ever look back on his life and find it empty
> and futile; I don't believe that Tolstoy, in the period when

he was writing his great novels, would ever have invented such a character.

This is simply put; it is also, simply, true. Ivan Ilyich would not have regarded his past life as empty and futile any more than Edmund Wilson, despite his aches and pains, could ever have found his life anything but fascinating and full, as through him marched the Iroquois, the protagonists of the Civil War, the Dead Sea Scrolls, recollections of Daisy and Hecate County, *Axel's Castle* and *To the Finland Station*, as well as these journals—first begun at Box Hill in Surrey, close to the small chalet where the great lost poet-novelist George Meredith wrote "half a dozen great novels."

The editor, Mr. Dabney, notes, I think correctly, that Wilson in his journals "was creating an art of portraiture in the tradition of Dr. Johnson, Taine and Sainte-Beuve." He is certainly at his best when he turns the lights on a literary figure whom he knows and then walks, as it were, all around him. He mentions occasionally that he is reading Jules Renard's journals; it is a pity that Wilson has none of that journalist's aphoristic wit. But he might have said, with Renard, "Be interesting! Be interesting! Art is no excuse for boring people," not to mention "I was born for successes in journalism, for the daily renown, the literature of abundance; reading great writers changed all that. That was the misfortune of my life." But their misfortune is our good fortune. They existed to give the dull a glimpse of unsuspected worlds hidden in the one that we daily look at. One admires in Wilson what he admired in Parkman, "the avoidance of generalization, the description of the events always in concrete detail. The larger tendencies are shown by a chronicle of individualized persons and actions. It is what I try to do myself." Successfully, one might add. In the four-volume *Literary Criticism: A Short History* (1957), by W. K. Wimsatt, Jr., and Cleanth Brooks, the *Almanach da Gotha* of critics, Wilson is cited in *three* footnotes. Three! Fame!

The New York Review of Books
4 November 1993

DAWN POWELL:
QUEEN OF THE GOLDEN AGE

In November 1987, after a year of reading the published works of Dawn Powell (1897–1965), I published my findings in *The New York Review of Books*.* There is now a somewhat blurred perception that she was always very much on the minds of such exciting critics and taste-makers as James Wolcott and John Updike, and that I had simply leapt onto a merrily moving bandwagon. Actually, all her books were out of print and her name was known only to those of us whose careers had overlapped hers. In the twenty-two years that had passed since her death, she had been thoroughly erased, as original writers so often are, in the United States of Amnesia. But then she had never had much success in her lifetime either. She was a wit, a satirist, and a woman, a combination that did not enchant the bookchatterers of that era. Worst of all, *she did not affirm warm mature family values.* She herself was the principal third of an interesting *ménage à trois* in Greenwich Village; the other two thirds were her lifelong (*his* life long) husband, Joseph Gousha, and Coburn Gilman, a man about town and sometime magazine editor. All three were serious drinkers but then so was everyone else in those days when she could (with no irony) write a book about Manhattan and call it *The Happy Island.*

Since my description of Powell's fifteen novels, she is now almost entirely in print, here and abroad, and some of her work is even, as she would say, compost for movies and television. As I con-

* *The New York Review of Books*, November 5, 1987.

template Dawn's posthumous victory, I feel incredibly smug. With sufficient diligence, bookchat *can* serve a purpose, indeed its only proper purpose: to persuade the few remaining voluntary readers to turn to a writer whom they have never heard of because authority for so long either ignored or disapproved of her. If I sound unduly proprietary, I am. Also, I liked not only the Powell novels but Dawn herself. ("Yes, I know I have the name of an unsuccessful stripper. It is my strong suit.") She was the best company in the world, with a fine savage wit, "that Irish strain in me." Now one Tim Page has taken on Powell's case and he is busy editing and republishing her work, most lately the diaries that she kept off and on from 1931 to her death in 1965, aged sixty-eight. He has, he tells us, "algebraically tightened many of the entries." Personally, I would have plane geometrically loosened them but then I am old school and would have kept some of the drunken entries. She is, he tells us, "one hell of a writer," the ultimate canonical praise from the likes of John Crowe Ransom and the New Critics of yesteryear. But so she is, Tim, so she is.

Biographical data: Powell was born at Mount Gilead, Ohio. Shunted about from relative to relative. Obliged to amuse the unamusable. When wicked stepmother destroys her writing, Dawn flees home. Works as a waitress. Eventually graduates from Lake Erie College and heads for New York City, where she writes anything to live. But always remains a novelist, writing either of her Ohio home, always further and further away, or tales of Manhattan life.

Now the diaries. For me, it is like having her back to life—very small, very plump—seated at a banquette in the Blue Angel, a long thin shiny black-walled night club, known to our friend John Latouche (of whom more later) as Juliet's Tomb, and presided over by its owner, Herbert Jacoby, a somber Frenchman who would introduce each comedy act with a melancholy sigh and then turn from Imogene Coca, let us say, with a look of absolute despair. Meanwhile, Dawn would be knocking back fiery waters and the wit would start to rise. It should be noted that she never complained to friends of her ongoing ill health, her retarded son, or chronic poverty. But occasionally in the diary she gives it to Fate for what Fate has done to her; yet at the end, she did have a degree of success with her last (and perhaps best) novels, *The Golden Spur* and *The Wicked Pavilion*. Astonishingly, she was nominated for a literary prize. She notes: "Will success spoil Dawn Powell? I don't see why not. I'm no better than anybody else, never said so." She failed to get the award.

Although Dawn was admired as a writer and bright companion by such contemporaries as Hemingway and Dos Passos, it was Edmund Wilson who helped her most, if a bit too late in the game. When finally he praised her in *The New Yorker*, he failed to elevate her to those heights where the important lady writers sunned themselves or, as Dawn characterized one lady writer with inherited money, "as she doesn't work for her success, therefore has it, along with prestige, handed to her on a silver platter with warning to God, 'Right Side Up.'" In 1934 she contemplates three fashionables of the day: Nancy Hale, Louise Bogan, Kay Boyle:

> I was impressed with how women now made their art serve their female purpose whereas once it warred with their femininity. Each page is squirming with sensitivity, every line—no matter how well disguised the heroine is—coyly reveals her exquisite taste, her delicate charm, her never-at-a-disadvantage body (which of course she cares nothing about and is always faintly amused at men's frenzies over her perfect legs, breasts, etc.). What gallantry, what equalness to any situation in the home, the camp, the yacht, the trenches, the dives—what *aristocrats* these women writers are, whose pen advertises the superiority of their organs. Fit companions and opposites of the he-man writers—Hemingway, Burnett, Cain—imitation he-manners whose words tersely proclaim their masculinity, every tight-lipped phrase shows the author's guts, his decency, his ability to handle any situation—insurrection (he is an instinctive leader or else too superior to show it), shipwreck, liquor, women.

Through the words shot out of the typewriter clip-clip one watches the play of his muscles; one sighs to lay one's head upon that hairy shoulder.

"Started job with Paramount doing over 'Quarantine' at $1000 a week." *Plus ça change*, as they say at the Beaux Arts. Dawn found the girls every bit as hilarious as the boys. This even-handedness is not the surest path to popularity.

"Happiness as a rule brings out the worst in people's characters. No longer afraid, they radiantly flaunt their smugness, small vices and worst sentimentalities. . . . Happiness has given [X] a sword; respectability has given her the right to be stupid." Although many of Dawn's novels deal with "career" women in New York who need each other for company between marriages and love affairs, Dawn is constantly suspicious of girlfriends. "Always be kind to strangers," she told Elaine Dundy at my house when they first met. "It's the friends to beware of." In the diaries she notes: "I am perpetually surprised at my own stupidity about women and cannot really blame men for the same lack of perception." But Dawn, though stringent, lacks all malice even when she zeroes in on someone she truly dislikes. She does a splendid send-up of Clare Boothe Luce, in *A Time to Be Born*, which "I have been denying for years . . . I insist it was a composite (or compost) but then I find a memo from 1939—'Why not do novel on Clare Luce?' Who can I believe—me or myself?"

There are few intimate revelations in the diaries. There is a hint that she and the Communist playwright John Howard Lawson once had an affair but one doubts that with the other points to her triangle— Joe and Coby—they would have bothered much about sex when wit and work and the company of each other and the passing parade of the Village was more than enough to occupy them. One is astonished at the amount of work that Dawn was obliged to do in order to pay for the institutionalized son, with not much help from Joe, himself feckless in money matters. She even made an obligatory trip or two to Hollywood to write for movies. Of Hollywood: "The climate picks you up and throws you down in the most amazing way." That was about it. She endures a production or two in the theater, dealing, usually unhappily, with the Group Theater and the Theater Guild. Except for Robert Lewis, a director very much on her wavelength, Dawn found the Strasbergs and Clurmans and Crawfords pretty lethal in their egotism and pomposity while actors regard "the author and his work as nasty stumbling blocks between them and the public." She was a good comic playwright who had the bad luck to fall into the hands of the Group Theater at its most didactic. After she saw what they had done to one of her plays, she hoped that they would get their heavy hands on Shaw and Pirandello and reduce those masters to agit-prop sermonizers.

Quite by chance, Dawn was at the center of the American Communist world. Friends of all sorts figure on the left, including a wealthy woman called Margaret de Silver, mistress of the Italian antifascist (and later murdered) Carlo Tresca. It was De Silver who came to Dawn's aid when she and Joe had been literally evicted from their apartment and left, along with their furniture, on the sidewalk. De Silver promptly created a trust fund for the retarded son. Dawn herself was apolitical. "Roosevelt dies" is a single entry in the diary: that was that.

In 1931 Dawn met Edmund Wilson and they remained friends, with the odd up and down, for thirty-four years. Lately, Wilson is being mysteriously attacked by peripheral literary folk as a drunken bully and general lout. It is true that the MLA disliked him as much as he did them, but at least there are good reasons on both sides, which he spelled out in a splendid work of demolition.* The current attacks on Wilson may simply be dismissed as "mere English": unfocused malice, combined with a well-earned sense of inferiority when faced with any powerful wide-ranging mind.

---

* "The Fruits of the MLA: I. Their Wedding Journey" (*The New York Review,* September 26, 1968); "II. Mark Twain" (October 10, 1968).

It seems unlikely that Dawn was one of the *femmes fatales des lettres* of the sort that Wilson was often drawn to. Two brilliant, tubby little creatures, deeply involved in literature of every kind, were bound to be companions rather than lovers. She made him laugh. He made her think. Sometimes it was the other way around, which could make him irritable; and make her sharp. Wilson was a man of the previous century and the idea of a brilliant woman as an equal was always intriguing (he married one, after all, Mary McCarthy, and duly suffered) but somehow against nature. On the other hand, he was that unusual phenomenon, the born teacher who never stops learning new things about everything, from the Iroquois Indians to the intricacies of Hungarian grammar. Inevitably their interests often overlapped (though not I suspect on the Iroquois).

March 23, 1943: "Reading for the first time a fine book (Flaubert's *Sentimental Education*) I am again impressed by the importance of satire as social history and my theory that what reviewers call satire is 'whimsy' and what they call realism is romanticism. . . . The only record of a civilization is satire—Petronius, Aristophanes, Flaubert." April 2: "Cocktails with Bunny [Edmund Wilson]. . . . I find Bunny a great devotee of [*Sentimental Education*], though he feels it loses in translation, being, like poetry, built on the cadences of its own language. . . ." Wilson then tells her that, from his own journal, he is about to extract " 'the greatest love story ever written' in pornographic detail. . . . It was exhilarating to spend time again with a sharp, creative literary mind, a balance so necessary in the hoodlum world I live in."

But there are clouds: Wilson wrote her a letter "depressing in its way. Men really dislike a literary woman (especially if she is good) and prefer not reading works of their women friends, hoping and even saying that they must be bad." She was distressed at Wilson's dim review of her best Ohio novel, *My Home Is Far Away*: "It is very discouraging to have someone (who actually has told me I'm infinitely better than John Marquand and equal to Sinclair Lewis at his best) do me so much genuine damage. I have enough damage done me already, merely by the desire to write. . . ."

By 1945 Dawn is seriously on the warpath: "All relations with Bunny are dictated by him—he is the one to name the hour, the place, the subject of conversation. . . . He is mystified and annoyed by the simple process of creation; he is furious at the things he does not understand—furious, blind and bored. What he does not understand is all life that is not in print. . . . He wants to see his ladies alone so he can attack them . . . [tell] them that everything they like is impossible. . . . He beams with joy and well-nourished nerves as he leaves, like a vampire returning from a juicy grave."

But there were autumnal joys between the old friends. Wilson's daughter, Rosalind, has said that of all the guests who stayed at Wilson's family place in upstate New York, only Dawn knew how to sit comfortably on the porch and do nothing but watch people pass. As Dawn remarks, "Bunny, Dos [Passos], etc., are so completely selfish that they allow it in others." There is one splendid drunken quarrel in a cab: Dawn blasted Bunny's wife Elena as a social climber, which, as Dawn promptly notes, "all this wrong, because [the previous wife] Mary McCarthy was the climber. . . . Sudden silence in cab as I raged, then Bunny said 'I wish you weren't so jealous of me, Dawn. It makes it very hard for you.' This was a wonderful switch, which I snatched at and said, 'It's because you keep me on that little back street and never let me meet your set and you're always going back to your wife and I have never seen you except when you're in town selling—' 'Yes I know it's been hard on you, dear,' he said. So we were saved from a real embarrassment." (For those who don't recognize the powerful scene they played, it is from the great best-seller of the day *Back Street* by Fannie Hurst.)

Next day I was ashamed but hardly could call and apologize for murder. So I sent wire to him—"Darling, what happened to us? Was it my money or your music? Was it the Club? Where did we go wrong, dear? Aurore." Today a postcard from him says 'Dear Aurore. Perhaps it might be as well for us not to see each other for awhile. The strain of our relationship is becoming difficult. I am leaving for Boston tomorrow. *Mille baisers*—Raoul."

They also conducted a correspondence in which she was the lofty Mrs. Humphrey Ward and he a seedy academic called Wigmore.

"There are so many kinds of fame for a writer that it is astonishing the number of us who never achieve one." A lifetime of near-misses depressed but did not discourage her. Also, the examination of such monsters as her friend Hemingway made her suspect that the first requisite of earthly glory was a total lack of humor or (the same thing?) self-knowledge. "I tried once again to read *Farewell to Arms* and it seems as clumsily written as ever to me. . . ." Of the protagonist of *For Whom the Bell Tolls*: "a fictional movie hero in Spain with the language neither Spanish nor English. When someone wishes to write of this age—as I do and have done—critics shy off—the public shies off. 'Where's our Story Book?' they cry. . . . This is obviously an age that Can't Take It." Dawn's conclusion is that "Success is a knack—like a knack for weaving something out of a few strings—which for the rest of us are nothing but a few strings." Nor was she about to ingratiate herself with book reviewers like the *New York Herald Tribune*'s Lewis Gannett, as serenely outside literature as his confrère in the daily *New York Times*, Orville Prescott, currently divided into two halves of equally bewildered density.

At Margaret's Lewis Gannett flung an affectionate arm around me and introduced me: "Dawn's a good girl except she drinks too much and one of these days she's going to do a good novel." "If I did, you wouldn't know it," I said. "As for drinking too much you've never seen me at these parties in the last five years where you were drinking more than anyone. That's why you can never be a writer or know good writing when you see it—generalizing about a person's habits from public performances instead of private understanding." He was mad. I lectured him that if ever I wrote something he considered "good" I would know I was slipping. "*Pas des mouches sur* Dawn," as Raoul would say.

But then, "All my life has been spent killing geese that lay golden eggs and it's a fine decent sport—superior to killing small birds, horses or lions."

It was Dawn Powell's fate to be a dinosaur shortly after the comet, or whatever it was, struck our culture, killing off the literary culture—a process still at work but no less inexorable—and replacing it with the Audiovisual, as they say at Film School. The Hemingway, Faulkner, Fitzgerald, Dreiser, and Powell American generation was the last to be central to the culture of that part of the world where Gutenberg reigned. By the next generation, it was clear to most of us that the novel had been superseded by the film while popular writing of the sort Dawn was reduced to turning out— stories and serials for slick mass magazines—has, in the last four decades, been replaced by television sitcoms and miniseries. Today few magazines publish fiction of any kind. Few people read fiction of any kind other than what those chains of bookshops in the bright malls of America feel that the mallsters are capable of grasping, which is not very much beyond thinly disguised stories about show-biz celebrities, competing with tell-all biographies or autobiographies of the few people that television has acquainted our unread public with. For Dawn Powell's generation, there was still the romantic, if somewhat sappy, notion of The Great American Novel that someone was bound to write—and altogether too many people did write. You were, if serious, a writer for life, with an ever-growing public if you were any good.

All that changed in the Fifties. Writers can still be minor celebrities, good to flesh out a talk show if they can be counted on not to say anything of interest. But the writer as definer of the prospect has no role at all in the "first world." Our serious writers teach other serious writers who in turn teach *them* in classrooms. But for the bright inventive woman who kept these diaries the scene was no different from what it was for George Sand—a novel one year, a play the next year, and a life in the stream of her time. When she noted that the reader wants his simple-minded Story Book, she had not realized that the story had already started its leap from dull page to bright moving picture, and when she mourned that this is the age that Can't Take It, she is quite right except that she thought the "it" was realistic observation—satire—that they couldn't take when the "it" they can't, and won't, take is literature itself.

The New York of the Golden Age (1945–1950—the only period when we were not kept at war) glitters in her diary, as she reflects on all sorts of wonders and novelties and even genius. Among the wonders was John Latouche, a short chunky Irish wit (with the obligatory Jewish mother). Although himself an outlander from Virginia he was, like Dawn herself, the personification of Manhattan, particularly its nightside, when ten thousand musicians in dives played songs for which he had written the lyrics—"Taking a Chance on Love," "Cabin in the Sky," "Lazy Afternoon" (written at my house on the Hudson one hot summer day). Latouche talked and talked and kept everyone excited and laughing. It was he who first told me of a writer with the unlikely name Dawn Powell; she had just written a novel called *The Locusts Have No King*. I met Dawn with him. They looked alike except that he had bright blue eyes in his disproportionately large head, while hers were, I think, brown.

> Latouche came out Saturday and Sunday and left me exhausted. He is so multi-gifted that he seems to leave people as worn as if they'd been to a circus, and while he shoots sparks in all directions, in the end it is the others who are depleted and he is renourished. . . . It is unconsciously deliberate on his part. He wants people not-to-do, just as he doesn't-do. He likes their doing well—no envy there—but it's actual *doing* he minds.

When, to survive, I wrote a dozen plays for live television in one year, Latouche was deeply saddened. "Whoever suspected that you would end up as the Lope de Vega of television?"

> March 11, 1954: Latouche's *Golden Apple* opened at Phoenix—thoroughly fresh and delightful. At end, saw him by stairs in middle of cheers. He was weeping. "They've ruined my second act—they've ruined it—spoiled everything! Come downstairs and have champagne!" Down was a vast Sardi's. Gore Vidal—Luciferian-looking young man who called a couple of times. Very gifted, brilliant, and fixed in facility as I am.

Thus, I first appear in her diaries: and though we saw each other far too seldom, the condition of an active life in the golden age, she—like Touche—made the weather for us all or, as she put it, "The way Latouche and I always knocked ourselves out to entertain morons. The more useless and blah they were, the harder we worked for their amusement—as if they were such a waste that only by converting these ciphers into something (in fact nothing more than audience) could they be endured."

Then the memorable August 7, 1956: "Latouche died!—in Calais, Vermont. Luckily his opera 'Baby Doe' had been a great peak last month in Central City, a peak he might not pass. Incredible that this dynamo should unwind and I think I can guess how. Talentless but shrewd users pursued him always . . . trying to get him in a corner room, lock him up and get out the gold when he wanted only to talk all day and all night. . . . I'm sure this was a desperate, hysterical escape from Lillian Hellman and others waiting for his output to finish up *Candide*." He was thirty-nine.

In later years Dawn reviewed books, shrewdly if somewhat wearily, in *Mademoiselle*. Although like every regular reviewer she was pretty much stuck with the daily output (Capote? "The Southern white trash and *crème de menthe* school as against the old mint julep school") but her own views on literature, particularly the superiority of Petronian satire to everything else in the prose line, are interesting. " 'Realism' is the only completely vague word. 'Satire' is the technical word for writing of people as they are: 'romantic' the other extreme of people as they are to themselves—but both of these are the truth. The ability to put in motive is called satire; the ability to put in vision is romanticism." She duly noted that the rich and the poor could be satirized with impunity (because they were—then—so few and never read books?) but "The middle class is wit-proofed. . . . If there is to be satire it must not bite at the bread-winner." And "the human comedy is always tragic but since its ingredients are always the same—dupe, fox, straight, like burlesque skits—the repetition through the ages is comedy."

Powell seems to have got the point to Edith Wharton long before others did. In 1951, "Read Edith Wharton's *The Reef* and struggling with *Wings of the Dove* by James simultaneously. Curiously alike, but she is so superior in this. Odd, her reputation for 'moralizing novels' when it was her *age* which read its own moralizing into her. Not one word could be called moralizing—no villains, no heroes in the noble sense. Villainy is done by a group of characters behaving in the only way they, in all honesty, feel they can decently behave. . . . I must write to Sophy Viner, I woke up thinking. I must tell her—tell her what? She never existed. What a precise miracle of illusion Edith Wharton created—never showing Sophy's room, giving her only one dress, one cloak, describing her only as fresh-faced—but she is *real*."

Dawn is very much on to Mary McCarthy: "Read Mary McCarthy's piece—another beginning of novel. . . . These last two starts are invigorating—like a brisk whiff of the stable on a clear wintry day. She has her two manners—her lace-curtain Irish, almost unbelievably genteel lady scholar torn between desire to be Blue Stocking without losing her Ladyship; and then her shanty Irish where she relaxes, whamming away at her characters like a Queen of the Roller

Derby, groin-kicking, shin-knifing, belly-butting, flailing away with skates and all arms at her characters and jumping on them with a hoarse whoop of glee when they are felled."

Finally, she comes to James through that curiously enchanting nouvelle *The Reverberator*, so prescient in its grasp of the general horror of publicity at the dawn of the age of the tabloid newspapers. "James's work nearly always stirs the writing imagination. Some object to 'involuted writing,' 'obtuseness'—but none of this is irrelevant. He is like a sculptor in wood, chopping his own trees, hacking and sawing to get to the exact core of his design, examining each branch and bit of sap for its effect on the inner meat. He is after his story for truth's sake, not yours. He is not a tailor, whipping up a pretty costume for your delight. Authors have been stealing his plots for years not because they are inventions (which always wear out with me) but because they are imperishable human truths. That is why he is caviar for the wise and old and experienced—nothing false."

A few months before death, Dawn wrote a definite non-Valentine to the rising generation of American writers.

Most important thing for novelist is curiosity and how curious that so many of them lack it. They seem self-absorbed, family-absorbed, success-absorbed, but the new social-climbing writer professes indifference to the couple across the aisle, the noise from the next apartment—as if a gentleman does not concern himself with things not his business.

I contend that a writer's business is minding other people's business. . . . The new writers disdain human curiosity; they wish only to explore and describe their own psyches; they are too egotistical and snobbish to interest themselves in neighbors. The urge to write now is no longer the love of storytelling or even the love of applause for a neat turn or dramatic twist. It is the urge to show off, the author as hero is a big sex success and leaves them gasping. The book's drive is only the desire to strip the writer's remembered woes and wrongs and show his superiority to the reader—not to communicate with him or entertain.

Since then, of course, text and context have been replaced by Theory, and Author—he dead. Dawn, if alive, would have been one of the first to make it to the Internet as rollicking Queen of the Cyber Punks, carefully digging potholes in the Information Highway.

In 1962 Joe Gousha dies, painfully, of cirrhosis. Dawn writes: "As for his death, this is a curious thing to say but after 42 years of life together—much of it precarious and crushing—we have been through worse disasters together, and I'm sure Joe would feel the same way about me." The next-to-last entry in the diaries records that "Bunny came in": Raoul faithful to the end to his Aurore. She died November 14, 1965, at St. Luke's Hospital. "I cannot exist without the oxygen of laughter," she wrote not long before the end. One might add that those who can (or must) exist without are—what else?—a sad lot.

The New York Review of Books
21 March 1996

By 1946 I had spent three years in the army, where the name of the daily *New York Times* book reviewer, Orville Prescott, struck not a bell, while, to the few who were literary-minded, Edmund Wilson meant everything. Wilson was The American Critic whose praise—or even attention—in *The New Yorker* meant earthly glory for a writer. When my first novel was published, I realized that he no longer bothered much with current novels or new writers. Although politely loyal to commercialite friends like Charles Jackson and Edwin O'Connor, he was now working up large subjects—most lately the suppurating wound of Philoctetes, the necessary archer. Also, he was known to have a not-so-secret passion for beautiful young women who wrote beautiful young prose that he might nurture with his generous praise and gentle advice (" 'i' before 'e' except after 'c,' dearest") and, indeed, if he could hack it, actual presence in their lives should the dice so fall. Even so, one still hoped. In my case, in vain—snake eyes.

It was the prissy Orville Prescott who praised me while Mr. Wilson astonished everyone that season with a Pythian ode to a beautiful young woman called Isabel Bolton, whose first book, *Do I Wake or Sleep*, he hailed as "school of Henry James . . . the device of the sensitive observer who stands at the center of the action and through the filter of whose consciousness alone the happenings of the story reach us . . . a voice that combines, in a peculiar way, the lyric with the dry; and is exquisitely perfect in accent; every syllable falls as it should. . . ." A star was born.

A comic legend was also born. Wilson, ravished by the beauty of Bolton's prose, hoped that its creator was equally beautiful and so . . . Well, Wilson was very much school of Montaigne. Like Montaigne, he was not exactly misogynistic but he felt that the challenge of another male mind was the highest sort of human exchange while possession of a beautiful woman was also of intense importance to him. Could the two ever be combined—the ultimate soulmate? Montaigne thought that if women endured the same education and general experience as men they would probably be no different and so intellectual equality might be achieved. But he gave no examples. By Wilson's time, many women had been similarly educated and luminous feminine minds—chock-a-block with *pensées*—were very much out there. But what about . . . well, to be blunt, Beauty? Could Mind as well as Beauty be found in one person?

Wilson's lifelong quest led him into some strange culs-de-sac. The strangest of all must have been when he discovered that Isabel Bolton—name deliberately reminiscent of Isabel Archer?—was, in reality, a majestic granddame of sixty-three, born Mary Britton Miller in 1883 at New London, Connecticut.

> Only five minutes, so legend goes, after my sister. This participation in identical twinship is the most valuable experience of my life. . . . Both of my parents died of pneumonia and within an hour of each other in the fourth year of my life. . . . In my fourteenth year my twin sister was drowned. After this there seems to be a kind of blotting out of life—everything became dim, unreal, artificial.

Perfunctory attendance at a boarding school. A well-off family made travels in Europe possible. "Three years in Italy were of profound importance. In 1911 New York became my permanent home."

As Miller, she published a half-dozen unmemorable works. Then, in 1946, she recreated herself under another name; and entered her kingdom. Wilson's was the first fanfare for a woman who was to write a half-dozen more novels of which two are as distinguished as her "first" (the three are now collected in *New York Mosaic*). Bolton died in 1979 at ninety-two, productive almost to the end. As practically nothing is now known of her, editor Doris Grumbach does her best with the odd facts: Bolton came from a "good" family; had two close lady friends; lived in pre-1914 Europe and then Manhattan. Attended the Writers' Colony at Yaddo. Died in Greenwich Village at 81 Barrow Street, not far from where Wilson's jolliest muse, Dawn Powell, lived. The rest is, so far, silence, secret—Sapphic?

So little is known of Bolton that one does not know if she and Wilson ever met. But I am fairly certain he saw to it that they did. A meeting only the prose of Henry James could have risen to, unlike the equally great Edith Wharton, who might have fallen upon it with terrible rending eagle's swoop:

> There had been—one wondered not so idly why—no photograph or other rendering of likeness or, even, dislikeness, on the homely paper "jacket" that embraced the ever, to Wilson, with each passing day, more precious volume, the distilled essence of all feminine beauty and sensibility, quite overpowering in its effect upon his perhaps too febrile adhesive system for which the names so boldly yet, by some magical art, demurely printed on this very same "jacket" convey to him the physical beauty of the divine girl who had "cut to roundness and smoothed to convexity a little crystal of literary form that concentrates the light like a burning glass"—his very own words in his *devoir* for *The New Yorker*, written with so much pounding of the heart as, to put it in a plain and vulgar fashion, a cry from that never *not* susceptible heart—in short, a love letter to the unknown girl—surely, a girl of genius rather than a woman like his handsome, brilliant, but—well, *incendiary* (literally) wife, Mary McCarthy, who had recently, when he had withdrawn

to his study and locked the door, slipped under that same door a single sheet of paper deliberately set aflame in order to smoke him, as it were, from his lair, all the while shouting in a powerful voice, not so much golden as a reverberating cymbal of purest brass, "Fuck you." The plangent voice resounded even now, unpleasantly, in his mind, as he rang the doorbell to a Greenwich Village residence set in a quarter not too—nor less than—fashionable.

The door opened. "Mr. Wilson." The voice was neither golden nor bronze but of another quality and substance entirely—honey from Hymettus, collected from blue and white Attic flowers—perhaps those very same asphodels which adorn the hill at Marathon that looks upon the sea, wine-dark sea like the eyes of Isabel Bolton into which he now so intensely gazed that he let fall the cluster of white violets he was holding and they scattered, as offering, at her shapely feet encased in crimson velvet with the sort of high instep that caused his heart to beat even more wildly than before. "Do forgive me," he said, collecting the fallen blossoms as the divine girl, all willowy with golden hair—no sign of chemical artifice in *those* massed curls—and the small exquisite poitrine like—what was it? gazelles? He must really get around to learning Hebrew one day.

Wilson's praise of the perfect book came in bursts of sound between articulated wheezes of emotion as he drank the perfectly made martini—plainly, there was to be no end to her genius—and his heart, that metaphor as well as vulnerable organ, rattled in his bosom like the unfortunate occupant in the fabled ferrous mask. Here, at last, she was. So entirely *there*, so real—man-brain in girl-shape. She was tantalizingly silent. So must Moira—Fate for the ancient Greeks—have appeared upon first encounter with a mere mortal.

An inner door of the tastefully decorated—all Englishy and yet impeccable—chamber opened, revealing a tall woman, old but majestic, with the creased brow of Juno beneath white hair parted in the middle. As the ancient Norn strode into the room, Wilson rose from his chair, saying to the perfect girl, "This then is your mother?" The powerful old lady smiled and held out her hand.

"No, Mr. Wilson. I am the Isabel Bolton you have lately written so amiably of in the popular press. This . . ." she indicated the girl of what had been his best dream, ever, "is my ward, Cherry." With that, Bolton shook Wilson's hand while her other arm enfolded lovingly, possessively, the narrow waist of the perfect girl.

As Wilson made his all too slow, it seemed to him, descent to the—yes, entirely clear at last, figure in the Persian carpet, he heard, from far-off, Bolton's voice—could it have been one of brass like Mary's? "I fear that Mr. Wilson has fainted. But then he is very stout. It is not uncommon at our age. Bring smelling salts." The last thing he saw were the heavy leather boots of the old lady, with their—what else? fallen insteps.

Needless to say, I have invented Cherry, yet there is often a Sapphic glow to Bolton's exchanges between women. In *Do I Wake or Sleep* the relationship between the exquisite Bridget (for whom Wilson fell as Bolton's surrogate) and the rough-hewn Millicent is lover-like in the teasing French manner rather than today's klutzy American style where each would have had to wear an auctorial label and, if sympathetic, behave correctly according to rules laid down by the heirs and heiresses of Cotton Mather. Happily, for Bolton, the amatory simply is; and, in general, gaiety (old meaning) rules and no one is assigned a label much less sold off in midseason to a team. In this, she is as alien to us as Ovid, and I suspect only a very few rare spirits ever took to her even when the books first came out in post-Hitler days, a time of stern *Julius Caesar* rather than her own *Midsummer Night's Dream*.

To read Bolton's three novels in sequence is to relive the three major moments of the American half century as observed by an unusual writer located aboard what Dawn Powell called "the happy island," Manhattan. The first novel takes place in 1939. War is wending its way toward the United States and the protagonist, the enchanting Bridget St. Dennis, is lunching blithely in the French Pavilion at Flushing Meadow's World's Fair. Although the chef, Henri Soulé, would later open what was regarded for many years as New York's best restaurant, it is a part of Bolton's magic that not only do you get quite a few good meals in her books but you get subtle distinctions as well. She shared everyone's delight in Le Pavillon's transfer from Flushing to Manhattan. But Bolton herself opts for the magical Chambord in Third Avenue where, as the cartoon used to say, the elite meet to eat or, as someone said to an ancient bon viveur who was recently extolling the long-vanished Chambord, "You are living in the past," to which the old man replied, "Where else can you get a decent meal?"

Bolton belongs to the James–Wharton school of transatlantic fiction or, perhaps, a new category should be invented—of *mid*-Atlantic literature that flourished, to put arbitrary dates like book-ends to its history, from Hawthorne's *Our Old Home* (1863) to T. S. Eliot's *Four Quartets*, published in 1943. It was a long and lively run and brought out the best in two literatures never destined to be one but each able to complement the other while even those profession-ally committed to the American side, like Twain and Howells, touched base regularly with their common old home. For a writer born in 1883, with sufficient family money but no Jamesian fortune, Europe would be as much a part of her life as Brookline, Massachu-setts, where the last of Bolton's protagonists hails from: a world of numerous servants, of courses at dinner, of changes of clothes, pre-sumably to give the servants more than enough to do in the pre-1914 world when Bolton was already a grown woman. As it turned out, pre-1914 continued well into the modern age of cocktails and movie stars—one of Edith Wharton's least-known novels, *Twilight Sleep*, deals with a Hollywood movie star in a way that must make the Collins sisters, the Bel-Air Brontës, quite nervous at how well the stately Mrs. Wharton depicts the life of one who lives on the screen everywhere on earth but nowhere at all in the flesh at home. Then, with Depression and Second War the old world expired. Good riddance, the modern thought. Bolton is of two minds. She is conscious of the *douceur de la vie* of the old time; also of the narrow callow brazen world that that time was rendering all gold, or trying to.

———

Wilson gets quite right Bolton's "Jamesian technique in *Do I Wake or Sleep*: the single consciousness that observes all." I missed it in the first chapter, which is all Bridget, lovingly observed, I thought, by author-god. Then, gradually, one realizes that it is the other woman at the table whose mind we've entered.

Plot: *Do I Wake or Sleep*. Bridget is having lunch at the French Pavilion with a besotted (by her) popular novelist, Percy Jones, equally besotted by martinis, and one Millicent, "a writer of witty articles and famous tales—beloved of Hollywood." A character perhaps influenced by Dorothy Parker and from whose point of view the story is told.

Bridget enchants at lunch; and her creator convinces us that she does so by what she says, not often quoted, and by the way that she includes everyone in a kind of vital intimacy. But she is unexpectedly evasive on the subject of her child, Beatrice. We learn that Bridget was born Rosenbaum; married Eric von Mandestadt, "an Aryan (she'd used the ridiculous word as though it had been incorporated into all the European tongues)." Percy is very much on the case: Beatrice is in Vienna with her paternal grandmother; the Nazis are there, too. Percy feels that it is urgent that the child be got out but Bridget ignores the subject. The first chapter is a very special example of the storyteller's art. It seems to be told in standard third person. But, gradually, with an aside here, a parenthesis there, one realizes that the consciousness taking all this in is the near-silent Millicent, who, in the next chapter, takes shape and autonomy. It is an elegant trick of narrative.

At lunch, Millicent observes and records Bridget as she hovers like a bright blur-winged hummingbird over many subjects. Wilson and Grumbach find much of James, Woolf, and the Elizabeth Bowen of *The Death of the Heart* in the prose but Bridget herself finesses that essential trio:

> She had been in her brief existence two distinctly different beings, and one of these was the creature she was before and the other she had become after reading the works of Marcel Proust. No, really, she wasn't joking. From the experience she'd emerged with all manner of extensions, reinforcements, renewals of her entire nervous system—indeed, she might say that she'd been endowed with a perfectly new apparatus for apprehending the vibration of other people's souls. . . . We were forced to take about with us wherever we went this extraordinary apparatus, recording accurately a thousand little matters of which we had not formerly been aware, and whether she was glad or sorry to be in possession of so delicate and precise an instrument, she had never been able to determine.

There is something to be said for putting off one's official first novel until the age of sixty-three. Certainly Bolton is not in the least diffident when it comes to putting the homegrown American product in its place, which is way out yonder in those amber fields of grain:

> Did [Percy] really believe that American novelists were ready to accept, to celebrate the same creature, the same human heart? It seemed to her that they were always trying to reshape, to remold the creature according to some pattern they desperately yearned to have it conform to— . . . would he agree with her that American novels seldom went deep into the realities of character—weren't they dealing more with circumstances, places—epochs, environments? They

came boiling up out of the decades—out of the twenties, out of the thirties—out of Pittsburgh. . . .

Poor novelist Percy is reeling by now. Yes, he is inclined to agree with her that American novelists are moralists but . . . Henry James, he makes the great name toll over the guinea hen. Bridget counterattacks—Dostoyevsky. "Who could really call Henry James in comparison a good psychologist? . . . matchless brilliance and probity . . . innocent, indignant and upright response to the vulgar, the brutal, the material aspects of society. . . . But if you tried to compare him with Dostoyevsky, he was a child, a holy innocent. [Dostoyevsky] was the traveler in the desert of the soul."

Fast forward, another restaurant: "I believe," said the head waiter, benignly, "this is Mr. Michael Korda's table. There's been some mistake. I do apologize. He is with," a conspiratorial whisper, "Mr. Stephen King."

Yes, to this day, the Four Seasons still echoes with that never-ending literary debate as the waiter shows them to their table in a shallow pool of water. "Mr. Kissinger's favorite table. But as it's Tuesday, he's lunching in Beijing."

The plot is simply the next day. Lunch again with Percy and Millicent. Percy obsessed by the child as putative victim of the Nazis. Bridget evasive. They meet at the Algonquin. Go on to Chambord. Dover sole newly arrived in brine aboard the *Normandie*. Later, to a cocktail party—*the* New York cocktail party of the Forties where the currently celebrated and fashionable mill about, grist for Millicent's eye and ear ever grinding them all up, finer and finer. Percy, drunk, misbehaves: gets knocked out. Doctor comes. No, he is not dead. The party ends—the denouement is that the child is somehow defective—the word "cretin" is used rather than "challenged" as they now say at the Four Seasons: in fact, a sort of monster. Then we learn that Bridget's evasiveness is due to the fact that she is currently penniless; even so, she will bring the child home.

———

What strikes one most is Millicent's deep-seated passion for America in general and for New York City in particular, understandable in the case of a provincial like Thomas Wolfe come wide-eyed to the web and the rock but odd in a partly Europeanized woman of her age. There has been a definite shift in mood since the generation before her: Mrs. Wharton shuddered at the sound of American voices and Henry James gave a murderously deadpan description of "American City" somewhere or other out there in the flat empty regions where the states are simply drawn on the national map with a ruler, and the buffalo roam.

Millicent contrasts New York with European cities: "Here you walked in a vacuum. There were no echoes, no reverberations." She looks at the Empire State Building.

It was one of the wonders of the world. Nevertheless she didn't (and how many people she wondered did) even know the name of its architect. It rose above you, innocent of fame or fable. . . . What a strange, what a fantastic city: and yet, and yet; there was something here that one experienced nowhere else on earth. Something one loved intensely. What was it? Crossing the streets—standing on the street corners with the crowds: what was it that induced this special climate of the nerves? . . . There was something—a peculiar sense of intimacy, friendliness, being here with all these people and in this strange place. . . . They touched your heart with tenderness and you felt yourself a part of the real flight and flutter-searching their faces, speculating about their dooms and destinies.

She has a sudden vision of Apocalypse. War. Towers crashing yet "an unchallenged faith and love and generosity, which . . . still lay deep-rooted in the American psyche to deliver us from death— remembering the Fair at the Flushing Meadow, the Futurama (sponsored by General Motors and displaying with such naive assurance the chart and prospect of these United States)." There is a kind of patrician Whitman at work here and one wonders does anyone now, nearly sixty years later, feel so intimately about Manhattan, the American fact?

In *The Christmas Tree*, Bolton has moved on to 1945. Mrs. Danforth wants her six-year-old grandson, Henry, to have a proper old-fashioned Christmas tree while all that he wants is to play with his bomber and fighter planes. She lives in a skyscraper overlooking the East River but a part of her is still anchored in the brownstone world of her youth, "the days when people really believed in their wealth and special privilege . . . the days of elegance, of arrogance, of ignorance and what a rashly planned security." Today Christmas is vast and mass-produced on every side unlike the days of her youth. She broods on her son Larry, father to Henry. He lives now in Washington with a male lover while Anne, his ex-wife, is en route to New York for Christmas, accompanied by her new husband, Captain Fletcher, an Army Air Force wing commander. (Bolton errs on this one: he would have been at least a full colonel if not brigadier general.) Mrs. Danforth admires Anne's resilience: the coolness with which she accepts the fact that she is often drawn to "the invert, the schizophrene, the artist. Men like that were never normal sexually."

Mrs. Danforth is sufficiently in the grip of the Freudians of the Forties—never again, happily, to be so ubiquitous or so serenely off-base—to wonder if she had loved her son too much when they lived in Paris and it was quite clear to her that, at fifteen, he was having an affair with a French boy a year or two older. "She'd felt no censure of the boys, she had no inclination to reproach them. She'd only felt an immense love, an overwhelming pity for them. And oh, she questioned passionately, how much could she herself be held responsible for Larry's inclinations? How much had she been implicated?" This was the era of the Oedipus Complex (something Oedipus himself did not suffer from since he didn't know that it was Mom he had married after killing what he hadn't known was Dad); also, of the era of popular books with titles like *Generation of*

Vipers—denouncing the American Mom for castrating her sons. Although Proust must have taught Bolton a lot more than Mrs. Danforth would ever learn, it is probably true to the time that mother would blame herself for her son's unorthodox sexual appetites.

Grumbach likes this the best of Bolton's novels. It is certainly the most tightly plotted; it would make a solid old-fashioned drawing-room comedy with a melodramatic twist. Unfortunately, Bolton's scenes between Larry and his lover are not quite all there on the page and what *is* there doesn't have the reverberation that a memory, say, of Mrs. Danforth's youth sets off in other pages. Bolton also makes the narrative more difficult for herself by shifting points of "view." Mrs. Danforth gives way to Larry, preparing to break up with a lover while brooding upon his Parisian past; finally, should he join his ex-wife Anne and her new husband beneath his mother's Christmas tree? We next shift to Anne on her way from Reno with her American husband; she is nostalgic for Larry,

> an exceptional human being, she sometimes suspected that he'd given very little to anyone and that, as a matter of fact, he'd taken from others even less. It was in his enormous concern for the general human plight that his affections were the most implicated; his love of humanity in the large impersonal sense was profound. . . . He was at the mercy of certain tricks and habits of bad behavior—nervous reflexes which apparently he could not control. . . .

There the fatal flaw is named and prepares us for what is to come.

Anne and her manly Captain make up the family scene with the child and Mrs. Danforth. Larry's presence is a dissonant note made worse by the arrival of his lover. Despite good manners all around, the collision between Larry and the Captain takes place over the child, who tells Larry that he hates him. The child prefers the war hero who has brought him numerous toy planes. The Captain then launches what is currently known as a "homophobic" rage at Larry, who tells him to get out. But instead they go out onto the terrace, sixteen stories above the street. The ladies hear loud voices, terrible epithets; silence. Larry comes back into the room, alone. He says that he has killed the Captain; pushed him over the railing. No, it was not an accident.

The others are willing to perjure themselves to save Larry. But he will not allow it; he rings the police; he confesses. *"Au revoir, Maman,"* he says, when they come to take him away. Mother and son have now reverted to their earlier happier selves. . . .

> With what pride, with what great pride she had watched him go!
>
> There was a flickering, a brightness, somewhere in the room. She turned; she lifted her eyes. The light was smiting the silver angel on top of Henry's Christmas tree, poised and trembling, with its wings and herald trumpet shining brightly, there it hung above the guttered candles and the general disarray.
>
> "Pardon us our iniquities, forgive us our transgressions— have mercy on the world," she prayed.

The Christmas Tree was published one year after the Kinsey Report furrowed a peasant nation's brow. The melodramatic ending meant that Bolton was responding, as so many of us did, to the fierce Zeitgeist. But her general coolness in dealing with the taboo probably accounts for the almost instant obscurity of her work amongst the apple-knockers.

Many Mansions was published when Bolton was close to seventy. She writes of Miss Sylvester, who is re-creating her own past by reading a memoir-like novel she had written years earlier. It is February 1, 1950, her birthday: she is eighty-four and Harry Truman's birthday present for her is to give the order to build the hydrogen bomb. She broods upon her great age:

The life of the aged was a constant maneuvering to appease and assuage the poor decrepit body. Why, most of the time she was nothing more than a nurse attending to its every need. As for the greater part of the night one's position was positively disreputable, all alone and clothed in ugly withering flesh—fully conscious of the ugliness, the ignominy—having to wait upon oneself with such menial devotion—here now, if you think you've got to get up mind you don't fall, put on the slippers, don't trip on the rug.

The body is now a perpetual sly nemesis, waiting to strike its mortal blow.

Meanwhile, Miss Sylvester has taken to pursuing lost time, that long-ago time when the body was a partner in a grand exercise known as life. She also frets about money. Has she enough if she should live to be ninety? Should she die soon, what about leaving her small fortune to the young Adam Stone whom "she had picked up in a restaurant . . . the only person in her life for whom she felt genuine concern"? Adam had been in the Second War; emerged bitter; devoured books "ravenously"; was at work upon a novel: "He had cast off his family. He had cast off one girl after another, or very likely one girl after another had cast him off." Miss Sylvester had spoken to him in an Armenian restaurant on Fourth Avenue. "I see you're reading Dante," was her opening gambit. She knows Italian and he does not; this proves to be an icebreaker though hardly a matchmaker.

Now she turns to her long-abandoned manuscript. Two families. Great houses. And the old century was still a splendid all-golden present for the rich. Seasons now come back to her. "Summer was that high field on the high shelf above the ocean . . . the surf strong, the waves breaking. Something pretty terrible about it—getting, in one fell swoop, the fury of the breakers carried back to crack and echo in the dunes . . . the wild cold smell of the salt spray inducing mania excitement." One suspects that Bolton is actually writing of her fourteen-year-old twin who drowned, but Miss Sylvester, her present alter ego, is single and singular and in wild nature more natural.

As an adolescent she lives among numerous grand relatives; but always set apart. Her father was an "Italian musician," a "Dago organ-grinder," she comes to believe, as the subject is unmentionable. Then, on a memorable Sunday Easter dinner, her grandfather makes a toast, "Let us drink to the burial of the feud." The organ-grinder, her father, Sylvester, is dead in southern Italy. He had been paid by the family to go away, leaving behind his daughter as a sort of boarder in their great houses.

Then, almost idly, she falls in love with a married relative; becomes pregnant. The resourceful family assigns yet another relative to her, Cecilia, who takes her to Europe, to fateful Italy, where she is treated as a respectable married woman in an interesting condition. The child, a boy, is born in Fiesole; but she never sees him; her positively Napoleonic family has promptly passed him on to an elegant childless New York couple who whisk him away to a new life, under a name that she will never learn. Cecilia raves about the anonymous couple's charm; their wealth; the guaranteed happiness of the boy's life. Grimly, the mother murmurs the phrase " 'tabula rasa,' . . . as though she'd coined it." She would now begin again as if nothing had ever happened.

The old lady finished her reading: "If her book should fall into the hands of others addicted as she was to the habitual reading of novels, what exactly would their feelings be?" One wonders—is there such a thing now as *a habitual reader* of novels? Even the ambitious, the ravenously literary young Adam seems to have a suspicion that he may have got himself into the stained-glass-window trade.

With a sufficient income, Miss Sylvester moves to New York. She becomes involved with another young woman, Mary (they live in a gentle ladies' pension near Fifth Avenue, presided over by yet another of the multitudinous cousins). "How passionately Mary loved the world and with what eagerness she dedicated herself to reforming it. . . ." The two young women study to be opera singers; but they have no talent. Then Mary involves them in settlement work and organizing women workers—it is the era of the young Eleanor Roosevelt, and Miss Sylvester realizes in old age that "with all the central founts of love—sexual passion and maternity—so disastrously cut off, had not this deep, this steadfast friendship for Mary been the one human relationship where love had never failed to nourish and replenish her?" But she loses Mary to marriage; then to death, which also claims, at Okinawa, Mary's son.

Miss Sylvester has a long relationship with a Jewish intellectual, Felix; but feels she is too old to marry him; then he announces that he is to marry his secretary, who has been his mistress for ten years: Miss Sylvester's decade of intimacy. They part fondly, for good.

She takes in, as a boarder, a young novelist. Son of a fashionable boring couple she once knew. Bolton is too elegant a novelist to reveal him as the old lady's son but sufficiently mischievous to find him, despite great charm, of indifferent character, even flawed.

The book concludes with Miss Sylvester in her flat, collecting some much needed cash for Adam, who is waiting for her at the Armenian restaurant. But even as he is telephoning, she is felled by a stroke. Angrily, Adam leaves the telephone booth "to go back in the dining-room to wait for his old lady, under the impression that she is on her way."

What then was the figure in the carpet that my highly imagined Edmund Wilson made out on his stately way to the floor? As I emerge from Bolton's world, I am sure that what he saw was the fourteen-year-old twin sister brought back from full fathom five— with pearls for eyes—by a great act of will and considerable art to replace the mediocre Mary Britton Miller with a magically alive writer whom she chose to call Isabel Bolton, for our delight.

Elmer Gantry. It Can't Happen Here. Babbitt. Main Street. Dodsworth. Arrowsmith. Sinclair Lewis. The first four references are part of the language; the next two are known to many, while the last name has a certain Trivial Pursuit resonance; yet how many know it is the name of the writer who wrote *Elmer Gantry*, played in the movie by Kirk Douglas—or was it Burt Lancaster?

Sinclair Lewis seems to have dropped out of what remains of world literature. The books are little read today, and he's seldom discussed in his native land outside his home town, Sauk Center, Minnesota. Although Sauk Center holds an annual Sinclair Lewis Day, the guide to his home recently admitted, "I've never read *Main Street*. . . . I've been reading the biographies." Elsewhere, the Associated Press (July 18) tells us, "About forty copies of Lewis's books are on the shelves of the town library. For the most part, that's where they stay."

"I expect to be the most talked-of writer," Lewis boasted before he was. But the great ironist in the sky had other plans for him. In the end, Lewis was not to be talked of at all, but his characters—as types—would soldier on; in fact, more of his inventions have gone into the language than those of any other writer since Dickens. People still say, in quotes as it were, "It can't happen here," meaning fascism, which probably will; hence, the ironic or minatory spin the phrase now gets. In the half century since Sinclair Lewis (one wants to put quotes about his name, too) what writer has come up with a character or phrase like Babbitt or Elmer Gantry that stands for an easily recognized type? There is "Walter Mitty" and Heller's "Catch-

22"; and that's that. Of course, much of this has to do with the irrelevance of the novel in an audiovisual age. It is "Murphy Brown"
not "Herzog" that registers, if only for the span of a network season.
Finally, even if the novel was of interest to the many, its nature has
certainly changed since the first half of the century when serious
novelists, committed to realism/naturalism, wrote about *subjects* like
the hotel business, the sort of thing that only pop novelists go in for
nowadays.

That said, it would seem impossible that a mere biographer could effectively eliminate a popular and famous novelist; yet that is exactly
what Mark Schorer managed to do in his 867-page biography, *Sinclair Lewis*.* Schorer's serene loathing of his subject and all his works
is impressive in its purity but, at the end, one is as weary of Schorer
himself as of Lewis. I once asked Schorer, an amiable man who liked
to drink almost as much as Lewis did, why he had taken on a subject that he so clearly despised. The long answer was money; the
short, too. In this Schorer did *not* resemble Lewis, who, as much
as he liked every sort of success, had a craving for Art in an *echt*-
American way, and a passion for his inventions; also, he believed that
somewhere over the rainbow there was a great good place that would
prove to be home. As it turned out, he was never at home anywhere;
and his restless changes of address take up altogether too many pages
in Schorer's survey, as they must have used up too much psychic energy in Lewis's life, where the only constant, aside from frantic writing and frantic drinking, was, as his first wife sadly observed,
"romance is never where you are, but where you are going." Since he
never stayed put, he never got there. Wives and women came and
went; there were hardly any friends left after the end of the great
decade of his life, 1920–1930.

    In 1920, the unadmired great man of American letters, William
Dean Howells, died, and Lewis published *Main Street*; then *Babbitt*
(1922); *Arrowsmith* (1925); *Elmer Gantry* (1927); *Dodsworth* (1929).

---

* *Sinclair Lewis: An American Life* (McGraw-Hill, 1961).

The Nobel Prize followed in 1930. That was the period when the Swedes singled out worthy if not particularly good writers for celebration, much as they now select worthy if not particularly interesting countries or languages for consolation. Although the next twenty-one years of Lewis's life was decline and fall, he never stopped writing; never stopped, indeed: always in motion.

"He was a queer boy, always an outsider, lonely." Thus Schorer begins. Harry Sinclair Lewis was born in 1885 in Sauk Centre, Minnesota, population 2,800. At the same time a couple of dozen significant American writers were also being brought up in similar towns in the Middle West and every last one of them was hell-bent to get out. Lewis's father, a doctor, was able to send him to Yale. Harry or Hal or Red was gargoyle ugly: red-haired, physically ill-coordinated, suffered from acne that was made cancerous by primitive X-ray treatments. He was a born mimic. He had a wide repertory of characters—types—and he was constantly shifting in and out of characters. But where Flaubert had only one act, The Idiot, Lewis had an army of idiots, and once started, he could not shut up. He delighted and bored, often at the same time.

Although Lewis had been born with all the gifts that a satirist needs to set up shop he was, by temperament, a romantic. Early writings were full of medieval fair ladies, gallant knights, lands of awful Poesie where James Branch Cabell was to stake out *his* territory, now quite abandoned. Lewis also had, even by American standards, absolutely no sense of humor. In a charming memoir his first wife, Grace Hegger, noted, "*Main Street* was not a satire until the critics began calling him a satirist, and then seeing himself in that role, is it possible that [his next book] *Babbitt* became true satire?" The question is double-edged. Like Columbus, Lewis had no idea where he had gone, but the trip was fun. He loved his high-toned heroine, Carol Kennicott, but if others thought her a joke, he was willing to go along with it.

In youth Lewis wrote yards of romantic verse, much of it jocose; yet he had heard Yeats at Yale and was much impressed by the early poetry. Like most born writers, he read everything: Dickens, Scott, Kipling were his first influences. But it was H. G. Wells's *The History of Mr. Polly* that became for him a paradigm for his own first novel. Like most writers, again, he later claimed all sorts of grand literary progenitors, among them Thoreau, but it would appear that he mostly read the popular writers of his time and on the great divide that Philip Rahv was to note—Paleface versus Redskin—Lewis was firmly Redskin; yet, paradoxically, he deeply admired and even tried to imitate those Edith Wharton stories that were being published when he was coming of age, not to mention *The Custom of the Country*, whose Undine Spragg could have easily served time in a Lewis novel.

The literary world before 1914 is now as distant from us as that of Richardson and Fielding. In those days novels and short stories were popular entertainment. They were meant to be read by just about everybody. Numerous magazines published thousands of short stories of every kind, and a busy minor writer could make as good a living as a minor bank president. Writing was simply a trade that, sometimes, mysteriously, proved to be an art. William Dean Howells had balanced commerce and art with such exquisite tact that he was invaluable as editor and friend to both the Paleface Henry James and the Redskin Mark Twain. Howells himself was a very fine novelist. But he lived too long. For the rising generation of the new twentieth century, he was too genteel, too optimistic (they had carelessly misread him); too much Beacon Street not to mention London and Paris and the Russia of Dostoevsky, whose first translations Howells had brought to the attention of those very conventional ladies who were thought to be the principal audience for the novel in America.

While still at Yale, Lewis headed straight to the action. Upton Sinclair had started a sort of commune, Helicon Hall, at Englewood, New Jersey, and in 1906 Lewis spent two months there, firing furnaces and writing. By 1909 he was at Carmel with his classmate William Rose Benét, another professional bookman. Lewis worked on the San Francisco *Bulletin*, and wrote. When Jack London had come to Yale to speak for socialism, Lewis had met him. Although Lewis was to be, briefly, a card-carrying Socialist, he was never much interested in politics, but he very much admired the great Redskin writer, and he got to know him at Carmel.

London wrote short stories for a living. Unfortunately, he had trouble thinking up plots. Although Lewis was not yet making a living from short stories, he had thought up a great many plots. So, in 1910, Lewis sold Jack London fourteen short story plots for $70. Two became published short stories; the third the start of a not-to-be-finished novel. Lewis later described London at that time as someone more interested in playing bridge than sea-wolfing. He also described how "Jack picked up James's *The Wings of the Dove* . . . and read aloud in a bewildered way. . . . It was the clash between Main Street and Beacon Street that is eternal in American culture." Well, eternity is a long time in bookchat land.

In 1910 Lewis moved on to Washington, D.C., which was to become, more or less, his home base in the United States. Meanwhile he worked for New York publishers as reader, copywriter, salesman. He was also selling fiction to the flagship of commercial publishing, *The Saturday Evening Post*, as well as to other magazines. From 1913 to 1914 he produced a syndicated book page that was carried in newspapers all around the country. By putting himself at the center of bookchat, he ensured good reviews for his own books in much the same way that in England now ambitious young writers not only review each other's books but also often act as literary editors in order to promote their future reviewers. Those destined for greatness will eventually review television programs in a Sunday newspaper, thus getting to know the television and film magnates who will, in due course, promote them personally on television as well as buy their products for dramatization. The English literary scene today is like that of the United States pre-1914.

Lewis's first novel, *Our Mr. Wrenn*, is very much school of Wells; it was, of course, well reviewed by his fellow bookmen. In the next four

years Lewis published four more novels. Each had a subject, of which
the most interesting was early aviation, *The Trail of the Hawk* (1915).
Lewis had got to know Paul Beck, one of the first army fliers, and the
novel presages, rather eerily, Lindbergh's career. In my memory these
books are rather like those of Horatio Alger that I was reading at the
same time, something of an agreeable blur. Since the Subject comes
before the Characters and since Lewis was a thorough researcher, there
are many little facts of the sort that pop writers today provide as they
take us on tours of the cosmetics or munitions businesses, subjects
they usually know very little about beyond idle, as opposed to dogged,
research. Only James Michener, through hard work, has mastered the
fictional narrative as a means of instruction in a subject of interest to
him, like Hawaii; and then to millions of others.

The first five novels established Sinclair Lewis as a serious if not
particularly brilliant novelist; but one with, as they say at *Billboard*,
a bullet. As a careerist, Lewis was an Attila. In his pursuit of blurbs,
he took no prisoners. He cultivated famous writers. *Main Street* is
dedicated to James Branch Cabell *and* Joseph Hergesheimer, the two
classiest novelists of the day. *Babbitt* is dedicated to Edith Wharton,
who took it all in her magnificent ruthless stride.

In 1915 his old mentor Upton Sinclair was invited to assess the
product. He did:

> You seem to me one of the most curiously uneven writers
> I have ever known. You will write pages and pages of in-
> teresting stuff, and then you will write a lot of conversa-
> tion which is just absolute waste, without any point or
> worthwhileness at all; and you don't seem to know the dif-
> ference. Everything of yours that I have read is about half
> and half . . . whenever you are writing about the under-
> world, you are at your best, and when you come up to your
> own social level or higher, you are no good.

Nicely, Upton Sinclair adds a postscript: "Don't be cross." Writers usually get other writers' numbers rather more quickly than critics ever

do. After all, as contemporaries, they have been dealt much the same cards to play with.

By 1929, the apprenticeship of Sinclair Lewis was over. He had married and become the father of a son, Wells, named for H.G., whom he had yet to meet (Lewis was deeply irritated when people thought that *he* had been named for Upton Sinclair when his father had named him after one Harry Sinclair, a dentist of the first rank).

The genesis of Lewis's ascent can be located in the year 1916 when he and his wife, Grace, came to stay in Sauk Centre with Dr. Lewis and his wife, Sinclair's stepmother. In her memoir, Grace Hegger Lewis is very funny about what must have been a fairly uncomfortable visit. "One morning when 'the curse' was upon me," Grace asked for breakfast on a tray. The Lewises said no, while Hal, Grace's name for her husband, was "furious. He had always taken for granted his affection for his parents and their behavior he had never questioned. But seeing his family through the eyes of New York and of marriage he was appalled by his father's overbearing rudeness." Grace suggests that this visit forced Lewis to see his hometown in an entirely new way and shift the point of view from that of a lonely offbeat lawyer in what was to be called *The Village Virus*, to that of Carol, a girl from outside the village who marries the local doctor, Will Kennicott, and so observes the scene with big city (in her case Minneapolis) eyes.

Grace reports that Dr. Lewis did apologize; the young couple stayed on; and the town magnates were brought to their knees when they learned just how much Lewis had been paid for a two-part serial in the *Woman's Home Companion* ($1,500). "When he told them that it had taken him two weeks to write the serial, the banker, dividing so much per diem, was visibly awed. . . . The young Lewises were to find that this measuring of talent by dollars was fairly universal, and Hal was hurt at first by the lack of interest in the writing itself."

Their later life in Washington sounds agreeable. She tells us how they would walk to the Chevy Chase Club with the young Dean Achesons and how Lewis also frequented the Cosmos Club and got to know General Billy Mitchell, Clarence Darrow, and the scarlet lady of our town, Elinor Wylie—murmur her name, as indeed people were still doing a few years later when I was growing up. The Lewises seem not to have known the Achesons' friend Grace Zaring Stone, author of *The Bitter Tea of General Yen*, who, when told by a lady novelist that she was writing a novel about Evil, sighed, "If only I had thought of that!"

Lewis maintained that the idea for a novel whose subject would be a small Midwestern market town came to him in 1905. I should suspect that it was always there. Village life was the first thing that he had known and, sooner or later, writers usually deal with their origins. The real-life lawyer Charles T. Dorion was to be the main character, an idealistic soul, able to see through the pretences, the hypocrisies, the . . . the . . . the absolute boredom of Sauk Centre (renamed by Lewis Gopher Prairie). But the 1916 homecoming gave Lewis a new point of view, that of his elegant New York wife, to be called Carol. Dorion was demoted to supporting cast, as Guy Pollock.

In July 1920, in a Washington heat wave, Sinclair Lewis finished *Main Street*. He gave the book to his friend Alfred Harcourt, who had started a new publishing house to be known, in time, as Harcourt, Brace, in which Lewis had invested some of his own money. In the business of authorship he seldom put a foot wrong.

October 23, 1920, *Main Street* was published and, as one critic put it, "if *Main Street* lives, it will probably be not as a novel but as an incident in American life." Even Schorer, not yet halfway through Lewis's career, concedes, a bit sadly, that the book was "the most sensational event in twentieth-century American publishing history." As of 1922 an estimated two million Americans had read the book; and they went right on reading it for years. With Howells gone, Lewis took his place as numero uno and reigned both at home and abroad until 1930, after which, according to Schorer, "with the increasing conformity at the surface of American life and the increasing fragmentation at its base, there have been no contenders at all." I'm not sure that Bill or Ernest or Scott or Saul or Norman or . . . would agree. The contenders are all in place. The problem is that fiction—stories intended to be read by almost everyone—ceased to be of much interest to a public "with no time to read" and movies to go to and, later, television to watch. The *Saturday Evening Post* serial, often well-written by a good writer, would now be done, first, as a miniseries on television or as a theatrical film. Today nonfiction (that is, fictions about actual people) stuffs our magazines and dominates best-seller lists.

In any case, *pace* Schorer, conformity in American life, whatever that means, would certainly be a spur to any writer. As for fragmentation, it is no worse now as the countryside fills up with Hispanics and Asians as it was when Lewis was describing the American hinterland full of Socialist Swedes and comic-dialect Germans. Actually, to read about the career of Sinclair Lewis is to read about what was a golden age for writing and reading; now gone for good.

Lewis's energetic self-promotion among the masters of the day paid off. His dedicatees Cabell and Hergesheimer wrote glowing testimonials. Predictably, the novel appealed to the English realists if not to Bloomsbury. The former wrote him fan letters—John Galsworthy, H. G. Wells, Rebecca West; presently he would be taken up by the monarch of bookchat and the master of the fact-filled realistic novel, Arnold Bennett. At home a fellow Minnesotan wrote him "with the utmost admiration," F. Scott Fitzgerald. But five years later Fitzgerald is wondering if *Arrowsmith* is really any good. "I imagine that mine [*Gatsby*] is infinitely better." Sherwood Anderson leapt on and off the bandwagon. Dreiser ignored the phenomenon but his friend H. L. Mencken was delighted with Lewis, and praised him in *Smart Set*. When Lewis's sometime model Edith Wharton won the Pulitzer Prize for *The Age of Innocence*, Lewis wrote to congratulate her. As for this uncharacteristic lapse on the part of a committee designed to execute, with stern impartiality, Gresham's Law, Mrs. Wharton responded with her usual finely wrought irony: "When I discovered that I was being rewarded by one of our leading Universities—for uplifting American morals, I confess I *did* despair." She praises Lewis vaguely; later, she is to prove to be his shrewdest critic.

While Mr. and Mrs. Sinclair Lewis toured restlessly about Europe, trying to enjoy his success, he was already at work on *Babbitt*.

★   The Library of America has now brought out both *Main Street* and *Babbitt* in a single volume, and it was with some unease that I stepped into the time-warp that is created when one returns after a half century not only to books that one had once lived in but almost to that place in time and space where one had read the old book— once upon a time in every sense. It was said of Lewis that, as a pre–1914 writer, he had little in common with the rising generation of post–World War writers like Hemingway, Dos Passos, Faulkner. It might equally be said that those of us who grew up in the Thirties and in the Second War made as great a break with what had gone before as today's theoreticians made with us. Literary history is hardly an ascending spiral, one masterpiece giving birth to an even greater one, and so on. Rather there are occasional clusters that occur at odd intervals each isolated from the others by, no doubt, protocreative dust. Lewis was pretty much his own small star set to one side of Twain, Crane, James, and Wharton, and the small but intense postwar galaxy which still gives forth radio signals from that black hole where all things end. In the Twenties, only Dreiser was plainly Lewis's superior but Dreiser's reputation was always in or under some shadow and even now his greatness is not properly grasped by the few who care about such things.

What strikes one first about *Main Street* is the energy of the writing. There is a Balzacian force to the descriptions of people and places, firmly set in the everyday. The story—well, for a man who supported himself by writing stories for popular magazines and selling plots to Albert Payson Terhune as well as Jack London, there is no plot at all to *Main Street*. Things just happen as they appear to do in life. In Minneapolis, Carol Milford meets Will Kennicott, a doctor from the small town of Gopher Prairie. There are events, some more dramatic than others, but the main character is Main Street and the intense descriptions of the place are most effective, while the people themselves tend to be so many competing arias, rendered by a superb mimic usually under control. Later, Lewis would succumb to his voices and become tedious, but in *Main Street* he is master of what Bakhtin (apropos Dostoevsky) called "the polyphonic novel. . . . There is a plurality of voices inner and outer, and they retain 'their unmergedness.' " Lewis is splendid on the outer voices but he lacks an idiosyncratic inner voice—he is simply a straightforward narrator without much irony—while his attempts to replicate the inner voices of the characters are no different, no more revelatory, than what they themselves say aloud.

"On a hill by the Mississippi where Chippewas camped two generations ago, a girl stood in relief against the cornflower blue of Northern sky." The first sentence is brisk; it places us in time— reminds us that this was Indian territory a half century ago, and so the white man is new to the scene, and his towns are still raw. "Cornflower" is *Saturday Evening Post*. "Corn" itself is a bit dangerous, as in corny. "Blue" isn't all that good either. Yet, paradoxically, Lewis had a lifelong hatred of the cliché in prose as well as a passion for sending up clichés in dialogue: this can cause confusion.

Anyway, he has now begun the story of Carol Milford, enrolled at Blodgett College, a girl full of dreams even more vivid than those of Emma Bovary—dreams rather closer to those of Walter Mitty than to Flaubert's Emma, though, in practice, as it later proves, Carol has more than a touch of Bouvard and Pécuchet in her when she takes to the field with one of her projects to bring beauty to a drab world. Lewis maintained that, as of 1920, he had read neither *Madame Bovary* nor Edgar Lee Masters's *Spoon River Anthology*, whose set of arias from the simple dead folk of a small-town cemetery inspired a generation of writers, achieving a peak, as it were, in Thornton Wilder's *Our Town*. Incidentally, there is some evidence that Lewis based her on the mother of Charles Lindbergh (cf. 132).

Carol is involved in the "tense stalking of a thing called General Culture." Ostensibly on her behalf, Lewis drops Culture names all over the place. First, Robert G. Ingersoll, the nineteenth-century agnostic, and then Darwin, Voltaire. One can't really imagine her liking any of them—she is too romantic; she dreams of truth and beauty. Ingersoll is a hard-bitten, dour freethinker. The other two are outside her interest. Later he tells us that she has read Balzac and Rabelais. Since she becomes a librarian, the Balzac would be inevitable but neither Carol nor Sinclair Lewis ever read Rabelais. There are some things that an experienced dispenser of bookchat knows without *any* evidence.

At a Minneapolis party, Carol meets Dr. Will Kennicott, a doctor in the small town of Gopher Prairie. He is agreeable, and manly, and adores her. In a short time: "He had grown from a sketched-in stranger to a friend." Will is "sincere" (a favorite word of Carol's is "insincere"). Carol meanwhile (as a result of Mrs. Wharton on interior decoration and *Italian Gardens?*) has dreamed that "what I'll do after college [is] get my hands on one of those prairie towns and make it beautiful. Be an inspiration. I suppose I'd better become a teacher then. . . . I'll make 'em put in a village green, and darling cottages, and a quaint Main Street!" Hubris is back in town. One doubts if the worldly Grace Hegger Lewis ever thought along those lines in Sauk Center in 1916. But Lewis has got himself a nice premise, with vast comic potentialities. But instead of playing it for laughs and making satire, he plays it absolutely straight and so achieved total popularity. Irony.

In 1912 Carol and Will get married. They take the train to Gopher Prairie. It is all very much worse than she expected. But Will exults in town and people. Although Lewis is noted for his voices, the best of the novel is the description of things and the author's observations of the people who dwell among the things.

The train was entering town. The houses on the outskirts were dusky old red mansions with wooden frills, or gaunt frame shelters like grocery boxes, or new bungalows with concrete foundations, imitating stone. Now the train was passing the elevator, the grim storage-tanks for oil, a creamery, a lumber-yard, a stock-yard muddy and trampled and stinking.

They are met by Will's friends, the elite of the village. There is a lot of kidding. Mock insults. Ho-ho-ho.

Main Street with its two-story brick shops, its story-and-a-half wooden residences, its muddy expanse from concrete walk to walk, its huddle of Fords and lumberwagons, was too small to absorb her. The broad, straight, unenticing gashes of the streets let in the grasping prairie on every side. She realized the vastness and emptiness of the land.

This is "home." She is in a panic. She notes "a shop-window delicately rich in error" (this is worthy of Wharton), "vases starting out to imitate tree-trunks but running off into blobs of gilt—an aluminum ash-tray labeled 'Greetings from Gopher Prairie.' " And so she makes her way down Main Street, all eyes, later ears.

Carol entertains the village magnates, only to discover "that conversation did not exist in Gopher Prairie . . . they sat up with gaiety as with a corpse." Nothing stirs them until one says, " 'Let's have some stunts, folks.' " The first to be called on is Dave, who gives a "stunt about the Norwegian catching a hen." Meanwhile, "All the guests moved their lips in anticipation of being called on for their own stunts." A stunt was usually an imitation or ethnic joke. One can imagine Lewis's own lips moving as he would prepare to hold captive some party with a monologue in a character not his own. As it turns out, there *is* conversation in Gopher Prairie—about "personalities," often in the form of lurid gossip, usually sexual. Carol is not happy.

Lewis is good at tracing Carol's ups and mostly downs. She puts on a play. Everything goes wrong. She joins the Library Board to encourage reading, only to find that the librarian believes that their function is not to lend but to preserve books. This, of course, was the ancestor of today's Sauk Center Library where Lewis's books are preserved but not read. Carol joins the Jolly Seventeen, the fashionable young matrons of the village in whose circle bridge is played and personalities dissected. Carol is thought a bit too citified and definitely stuck-up when she tries to talk of General Culture and town improvements. She does her best to fit in but she "had never been able to play the game of friendly rudeness."

In time, Carol flirts with the lawyer, Guy Pollock. He loves literature and disdains the town and one can see that Lewis had it in mind to bring them together but Guy is too damp a character. She drops him; then she goes off in two unexpected directions. A beautiful young Swedish tailor has come to town, Erik Valberg. A townswoman soliloquizes: "They say he tries to make people think he's a poet—carries books around and pretends to read 'em, says he didn't find any intellectual companionship in this town. . . . And him a Swede tailor! My! and they say he's the most awful mollycoddle—looks just like a girl. The boys call him Elizabeth. . . ." Plainly, the influence of Willa Cather's curiously venomous short story "Paul's Case" of 1905 was still strong enough for Lewis to ring changes on the sissy boy who dreams of art and civilization and beauty.

As it turns out, Erik is not hot for Will but for Carol. They talk about poetry; they lust for each other. They are two against the town. He is randy Marchbanks to her Candida. But nothing happens except that everyone suspects, and talks; and Lewis is at his best when he shows Carol's terror of public opinion in a place where it is not physically possible to escape from eyes at windows. This sense of claustrophobia and of no place to hide is the heart of the book. Even the metaphor of the unending "grasping" prairie contributes to the stifling of the individual.

Erik is a farm boy turned tailor turned autodidact: he has got the point. "It's one of our favorite American myths that broad plains necessarily make broad minds, and high mountains make high purpose. They do just the opposite." Carol's attempts to integrate him in the town fail. Will observes them walking together at night. There is no scene, but it is clear that Erik must leave town, which he does.

The other counterpoint voice to Gopher Prairie is Miles Bjornstam, unfondly known as "the Red Swede." He is a self-educated laborer; he cuts wood, does odd jobs, lives in a shack like Thoreau. He reads Veblen. Reading lists of the characters are all-important to Lewis. Carol has not only read but *bought* "Anatole France, Rolland, Nexe, Wells, Shaw, Edgar Lee Masters, Theodore Dreiser, Sherwood Anderson, Henry Mencken." Of those on this list, three subsequently gave Lewis blurbs. Ambitious penpersons take note.

Daringly, Carol pays Miles a call; he shocks and delights her by putting into words her own thoughts about the village. Then he goes into business for himself; prospers with a dairy; marries Carol's best friend, her maid-of-all-work, Bea Sorenson, who comes from the hinterland and though she peaks with a comic Scandinavian accent her heart is gold. Earlier, the village was scandalized that Carol had treated her as an equal. Now, although Mr. and Mrs. Bjornstam are hardworking and prosperous, they are still shunned, partly because of their foreignness and low class but mostly because the agnostic Miles has been "lippy" about God's country and the most perfect of its Main Streets. With the arrival of the First World War everyone is now a super-American, busy demonizing all things foreign—like Miles and Bea. But Carol continues to see the Bjornstams and their child. She, too, has a son.

It is during these scenes that Lewis must do a fine balancing act between melodrama and poetic realism in the Hardy vein (sometimes Hardy, too, lost his balance). The Bjornstams are the only people Carol—and the reader—likes. But the villagers continue to hate them even though Miles has done his best to conform to village ways.

Bea and her child get typhoid fever, from the bad water that they must drink because the neighbor with the good water won't share. Will Kennicott does his best to save Bea and her child but they die. Carol is shattered. Miles is stoic. When the ladies of the village unexpectedly call with gifts, not knowing that mother and child are dead, Miles says, "You're too late. You can't do nothing now. Bea's always kind of hoped that you folks would come see her. . . . Oh, you ain't worth a God-damning." Like Erik, he, too, leaves town.

Set piece follows set piece. There is a trip to California, where Will searches for fellow villagers and, unhappily for Carol, finds them. She is now ready to leave Gopher Prairie, "Oh, is all life always an unresolved but?" She resolves the "but." She will get out into the world, *any* world but that of the claustrophobic censorious village folk. Will accepts her decision even though he continues to be In Love With Her. (Rather unlikely this.) Carol and son set out for Washington, D.C.—the city from which we locals used to set out for New York as soon as we could. On the train east, the boy asks where they are going and Carol says, "We're going to find elephants with golden howdahs from which peep young maharanees with necklaces of rubies, and a dawn sea colored like the breast of a dove . . ." John Cheever would, years later, redo this bit of purple most tastefully.

The elephants turn out to be the Bureau of War Risk Insurance, where she does clerical work, and in mythical, magical Washington "she felt that she was no longer one-half of a marriage but the whole of a human being." She moves among army, navy, minor officialdom. She revels in "the elm valley of Massachusetts Avenue . . . the marble houses on New Hampshire Avenue . . ." and the splendors of the restaurant on the roof of the Powhatan Hotel.

Will pays her a call; she is now a whole woman and so able to return to Gopher Prairie; she is, somehow, mysteriously, at peace with its boredom and mean-spiritedness. But she will not be coopted; she will not be a booster. She has another child. She sees Erik again—at the movies, up there on the silver screen; he had found his way to Hollywood. "I may not have fought the good fight," Carol says at the end to Will, "but I have kept the faith." On those words of the great Populist William Jennings Bryan, the book ends.

Babbitt was intended to be the account of a single day in the life of the eponymous protagonist, a realtor in the great city of Zenith, an extension and enlargement of Gopher Prairie, with elements of sultry Duluth where the Lewises had lived for a season and were—what else?—the cynosure of all eyes. The day that Lewis had picked was one in April 1920, and we follow George F. Babbitt from the moment that he awakens with, significantly, a hangover to the end of the day, but by that time Lewis had decided that one day wasn't going to be enough for him to do his stunts in, so the story continues another year or two, and a Midwestern Bloom was not to be.

Lewis's eye for detail is, as always, precise. We get an inventory of bathroom and house and sleeping porch, a fad of the day that I have just recalled with the sense of having slipped several notches back in time. There is a long-suffering wife, a son, two daughters— one at Bryn Mawr. Babbitt is forty-six years old. Prohibition has been in place for a year, so everyone drinks too much. There is talk of the coming election, and the great shadow of Warren Gamaliel Harding is already darkening the land and his famous injunction "Don't knock, boost" is on every Zenith businessman's lip. Babbitt himself is vaguely unhappy: "the Babbitt house," apparently, "was not a home." But all the latest gadgets are on display. There is chintz, but no heart. The real estate business is booming.

Even so, he dreams of "a fairy child," a recurring dream that somehow underscores Lewis's uneasiness with sex, mature or otherwise. Babbitt has been true to his wife, Myra, since he married her, something that is hard for us plague-ridden *fin de siècle* types to fathom. As a result, he lusts for other women in his heart, and, sooner or later, lust must be served. This gives the story what small impetus it has: how—and for whom—will he fall, and what kind of mess will he make?

As in *Main Street* there is no plot, only set scenes. Lewis notes the class divisions. There is the class above Babbitt that belongs to the Union Club as best emblemized by Charles McKelvey; then there is the Athletic Club where Babbitt and his fellow boosters hang out and denounce socialism and labor unions and anarchists. Meanwhile, at the wheel of his new car, a "perilous excursion," Babbitt daydreams en route to his office, the "pirate ship." He has had his first conversation of the day with a neighbor, and they have talked of the weather in great detail and though their exchange should be as tedious as the real thing, Lewis is a master of those grace notes of boring speech that put one in mind of Bach. "There was still snow at Tiflis, Montana, yesterday," says the neighboring Bore; then goes for a crescendo: "Two years ago we had a snow-squall right here in Zenith on the twenty-fifth of April."

Next, a loving description of Zenith—skyscrapers now—and old houses, movie billboards, drugstores, factory suburbs, a proper city where once the Chippewas roamed. At the office there is a young partner, a secretary—Babbitt's father-in-law is senior partner, and seldom seen. Babbitt is having what now would be called a midlife crisis of a sexual nature: "In twenty-three years of married life he had peered uneasily at every graceful ankle, every soft shoulder; in thought he had treasured them; but not once had he hazarded respectability by adventuring." Plainly, Lewis is not drawing on autobiography. Although he preferred drink to sex, he had, at least once, in Italy, cheated on Grace, and one does not suppose him to have been pure premarriage. What is interesting about Lewis's description of Babbitt's sex life is whether he is distorting it deliberately to give American readers, a high-toned, censorious, prudish lot, this picture of an average American businessman, true as steel to the little lady, or whether he has some arcane knowledge of how Zenith males denied themselves. It is hard to know what to think. Even in the Gopher Prairie of Springfield, Illinois, in the 1840s there were girls to be rented by young lawyers like A. Lincoln and J. Speed. Yet in 1920 Babbitt has only masturbatory images, and the recurring mawkish dream of the "fairy girl."

Babbitt has only one actual friend, even though he himself is a pro-totypical gregarious regular fellow and very well liked. But he had been at a school with Paul Riesling, who had wanted to be a musi-cian; instead Paul married a virago (whom he will later shoot but not, alas, kill—he does serve time). Paul and Babbitt revert to ado-lescence when together. They romanticize their common past. Bab-bitt was to have been a powerful tribune of the people and Paul a world-class violinist. But since neither is articulate, when they are to-gether they can only tell jokes, as they try, rather wistfully, to go back in time to where they had been, if nothing else, real. They dream now of going off together on a hunting trip.

Babbitt has lunch at the Athletic Club. Lewis delights in repro-ducing the banalities of the Joshers, Good Fellows, Regular Guys. Kidding, chaffing, "stunts"—all these pass for communication and the fact that Lewis could reproduce this sort of conversational filler delighted those who went in for it, which was most Americans, while British book reviewers acknowledged that Lewis's Joshers con-firmed their worst fears about the collective cretinism of the sepa-rated cousinage. I cannot think how the French took Lewis's dialogue in translation. Bouvard and Pécuchet are like figures from Racine when compared with the Boosters of the Athletic Club. In any case, Lewis had somehow struck a universal class nerve and, for a time, everyone was delighted by his hyperrealism. Even so, Edith Wharton struck a warning note. She was, she wrote, duly grateful for the dedication to herself of *Babbitt* but she saw fit to make one sug-gestion: "In your next book, you should use slang in dialogue more sparingly. I believe the real art in this respect is to use just enough to *colour* your dialogue, not so much that in a few years it will be al-most incomprehensible." She admired his "irony," wondering how much of it Americans got.

I suspect they got none; the book was taken as just like life and Lewis was hardly more critical of Americans and their values than his readers were. They, too, hankered after fairy girls in dreamland as well as magic casements elsewhere, preferably in Europe, through which they might, like Alice, step into Wonderland. The secret of Lewis and his public was that he was as one with them. Grace thought that the crown of ironist he had been mistakenly awarded by those who read *Main Street* obliged him to go for the real diadem in *Babbitt*. But I think he just kept on recording.

The story proceeds with random events. Babbitt becomes an orator for the realtors; he takes part in the election of a Republican mayor; tries to move up socially and fails; he drinks more and more; the most vivid description in the book is the way booze was sold clandestinely at an ex-saloon, a sordid place, "giving that impression of forming a large crowd which two men always give in a saloon."

Lewis makes an odd obeisance to Howells, whom he will dismiss, so foolishly, at the Nobel Prize ceremony of 1930. Lewis calls the state capital Galop de Vache, in memoriam of the hometown of the journalist hero of Howells's Florentine tale *Indian Summer*, who hailed from Des Vaches, Indiana.

Babbitt is essentially a *roman fleuve* despite its snappy scenes and bright "stunts." In due course, the river deposits Babbitt on the not-so-wild shore of love. He meets a demimondaine lady of a certain age, Mrs. Tanis Judique. She is arty; she has a salon of marginal types. Tactfully, Myra Babbitt has retreated, temporarily, to her family and so Babbitt is able to conduct his love affair in relative peace while drinking more and more in the company of the feckless young. Business is affected: deals are lost. He falls in with the town radical, Seneca Doane, another variation on the original Dorion, with a bit of Upton Sinclair thrown in. Doane has been defeated for mayor. He now supports a local strike. Babbitt falls under his spell for a time (they had known each other in college). Then the town turns on Babbitt. Adultery does not disturb the boosters so much as Babbitt's timid support of the strikers. In a series of confrontations almost as terrible as the ones at the end of *The Age of Innocence* Zenith threatens to destroy him; and Babbitt caves in. He has not fought the good fight, and he has not kept much of any faith to anything but, at the end, he will " 'start something', he vowed, and he tried to make it valiant." Meanwhile, happy ending. Tanis and Seneca slink away; wife comes home. Valiant.

March 26, 1925, Lewis wrote his publisher, "Any thoughts on pulling wires for [*Arrowsmith*] for Nobel Prize?" There were such thoughts, there were such wires. By 1930 the Swedes were at last ready to pick an American. Earlier, Henry James had been airily dismissed in favor of Maurice Maeterlinck, the Belgian beemaster. The choice was now between Dreiser and Lewis and, as these things are ordered in the land of the great white night, Lewis was inevitably chosen. Mark Schorer writes of all this with distinct sadness. Even the President of the United States, a New England wit called Calvin Coolidge, broke his usual silence—he was a school of Buster Keaton comic—to declare, "No necessity exists for becoming excited."

Lewis lived for twenty-one more years. He produced a great amount of work. He turned to the theater; even acted onstage. He married the splendid journalist Dorothy Thompson, who never stopped talking either. They opposed America's entry into World War Two, a war in which his son Wells was killed. It is painful to read of Lewis's last days as recorded by Schorer. Drink had estranged him from most people; and so he was obliged to hire young secretaries to play chess with him and keep him company; among those paid companions were the writers-to-be Barnaby Conrad and John Hersey, who has prepared the exemplary Library of America *Sinclair Lewis*.

Mr. Schorer, enraged to the end, notes, finally, "He was one of the worst writers in modern American literature, but without his writing one cannot imagine modern American literature. That is because, without his writing, we can hardly imagine ourselves." This is not a left-handed compliment so much as a rabbit-punch. Whatever Lewis's faults as a writer he never knowingly wrote a bad book or, indeed, one on any subject that he could not at least identify with in imagination. Curiously enough, his ex-wife, Grace Hegger, is more generous (and writes rather better prose) than the biographer:

> Even though Lewis's first successful novels can be recognized as written by him, it is significant that he created no school of writing as have Hemingway and Faulkner, Henry James and Flaubert. He influenced public thinking rather than public writing.

Surely, that is something. As for the man, after his ashes were returned to Sauk Center, she writes, "Dear, dear Minnesota Tumbleweed, driven by the winds of your own blowing, rootless to the day when your ashes were returned to the soil which had never received your living roots, I offer you these memories. With love from Gracie."

The New York Review of Books
8 October 1992

Both Mark Twain and his inventor, Samuel Clemens, continue to give trouble to those guardians of the national mythology to which Twain added so much in his day, often deliberately. The Freudians are still on his case even though Dr. Freud and his followers are themselves somewhat occluded these days. Yet as recently as 1991, an academic critic* tells us that Clemens was sexually infantile, burnt-out at fifty (if not before), and given to pederastic reveries about little girls, all the while exhibiting an unnatural interest in out-house humor and other excremental vilenesses. It is hard to believe that at century's end, academics of this degraded sort are still doing business, as Twain would put it, at the same old stand.

As is so often the case, this particular critic is a professor emeritus and emerituses often grow reckless once free of the daily grind of dispensing received opinion. Mr. Guy Cardwell, for reasons never quite clear, wants to convince us that Twain (we'll drop the Clemens because he's very much dead while Twain will be with us as long as there are English-speakers in the United States) "suffered from erectile dysfunction at about the age of fifty. . . . Evidence that he became impotent ranges from the filmy to the relatively firm." This is a fair example of the good professor's style. "Filmy" evidence suggests a slightly blurred photograph of an erection gone south, while "relatively firm" is a condition experienced by many men over fifty

---

* Guy Cardwell, *The Man Who Was Mark Twain* (Yale University Press, 1991). This oddly repellent work might have been more accurately—and more modestly— called *The Mark Twain Nobody Else Knows*.

who drink as much Scotch whisky as Twain did. But filmy—or flimsy?—as the evidence is, the professor wants to demolish its owner, who, sickeningly, *married above his station* in order to advance himself socially as well as to acquire a surrogate mother; as his own mother was—yes!—a strong figure while his father was—what else?—cold and uncaring.

No Freudian cliché is left unstroked. To what end? To establish that Twain hated women as well as blacks, Jews, foreigners, American imperialists, Christian missionaries, and Mary Baker Eddy. Since I join him in detesting the last three, I see no need to find a Freudian root to our shared loathing of, say, that imperialist jingo Theodore Roosevelt. Actually, Twain was no more neurotic or dysfunctional than most people and, on evidence, rather less out of psychic kilter than most other figures in the American literary canon.

Twain was born November 30, 1835, in Missouri. He spent his boyhood, famously, in the Mississippi River town of Hannibal. When he was twelve, his father died, becoming *truly* absent as Dr. Freud might sagely have observed, and Twain went to work as a printer's apprentice. Inevitably, he started writing the copy that was to be printed and, in essence, he was a journalist to the end of his days. Literature as such did not really engage him. *Don Quixote* was his favorite novel (as it was Flaubert's). He could not read Henry James, who returned the compliment by referring to him only once in his own voluminous bookchat, recently collected and published by the Library of America.

Exactly where and how the "Western Storyteller," as such, was born is unknown. He could have evolved from Homer or, later, from the Greek Milesian tales of run-on anecdote. In any case, an American master of the often scabrous tall story, Twain himself was predated by, among others, Abraham Lincoln, many of whose stories were particularly noisome as well as worse—worse!—*politically incorrect.* Our stern Freudian critic finds Twain's smutty stories full of "slurs" on blacks and women and so on. But so are those of Rabelais and Ariosto and Swift, Rochester and Pope and . . . Whatever the "true" motivation for telling such stories, Twain was a master in this line both in print and on the lecture circuit.

Primarily, of course, he was a popular journalist, and with the best-seller *Innocents Abroad* (1869) he made the hicks back home laugh and Henry James, quite rightly, shudder. Yet when the heavy-handed joky letters, written from the first cruise liner, *Quaker City*, became a text, it turned out to be an unusually fine-meshed net in which Twain caught up old Europe and an even older Holy Land and then, as he arranged his catch on the—well—deck of his art, he Americanized it in the most satisfactory way ("Lump the whole thing! Say that the Creator made Italy from designs by Michael Angelo!"), and made it possible for an American idea to flourish someday.

Twain was far too ambitious to be just a professional hick, as opposed to occasional hack. He had social ambitions; he also lusted for money (in a banal anal way, according to the Freudian emeritus—as opposed to floral oral?).

In the great tradition of men on the make, Twain married above his station to one Olivia Langdon of the first family of Elmira, New York. He got her to polish him socially. He also became a friend of William Dean Howells, a lad from the Western Reserve who had superbly made it in Boston as editor of *The Atlantic Monthly*. Howells encouraged Twain to celebrate the American "West" as the sort of romanticized Arcadia that Rousseau might have wanted his chainless noble savage to roam.

While knocking about the West and Southwest, Twain worked as pilot on Mississippi steamboats from 1857 to 1861; he joined the Civil War, briefly, on the Confederate side. When he saw how dangerous war might be, he moved on to the Nevada Territory, where his brother had been made secretary to the governor. He wrote for newspapers. In 1863, he started to use the pseudonym "Mark Twain," a river pilot's measurement of depth, called out on approaching landfall—some twelve feet, a bit on the shallow side for a proper ship.

After the war, Twain began to use life on the river and the river's bank as a background for stories that were to place him permanently at the center of American literature: *The Adventures of Tom Sawyer* (1876); *Life on the Mississippi* (1883); *The Adventures of Huckleberry Finn* (1884). He liked fame and money, the last perhaps too much since he was forever going broke speculating on experimental printing presses and underfinanced publishing houses. He lived in considerable bourgeois splendor at Hartford, Connecticut; oddly for someone who had made his fortune out of being *the* American writer, as he once described himself, Twain lived seventeen years in Europe. One reason, other than *douceur de la vie*, was that he was admired on the Continent in a way that he never was, or so he felt, by the eastern seaboard gentry, who were offended by his jokes, his profanity, his irreligion, and all those Scotch sours he drank. Fortunately, no one then suspected his erectile dysfunction.

Whenever cash was needed and a new book not ready to be sold to the public, Twain took to the lecture circuit. An interesting if unanswerable question: Was Mark Twain a great actor who wrote, or a great writer who could act? Or was he an even balance like Charles Dickens or George Bernard Shaw? Much of what Twain writes is conversation—dialogue—with different voices thrown in to delight the ear of an audience. But, whichever he was, he was always, literally, a journalist, constantly describing daily things while recollecting old things. In the process, he made, from time to time, essential literature, including the darkest of American novels, *Pudd'nhead Wilson* (1894).

Mark Twain's view of the human race was not sanguine, and much has been made of that Calvinism out of which he came. Also, his great river, for all its fine amplitude, kept rolling along, passing villages filled with fierce monotheistic folk in thrall to slavery, while at river's end there were the slave markets of New Orleans. Calvinist could easily become Manichean if he brooded too much on the river world of the mid-1800s. In *Pudd'nhead Wilson*, Twain's as yet unarticulated notion that if there is a God (*What Is Man?*, 1906) he is, if not evil in the Manichean sense, irrelevant, since man, finally, is simply a machine acted upon by a universe "frankly and hysterically insane" (*No. 44, The Mysterious Stranger*): "Nothing exists but You. And You are but a *thought*."

The agony of the twin boys in *Pudd'nhead Wilson*, one brought up white, the other black, becomes exquisite for the "white" one, who is found to be black and gets shipped downriver, his question to an empty Heaven unanswered: "What crime did the uncreated first nigger commit that the curse of birth was decreed for him?" All this, then, is what is going on in Mark Twain's mind as he gets ready for a second luxury tour, this time around the world.

When one contemplates the anti-imperialism of Mark Twain, it is hard to tell just where it came from. During his lifetime the whole country was—like himself—on the make, in every sense. But Mark Twain was a flawed materialist. As a Southerner he should have had some liking for the peculiar institution of slavery; yet when he came to write of antebellum days, it is Miss Watson's "nigger," Jim, who represents what little good Twain ever found in man. Lynchings shocked him. But then, *pace* Hemingway, so did Spanish bullfights. Despite the various neuroses ascribed to him by our current political correctionalists, he never seemed in any doubt that he was a man and therefore never felt, like so many sissies of the Hemingway sort, a need to swagger about, bullying those not able to bully him.

In 1898, the United States provoked a war with Spain (a war with England over Venezuela was contemplated but abandoned since there was a good chance that we would have lost). The Spanish empire collapsed more from dry rot than from our military skills. Cuba was made "free," and Puerto Rico was attached to us while the Spanish Philippines became our first Asian real estate and the inspiration for close to a century now of disastrous American adventures in that part of the world.

Mark Twain would have had a good time with the current demise of that empire, which he greeted, with some horror, in the first of his meditations on imperialism. The pamphlet "To the Person Sitting In Darkness" was published in 1901, a year in which we were busy telling the Filipinos that although we had, at considerable selfless expense, freed them from Spain they were not yet ready for the higher democracy, as exemplified by Tammany Hall, to use Henry James's bitter analogy. Strictly for their own good, we would have to kill one or two hundred thousand men, women, and children in order to make their country into an American-style democracy. Most Americans were happy to follow the exuberant lead of the prime architect of empire, Theodore Roosevelt—known to the sour Henry Adams as "our Dutch-American Napoleon." But then, suddenly, Mark Twain quite forgot that he was *the* American writer and erupted, all fire and lava.

The people who sit in darkness are Kipling's "lesser breeds," waiting for the white man to take up his burden and "civilize" them. Ironically, Twain compares our bloody imperialism favorably with that of the white European powers then abroad in the "unlit" world, busy assembling those colonial empires that now comprise today's desperate third world. Twain, succinctly for him, lists who was stealing what from whom and when, and all in the name of the "Blessings-of-Civilization Trust." But now the American writer is so shocked at what his countrymen are capable of doing in the imperial line that he proposes a suitable flag for the "Philippine Province": "We can have just our usual flag, with the white stripes painted black and the stars replaced by the skull and crossbones."

In 1905, Twain published a second pamphlet (for the Congo Defense Association), "King Leopold's Soliloquy," subtitled "A Defence of His Congo Rule." On the cover there is a crucifix crossed by a machete and the cheery inscription "By this sign we prosper."

The soliloquy is just that. The King of the Belgians is distressed by reports of his bloody rule over a large section of black Africa.

Leopold, an absolute ruler in Africa if not in Belgium, is there to "root out slavery and stop the slave-raids, and lift up those twenty-five millions of gentle and harmless blacks out of darkness into light. . . ." He is in rather the same business as Presidents McKinley and Roosevelt of the earlier pamphlet.

Leopold free-associates, noting happily that Americans were the first to recognize his rule. As he defends himself, his night-mind (as the Surrealists used to say) gets the better of him and he keeps listing his crimes as he defends them. He notes that his enemies "concede—reluctantly—that I have *one* match in history, but only one—the *Flood*. This is intemperate." He blames his current "crash" on "the incorruptible *kodak* . . . the only witness I have encountered in my long experience that I couldn't bribe." Twain provides us with a page of nine snapshots of men and women each lacking a hand, the King's usual punishment. Twain's intervention was not unlike those of Voltaire and Zola or, closer to home, Howells's denunciation of the American legal system—and press—that had found guilty the non-perpetrators of the Haymarket riots. Imperialism and tyranny for Twain were great evils but the more he understood—or thought he understood—the human race, the darker his view of the whole lot became, as he would demonstrate in the epigraphs from *Pudd'nhead Wilson's New Calendar* at the head of each chapter of his travel book *Following the Equator* (1897).

In Paris, 1895, Twain, his wife, Olivia, and their daughter Clara started on a round-the-world lecture tour. They crossed the Atlantic; then the United States; then, on August 23, they set sail from Vancouver bound for Sydney, Australia. For several years Twain had suffered a series of financial setbacks. Now the lecture tour would make him some money, while a look at the whole world would provide him with a great deal of copy, most of which he was to use in *Following the Equator*.

At the start of the tour, Twain seems not to have been his usual resilient self. "Mr. Clemens," wrote Olivia to a friend, "has not as much courage as I wish he had, but, poor old darling, he has been pursued with colds and inabilities of various sorts. Then he is so impressed with the fact that he is sixty years old." Definitely a filmy time for someone Olivia referred to as "Youth."

The pleasures of travel have not been known for two generations now; even so, it is comforting to read again about the soothing boredom of life at sea and the people that one meets aboard ship as well as on shore in exotic lands. One also notes that it was Twain in Australia, and not an English official recently testifying in an Australian court, who first noted that someone "was economical of the truth."

In Twain's journal, he muses about the past; contemplates General Grant, whose memoirs he had published and, presumably, edited a decade earlier. One would like to know more about that relationship since Gertrude Stein, among others, thought Grant our finest prose writer. When the ship stops in Honolulu, Twain notes that the bicycle is now in vogue, and "the riding horse is retiring from business everywhere in the world." Twain is not pleased by the combined influences of Christian missionaries and American soldiers upon what had once been a happy and independent Pacific kingdom.

They pass the Fiji Islands, ceded to England in 1858. Twain tells the story that when the English commissioner remarked to the Fiji king that it was merely "a sort of hermit-crab formality," the king pointed out that "the crab moves into an unoccupied shell, but mine isn't."

A great comfort to Twain aboard ship is *The Sentimental Song Book* of the Sweet Singer of Michigan, one Mrs. Julia A. Moore, who has, for every human occasion, numerous sublimely inapt verses that never, even by accident, scan.

> *Frank Dutton was as fine a lad*
> *As ever you wish to see,*
> *And he was drowned in Pine Island Lake*
> *On earth no more will he be,*
> *His age was near fifteen years,*

And he was a motherless boy,
He was living with his grandmother
When he was drowned, poor boy.

As one reads Twain's own prose, written in his own character, one is constantly reminded that he is very much a stand-up comedian whose laugh lines are carefully deployed at the end of every observation, thus reducing possible tension with laughter. Of the colonists sent out to Australia by England, Twain observes that they came from the jails and from the army. "The colonists trembled. It was feared that next there would be an importation of the nobility."

In general, Australia gets high marks. Twain and family travel widely; he lectures to large crowds: "The welcome which an American lecturer gets from a British colonial audience is a thing which will move him to his deepest deeps, and veil his sight and break his voice." He is treated as what he was, a Great Celebrity, and "I was conscious of a pervading atmosphere of envy which gave me deep satisfaction."

Twain continually adverts to the white man's crimes against the original inhabitants of the Pacific islands, noting that "there are many humorous things in the world; among them the white man's notion that he is less savage than the other savages." The Freudian critic cannot quite fathom how the Twain who in his youth made jokes about "Negroes" now, in his filmy years, has turned anti-white and speaks for the enslaved and the dispossessed. Dr. Freud apparently had no formula to explain this sort of sea change.

New Zealand appeals to Twain; at least they did not slaughter the native population, though they did something almost as bad: "The Whites always mean well when they take human fish out of the ocean and try to make them dry and warm and happy and comfortable in a chicken coop," which is how, through civilization, they did away with many of the original inhabitants. Lack of empathy is a principal theme in Twain's meditations on race and empire. Twain notes with approval that New Zealand's women have been able to vote since 1893. At sixty, he seems to have overcome his misogyny; our Freudian critic passes over this breakthrough in dark silence.

Ceylon delights. "Utterly Oriental," though plagued by missionaries who dress the young in Western style, rendering them as hideous on the outside as they are making them cruelly superstitious on the inside. Twain broods on slavery as he remembered it a half-century before in Missouri. He observes its equivalent in Ceylon and India. He meets a Mohammedan "deity," who discusses Huck Finn in perfect English. Twain now prefers brown or black skin to "white," which betrays the inner state rather too accurately, making "no concealments." Although he prefers dogs to cats, he does meet a dog that he cannot identify, which is odd since it is plainly a dachshund. He tries to get used to pajamas but goes back to the old-fashioned nightshirt. Idly, he wonders why Western men's clothes are so ugly and uncomfortable. He imagines himself in flowing robes of every possible color. Heaven knows what this means. Heaven and a certain critic. . . .

Benares has its usual grim effect. Here, beside the Ganges, bodies are burned; and people bathe to become pure while drinking the polluted waters of the holiest of holy rivers. It is interesting that Twain never mentions the Buddha, who became enlightened at Benares, but he does go into some detail when he describes the Hindu religion. In fact, he finds the city of Benares "just a big church" to that religion in all its aspects. In Calcutta, he broods on the Black Hole, already filled in. The Taj Mahal induces an interesting reverie. Twain notes that when one has read so many descriptions of a famous place, one can never actually see it because of all the descriptions that crowd one's mind. In this perception, Twain anticipates the latest—if not the last—theory of how memory works. He also broods on the phenomenon of Helen Keller, born deaf, dumb, and blind; yet able to learn to speak and think. How *does* the mind work?

From India, Twain and company cross the Indian Ocean to Mauritius. Although he often alludes to his lecturing, he never tells us what he talks about. He does note, "I never could tell a lie that anybody would doubt, nor a truth that anybody would believe." We learn that he dislikes Oliver Goldsmith and Jane Austen. As a prose writer, the imperialist Kipling beguiles him even though Twain likens empires to thieves who take clothes off other people's clotheslines. "In 800 years an obscure tribe of Muscovite savages has risen to the dazzling position of Land-Robber-in-Chief." He is more tolerant of the English. But then he is a confessed Anglophile.

Meanwhile, the ship is taking Twain and family down the east coast of Africa. South Africa is in ferment—Boers against English settlers, white against black. Cecil Rhodes is revealed as a scoundrel. But Twain is now writing as of May 1897, one year after his visit to South Africa, and so the outcome of all this is still unclear to him. He sides with the English, despite reservations about Rhodes and company. "I have always been especially fond of war. No, I mean fond of discussing war; and fond of giving military advice." As for that new territorial entity, Rhodesia, Twain remarks that it is "a happy name for that land of piracy and pillage, and puts the right stain upon it"; and he also has Pudd'nhead Wilson observe: "The very ink with which all history is written is merely fluid prejudice."

Finally, "Our trip around the earth ended at Southampton pier, where we embarked thirteen months before. . . . I seemed to have been lecturing a thousand years. . . ." But he had now seen the whole world, more or less at the equator, and, perhaps more to the point, quite a few people got to see Mark Twain in action, in itself something of a phenomenon, never to be repeated on earth unless, of course, his nemesis, Mary Baker Eddy, were to allow him to exchange her scientific deathless darkness for his limelight, our light.

The New York Review of Books
23 May 1996

While writing about Mark Twain's views on imperialism, I checked some recent "scholarly" works to see how his reputation is bearing up under the great fiery cross of political correctness. We were all astonished, some years ago, when a squad of sharp-eyed textual investigators discovered, to their manifest surprise and horror, that the noblest character in Twain's fiction was called "Nigger" Jim. There was an understandable outcry from some blacks; there was also a totally incomprehensible howl from a number of fevered white males, many of them professors emeritus and so, to strike the tautological note, career-minded conservatives unused to manning barricades.

In an apparently vain effort at comprehension, I quoted a number of malicious and, worse, foolish things that these silly-billies are writing about Twain. Thanks to an editorial quirk, one hothead was mentioned by *name*, for which I apologize. I always try to shield the infamous from their folly in the hope that they may, one day, straighten up and fly right. But a single name *was* mentioned and now we have its owner's letter at hand. For serene duplicity and snappy illogic it compares favorably to some of the screeds, I believe they are called, from my pen pals in the Lincoln priesthood.

Although my new pen pal does acknowledge that I am reporting the views of other critics on Twain's impotence, sexual infantilism, fondness for small girls, he declares mysteriously that this is "not what I say." But it is what he says and presumably means. The Jesuits like to say: "The wise man never lies." But in the army of my day, any soldier (or indeed discomfited general) who spent too much time twisting about the language of regulations in his own favor was called a guardhouse lawyer. I now put the case on the evidence at hand, that we have here a compulsive guardhouse lawyer or quibbler. Straight sentences must be bent like pretzels to change meanings to score points. But then much of what passes for literary discourse in these states is simply hustling words to get them to mean what they don't. "That Clemens dreamed of little girls is well known." Thus Quibbler wrote but now he has—tangential?—second thoughts. Actually who knows what Twain's dreams were. But let us agree that he doted on the company of Dodgsonesque girls and so may well have dreamed . . . fantasized about them in a sexual way. Why not? But Quibbler is getting a bit edgy. He thinks, too, that I have given him a splendid chance to open the guardhouse door. Now we improvise: "that his dreams and reveries were pederastic is not said in my book by me or by anyone else." But, of course, that's what the professor (and presumably, those whom he adverts to) means in the course of a chapter entitled "Impotence and Pedophilia."

But Quibbler has leapt at the adjective "pederastic." Like so many Greekless Americans with pretensions, he thinks that the word means a liking for boys by men with buggery on their mind. But I had gone back to the original noun root, *paid*, from which comes pederasty, pedophilia, etc.; and *paid* means not boy but child. A quibble can be made that, as vulgar usage associates the word with boys, that's what I mean but, as context makes clear, it is Lolita-*paid*—not Ganymede-*paid*—that Twain *may* be dreaming of. So this quibble is meaningless.

"The idea of impotence excited Clemens's anxious interest: apparently he suffered from erectile dysfunction at about the age of fifty." I noted in my review that "so do many men over fifty who drink as much Scotch whisky as Twain did." Next: "Psychoanalysts have noted many cases in which diminished sexual capacity . . . has been related to a constellation of psychic problems like those which affected Clemens." All right. Which psychoanalysts? Did any know him? As for his psychic problems, did he really have a constellation's worth? "Evidence that he became impotent ranges from the filmy to the relatively firm"—I had some fun with those two loony adjectives. "Likelihood is high that diminished capacity may be inferred . . ." All these "apparentlys," "likelihoods," "inferreds" as well as filmy to firm "evidence" appear in one short paragraph.

What we have here is not a serious literary—or even, God help us, psychoanalytic—view of Twain's sex life as imagined by a politically correct schoolteacher but what I take to be outright character assassination of a great man who happens to be one of the handful— small hand, too—of good writers our flimsy culture has produced. ("Filmy," of course, may be the *mot juste* if we count the movies.) At one point, in the midst of a prurient flow of nonsense, the professor suddenly concedes, "We do not know the intimate details of Clemens's life very well. . . ." I'll say we don't, so why go to such imaginative length to turn him into an impotent pederast, or pedophile?

Point two. Here we get the denial-of-meaning quibble based on Absence of Quotation Marks. I remark on Twain's having, sickeningly, in the professor's view, "*married above his station* in order to advance himself socially." Blandly, the professor quibbles that he never used the italicized words. Yet they are an exact paraphrase of how he interprets Twain's marriage to Olivia Langdon. Quibbler has reinvented his own text. Actually, it is his view that Twain did not marry above his station in any but the economic sense, although "like the most bourgeois of the bourgeois he delighted in money, and high living, and he fervently wished to become a member of the eastern establishment." Surely, to get from Hannibal, Missouri, to the Gold Coast of Hartford was going to take a bit of social climbing, which he did by marrying into the Langdon family.

"Clemens was what Freud would call a narcissistic suitor." Quibbler acts as if he is quoting some sort of authority in these matters. Ward McAllister might have been more to his point on American social climbing. "[Clemens] ardently wished to marry a woman who typified not what he was but what he wished to be—rich and possessed of status, a member of the eastern social order." So, as I said in a phrase to which Quibbler objects, for no clear reason, "he married above his station." (I'm surprised he does not make the point that Grand Central *Station* was not in use that hymenal year.) My use of the adverb "sickeningly" was meant to be ironic, something to which the teaching of school tends to make impervious even the brightest and the best. Anyway, Twain's hypergamous marriage was a happy one, so what's the big deal?

A lust for money that is banal anal (as opposed to floral oral) is simply a verbally symmetrical way of setting up Freud's notion of money as "faeces." How did I happen to get this juxtaposition in my head? At one point, our author suddenly quibbles that Twain didn't marry Olivia for her money, at least "not in any banal sense of the phrase; but he very much wanted to be rich." As I read the word "banal," I knew that Freud's theory of anality was coming up. I turned the page. There it was. "Freud stresses the anal character of money and equates money and feces: it means power, vitality, potency." The one good thing about bad writing is that one is never surprised by any turn an argument, much less a cliché, may take.

Let me now indulge in quibbler creativity. Freud would never have characterized Twain as narcissistic—an adjective currently used to describe anyone better-looking than oneself. As performer-writer Twain took by storm Vienna in general and Freud in particular. Freud was also something of a connoisseur of jokes and he enjoyed Mark Twain in person and on the page quite as much as he would have reveled in the letter of Professor Emeritus Guy Cardwell. *Ich kann nicht anders*, I can hear Sigmund chuckle through his cigar smoke. (Cf. *The Strange Case of Dr. Luther Adler* by an Unknown Actress—op. cit. Just about anywhere.)

Reporting for the BBC during the election campaign, I stood in front of the Albert Hall, the voice of the crown in parliament incarnate, John Major, still ringing in my ears as, inside, a recording of Elgar caused a thousand gorges to rise, including that little part of me which is forever Dimbleby. I faced the BBC cameras. A *petit* mini-mini-documentary was in progress. "Here," I said, head empty of all but emotion, "is the proof that only through England's glorious past can a bright future be secured for this land of Drake and Nelson, of Clive—and Crippen."

The BBC crew was ecstatic: like television crews everywhere, nobody ever listens to what the talking head is actually saying. What had come over me? What on earth was I doing? Well, like most American writers at one time or another, I was playing Mark Twain. The deadpan sonorous delivery. Then the careful dropping of the one fatal name. With Twain's description of the Albert Hall flashing in my head, "a dome atop a gasometer," I dimbled on to the safe ground of the understated cliché.

Mark Twain is our greatest . . . Mark Twain. He is not, properly speaking, a novelist nor "just" a journalist nor polemicist. He is simply a voice like no other. The only mystery to him is this: was he a great comic actor who could also write much as he acted, or was he a great writer who could also act, like Dickens? Some evidence of how he did both is now at hand in the form of the 309 letters that he wrote in the years 1872–3, when he first visited England and took the country by storm as a performer (the books *Innocents Abroad* and *Roughing It* had already, despite—or because of—their

Americanness, been popular). England also took hugely to the 36-year-old Twain (a.k.a. Samuel Clemens of Hannibal, Mo., and Hartford, Conn.). To his wife, Olivia, he wrote, after six months' residence in the Langham Hotel (later to contain the BBC's secret abattoir), "I would rather live in England than America—which is treason." The fact of the matter is that he was having a wonderful time being lionized by London's tamers, ever on the lookout for a good joke. But then, as he himself put it, he was "by long odds the most widely known and popular American author among the English." This was true too.

On Twain's first trip he did not lecture. On his second, accompanied by wife and daughter, he filled halls with a lecture on the Sandwich Islands, which he eventually tired of and replaced with one on his early days in Nevada, based on *Roughing It*.

The liking for a country not one's own (or for a celebrity not one's own) is usually based on serious misunderstandings all around. Twain's comedy was based on a Manichaean view of life. But neither audiences nor readers suspected the darkness that was at the core of his curious sensibility. As for Twain himself, in England he was very much the passionate pilgrim, to appropriate Henry James's phrase (it can safely be said that the two writers could not abide each other). Each in his own way had found American society a bit on the thin side. But where James was after very big game indeed, psychologically, Twain simply preferred local color, while reveling in a sense of the past that often came rather too close to ye olde. "Spent all day yesterday driving about Warwickshire in an open barouche. We visited Kenilworth ruins, Warwick Castle (pronounce it Warrick) and the Shakespeare celebrities in and about Stratford-on-Avon (pronounce that 'a' just as you would in Kate)." All in all, "I would rather live here if I could get the rest of you over." As it turned out, by the end of his life he had lived 17 years abroad, much of the time in England.

But there are some marked oddities in these love letters to England. For one thing there are hardly any people in them, any English people, that is. Trollope had him to dinner at the Garrick, but he gives no description of this occasion even when writing to his bookish mother. He met Browning: no serious mention. He does ask the poet laureate to one of his lectures and, thoughtfully, sends along a ticket. Return post: "Dear Sir, I saw some of your countrymen last Sunday who spoke so highly of your Lectures that I longed to come and hear you; but whether I come or not I am equally beholden to you for your kindness. Yours with all thanks, A. Tennyson." Not quite in the class of Disraeli, thanking an author for sending him a book "which I shall waste no time in reading."

Where are the London hostesses of the day? Did they pursue him? He hated staying in other people's houses so there are no descriptions of Bitter Homes and Gardens. For someone who had just finished a political satire, *The Gilded Age* (a "partnership" novel, he called it, with Charles Dudley Warner), he does not seem to have met any politicians other than the MP Douglas Straight, whose family was soon to be transatlantic. He does not mention what, if anything, he is reading. During his first London seasons he is simply absorbing color and drawing strength from the great crowds that come to hear him; first in Hanover Square and, later, around England.

These are very much the letters and thoughts of a businessman-actor-writer with a gift for comedy. He is, in short, a star on tour as well as a writer with an ever-alert eye for incidents to be used in such later books as *A Connecticut Yankee* and *The Prince and the Pauper*. Current productions by others (Samuel Butler's *Erewhon*, Thomas Hardy's *Under the Greenwood Tree*, and John Stuart Mill's *Autobiography*) go unremarked.

So what then did British audiences actually see and hear? London *Daily News*: "Mr. Twain is a comparatively young man, small in form and feature, dark-haired and dark complexioned." Actually, he was ginger-haired with a ruddy face. "He has a good deal of the nasal tone of some portion of the Americans." London *Examiner*: "His dry manner, his admirable self-possession, and perfectly grave countenance formed a background that made the humorous portion of the lecture irresistible." Often with no more than a carefully positioned pause, he would set up his joke, let the audience do the rest. "A smile never appears on his lips and he makes the most startling remarks as if he were uttering merest commonplace."

But a predictably sour note was struck by the expatriate secretary to the American legation: "He [Twain] is a wiry man, with brown, crisp, wiry hair: a narrow forehead, Roman nose and sinister expression, and does not seem to know as much as would hurt him." The secretary had once had literary longings.

Mark Twain's Letters covers two years in 691 pages, of which one is blank except for the ominous phrase "Editorial Apparatus." To come? One trembles. This is hardly a labor of love for the common reader. There are footnotes upon footnotes. Nothing is not explained. Twain meets a gentleman who affects a Plantagenet connection. The irrelevant history of that broomish family is flung at the reader.

American scholarship is now a sort of huge make-work program for the conventionally educated. In a case like this, scholar squirrels gather up every scrap of writing they can find and stuff these bits into volume after volume, with metastasizing footnotes. The arrangements that Mr. and Mrs. Clemens made to have their laundry and dry-cleaning done by mail (no, I won't explain how that worked) is a joy for those of us who revel in dry-cleaning, but what of the unkempt many who sit in darkness? No matter. We are dealing here with ruthless collectors. To them, one "fact" is equal to any other. I accept this thoroughness. But is it necessary to note every phrase—indeed every letter of the alphabet that Twain and his various correspondents saw fit to cross out? ~~Like this.~~ No.

The Sunday Times
11 May 1997

A decade ago, thanks to the success of America's chain bookstores with their outlets in a thousand glittering malls, most "serious" fiction was replaced by mass-baked sugary dough—I mean books—whose huge physical presence in the shops is known, aptly to the trade, as "dumps": outward and visible sign of Gresham's Law at dogged work. In spite of this, the fact that John Updike's latest novel, *In the Beauty of the Lilies*, briefly made it to the bottom of the *New York Times* best-seller list is remarkable. As it is a rare week when any "serious" novel is listed, one is usually so grateful that there are still those who want to read an even halfway good novelist, one ought never to discourage those readers whom he attracts. Also, what is the point of attacking writers in a period where—save for prize-mad pockets of old London—they are of so little consequence?

In observance of this law of a dying species, I have hardly mentioned, much less reviewed, Updike in the past, and he has observed the same continence with regard to me. But, lately, as I turn the pages of *The New Yorker*, where his poems, short stories, and book reviews have been appearing for so many years, I note an occasional dig at me. Apparently, I do not sufficiently love the good, the nice America, is the burden of his *épingles*. In sere and yellow leaf, Updike is now in superpatriot mood and on the attack. For instance, apropos the movie star Lana Turner (whom, to his credit, he appreciates): "Fifty years ago we were still a nation of builders and dreamers, now whittlers and belittlers set the cultural tone." O vile Whittlers! O unGodly Belittlers! Of whom, apparently, I am one.

Although I've never taken Updike seriously as a writer, I now find him the unexpectedly relevant laureate of the way we would like to live now, if we have the money, the credentials, and the sort of faith in our country and its big God that passes all understanding. Finally, according to the mainline American press, Updike has now got it all together, and no less an authority than *The New Yorker*'s George Steiner (so different from Europe's one) assures us that Updike now stands alongside Hawthorne and Nabokov, when, surely, he means John P. Marquand and John O'Hara.

Prior to immersion in next year's Pulitzer Prize novel, I read Updike's memoir, *Self-Consciousness* (1989), written in the writer's fifty-seventh year. Self-consciousness is a good theme, if meant ironically. After all, save to self, we are, none of us, worth much fussing about, run-of-the-mill poor, bare forked animals—or was it radishes?—that we are. Anyway, I hoped that he would make some self-mocking play on his own self-consciousness as opposed to Socrates' examined life. Hope quickly extinguished. There is no examination of the self, as opposed to an unremitting self-consciousness that tells us why he was—is—different—but not too much different—from others and what made him the way he is—always *is*, as he doesn't much change in his own story, a small-town Philoctetes whose wound turns out to be an unpretty skin condition called psoriasis. "Yet what was my creativity, my relentless need to produce but a parody of my skin's embarrassing overproduction?"

John Updike's father was of Dutch-American stock; his mother German. He was born in 1932, in modest circumstances at Shillington, Pennsylvania. The mother was a would-be writer, constantly typing away and sending out stories that returned to her like so many boomerangs. The son would soon outdo the mother, *his* stories returning home in the pages of *The New Yorker*.

The Shillington that he describes is a sunny place, despite the Depression of the 1930s and some labor strikes; more than once, Updike edgily refers to the election by the nearby city of Reading of a *socialist* mayor. Happily, for his school of Biedermeier novels, the world outside himself seems never to have caught his proper interest until the dread 1960s, when "bright young men who are born with silver spoons in their mouth . . . were selling this nation out." But that was long after he was a "plain child, ungainly youth. Lacking brothers and sisters, [he] was shy and clumsy in the give and take . . . of human exchange." Of contemporaries who did not care for school, "I could not understand how anybody could rebel against a system so clearly benign." But then he is always true to his "docile good child nature."

Yet under all this blandness and acceptance of authority in any form, there is a growing puzzlement. "Social position in America is not easy to be precise about," he notes; then, warily, he tries to place his high-school teacher father: "My family sold asparagus and pansies for odd money, embarrassing me." But unlike a Fitzgerald or an O'Hara (most Irish Catholic writers in America are born with perfect radar on how to make it all the way to the blue light at landing's end—or pass out at the bar in the attempt), Updike seems to have missed whatever gentry there may have been in the neighborhood. All he knows is that his mother says that we are much "nicer" than a lot of other people, which is important if not very useful, as his father is a definite nonsuccess, and so Updike concludes that:

> Life breeds punchers and counterpunchers, venturers like my father and ambushers like me: the venturer risks rebuff and defeat; the ambusher . . . risks fading away to nothing. . . . All those years in Shillington, I had waited to be admired, waited patiently . . . burrowing in New York magazines and English mystery novels for the secret passageway out, the path of avoidance and vindication. I hid a certain determined defiance. . . . I would "show" them, I would avenge all the slights and abasements visited upon my father—the miserly salary, the subtle tyranny of his overlords at the high school, the disrespect of his students, the laughter in the movie house at the name of Updike.

Not exactly Richard III. Rather the inner rebellion of a shy, ambitious, small creature—a rabbit?—preparing to abandon its nice safe burrow for a world elsewhere, for a place across the water in nearby sinful Manhattan.

Shillington was to remain central to Updike's intense consciousness of self. In footnotes to his memoir, he solemnly quotes from his own work to show just how he has used the "real" life of his small town in fiction. Over and over again he writes of the Lutheran Grace Church, the elementary school, the post office, of youthful revels at Stephens' Luncheonette. Not since Sinclair Lewis has a naturalistic writer been so merciless to his reader as Updike. Endlessly, he describes shops and their contents, newspaper advertisements, streets that go here, there and everywhere except into the—this—reader's mind. Places and people seem to interest him only when reduced, as cooks say, to receipts not dishes. Certainly all the words he uses are there on the page, but what they stand for is not. Only he himself is recorded with careful attention, as he notes his aim of "impersonal egoism," and "always with some natural hesitation and distaste" when it comes to memoir-writing; yet he soldiers on, and we learn that only after the family moved from Shillington does he masturbate—and so a lifelong adhesion to heterosexuality begins, at least in the mind. With *jouissance*, he comes into his kingdom, love in hand.

As a fellow *New Yorker* writer, S. J. Perelman, puts it in a letter to Ogden Nash in 1965, "J. Updike . . . read extracts from three works of his to the assembled scholars, which I didn't personally hear as I was overtaken by the characteristic nausea that attacks me when this youth performs on the printed pages. But Cheever brought me tidings that all dealt with masturbation, a favorite theme of Updike's." Of course, Perelman was a bit of a grouch; and who could have foretold that in three years' time this onanistic "youth" would write *Couples*, a celebration of marriage and its saucy twin, adultery, the only important subjects of middlebrow fiction, saving God Himself and His America? It should be noted that Christianity seems always to have been a fact for Updike, starting with the Grace

Lutheran and other churches of Shillington; later, as an outward and visible sign of niceness and of belongingness, he remains a church-goer when he moves up the social scale to Ipswich, Massachusetts, where he achieves that dream of perfect normality which is not only American and Christian but—when in the company of other up-wardly mobile couples—ever so slightly bohemian.

Although Updike seems never to have had any major psychic or physical wound, he has endured all sorts of minor afflictions. In the chapter "At war with my skin," he tells us in great detail of the skin condition that sun and later medicine would clear up; for a long time, however, he was martyr to it as well as a slave to his mirror, all the while fretting about what "normal" people would make of him. As it proved, they don't seem to have paid much attention to an af-fliction that, finally, "had to do with self love, with finding myself ac-ceptable . . . the price high but not impossibly so; I must pay for being me." The price for preserving me certainly proved to be well worth it when, in 1955, he was rejected for military conscription, even though the empire was still bogged down in Korea and our forces were increased that year from 800,000 to three million—less Updike, who, although "it pains me to write these pages," confesses that he was "far from keen to devote two years to the national de-fense." He was later to experience considerable anguish when, al-most alone among serious writers, he would support the Vietnam War on the ground that who am I "to second-guess a president?" One suspects that he envies the clear-skinned lads who so reluctantly fought for the land *he* so deeply loves.

"I had a stammer that came and went." But he is ever game: "As with my psoriasis, the affliction is perhaps not entirely unfortunate." Better than to be born with a silver spoon in one's mouth is to be born at the heart of a gray cloud with a silver lining. The stammer does "make me think twice about going onstage and appearing in classrooms and at conferences," but "Being obliging by nature and anxious for approval, I would never say no if I weren't afraid of stut-tering. Also, as I judge from my own reactions, people who talk too easily and comfortably . . . arouse distrust in some atavistic, pre-speech part of ourselves; we turn off." Take that, Chrysostom Chatterbox! Characteristically, he is prompt to place a soothing Band-Aid on his own wound: he quotes Carlyle, who observes of Henry James: "a stammering man is never a worthless man." Whatever that means. (Also, *pace* Carlyle, the Master did not stammer; he filibustered elaborately, cunningly, with pauses so carefully calculated that if one dared try to fill one, he would launch a boa-constrictor of a sentence at the poor mesmerized, oh, dear, rabbit! of an auditor.) Finally, Updike confesses to unease with certain groups that your average distinguished author must address. He is afraid of New York audiences especially: "They are too smart and left wing for me. . . ." This seems to mean politically minded Jews, so unlike the *nice* Southern college audiences with whom he is most at home.

Dental problems occupy many fascinating pages. But then I am a sucker for illness and debilities and even the most homely of exurban *memento mori*. Finally, relatively late in life, he develops asthma! This splendid coda (to date) of the Updike physical apparatus is something of a master stroke, and, as I once coughed along with Hans Castorp and his circle, I now find myself wheezing along with Updike; but then I, too, am mildly asthmatic.

The psychic Updike is dealt with warily. The seemingly effortless transition from the Shillington world to Harvard and then to the *New Yorker* staff is handled with Beylesque brevity. He notes, but does not demonstrate, the influence on him of such Christian conservative writers as G. K. Chesterton and C. S. Lewis and Jacques Maritain, while the names Karl Barth and Kierkegaard are often treated as one word, Barthegaard. He tells us that, as a novelist, "my models were the styles of Proust and Henry Green—dialogue and meditation as I read them (one in translation)." Which one? We shall never know. But for those of us who reveled in the French translations of Green, I can see how attractive those long irregular subjunctive-laden "tender explorations" must have been for Updike, too. Although every other American novelist of the past half-century seems to regard Proust as his "model," one finds no trace of Proust in Updike's long lists of consumer goods on sale in shops as well as of human characteristics that start with external features, followed by internal "meditations" on the true character of the Character.

Despite all of Updike's book-reviewing, one gets the sense that books have not meant much to him, young or old; but then he was originally attracted to the graphic arts (he attended the Ruskin School at Oxford), and the minor technical mysteries of lettering nibs and scratchboard. . . . "And my subsequent career carries coarse traces of its un-ideal origins in popular, mechanically propagated culture." This is endearing; also, interesting—"I was a cultural bumpkin in love not with writing, but with print." And, like everyone else of the time, with the movies, as he will demonstrate in his latest novel.

Easily, it would appear, he became an all-round writer for *The New Yorker* "of the William Shawn era (1951–87) . . . a club of sorts, from within which the large rest of literary America . . . could be politely disdained. . . . While I can now almost glimpse something a bit too trusting in the serene sense of artistic well-being, of virtual invulnerability, that being published in *The New Yorker* gave me for over thirty years. . . ." During much of this time, he seemed unaware that the interesting, indeed major, writers of the period did not belong to his club, either because they were too disturbing for the mild Shawn or because they could not endure the radical editing and rewriting that the quintessential middlebrow magazine imposed on its writers. "I shook with anger," Perelman wrote in 1957, "at their august editorial decisions, their fussy little changes and pipsqueak variations on my copy." Nabokov, published at Edmund Wilson's insistence, needed all of Wilson's help in fighting off editorial attempts to make his prose conform to the proto–Ralph Lauren house impersonation of those who fit, socially, in the roomy top-drawer-but-one. Unlike that original writer, Nabokov, Updike, ever "the good child," throve under strict supervision and thought himself on Parnassus, a harmless, even beguiling misunderstanding so long as the real world never confronted him, which, of course, it did.

————

The Vietnam war jolted Updike into the nearest he has yet come to self-examination as opposed to self-consciousness. "I was a liberal," he notes at some point. That is, he didn't like Nixon when he was at Harvard, and he voted for Kennedy. But now he strikes the Pecksniffian note as he invokes class distinctions. Of liberals at Harvard, "they, Unitarian or Episcopalian or Jewish, support Roosevelt and Truman and Stevenson out of enlightenment, *de haut en bas*, whereas in my heart of hearts, I however, veneered with an education and button-down shirts, was *de bas*. They, secure in the upper-middle class, were Democrats out of human sympathy and humanitarian largesse, because this was the party that helped the poor. Our family had simply *been* poor, and voted Democrat out of crude self-interest." He is now moving into McCarthy, Wallace, Buchanan country. Resentment, for Updike a slow-blooming plant, is starting to put forth lurid flowers, suitable for funeral wreaths to be laid upon his carefully acquired affluent niceness as well as upon the sort of company that it had earned him, which, almost to a man, stood against the war that he accepts and even, for a time, favors. Suddenly he starts scrabbling in search of peasant roots to show that he is really *dans le vrai*—unlike those supercilious silver-spoon-choked snobs who dare "second-guess" presidents.

"Was I conservative? I hadn't thought so, but I did come from what I could begin to see" (after a third of a century?) "was a conservative part of the country. . . . The Germans of Berks County didn't move on, like the typical Scots-Irish frontier-seeking Americans. They stayed put, farming the same valleys and being buried in the same graveyards. . . ." Presumably, this stay-put mindset ought to have made him isolationist and antiwar when it came to military adventures in far-off places where other Americans, whom he knew little of, fought Asians, whom he knew nothing of. But, startlingly, he chooses to interpret the passivity of his ancestral tribes as the reason for his own unquestioning acceptance of authority: if the president wants you to go fight the Viet Cong in order to contain the Viet Cong's mortal enemy, China, you must not question, much less second-guess him. You will go fight when and where he tells you to, unless you are lucky enough to be kept safe at home by psoriasis. For the first time, the apolitical, ahistorical Updike was faced with what pop writers call an Identity Crisis.

"By my mid-thirties, through diligence and daring" (if one did not know better, one might think the second adjective ironic), "I had arrived at a lifestyle we might call genteel bohemian—nice big house (broad floorboards, big fireplaces). . . . We smoked pot, wore dashikis and love beads, and frugged ourselves into a lather while the Beatles and Janis Joplin sang away on the hi-fi set. I was happy enough to lick the sugar of the counterculture; it was the pill of antiwar, anti-administration, anti-'imperialist' protest that I found oddly bitter." He notes that the frugging technocrats *et al.* of his acquaintance simply sloughed off the war as an "administration blunder." But writers, artists, even the very voices to whose sound Updike frugged, began very early to object to the war, while "I whose stock in trade as an American author included an intuition into the mass consciousness and an identification with our national fortunes—thought it sad that our patriotic myth of invincible virtue was crashing, and shocking that so many Americans were gleeful at the crash." This is worthy of Nixon at his unctuous best; yet to give that canny old villain his due, Nixon wouldn't have believed a word he was saying. Incidentally, who was "gleeful" at so much mindless carnage? And what honest citizen would *not* be grateful that a "myth" of any kind, no matter how "patriotic," be dispelled?

When intellectuals, for want of any other word, were asked to contribute their views to a book called *Authors Take Sides on Vietnam*, Updike admitted that he was "uncomfortable" about our military adventure, but wondered "how much of the discomfort has to do with its high cost, in lives and money, and how much with its moral legitimacy." This is wondrously callous. Of course, television had not yet shown us too many lives, much less money, being lost on prime time, but Updike weighs them as nothing in the balance when compared to the moral decision made by our elected leaders, who must know best—otherwise they would not be our elected leaders. Loyal to authority, he favors intervention "if it does some good," because "the crying need is for genuine elections whereby the South Vietnamese can express their will. If their will is for Communism, we should pick up our chips and leave." But the American government had stopped the Vietnamese from holding such elections a decade earlier, because, as President Eisenhower noted in his memoirs, North and South Vietnam would have voted for the Communist Ho Chi Minh and "we could not allow that." Updike's ignorance—innocence, to be kind—is not very reassuring, even when he echoes Auden on how "it is foolish to canvass writers upon political issues." Our views, as he says, "have no more authority than those of any reasonably well-educated citizen." Certainly, the views of a writer who knew nothing of the political situation in Vietnam weren't worth very much, but, as an American writer identified with our national fortunes, Updike does acknowledge that writers are supposed to be attuned to the human as well as to the moral aspects of engaging in war, particularly one so far from our shores, so remote from our interests. As Updike's wife at the time told him, "It's their place." But by then it was too late. Mild Rabbit had metamorphosed into March Hare.

Letter to *The New York Times*: "I discover myself named . . . as the lone American writer 'unequivocally for' the United States intervention in Vietnam." He notes that he is not alone. Apparently James Michener, "an old Asia hand," and Marianne Moore, an old baseball hand, thought that the Commies should be stopped by us anywhere and everywhere . . . or, in Updike's case, by *them*, the Americans obliged to fight. He finds such opponents as Jules Pfeiffer and Norman Mailer "frivolous." Mailer had written, "The truth is maybe we need a war. It may be the last of the tonics. From Lydia Pinkham to Vietnam in sixty years, or bust." Mailer was being Swiftian. But Updike is constitutionally unable to respond to satire, irony, wit, rhetorical devices that tend to be offensive to that authority which he himself means to obey.

Updike takes offense at a "cheerful thought by James Purdy: 'Vietnam is atrocious for the dead and maimed innocent, but it's probably sadder to be a live American with only the Madison Ave-

nue Glibbers for a homeland and a God.' " Rabbit will go to his final burrow without ever realizing the accuracy of Purdy's take on the
society in which Updike was to spend his life trying to find a nice
place for himself among his fellow Glibbers.

For a certain kind of quotidian novelist, there is nothing wrong
in leaving out history or politics. But there is something creepy
about Updike's overreaction to those of us who tried to stop a war
that was destroying (the dead to one side) a political and economic
system that had done so well by so many rabbits. Updike is for the
president, any president, right or wrong, because at such a time "it
was a plain citizen's duty to hold his breath and hope for the best."
For thirteen years? Then, with unexpected passion, he sides with
what he takes to be the majority of Americans against those members of the upper class whom he once emulated and now turns upon:
"Cambridge professors and Manhattan lawyers and their guitar-
strumming children thought they could run the country and the
world better than this lugubrious bohunk from Texas (Johnson).
These privileged members of a privileged nation . . . full of aesthetic
disdain for their own defenders." At some point, unclear to me, the
Viet Cong must have bombed San Diego. "At a White House
dinner in June of 1965, I saw what seemed to me a touching
sight: Johnson and Dean Rusk . . . giving each other a brief hug in
passing—two broad-backed Southern boys, trying to hold the fort."

After the thrill of watching those whom Unser Gott had placed over
us, Updike turns manic ("My face would become hot, my voice high
and tense and wildly stuttery"). He grieves for "the American soldiers, derided and mocked at home. . . ." This is purest Johnson.
Whenever LBJ was attacked for having put the troops in Vietnam
for no clear reason, he would charge those who questioned presidential mischief with disloyalty—even treason—against our brave
boys, when, of course, it was he and Eisenhower and Kennedy and
Ford and Nixon who supported the sacrifice of our brave boys in a
war that none of these presidents could ever, with straight face, explain; a war whose longtime executor, Robert McNamara, now tells

us that he himself never did figure out. But in the presence of Authority, Updike is like a bobby-soxer at New York's Paramount Theater when the young Frank Sinatra was on view. Out of control, he writes, "Under the banner of a peace-movement . . . war was being waged by a privileged few upon the administration and the American majority that had elected it." The reverse was true. Finally Wall Street marched against the war, and Nixon surrendered, weightier matters, like impeachment, on his mind.

"Reading a little now, I realize how little I knew, for all my emotional involvement, about the war itself, a war after all like other wars. . . ." But it was not like other wars. No matter, the March Hare has turned his attention to other legitimacies, such as God. "Western culture from Boethius to Proust had transpired under the Christian enchantment." What an odd pairing! Plainly, Updike doesn't know much about Boethius. It is true that after his execution by the Emperor Theodoric in A.D. 525, he was taken over by the Christian establishment (Latin team) as a patristic authority, even though, in his last work, *The Consolation of Philosophy* (a "golden volume," according to Gibbon), he is mostly Platonist except when he obeys the injunction "follow God" in imitation not of the tripartite Christian wonder but of Pythagoras. As for the half-Jew Proust, so emotionally and artistically involved in the Dreyfus case, Christianity in action could hardly have been "enchanting." But Updike, in theological mood, is serenely absolutist: "Among the repulsions of atheism for me has been its drastic uninterestingness as an intellectual position." This is very interesting.

At times, reading Updike's political and cultural musings, one has the sense that there is no received opinion that our good rabbit does not hold with passion. "The fights for women's rights and gay rights emerged enmeshed with the Vietnam protest and have outlived it. Though unconsciously resisting the androgyny, which swiftly became—as all trends in a consumer society become—a mere fashion, I must have felt challenged." As American women have been trying to achieve political and economic parity with men for two centuries, how can these activities be considered "mere fashion" or a new consumer trend? For Updike, fags and dykes are comical figures who like their own sex and so cannot be taken seriously when they apply for the same legal rights under the Constitution that fun-loving, wife-swapping exurbanites enjoy. Reality proved too much for him. "I found the country so distressing in its civil fury" that he, along with current wife and Flopsy, Mopsy, and Cottontail, fled to London "for the school year of 1968–69." The year, one should note, of the three "decadent" best-sellers, *Portnoy's Complaint*, *Myra Breckinridge*, and his own *Couples*.

Today, Rabbit seems at relative peace. He addresses a letter to his grandchildren full of family lore. Along the way, he has acquired an African son-in-law. He is full of Shillington self-effacing gracefulness on what—if any—race problem there might still be in the grand old United States, converted during the Reagan years—golden years for bunnies—to a City on a Hill where he can now take his ease and en-joy the solace of Religion, pondering "the self [which] is the focus of anxiety; attention to others, self-forgetfulness and living like [*sic*] the lilies are urged."

Between *Self-Consciousness* (1989) and the current *In the Beauty of the Lilies*, Updike has published three novels, a book of short sto-ries, and one of critical pieces. He is, as Dawn Powell once said of herself, "fixed in facility," as are most writers-for-life; a dying breed, I suspect, as, maw ajar, universal Internet swallows all. Meanwhile, Updike has written his Big Book, the story of four generations of American life, starting in 1910 and ending more or less today in—and on—television, as practically everything does in what the be-mused Marx thought might be our "exceptional" republic.

Before the outbreak of the Civil War, John Brown, a yeoman from Connecticut, destined to be forever connected with Os-awatomie, Kansas, set himself up as a unilateral abolitionist of slav-ery in a state torn between pro- and antislavery factions. Updike probably first encountered him, as I did, in the film *Santa Fe Trail* (1940), where he was made gloriously incarnate by Raymond Massey. With a band of zealots, Brown occupied the federal arsenal at Harpers Ferry, Virginia. The nation suddenly was afire. Inevitably,

Brown was defeated and hanged by the state of Virginia, thus making him a martyr for the North, while a song, "John Brown's Body," was set to a rousing old English folk tune. The poet Julia Ward Howe, listening to troops sing the demotic words to "John Brown's Body," in a Delphic fever of inspiration, wrote her own words for what would later be known as "The Battle Hymn of the Republic," one of the few stirring pieces of national music to give the "Marseillaise" a run for its Euro-francs.

Updike has chosen for his title one of the least mawkish, if not entirely coherent, quatrains from Howe's lyrics. "In the beauty of the lilies Christ was born across the sea / With a glory in his bosom that transfigures you and me / As he died to make men holy, let us die to make men free / While God is marching on." Precisely why God has chosen this moment to go marching—on to where?—is a secret as one with the source of the sacred river Alph. But, no matter, this is rousing stuff. It is patriotic; it favors the freedom of black slaves at the South; it is botanically incorrect—no lilies at Bethlehem in December, as opposed to all those iconographic lilies during April's immaculate conception. But the text fits Updike's evening mood; it also provides him with an uplifting sonorous title, though a more apt title could have been found in the quatrain that begins, "I have seen Him in the watch-fires of an hundred circling camps; / They have builded Him an altar in the evening dews and damps." Updike has well and truly builded us a novel that might well and truly be called "The Evening Dews and Damps." He has also written easily the most intensely political American novel of the last quarter-century.

The story begins in the grounds of a baronial estate in Paterson, New Jersey. Shillington territory. But this is not your usual Rabbit story. On the lawn, D. W. Griffith is making a film with Mary Pickford. We hear little more about this film, but the modern note has been struck. Now we must defer satisfaction, as Updike gives us a list of things, visible and invisible, in the immediate neighbourhood—like New York City only fifteen miles to the east of Paterson "lying sullenly snared within the lowland loop of the Passaic River." One wonders what editor Shawn might have made of that "sullenly." Surely, there must have been a house ukase against the pathetic fallacy. But Updike has always liked to signal with his adverbs as he conforms with his adjectives. Besides, he is now off the *New Yorker* page and on to his very own page.

The first section is titled "Clarence." The Reverend Clarence Arthur Wilmot of the Fourth Presbyterian Church, whose address we are given as well as the church's dimensions, physically and spiritually, along with those of Clarence himself, "a tall narrow-chested man of forty-three," etc., etc., who has, at this moment, suddenly, almost idly, lost his faith. A promising beginning which might have been more effective without the weeds of description that precede it. Even so, there *it* is, on the third page—the Problem. In order to refute a lapsing parishioner, Clarence has been reading the atheist Robert Ingersoll's *Some Mistakes of Moses*, and, in the process, in a flash of utter darkness, he comes to the conclusion that Ingersoll was "quite right." Shaken, Clarence makes his way home through a forest of description and into his house with its "leaded rectangles of stained glass the color of milky candies and the foot of the dark walnut staircase that, in two turnings punctuated by rectangular newel posts whose point had been truncated . . ." We are spared nothing, rectangular or otherwise.

Clarence ponders free will versus predestination, the sort of thing that at a church school like St. Albans, to the south of Paterson in Washington, D.C., most boys had pretty much wrapped up before the onset of puberty   or Grace, whichever took place first. We meet wife and mother, Stella, supervising the cook in the kitchen. Tonight there will be supper for some important Presbyterians. Money for the church will be discussed. Clarence listens to kitchen chatter: "The eavesdropping clergyman, numbed by his sudden atheism . . ." Then we're off to a description of lots and lots of things in the house including a Tiffany-glass chandelier, with scalloped edges. Updike never quite knows what to do with his lists of random objects or physical human characteristics. In this, he resembles a more graceful James Michener, whose huge books are simply compendia of thousands of little facts collected by researchers and deposited helter-skelter in his long "novels."

Updike also provides us with reading lists of those books that encourage and discourage Christian faith. Clarence is suffering from a mini-vastation, somewhat diluted by Updike's sudden introduction of "real people" into the book, or at least of real names culled from contemporary newspapers. There is Mary Pickford at the start. Then a son of Theodore Roosevelt gets married. We are given the list of ushers, dazzling society names of the day. Updike will keep on doing this for the entire sixty-year period covered by his narrative. But a technique that worked so well for John Dos Passos in *USA* simply stops dead what story Updike has to tell.

Updike, unlike his alleged literary models, Henry Green and Proust, describes to no purpose. In fact, Green, as I recall, describes hardly anything, relying on a superlative ear for a wide variety of speech patterns, while Updike's characters all speak in the same tone of voice, their dialogue a means to get them from one plot point to the next. As one trudges through these descriptions, one wishes that Updike had learned less from his true models, Marquand and O'Hara, and more from the middle James, who, as a lord of the pertinent and the relevant, knew that nothing need be described or, indeed, *told* unless it suggests, while never naming, the presence in the deep of monsters, as the author, off-page, turns ever tighter the screw.

Although in *The Spoils of Poynton* mother and son fight over the contents of a great house, we are never told just *what* is being fought over. James leaves the details to the reader's imagination. But such continence has never been the way of the commercial American writer, no matter how elevated his theme or resourceful his art. For Updike, Poynton is a Sotheby's catalog.

James only needed to describe—was it one crucifix?—to represent a house full of rare furniture and objects worth killing for. The naturalistic Dos Passos used movielike cuts and intercuts of headlines to act as useful counterpoint to a narrative that takes place in public, as opposed to strictly private, time. Since most people get the news of their day through press and television, why not use or at least mimic these sources? The naturalistic Updike seems to think that just about any item will do in the way of color, and, in a sense, he is right; one has only to consider the huge popularity of Michener's myriad-fact novels with an unsophisticated reading public that likes to think that valuable time is not being wasted on a made-up story, that the reader is really getting the inside dope on, let's say, Detroit and the auto business or, in Updike's case, on the United States' second most profitable export after aerospace—showbiz and Hollywood. But whereas a few million small facts are the object of the Michenerian enterprise, Updike is more conventionally ambitious. He wants to dramatize the forces that have driven the United States ever leftward, even further away from the marching, lily-born God, away from family values and obedience to Authority, away from *The New Yorker*'s benign fact-checkers and sentence-polishers, so sadly absent now when he really needs them.

After James's disasters in the theater, he famously returned to prose with a new sharp intensity. He had learned that nothing is to be noted unless it is absolutely essential to the dramatic revelation of even the vaguest figure in the carpet. As far as I know, Updike has never submitted himself to the strict discipline of relevance one learns from theater. And yet, parenthetically, his one attempt at a play, *Buchanan Dying* (1974), though probably unstageable as written, is a superb work of mimesis, the last thoughts of the enigmatic president from Pennsylvania whose cautious inertness helped bring on the Civil War and imperial Lincoln. The effect is startling and unique, unlike . . .

"Dialogue and meditation" is how Updike, inaccurately, describes the manner of his early "model," Henry Green. Updike himself writes long, long descriptions interspersed with brief snatches of dialogue. In theory . . . no, no theory! . . . *ideally*, both description and dialogue should forward narrative, as in most pop writing. Realistic storytellers in English oscillate between the *démeublement* of Raymond Carver and the richly detailed settings, physical and psychic, of James Purdy. For a true master of effects, either way works. But if, like Updike, one means to go into the wholesale furniture business, one had better be prepared to furnish, in appropriate manner, great Poynton itself. I realize that in a world where democracy is on the rise everywhere except in American politics, one style can never be better than another, 'cause my feelings are just as deep as yours and how can you criticize my voice, my style which is Me? To which some of us old meanies must respond, well, dear, if you choose to send your letter to the world then here's the answer, assuming the letter was not returned to sender for lack of correct address or sufficient postage.

Years ago, in unkind mood, Norman Mailer referred to Updike's writing as the sort of prose that those who know nothing about writing think good. Today, theory, written preferably in near-English academese, absorbs the specialist, and prose style is irrelevant. Even so, what is one to make of this sentence: "The hoarse receding note drew his consciousness . . . to a fine point, and while that point hung in his skull starlike he fell asleep upon the adamant bosom of the depleted universe"? Might Updike not have allowed one blind noun to slip free of its seeing-eye adjective?

Plot, four generations of the Wilmot family. After Clarence's loss of faith, he sells encyclopedias, perseveres in his failure, as did Updike's own father, each to be avenged by a descendant; though not by Clarence's son, Teddy, who occupies the next chunk of time—and novel-space. Now we go into the Updike time machine. "And then it was a new decade, and drinking was illegal all across the nation, and Attorney General A. Mitchell Palmer accused the IWW of causing the railroad strikes. . . . Mary Pickford and Douglas Fairbanks were married in a Hollywood dream come true, and Europe twisted and turned with coups and riots and little wars" (which ones?), "and the Democrats at their convention put up James Cox and another Roosevelt, and Bill Tilden . . . and . . . and . . . and . . ."

Teddy doesn't know what to do with his life. He is passive and not very bright. He works in a bottle-top factory; studies accounting. Meanwhile, he struggles for light beneath his author's thick blankets of research, intended to give us the sense of a world and a time in which Teddy himself has neither place nor perceptible interest: "And now the sordidness of illusions was leaking out of Hollywood itself. . . . Fatty Arbuckle, unsolved mystery of director William Desmond Taylor . . ." But there is some point to all this news from outside, because, in the next slice of the Wilmot saga, Teddy's daughter, Esther or Essie, will become a Movie Star and avenge—"ambush," as Updike did—a world that paid no attention to his father, her grandfather. When Teddy goes to work in Addison's Drug Store (Stephenson's back in Shillington), we are given page after page of what is sold in the store. Then Teddy marries a crippled girl with a strong character. Teddy gives up being a soda jerk and becomes a career postman. He endures a happy marriage, until his wife, as fictional characters tend to do, falls through one of the interstices in Updike's web of Passing Parade notes on world events: "Jews and Arabs fought in Jerusalem; Chinese and Russians battled along the Manchurian border." Social notes from all over. Teddy smokes Old Golds.

Part Three. We shift from Teddy to Essie/Alma. I found myself curious that Updike did not choose to shift from third to first person in his studies of four generations. Since all his character writing is in essentially the same tone of voice, he might have dramatized—well, differentiated—his four protagonists by giving each a distinctive voice. But he remains in the lazy third person: Now she thinks this . . . now she does that . . . now Japan invades Manchuria.

In Essie's section, the Shillington/Basingstoke movie house is central, and Essie, now a beauty, is thrilled by what she sees on the screen, ideal life writ large in celluloid. Ambitious, for a dull Wilmot, she enters a beauty contest, where she meets a photographer from New York. "There was something mystical in the way the camera lapped up her inner states through the thin skin of her face. She had known as a child she was the center of the universe and now proof was accumulating, click by click." She becomes a model. An actress. A star, as Alma De Mott.

But for Updike, Essie is early blighted. Even before Hollywood and stardom she is taken in by liberals—Commies, too. Plainly, sinister osmosis was taking place at the movie house in her hometown. The liberal image of America the Bad was like some insidious virus contained in the celluloid, bacteria which, under the optimum condition of hot light projected through its alien nesting ground on to the screen, bred discontent in those not sufficiently vaccinated against Doubt by benign school and good church. So ravaged was Essie by Red films like *Now, Voyager* ("Why ask for the moon when we have the stars?") that she actually objected to the loyalty oaths inflicted on so many Americans by President Truman's administration, oaths that the self-conscious Updike cannot, like his father, find objectionable. When Essie's little brother, Danny, says, "I hate Communists," she says, "What do you know about anything? Who do you think beat Hitler's armies?" And so the green twig was bent by the product of MGM and the Brothers Warner.

Before Essie leaves New York for Hollywood, Updike helpfully tells us the names "of the big Hollywood movies at the end of the Forties." He also lists the foreign films that ravished Essie. Curiously, he forgets to rate the Italian neorealists for Leftist content. In New York, Essie is taken up by a queer cousin, Patrick. He is worldly, knows his Manhattan: like all homosexuals, he is "sensitive" but "frustrating . . . and not just sexually; some inner deflection kept him on the sidelines of life, studying painting but not wanting to paint himself, and even sneering at those that did try"; but then "the arts, especially minor arts like window dressing, were dominated by them." Patrick manages her career for a time: "A comforting accreditation . . . to have a poof bring her in."

Before Alma makes it to the silver screen, she serves time in live television. Updike tells us all about what it was like; but then there is a firm in New York that will do intensive research on any subject a writer might want—from the Golden Age of Television, say, to the flora and fauna of Brazil. I am certain that Updike, the artist, would never resort to so brazen a crib; even so, many of his small piled-up facts are so rotelike in their detail and his use of them so completely haywire that—well, *vichyssoise qui mal y pense.*

"Alma would play opposite, within the next few years, both Gary Cooper and . . . Clark Gable." Boldly, Updike tells us a lot of personal things about Cooper and Gable which he could only have got from fan magazines or showbiz biographies. Updike is now frugging wildly into Collins Sisters territory. But where the Bel-Air Brontës are well advanced in the art and arts of popular fiction and write *romans à clef* with phallic keys, Updike, ever original, disposes with the keys. Confidently, he tells us about "Coop's" aches and pains, about Clark's career anxieties and sex. Updike has now made it to the heart of the heart of pop fiction: "there was in Gable a loneliness too big for Alma to fill. Where Cooper was a sublime accident (he reached over, while the wind rushed past and the sun beat sparkling dents in the Pacific below, and cupped his hand around her skull) . . . Gable had never been anything but an aspiring actor. . . . He had been so long a star he had forgotten to find mortal satisfactions." Why ask for the butterscotch when we can have the fudge?

For a beautiful heroine like Alma, sex is *de rigueur,* but though she fucks like a minx, the sexagenarian Updike has lost some of his old brio. Alma marries a nobody with a body; he never makes it in the business but makes a baby. Meanwhile, she grows more and more un-American. Proud to be a Hollywood liberal, she is prone to quarrel with her kid brother, Danny, now a CIA honcho. "Well, Danny darling, the movies have never pretended to be anything except entertainment. But what you're doing pretends to be a great deal more."

"It pretends to be history," he said quickly. "It *is* history. Cast of billions. The future of the globe is at stake. I kid you not." Nice touch, this last. Television slang of the 1950s.

Alma De Mott rises and falls and rises again. She is clearly based—research to one side—on Yvonne de Carlo's performance as an up-down-up movie star of a certain age in Sondheim's musical comedy *Follies,* whose signature song was "I'm Still Here."

Time now to shift to Alma's son, Clark, named for . . . you guessed it. In the family tradition, he is a born Shillington loser. He is, of course, conscious of being a celebrity as a star's son. But the connection does him no particular good. He also has a stepfather called Rex. When he asks Alma why she married Rex, she "told him calmly, Because he is all cock."

Clark is in rebellion against the Communism of his mother and her friends—pinks if not reds—and, worse, unabashed enemies of the United States in the long, long, war against the Satanic Ho Chi Minh. "Mom, too, wanted North Vietnam to win, which seemed strange to Clark, since America has been pretty good to her." As irony, this might have been telling, but irony is an arrow that the Good Fiction Fairy withheld from the Updike quiver. Consequently, this *non sequitur* can only make perfect sense to a writer who believes that no matter how misguided, tyrannous, and barbarous the rulers of one's own country have become, they *must* be obeyed; and if one has actually made money and achieved a nice place in the country that they have hijacked then one must be doubly obedient, grateful, too. Under Hitler, many good Germans, we are told, felt the same way.

There is nothing, sad to say, surprising in Updike's ignorance of history and politics and of people unlike himself; in this, he is a standard American and so a typical citizen of what Vice-President Agnew once called the greatest nation in the country. But Updike has literary ambitions as well as most of the skills of a popular writer, except, finally, the essential one without which nothing can ever come together to any useful end as literature, empathy. He is forever stuck in a psychic Shillington-Ipswich-New York world where everything outside his familiar round is unreal. Because of this lack of imagination, he can't really do much even with the characters that he does have some feeling for because they exist in social, not to mention historic, contexts that he lacks the sympathy—to use the simplest word—to make real.

Many of Updike's descriptions of Hollywood—the place—are nicely observed. Plainly, he himself *looked* at the Three B's—Beverly

Hills, Bel-Air, Brentwood—"the palm trees, the pink low houses, the Spanishness, the endlessness . . . the winding palm-lined streets of Beverly Hills, where there was no living person in sight but Japanese and Mexican gardeners wheeling dead palm fronds out from behind hedges of oleander and fuchsias." "The wealth here was gentle wealth, humorous wealth even; these fortunes derived from art and illusion and personal beauty and not, as back home, from cruel old riverside mills manufacturing some ugly and stupid necessity like Trojans or bottlecaps." The "humorous" is an inspired adjective, proving there is a lot to be said for firsthand observation. But then, alas, he must tell us about *how* films were made in the 1950s and what the makers were like, including Columbia's Harry Cohn, a much-written-about monster. Once inside the celluloid kitchen, Updike falls far, far behind the Bel-Air Brontës at their cuisine-art.

Alma is still here, as the song goes, while the son, Clark, works at a Colorado ski resort, owned by his great-uncle. Clark has gone through the usual schools and done the usual drugs and had the usual run-of-the-mill sex available to a movie star's child. Now he must *find* himself—if there is a self to find—in a partially pristine Colorado rapidly being undone by ski resorts and the greenhouse effect.

Except for Alma, who knew from the beginning that she was unique in her beauty and sweet self-love, none of Updike's protagonists has any idea of what to do with himself during the seventy years or so that he must mark time in this vale of tears before translation to sunbeam-hood in Jesus' sky-condo. Happily, if tragically, true meaning comes to Clark in Colorado.

Updike, nothing if not up-to-date, re-creates the celebrated slaughter at Waco, Texas, where the charismatic David Koresh and many of his worshipers were wiped out in their compound by federal agents. In Updike's fiction, a similar messiah and his worshipers withdraw to Colorado in order to live in Christian fellowship until the final trump, due any day now. An attractive girl leads Clark to the Lower Branch Temple and to Jesse, a Vietnam veteran who is now a "high-ranch messiah." As a novelist, Updike often relies on the wearisome trick of someone asking a new character to tell us about himself. Within the rustic temple, skeptical Clark and primitive Scripture-soaked Jesse tell us about themselves. Clark: "Yeah, well. What was I going to say? Something. I don't want to bore you." Jesse: "You will never find Jesse bored. Never, by a recital of the truth. Weary, yes, and sore-laden with the sorrows of mankind, but never bored." A good thing, too, considering the level of the dialogue. Jesse fulminates with biblical quotes from the likes of Ezekiel, while Clark wimps on and on about the emptiness of gilded life in the Three B's.

The actual events at Waco revealed, terribly, what a paranoid federal apparatus, forever alert to any infraction of its stern prohibitions, was capable of when challenged head-on by nonconformists. How, I wondered, will Updike, a born reactionary, deal with the state's conception of itself as ultimate arbiter of everything, no matter how absurd? Even "the good child" must be appalled by the slaughter of Jesse and his fellow believers by a mindless authority.

Since we shall witness all this through Clark's eyes, Updike has made him even more passive than his usual protagonists. Too much acid in the Vipers Lounge? Clark does have a scene with Uncle Danny, who explains the real world to him in terms that the editorial page of *The Wall Street Journal* might think twice about publishing. Danny: "Vietnam was a hard call. . . . But somebody always has to fight." (In the case of Vietnam, somebody proved to be poor white and black males.) "You and I walk down the street safe, if we do, because a cop around the corner has a gun. The kids today say the state is organized violence and they're right. But it matters who's doing the organizing . . . Joe Stalin . . . or our bumbling American pols. I'll take the pols every time." Thus, straw villain undoes straw hero; neither, of course, relevant to the issue, but Updike—Danny (true empathy may have been achieved at last) is now in full swing: "The kids today . . . grow long hair . . . smoke pot and shit on poor Tricky Dicky" only because of "the willingness of somebody else to do their fighting for them. What you can't protect gets taken away. . . ." Hobbesian world out there. Danny does admit that we got nothing out of Vietnam, not even "thanks"—one wonders from whom he thinks gratitude ought to come. But, no matter. Danny hates Communism. Hates Ho Chi Minh. Hates those "Hollywood fatcats and bleeding hearts" who oppose the many wars. Even so, "I try to be dispassionate about it. But I love this crazy, wasteful, self-hating country in spite of myself." It would seem that Updike–Danny has not got the point. The people of the country don't hate the country, only what has been done to it by those who profit from hot and cold wars and, in the process, bring to civilian governance a murderous military mentality, witness Waco.

How does Clark take all this? "To Clark, Uncle Danny seemed a treasure, a man from space who was somehow his own. . . ." Clark has not known many employees of the CIA, for whom this sort of bombast is the order of the day. That order flows not only through the pages of *The Wall Street Journal* but throughout most of the press, where Hume's Opinion is shaped by the disinformation of a hundred wealthy tax-exempt American foundations such as Olin, Smith-Richardson, Bradley, Scaife and Pew, not to mention all the Christian coalitions grinding out a worldview of Us against Them, the Us an ever-smaller group of propertied Americans and the Them the rest of the world.

Clark would now be ripe for neo-conhood, but for the fact that he was never a con or anything at all until he drifted into Jesse's orbit, already set on a collision course with the U.S. government, which allows no group the pleasure of defiance even in the name of the One in whose Image we were fashioned. Jesse has been stockpiling weapons for "The Day of Reckoning." Lovingly, Updike lists the arsenal. Clark suddenly realizes that here, at last, is the perfect orgasm, something well worth dying for. "The gun was surprising: provocative like a woman, both lighter and heavier than he would have thought." The ultimate love story of a boy and his gun, "ready to become a magic wand." Disappointingly, at the end, Updike is too patriotic or too timid to allow federal law-enforcement officers to destroy the temple along with the men, women, and children that Jesse has attracted to him. Colorado State Troopers do Caesar's work, unlike Waco, where Caesar himself did the deed.

At the end, Clark turns on Jesse and betrays him. In order to save the children from the Conflagration, Clark "shot the false prophet twice." Although Clark himself perishes, he dies a hero, who saved as many lives as he could from the false prophet whom he had, for no coherent reason, briefly served. Finally, world television validates Clark's life and end. Who could ask for anything more?

Stendhal's view that politics in a work of art is like a pistol shot at a concert is true, but what is one to do in the case of a political work that deals almost exclusively with true patriot versus nonpatriot who dares criticize the common patria? I quoted at length from Updike's *Self-Consciousness* in order to establish what human material this inhuman novel is based on. I have also tried to exercise empathy, tried to feel, as President Clinton likes to say, the author's pain. Actually, to find reactionary writing similar to Updike's, one must turn back to John Dos Passos's *Midcentury*, or to John Steinbeck's *The Winter of Our Discontent*. But Updike, unlike his predecessor Johns, has taken to heart every far-out far-right piety currently being fed us.

Also, despite what Updike must have thought of as a great leap up the social ladder from Shillington obscurity to "Eliotic" Harvard and then on to a glossy magazine, he has now, Antaeus-like, started to touch base with that immutable Dutch-German earth on which his ladder stood. Recent American wars and defeats have so demoralized our good child that he has now come to hate that Enlightenment which was all that, as a polity, we ever had. He is symptomatic, then, of a falling back, of a loss of nerve; indeed, a loss of honor. He invokes phantom political majorities, righteous masses. Time to turn to Herzen on the subject: "The masses are indifferent to individual freedom, liberty of speech; the masses love authority. They are still blinded by the arrogant glitter of power, they are offended by those who stand alone . . . they want a social government to rule for their benefit, and not against it. But to govern themselves doesn't enter their heads."

Updike's work is more and more representative of that polarizing within a state where Authority grows ever more brutal and malign while its hired hands in the media grow ever more excited as the holy war of the few against the many heats up. In this most delicate of times, Updike has "builded" his own small, crude altar in order to propitiate—or to invoke?—"the fateful lightning of His terrible swift sword."

The Times Literary Supplement
26 April 1996

A Note on *The City and the Pillar* and Thomas Mann

Much has been made—not least by the Saint himself—of how Augustine stole and ate some pears from a Milanese orchard. Presumably, he never again trafficked in, much less ate, stolen goods, and once this youthful crime ("a rum business," snarled the unsympathetic American jurist Oliver Wendell Holmes, Jr.) was behind him, he was sainthood-bound. The fact is that all of us have stolen pears; the mystery is why so few of us rate halos. I suspect that in certain notorious lives there is sometimes an abrupt moment of choice. Shall I marry or burn? Shut the door on a life longed for while opening another, deliberately, onto trouble and pain because . . . The "because" is the true story seldom told.

Currently, two biographers are at work on my sacred story, and the fact that they are trying to make sense of my life has made me curious about how and why I have done—and not done—so many things. As a result, I have begun writing what I have said that I'd never write, a memoir ("I am not my own subject," I used to say with icy superiority). Now I am reeling haphazardly through my own youth, which is when practically everything of interest happened to me, rather more soon than late, since I was force-fed, as it were, by military service in the Second World War.

My father once told me, after reviewing his unpleasant period in public office, that whenever it came time for him to make a crucial decision, he invariably made the wrong one. I told him that he must turn Churchill and write his own life, demonstrating what famous victories he had set in motion at Gallipoli or in the "dragon's soft underbelly" of the Third Reich. But my father was neither a writer nor a politician; he was also brought up to tell the truth. I, on the other hand, was brought up by a politician grandfather in Washington, D.C., and I wanted very much to be a politician, too. Unfortunately, nature had designed me to be a writer. I had no choice in the matter. Pears were to be my diet, stolen or homegrown. There was never a time when I did not make sentences in order to make those things that I had experienced cohere and become "real."

Finally, the novelist must always tell the truth as he understands it while the politician must never give the game away. Those who have done both comprise a very short list indeed. The fact that I was never even a candidate for the list had to do with a choice made at twenty that entirely changed my life.

At nineteen, just out of the army, I wrote a novel, *Williwaw* (1946): it was admired as, chronologically at least, the first of the war novels. The next year I wrote the less admired *In a Yellow Wood* (1947). Simultaneously, my grandfather was arranging a political career for me in New Mexico (the governor was a protégé of the old man). Yes, believe it or not, in the greatest democracy the world has ever known—freedom's as well as bravery's home—elections can be quietly arranged, as Joe Kennedy somewhat showily demonstrated.

For someone twenty years old I was well situated in the world, thanks to two published novels and my grandfather's political skills. I was also situated dead center at a crossroads rather like the one Oedipus found himself at. I was writing *The City and the Pillar*. If I published it, I'd take a right turn and end up accursed in Thebes. Abandon it and I'd turn left and end up in holy Delphi. Honor required that I take the road to Thebes. I have read that I was too stupid at the time to know what I was doing, but in such matters I have always had a certain alertness. I knew that my description of the love affair between two "normal" all-American boys of the sort that I had spent three years with in the wartime army would challenge every superstition about sex in my native land—which has always been more Boeotia, I fear, than Athens or haunted Thebes. Until then, American novels of "inversion" dealt with transvestites or with lonely bookish boys who married unhappily and pined for Marines. I broke that mold. My pair of lovers were athletes and so drawn to the entirely masculine that, in the case of one, Jim Willard, the feminine was simply irrelevant to his passion to unite with his other half, Bob Ford: unfortunately for Jim, Bob had other sexual plans, involving women and marriage.

I gave the manuscript to my New York publishers, E. P. Dutton. They hated it. One ancient editor said, "You will never be forgiven for this book. Twenty years from now you will still be attacked for it." I responded with an uneasy whistle in the dark: "If any book of mine is remembered in the year 1968, that's real fame, isn't it?"

To my grandfather's sorrow, on January 10, 1948, *The City and the Pillar* was published. Shock was the most pleasant emotion aroused in the press. How could our young war novelist . . . ? In a week or two, the book was a best-seller in the United States and wherever else it could be published—not exactly a full atlas in those days. The English publisher, John Lehmann, was very nervous. In his memoirs, *The Whispering Gallery*, he writes, "There were several passages in *The City and the Pillar*, a sad, almost tragic book and a remarkable achievement in a difficult territory for so young a man, that seemed to my travellers and the printers to go too far in frankness. I had a friendly battle with Gore to tone down and cut these passages. Irony of the time and taste: they wouldn't cause an eyebrow to be lifted in the climate of the early sixties." Nevertheless, even today copies of the book still fitfully blaze on the pampas and playas of Argentina and other godly countries. As I write these lines, I have just learned that the book will at last appear in Russia, where a Moscow theater group is adapting it for the stage.

What did my confrères think? I'm afraid not much. The fag writers were terrified; the others were delighted that a competitor had so neatly erased himself. I did send copies to two famous writers, fishing, as most young writers do, for endorsements. The first was to Thomas Mann. The second was to Christopher Isherwood, who responded enthusiastically. We became lifelong friends. Through Joseph Breitbach I was told that André Gide was planning to write an "appreciation," but when we finally met he spoke only of a handwritten, fetchingly illustrated pornographic manuscript that he had received from an English clergyman in Hampshire.

At fourteen I had read Thomas Mann's *Joseph* books and realized that the "novel of ideas" (we still have no proper phrase in English for this sort of book, or, indeed, such a genre) could work if one were to set a narrative within history. Later, I was struck by the use of dialogue in *The Magic Mountain*, particularly the debates between Settembrini and Naphta, as each man subtly vies for the favors of the dim but sexually attractive Hans Castorp. Later, there would be complaints that Jim Willard in *The City and the Pillar* was too dim. But I deliberately made him a Hans Castorp type: what else would someone so young be, set loose on the world—the City—that was itself the center of interest? But I did give Jim something Hans lacked: a romantic passion for Bob Ford that finally excluded everything else from his life, even, in a sense, the life itself. I got a polite, perfunctory note from Thomas Mann, thanking me for my "noble work": my name was misspelled.

Contemplating the American scene in the 1940s, Stephen Spender deplored the machinery of literary success, remarking sternly that "one has only to follow the whizzing comets of Mr. Truman Capote and Mr. Gore Vidal to see how quickly and effectively this transforming, diluting, disintegrating machinery can work." He then characterized *The City and the Pillar* as a work of sexual confession, quite plainly autobiography at its most artless. Transformed, diluted, disintegrated as I was, I found this description flattering. Mr. Spender had paid me a considerable compliment; although I am the least autobiographical of novelists, I had drawn the character of the athlete Jim Willard so convincingly that to this day aging pederasts are firmly convinced that I was once a male prostitute, with an excellent backhand at tennis. The truth, alas, is quite another matter. The book was a considerable act of imagination. Jim Willard and I shared the same geography, but little else. Also, in the interest of verisimilitude I decided to tell the story in a flat gray prose reminiscent of one of James T. Farrell's social documents.

In April 1993, at the University of New York at Albany, a dozen papers were read by academics on *The City and the Pillar*. The book has been in print for close to half a century, something I would not have thought possible in 1948, when *The New York Times* refused to advertise it and no major American newspaper or magazine would review it or any other book of mine for the next six years. *Life* magazine thought that God's country was being driven queer by the young army first mate they had featured only the previous year, standing before his ship. I've not read any of the Albany papers. For one thing, it is never a good idea to read about oneself, particularly about a twenty-one-year-old self who had modeled himself, perhaps too closely, on Billy the Kid. I might be shot in the last frame, but I was going to take care of a whole lot of folks who needed taking care of before I was done.

There were those who found the original ending "melodramatic." (Jim strangles Bob after an unsuccessful sexual encounter.) When I reminded one critic that it is the nature of romantic tragedy to end in death, I was told that so sordid a story about fags could never be considered tragic, unlike, let us say, a poignant tale of doomed love between a pair of mentally challenged teenage "heteros" in old Verona. I intended Jim Willard to demonstrate the romantic fallacy. From too much looking back, he was destroyed, an unsophisticated Humbert Humbert trying to re-create an idyll that never truly existed except in his own imagination. Despite the title, this was never plain in the narrative. And of course the coda *was* unsatisfactory. At the time it was generally believed that the publishers forced me to tack on a cautionary ending in much the same way the Motion Picture Code used to insist that wickedness be punished. This was not true. I had always meant the end of the book to be black, but not as black as it turned out. So for a new edition of the book published in 1965 I altered the last chapter. In fact, I rewrote the entire book (my desire to imitate the style of Farrell was perhaps too successful), though I did not change the point of view or the essential relationships. I left Jim as he was. I had no choice: he had developed a life of his own outside my rough pages. Claude J. Summers, in his book *Gay Fictions*, recently noted that of the characters:

> only Jim Willard is affecting, and he commands sustained interest largely because he combines unexpected characteristics. Bland and ordinary, he nevertheless has an unusually well-developed inner life. Himself paralyzed by romantic illusions, he is surprisingly perceptive about the illusions of others. For all the novel's treatment of him as case history, he nevertheless preserves an essential mystery. As Robert Kiernan comments (*Gore Vidal*), Jim Willard is Everyman and yet he is l'étranger . . . the net effect is paradoxical but appropriate for it decrees that, in the last analysis, we cannot patronize Jim Willard, sympathize with him entirely, or even claim to understand him. Much more so than the typical character in fiction, Jim Willard simply exists, not as the subject of a statement, not as the illustration of a thesis, but as himself.

Recently, I received a note from a biographer of Thomas Mann. Did I know, he asked, the profound effect that my book had had on Mann? I made some joke to the effect that at least toward the end of his life he may have learned how to spell my name. "But he didn't read the book until 1950, and as he read it he commented on it in his diaries. They've just been published in Germany. Get them." Now I have read, with some amazement, of the effect that Mann's twenty-one-year-old admirer had on what was then a seventy-five-year-old world master situated by war in California.

Wednesday 22, XI, 50
. . . Began to read the homoerotic novel "The City and the Pillar" by Vidal. The day at the cabin by the river and the love-play scene between Jim and Bob was quite brilliant.—Stopped reading late. Very warm night.

Thursday 23, XI, 50
. . . Continued "City and Pillar."

Friday 24, XI, 50
. . . In the evening continued reading "The City and the Pillar." Interesting, yes. An important human document, of excellent and enlightening truthfulness. The sexual, the affairs with the various men, is still incomprehensible to us. How can one sleep with men—[Mann uses the word *Herren*, which means not "men" but "gentlemen." Is this Mann being satiric? A rhetorical question affecting shock?]

Saturday evening 25, XI, 50
. . . in May 1943, I took out the *Felix Krull* papers only to touch them fleetingly and then turn to *Faustus*. An effort to start again must be made, if only to keep me occupied, to have a task at hand. I have nothing else, no ideas for stories; no subject for a novel. . . . Will it be possible to start [*Felix Krull*] again? Is there enough of the world and are there enough people, is there enough knowledge available? The homosexual novel interests me not least because of the experience of the world and of travel that it offers. Has my isolation picked up enough experience of human beings, enough for a social-satirical novel?

Sunday 26, XI, 50
Busy with [the *Krull*] paper, confusing.
Read more of Vidal's novel.

Wednesday 29, XI, 50
. . . The *Krull* papers (on imprisonment). Always doubts. Ask myself whether this music determined by a "yearning theme" is appropriate to my years. . . . Finished Vidal's novel, moved, although a lot is faulty and unpleasant. For example, that Jim takes Bob into a Fairy Bar in New York.

I am pleased that Mann did not find the ending "melodramatic," but then what theme is more melodramatically "yearning" than *Liebestod*? In any case, the young novelist who took what seemed to everyone the wrong road at Trivium is now saluted in his own old age by the writer whom he had, in a certain sense, modeled himself on. As for Mann's surprise at how men could sleep with one another, he is writing a private diary, the most public act any German master can ever do, and though he often refers to his own "inversion" and his passions for this or that youth, he seems not to go on, like me, to Thebes but to take (with many a backward look) the high road to Delphi, and I am duly astonished and pleased that, as he read me, he was inspired—motivated—whatever verb—to return to his most youthful and enchanting work, *Felix Krull*.

Some of my short stories are almost as lighthearted as Thomas Mann in his last work. One of them, "The Ladies in the Library," is an unconscious variation on *Death in Venice*. Three variations on a theme: Mann's Hans Castorp; then my own, Jim Willard; then a further lighter, more allegro version of Jim in the guise of a character whom Mann appropriately called Felix—Latin for "happy."

The Threepenny Review
Summer 1995

Although in life Anthony Burgess was amiable, generous, and far less self-loving than most writers, I have been disturbed, in the last few years, to read in the press that he did not think himself sufficiently admired by the literary world. It is true, of course, that he had the good fortune not to be hit, as it were, by the Swedes, but surely he was much admired and appreciated by the appreciated and admired.

In my lifetime he was one of the three "best" novelists to come out of England (all right, the other two are the Swedized Golding, and Iris Murdoch) but he was unlike the whole lot in the sense that one never knew what he would do next. He resisted category.

To me this is a great virtue, and a tiny source of income for him because he was the only writer of my time whose new book I always bought and always read. On or off form, there was bound to be something that he had come up with that I did not know—or even dream of—while his Enderby series are even finer comedies than those by the so much admired E. Waugh.

I was both moved and alarmed that one of his own last reviews in *The Observer* was of my collected essays in which appeared a long piece on his first volume of memoirs: I recalled him personally, with fondness; reported on his life and work; remarked, of the memoir, that he had no sense of humor.

In his review of me he quotes this, remarking that, once, he did have a sense of humor. I almost wrote him to say that I was referring only to the autobiography. Now I know that he had known for some time that he was dying of cancer, no rollicking business.

I cannot think what English book reviewing will do without him. He actually read what he wrote about, and he was always interesting on what he read. He did not suffer from the English disease of envy that tends to make so much English reviewing injurious to the health of literature.

When I first met him in 1964, he was about to be famous for *A Clockwork Orange*. He was, however, truly notorious because he had reviewed, pseudonymously, several of his own books in a provincial newspaper. "At least," I said at the time, "he is the first novelist in England to know that a reviewer has actually read the book under review."

Shakespeare, Joyce, Roman Empire (of the imagination), Malaysia; the constipated Enderby, whose fine poems were often included in the prose text. He ranged throughout language, a devoted philologist, and throughout music as a composer.

Once his first wife snarled—when it became clear that I was eight years younger than he—that I ought not to have got some Book Club selection when he had written so much more than I. Neither of us quite sober, we began to compare units of production. When it became clear that I was ahead, he said with quiet pomp, "I am really a composer." I was left without a single choral work, much less a fanfare, to put in the scales.

At one point when we were both living in Rome, whenever I would be offered a twelve-part television miniseries on the Medici or the Huns, I'd say, "Get poor Burgess," and so they did. When I made the mistake of using the phrase "poor Burgess" in an interview, he wrote, "I can't say that I liked that 'poor Burgess' bit. Happily, I left Gore out of the Encyclopedia Britannica on the contemporary novel." In due course, he transcended Italian television and did, for the RSC, the finest version I have ever seen of *Cyrano de Bergerac*. Many parts, not so poor Burgess.

I ended my review of Anthony's autobiography—much of it about how he lost faith in God—by making a play on the title *Little Wilson* (Burgess's real name) *and Big God*. I suggested that the book might better have been called *Little Wilson and Big Burgess*, "who did it his, if not His, way."

I saw him a year or two ago. We were being jointly interviewed by BBC Radio. "Odd," he said, "I keep looking at my watch. It's like a tic. I wonder why?" For once, I made no answer.

The Observer
28 November 1993

★ PRIDE

Is pride a sin at all? The *Oxford English Dictionary* strikes a primly English note: "A high or overweening opinion of one's own qualities, attainments or estate," or too clever by half, the ultimate put-down in those bright arid islands where ignorance must be lightly worn.

Apparently, the Romans and the Greeks had other, by no means pejorative, words for it. The quintessential Greek, Odysseus, reveled in being too clever by any number of halves. Of course, neither Greeks nor Romans had a word for sin, a Judeo-Christian concept that the Germans did have a word for, *Sünde,* which Old English took aboard. Obviously, in any time and place an overweening person is tiresome, but surely laughter is the best tonic for restoring him to our common weeniness. He hardly needs to be prayed for or punished as a sinner. Yet pride is listed as the first of the seven deadly sins, and only recently—by accident, not design—did I figure out why.

Over the years I have taken some . . . well, pride in never reading my own work, or appearing with other writers on public occasions, or joining any organizations other than labor unions. In 1976, when I was elected to the National Institute of Arts and Letters, I promptly declined this high estate on the ground that I was already a member of the Diners' Club. John Cheever was furious with me: "Couldn't you at least have said Carte Blanche? Diners' Club is so tacky." A couple of months ago I declined election to the Society of American Historians—politely, I hope.

James Joyce's "silence, exile, and cunning" is the ultimate in artist's pride. But for someone politically inclined, that was not possible;

even so, one could still play a lone hand, as a writer if not as an engaged citizen. Recently, Norman Mailer asked me if I would join him and two other writers in a reading of George Bernard Shaw's *Don Juan in Hell*. The proceeds would go to the Actors Studio. I would play the Devil, who has most of the good lines.

So, out of Charity—Vanity?—I set to one side my proud rule and shared a stage with three writers and the fading ghost of a very great one; fading because Shaw can appeal only to those who think that human society can be made better by human intelligence and will. I am of Shaw's party; the Devil's, too, I found, as I began to immerse myself in the part.

In a very long speech, the Devil makes an attractive case for himself; he also explains the bad press that he has got from the celestial hordes and their earthly admirers. The Devil believes that the false view of him in England is the result of an Italian and an Englishman. The Italian, of course, is Dante, and the Englishman is John Milton. Somewhat gratuitously, Shaw's Devil remarks that like everyone else he has never managed to get all the way through *Paradise Lost* and *Paradise Regained*. Although I had my problems with the second, the first is *the* masterpiece of our language, and Lucifer, the Son of Morning, blazes most attractively while God seems more arbitrary and self-regarding than ever, eager in His solipsistic pride to hear only praise from the angelic choirs, as well as from Adam and Eve, two mud pies He liked to play with.

It is Milton's conceit that proud Lucifer, a bored angel, tempts Adam and Eve with the only thing a totalitarian ruler must always keep from his slaves, knowledge. Rather surprisingly, the First Couple choose knowledge—well, she chooses it; they lose Eden; go forth to breed and die while Lucifer and his party, expelled from heaven, fall and fall and fall through Chaos and Old Night until they reach rock bottom, hell:

> *Here we may reign secure, and in my choice*
> *To reign is worth ambition though in hell:*
> *Better to reign in hell than serve in heav'n.*

I first heard those words in 1941, spoken by Edward G. Robinson in the film of Jack London's *Sea Wolf*. It was like an electric shock. The great alternative. I can do no other. Bright world elsewhere. To reign and not to serve. To say, No. This was my introduction to Milton and to Lucifer's pride.

I was brought up in a freethinking Southern family where pride of clan could lead to all sorts of folly as well as to exemplary self-sacrifice.

My great-grandfather sat for a whole day on the steps of the courthouse at Walthall, Miss., debating whether to go fight with the rest of the clan in a civil war that he knew could not be won, and for a cause that he despised. Pride required him to fight with his clan; he fell at Shiloh.

Fifty years later in the Senate, his son defied the leader of his party, President Woodrow Wilson, on the issue of whether or not the United States should fight in World War I. The Chamber of Commerce of Oklahoma City sent him a telegram saying that if he did not support the war, he would be an ex-senator. He sent them a telegram: "How many of your membership are of draft age?" He fell from office, as they had promised.

There is a whiff of sulfur here, perhaps; but there is also the sense that one is the final judge of what must be done despite the seductive temptations and stern edicts of the gods. In the absence of a totalitarian sky-god or earthly ruler, there is the always troubling dictatorship of the American majority, which Tocqueville saw as the dark side to our "democracy."

Very much in the family tradition, in 1948, I ran counter to the majority's loony superstitions about sex and fell quite far indeed. (This newspaper's regular daily critic not only did not review the offending novel, *The City and the Pillar*, but told my publisher that he would never again read, much less review, a book of mine: six subsequent books were not reviewed in the daily paper.) But pride required that I bear witness, like it or not, and if the superstitious masses—or great Zeus himself—disapproved, I would go even deeper into rebellion, and fall farther. Understandably, for the cowed majority, pride is the most unnerving "sin" because pride scorns them quite as much as Lucifer did God.

Significantly, a story that keeps cropping up from culture to culture is that of the man who steals fire from heaven to benefit the human race. After Prometheus stole the fire for us, he ended up chained to a rock, an eagle gnawing eternally at his liver. Zeus' revenge was terrible, but the Prometheus of Aeschylus does not bend; in fact, he curses Zeus and predicts: "Let him act, let him reign his little while as he will; for he shall not long rule over the gods."

So let us celebrate pride when it defies those dominations and powers that enslave us. In my own case, for a quarter-century I have refused to read, much less write for, this newspaper, but, as Prometheus also somewhat cryptically observes, "Time, growing ever older, teaches all things." Or, as Dr. Johnson notes, reflecting Matthew's Gospel, "Pride must have a fall"; thus proving it was the real thing and not merely the mock.

The New York Times
4 July 1993

On May 20–21, 1927, in thirty-three and a half hours, Charles A. Lindbergh, Jr., flew nonstop from New York City to Paris's Le Bourget airport. At the age of twenty-five, Slim, as he was known to associates, became the most famous person in the world, and so he remained for much of a life that ended in 1974. As is usual with heroes, his popularity waxed and waned; also, as is not usual with ordinary heroes, he was much more than just the one adventure. He was also an engineering genius with a mystical bent that, by the time of his death, had made him regret the world he had helped create—*Modern Times* (starring the world's second most recognized man, Charlie Chaplin). Slim was drawn more and more to Thoreau and to primal nature as well as to Lao Tzu, who saw essential change in those waters and tides that are able to wear down rock surfaces, no matter how adamantine, in order to make a new world. Finally, he turned himself into a good writer; school of Julius Caesar, yes, but Caesar crossed with Lucretius' sense of the beauty of "things" and their arrangement, precisely described. Lindbergh was a very strange sort of American for the first part of the century now ending. He is practically incomprehensible today.

A. Scott Berg has produced a characteristically workmanlike survey of the many things that Lindbergh did, and of some of the things that he was. Aside from the creation of airlines in the 1930s, he invented a "perfusion pump," variations of which now keep alive bodily organs until they are ready to be transplanted. Also, as early as 1929, the prescient Lindbergh befriended Robert Goddard, whose rocket research could have given the United States the unmanned missile long before Hitler's V-2, which nearly won the war for the Nazis.

In 1932, when the Lindberghs' two-year-old son was kidnapped and killed, fearful for their growing family and hounded by a press every bit as dreadful then as now, Lindbergh and his wife, Anne Morrow, moved to Europe, where they stayed for three years.

At the request of the American military, Lindbergh checked out the German Luftwaffe, which he found alarmingly advanced in both design and production, while the French and British air forces combined were not in the same league. In 1939 Lindbergh came home to call for "an impregnable system of defense." Also, between 1939 and 1941, he was the chief voice raised against U.S. intervention in the Second World War. In a notorious speech at Des Moines in 1941, he identified America's three interventionist groups: the Roosevelt administration, the Jews, and the British. Although the country was deeply isolationist, the interventionists were very resourceful, and Lindbergh was promptly attacked as a pro-Nazi anti-Semite when he was no more than a classic Midwestern isolationist, reflective of a majority of the country. But along with such noble isolationists as Norman Thomas and Burton K. Wheeler, not to mention Lindbergh's friend Harry Guggenheim's foundation, the "America First" movement, as it was called, did attract some genuine homegrown fascists who would have been amazed to learn that there was never a "Jewish plot" to get the United States into the Second World War. Quite the contrary. Before Pearl Harbor, as Berg notes, "though most of the American motion-picture studios were owned by Jews, most were virtually paranoid about keeping pro-Jewish sentiment off the screen." Also, Arthur Hayes Sulzberger, publisher of *The New York Times*, confided as late as September 1941 to the British Special Operations Executive agent Valentine Williams "that for the first time in his life he regretted being a Jew because, with the tide of anti-Semitism rising, he was unable to champion the anti-Hitler policy of the administration as vigorously and as universally as he would like, as his sponsorship would be attributed to Jewish influence by isolationists and thus lose something of its force."

It was not until November 25, 1996, that an American academic, Thomas E. Mahl, researching Britain's various secret service archives, came across the Williams file. He has now published *Desperate Deception*, as full a story as we are ever apt to get of "British Covert Operations in the United States 1939–44." Although media and schools condition Americans to start giggling at the mention of the word "conspiracy," there are, at any moment, all sorts of conspiracies crisscrossing our spacious skies and amber fields of grain, and of them all in this century, the largest, most intricate and finally most successful was that of the British to get us into the Second World War. Mahl shows us just how busy their operatives were, from Ronald Colman, starring in pro-British films and the Korda brothers making them, to Walter Winchell reading on his Sunday broadcast pro-British messages written for him by Ernest Cuneo, who also ghosted pro-British newspaper columns for Drew Pearson. There was indeed a vast conspiracy to maneuver an essentially isolationist country into war. There was also a dedicated conspiracy to destroy Lindbergh's reputation as hero.

Meanwhile, just who was the hero? In 1932 the rococo English journalist Beverly Nichols met Lindbergh. "What is all this fuss about flying the Atlantic?" Nichols later marveled. "Isn't that just the sort of thing a bore like that *would* do? Now if Noel or I had flown, you would have a real story!" So one would. But Slim did fly, alone, and thereby hangs a century's great story, The Lone Eagle.

Lindbergh's daughter, Reeve, has now written a charming memoir of her father and mother, *Under a Wing*. She sets out to place her father in his native country, specifically, at Little Falls, above the Mississippi River in northern Minnesota. For reasons that have to do with the nature of the sky in the upper Midwest, a great many of the early—I almost wrote *real*—fliers came from that part of the world: from the Ohio Wright brothers, who pretty much started it all at the turn of the century, to Minnesota Lindbergh and Kansas Earhart to my South Dakota father, an army flier since 1917 and from 1927 to 1930 general manager of Transcontinental Air Transport (TAT, later TWA), for which Lindbergh acted as consultant and general publicist.

On my one visit to South Dakota, as I drove from Madison to Sioux Falls, I was conscious of an all-enveloping bowl of light, as if one were at the bottom of a vast goldfish bowl; odder still, the light also seemed to be coming as much from below as from above. Then I noticed how flat the plain was that I was crossing, how tall sky and low horizon made a luminous globe. In such a landscape, aerial flight seems, somehow, inevitable. So Lindbergh must have felt of his native country over which he was to fly for much of his youth as one of the first airmail carriers.

Earthly geography aimed him for the sky. Family, too. A paternal grandfather left Sweden during a political-financial scandal that Berg handles the best of anyone I've read. Ola Mansson was a farmer with a large family. Elected to the Swedish Parliament in 1847, he had an illegitimate child by a Stockholm waitress. Thanks to a scandal that involved the king, he fled Sweden, leaving behind his first family but taking with him the mother of his young son, Karl August. By 1859 he had changed his name to August Lindbergh; he had also become a farmer near Sauk Center, Minnesota, where Sinclair Lewis would be born in 1895. A politician in the old country, August became something of one in the new, but it was his eldest son, now called Charles August, who was to rise in that line of work. C.A. became a lawyer, married and had two children. After the death of his wife, he married a doctor's daughter. Evangeline Land was twenty-four; C.A. was forty. They were considered the best-looking couple in the heart of the heart of the country.

Enter American literature. Evangeline was a schoolteacher, well educated for the time, with fanciful artistic leanings. She loved amateur theatricals. Beauty, too. She wanted to "be an inspiration. I suppose I'd better become a teacher then . . . I'll make 'em put in a village green, and darling cottages. . . ." Thus speaks Carol Kennicott, heroine of Sinclair Lewis's *Main Street*. Thus spake, it would appear, Evangeline Lindbergh, on whom Carol appears to be based.

Most intriguingly, Lewis wrote his novel seven years before Carol-Evangeline's son became world-famous.

Although Lindbergh (born 1902) was to remain as close to his mother as two cool Scandinavians could ever be (or so she termed them when they refused to embrace for the press as he left for Paris), she was never to be the influence that his father was. In 1906, C.A. was elected to the House of Representatives as a Progressive on the Republican ticket, very much in the Robert La Follette populist isolationist tradition.

To understand the son's politics—or, perhaps, tropisms, reflexes to the public business—one must understand C.A. and his world.

Although Berg's book is well assembled and full of new detail, *Loss of Eden* by Joyce Milton is still, perhaps, the liveliest biography in the sense that she manages to bring alive her cast in a way not usual in contemporary biographies. But finally, it is Lindbergh himself, particularly in his posthumous *Autobiography of Values*, who bears the most interesting witness to a life so extraordinary that it becomes, paradoxically, emblematic of the American character at its most fulfilled.

Of his childhood, Lindbergh wrote:

My father grew up on the frontier. His parents had brought him there from Sweden when he was six years old. They staked out a homestead and from it axed a clearing and plowed a field. His early boyhood had been spent in constant fear of Indians and reliance upon soldiers. On one occasion when the Sioux had taken the warpath, my grandfather abandoned his homestead and with his family fled by ox-cart to the fort at St. Cloud. A massacre of settlers took place in a village to the south and reasonable security was not regained until soldiers came with their rifles. . . . During the early years of my life, I lived under the influence of three environments: our farm and town, my grandfather's Detroit laboratory (Dr. Land invented the porcelain tooth), and the city of Washington, D.C., where my father served for ten years in Congress and where I attended school. My interests were divided between the farm and the laboratory, for I disliked school and had little curiosity about the politics of Washington.

It is hard to think of the boy Lindbergh serving two years at Friends School, where so many of us were to do time in later years, including Mrs. Ronald Reagan.

In Congress, C.A. was the people's man or, as Milton puts it:

> If there was a single event that symbolized for the Progressives all that was wrong with unfettered capitalism, it was a meeting held in the library of the Madison Avenue home of New York financier J. P. Morgan in December 1890. At that conference Morgan had convinced the presidents of seven major railroads to call a halt to their cutthroat competition and form a cartel. The meeting marked the beginning of the era of the trusts, and during the next fifteen years Morgan would personally preside over the organization of more than a half-dozen mega-corporations— among them United States Steel, the Guggenheim copper trust, etc.

Most Progressives glumly accepted things as they were, but C.A. declared war on what he called the Money Trust, centered on the house of Morgan. Needless to say, the Money Trust survived his attacks but his marriage did not. C.A. and Evangeline separated. By 1907, she and Charles were in Detroit with her parents. Dr. Land was, like so many of the livelier figures of that age, an inventor. Charles would also become an inventor, a natural sort of activity at the dawn of the age of technology, whose presiding genius was Henry Ford.

In the end, Evangeline agreed to live in Washington, but not with C.A. At the age of eleven, Charles mastered Ford's invention and drove C.A. about his Minnesota district. Although more interested in the combustion engine than C.A.'s attacks on the Money Trust, Charles was bound to absorb a good deal of the populist faith. C.A. blasted the gold standard, the "subsidized press," the "anglophiles" who, by 1914, were eager for us to enter the European war, aided and abetted by J. P. Morgan, who supported the British and French currencies while supplying the Allies with arms. During all this, President Wilson was quietly maneuvering the United States into the war while running for reelection in 1916, using Senator T. P. Gore's slogan, "He kept us out of war." Representative Lindbergh and Senator Gore were not only allies in this, but each admired LaFollette, who also opposed, along with a majority of the American people, foreign entanglements and adventures. But the bankers' war, as the isolationists thought of it, was inevitable. The subsidized press that would later so damage Charles's reputation beat the drums for war, and, according to C.A.'s hyperbole, "at no period in the world's history has deceit been so bold and aggressive as now [sic] attempting to engulf all humanity in a maelstrom of hell." Little did the apolitical, science-loving Charles suspect that a generation later he would be making the same sort of speeches in the face of a conspiracy that neither he, nor anyone else much, understood at the time.

Berg is at his best with the two great news stories of Lindbergh's life—the 1927 flight to Paris and subsequent fame; and the 1932 kidnapping and killing of his two-year-old son and the chaotic search for the murderer, a German immigrant called Bruno Richard Hauptmann. (These sections read most excitingly, and despite the work of the inevitable revisionists, it seems more than ever clear that Hauptmann was indeed the kidnapper.) Berg dutifully notes that the first question King George V asked Lindbergh after his Atlantic flight was, "How did you pee?" Lindbergh was already used to the question. He had used paper cups. My father, Gene Vidal, his colleague, was more probing. "How did you . . . ?" Lindbergh laughed. "Well," he said, "I sort of felt sorry for those Frenchmen who were carrying me on their shoulders."

Neither Berg nor Milton is particularly good on the early days of aviation, a period awaiting its historian. By 1928, Lindbergh and Gene were involved in the first transcontinental airline, which took two days to cross the country (no night flying) by rail and air, landing at Glendale. The company's name, TAT, was an acronym, according to cynics, for Take A Train. Since Lindbergh virtuously refused to capitalize on his name (he rejected the fortune that William Randolph Hearst offered him to appear in a movie about his life), he settled for being a publicist for commercial aviation in general and TAT in particular.

"But what did he do?" I once asked my father. "He let us use his name. The Lindbergh line we called ourselves. Then he visited all around the country, sometimes checking out sites for landing fields. But then we all . . . those of us who were pilots . . . did that. We'd also taken on Amelia Earhart. We called her Assistant Traffic Manager. But, basically, it was all public relations. Everyone in the world wanted to look at those two. Amelia's main function for us was to convince women that it was safe to fly." "You mean you wanted more women pilots?" Gene was amused. "No. We were trying to get the women to let the men—their husbands, relatives, friends—fly. Amelia had such a cool and serene disposition that she really put people at ease, and so made the whole thing look a lot safer than it really was."

Milton is amusing about the somewhat edgy relations between the god of flight and, as of 1928, the goddess of flight. Much was made of the physical resemblance between Charles and Amelia. Milton seems to think that publisher-publicist George Palmer Putman had "plucked her from obscurity . . . impressed by her striking resemblance to the hero of 1927 and promoted her as 'Lady Lindy.' " It was always my impression that she had plucked herself from obscurity by becoming a flier and that Putman proceeded to commercialize her. Amelia was very much a proto-feminist whose Bible was Virginia Woolf's *A Room of One's Own*. Anne Morrow, Lindbergh's new wife, was also an enthusiast of Woolf, but Anne disappointed

Amelia by insisting that she was not "a modern career woman but rather the wife of a modern man."

According to Milton, while the two women were first bonding at a kitchen table, the practical joker Slim sneaked up behind his wife and began to dribble water on her silk dress. Amelia was delighted when Anne turned around and threw a glass of buttermilk in his face. But there was always a certain edginess between the Yin and Yang of flight. As Gene once said, tactfully, "Amelia was not a natural seat-of-the-pants flier like Slim." While Berg tells a joke that I'd not heard before. After Amelia soloed to Ireland in 1932, Lindbergh is supposed to have said, "I hear that Amelia made a good landing— once."

Berg gives almost equal space to Anne Morrow, as does Milton. Anne was born into the enemy camp. She was the daughter of a wealthy Morgan partner, Dwight Morrow, who was serving as his friend President Coolidge's ambassador to Mexico, where she first got to know her husband from the sky. Anne had graduated from Smith; published poetry; despite shyness, she enjoyed social life. Farm boy and society girl ought not to have got on at all, and, in a sense, the marriage was unbalanced, but she had wanted to marry a hero, and that meant accommodating herself to a hero's personality, Swedish division. As it was, she never ceased to admire him, something of a record in any marriage. They were to have six children.

In many ways, the marriage was a successful partnership; he taught her to fly, to be a navigator, while she encouraged him to become a serious writer. It is hard now to realize that, for years, each was one of the most popular writers in the world, a world that they saw from so far above that they were a bit like observant gods, hovering over all our seas and lands and noticing what the earthbound do not, the unity of things. They also raised a family, which their youngest daughter, Reeve, now describes in *Under a Wing*. The ethereal but tough Anne needed someone perhaps more sensitive to her moods—not to mention, more often at home; Slim was forever in motion. Later, Anne seems to have found a soulmate, first, briefly and intensely, in another poet-flier, Antoine de Saint-Exupéry, and, later, in her doctor. Interestingly, the twenty-seven-year-old Charles and the twenty-three-year-old Anne appear to have been virgins at the time of their wedding. We learn from Milton that, before the Paris flight, Slim had never attended a dinner party, never learned to dance, never gone out with a girl—because he'd had no time to learn what he regarded as the separate language of women. From the photographs, his love life seems to have involved a series of dogs, by no means an affective deprivation.

In 1933, Gene Vidal became Roosevelt's Director of Air Commerce, and for four years he systematized commercial aviation, issuing the first pilot's licenses (thoughtfully giving himself number one); he standardized the national system of airports. He also worked closely with his former colleague at TAT, now a consultant to Juan Trippe's Pan American Airways. During this period, the Lindberghs moved to Europe—but not before the opening gun in what would prove to be the most significant *mano a mano* duel of the hero's life.

It was the not unnatural view of Franklin Delano Roosevelt that in a time of crisis there could not be two heroes in the United States at the same time. As a mere governor, he had asked Slim for an autographed picture. But in 1932, when the mandate of Heaven was bestowed upon FDR, he became the embodiment of a nation's fears and hopes. He was alone . . . well, almost. Unfortunately, the Lone Eagle could always draw a bigger crowd. Fortunately, for FDR, Lindbergh genuinely hated the limelight, and after the death of his child, he vanished as much as he could within the New York laboratory of Dr. Alexis Carrel, where he worked on the perfusion pump, far from the rabid eyes of the press. With hindsight, one now sees how dramatically inevitable it was that the two largest figures on the national stage must eventually confront each other. To that end, the great dramaturge in the sky carefully set the scene, using Gene, at times, as third character.

The Hoover administration had awarded airmail contracts in a somewhat questionable manner, favoring rich conglomerates over independent airlines. When Gene Vidal's Ludington airline was passed over in favor of a conglomerate, Gene went public to denounce "Hoover socialism," something truly new under the sun. Once in office, FDR saw a neat way of scoring points off the Republican Party. He got the postmaster general to accuse his predecessor of "conspiracy and collusion" in the awarding of contracts, then, on February 9, 1934, by executive order, FDR canceled all airmail contracts. The Army had flown the mail in 1918; they would do so again. The Director of Air Commerce objected. Army pilots did not have the wildcat skills of mail pilots. Gene knew. He was an Army pilot. But FDR would not budge. I've always suspected that Gene got secretly to Lindbergh, who was both an Army pilot and an ex-mail pilot, and urged him to speak out before things got even worse—if that was possible: by the end of the first week, five Army pilots were dead, six critically injured, eight planes totaled. Meanwhile, airlines without mail contracts faced abrupt ruin.

Lindbergh sent off a 275-word telegram to the President while, simultaneously, releasing a copy to the press. This was *lèse majesté*. The White House attacked Lindbergh. The Senate called him before one of its committees. The hero was accused of publicity-seeking. This occasioned the only genuine laugh in the whole mess. Privately, Gene observed that FDR's state of denial over his blunder now required that Lindbergh be made the villain of the piece. In this the President was aided by another paladin of air, General Billy Mitchell, the apostle of military air power. Mitchell thought FDR should have taken over TWA to fly the mail until new—"honest"—contracts had been awarded. Meanwhile, Mitchell smeared Lindbergh as "a front of the Air Trust" and, worse, identified him as "that son-in-law of Dwight Morrow." So C.A., enemy for life of the Money Trust and the House of Morgan, now had a son said to be in thrall to the moneyed powers of darkness. Luckily, C.A. had died before his son married Anne Morrow.

As Army pilots kept falling from the skies, Roosevelt backed down. The mail, he declared, would be flown by any commercial airline that had not benefited from the previous regime. The old TAT, now Transcontinental and Western Air, became Trans World

Airlines. Lindbergh found this semantic solution "reminiscent of something to be found in *Alice in Wonderland.*"

The obligatory Schilleresque scene between the antagonists did not take place until April 1939. Lindbergh had been impressed—hoodwinked, some thought—by the German air forces. He had also, for the American military, gone to the Soviet Union, where he was appalled by the general military incompetence; and depressed by the political system. Like so many American conservatives of the day, he feared "Asian" Communism more than he did Nazi efficiency. In any case, after nearly four years of exile, he came home to ask for a military buildup by the United States, just in case; he had also come home to preach against involvement in the approaching European war. On the buildup, as the two heroes were wary allies, they met for the first and last time.

From Lindbergh's diary:

I went to see the President about 12:45. . . . He was seated at his desk at one end of a large room. There were several model ships around the walls. He leaned forward from his chair to meet me as I entered, and it is only now that I stop to think that he is crippled. I did not notice it and had not thought of it during our meeting. He immediately asked me how Anne was and mentioned the fact that she knew his daughter in school. He is an accomplished, suave, interesting conversationalist. I liked him and feel that I could get along with him well. Acquaintanceship would be pleasant and interesting.

But there was something about him I did not trust, something a little too suave, too pleasant, too easy. Still, he is our President, and there is no reason for any antagonism between us in the work I am now doing. The airmail situation is past—one of the worst political maneuvers I know of, and unfair in the extreme, to say the least. But nothing constructive will be gained by bringing it up again at this time.

Roosevelt gave me the impression of being a very tired man, but with enough energy left to carry on for a long time. I doubt that he realizes how tired he is. His face has that gray look of an over-worked businessman. And his voice has that even, routine tone that one seemed to get when mind is dulled by too much and too frequent conversation. It has that dull quality that comes to any one of the senses when it is overused: taste, with too much of the same food day after day; hearing, when the music never changes; touch, when one's hand is never lifted.

Roosevelt judges his man quickly and plays him cleverly. He is mostly politician, and I think we would never get along on many fundamentals. But there are things about him I like, and why worry about the others unless and until they necessitate consideration. It is better to work together as long as we can; yet somehow I have a feeling that it may not be for long.

Thus the great dramaturge keeps the plot aboil. Also, Lindbergh's impressions are as interesting and "accurate" a take on FDR as anything written by a contemporary. Certainly, it is unique in Lindbergh's diary because he—who was observed constantly by everyone else—seldom observes anyone, not so much due to lack of interest but of opportunity. Happily, for gossips, he did note how astonishingly boring the Duke of Windsor was at dinner when he discussed at length how much higher the Etoile was than the Place de la Concorde, plainly an all-time room-emptier.

The truce with FDR was short. That summer, Lindbergh worked with the commanding general of the Army Air Force, H. H. Arnold; research and development was the Lindbergh assignment. On September 1, the Germans invaded Poland. The European war had begun. On September 15, Lindbergh took to the airwaves to speak on "America and the European Wars." Of this, he writes, "An interesting incident relating to the address had occurred earlier in the day."

A colonel had been sent to him to say "the Administration was very much worried by my intention of speaking over the radio and opposing actively this country's entry into a European war. [He] said that if I did not do this, a secretaryship of air would be created in the Cabinet and given to me! . . . This offer on Roosevelt's part does not surprise me after what I have learned about his Administration. It does surprise me, though, that he still thinks I might be influenced by such an offer. It is a great mistake for him to let the Army know that he deals in such a way."

This is very prim indeed, but Lindbergh knew that, from Arnold on down, the President had been told Lindbergh wouldn't accept. "Regardless of the fact that [FDR] had publicly advocated a policy of neutrality for the United States, it seemed to me apparent that he intended to lead our country into the war. The powers he influenced and controlled were great. Opposing them would require planning, political skill, and organization. For me, this meant entering a new framework of life."

For nearly three years, the son of C.A. galvanized the country with his speeches and rallies. The first and, thus far, last great debate of the "American Century" was now engaged. Although Lindbergh had many formidable allies, the President had not only great skills and powers, he had, as we now know, the British secret services at work throughout the land, and their first task was the deconstruction of a hero.

To swing American opinion towards war, the British knew that they could count on the wily Roosevelt only up to a point. He had a third term to win in 1940; he also had a country with an isolationist majority, and a Lone Eagle pecking away at him. He could still launch trial balloons like his 1937 "Quarantine the Aggressors" speech, which was, according to Canada's Governor-General, Lord Tweedsmuir, "the culmination of a long conspiracy between us (this must be kept secret)!" Unfortunately, that balloon burst and FDR retreated, for the moment. He always had the same advice for enthusiasts whose aims he shared but dared not support openly in the absence of a political majority. "You must *force* me to act," he would say blithely. When a denunciation of his inaction was being prepared by the interventionists, he suggested "pusillanimous" as a nice word to describe his cautious public policies.

C.A.'s son was now beginning to see, if not the covert hand of the British in our affairs, the overt hand of the House of Morgan, not to mention his own father-in-law, Dwight Morrow. Lindbergh had never much minded the Money Trust that had so incensed his father. He had gone from being a farm boy, to stunt flier, to Army flier and then to world hero. Social injustice seemed never to have concerned him. After all, he had looked after himself and everything had turned out rather more than well. He had allowed himself to be taken up by Dwight Morrow and the Morgan partners who invested his money for him and made him rich without ever commercializing his name. Incidentally, Berg made a gentlemanly treaty with Anne Morrow Lindbergh (still alive in her nineties) to use her diaries and correspondence. One *quid* for this *quo* is that Berg never mentions the fact that the brilliant, self-made Morrow was an alcoholic. It is here that Milton is much more interesting than Berg about the family that Lindbergh married into.

One fact of the national condition that can never be discussed with candor is the class system. At the peak of the American pyramid—the one with that awful unblinking eye in it—is the WASP eastern establishment. Mahl notes that C. Wright Mills took considerable flak when

> he identified [it] in his book *The Power Elite* (1956). The United States, wrote Mills, was controlled not by the mass of its citizens as described by democratic theory, but by a wealthy Anglo-Saxon Protestant elite from Ivy League schools. In a flurry of caustic reviews, critics, often Cold War liberals, heatedly denied that there was such an elite. That debate now seems over, as Douglas Little noted in a recent review article in *Diplomatic History*: "Far from

rejecting the idea of a power elite . . . [the books under re-
view] celebrate its short lived Periclean age during the quarter century after 1945. . . ."

The British had never displayed any similar doubts about the
existence of an American "power elite." As early as 1917, Lord
Robert Cecil in Cabinet noted that "though the American people are
very largely foreign, both in origin and modes of thought, their
rulers are almost exclusively Anglo-Saxons, and share our political
ideals."

The Swedish Lindberghs were as foreign to this establishment as
the Sulzbergers. But in the instance of war or peace the Sulzbergers
sided with the WASP elite, while Charles Lindbergh missed the
point which Anne swiftly got the moment he showed her the medal
that Goering had unexpectedly handed him at dinner in Berlin.
"Your albatross," she said. Lindbergh seems never to have got it.

Meanwhile, between WASP elite and British agents, the United
States was being totally transformed. From President Washington's
day to Pearl Harbor, isolationism was the honorable, if sometimes
opportunistically ignored, national creed. But by 1940, one of the
two leading isolationist senators, Arthur Vandenberg, had been converted to war and, later, to global hegemony, by three enchanting
ladies in the pay of the British. Mahl gives names, addresses. One of
them, wife to a British diplomat, code name "Cynthia," was the
heroine of an eponymous study by H. Montgomery Hyde in 1965.
Finally, just in case FDR was defeated in 1940, the other great isolationist, Senator Robert A. Taft, was overwhelmed at the Republican convention by the British candidate, the previously unknown
Wendell Willkie.

After Pearl Harbor, Lindbergh offered his services to the Air
Force. FDR, never one to forgo an enmity, took pleasure in turning
him down, despite the *New York Times* editorial to the effect that he
should be used as "he is a superb air man, and this is primarily and
essentially an air war." But Roosevelt could not allow his competi-

tion to regain hero status, which, indeed, despite the best efforts of many interested parties, he never did lose for most of the people. Lone Eagles tend to outsoar presidents, no matter how bad the weather. As it was, Lindbergh got to the South Pacific, where he flew clandestine combat missions with men half his age. As he was only an observer, this was illegal, but commanders in the field were delighted to have so consummate and useful an airman in their midst.

Once the war was over, Lindbergh continued his travels with Anne; they also raised their five surviving children. It appears that Lindbergh was a conscientious father, with a tendency to reinvent the wheel when there was something to be explained. He was also a bit of a martinet with checklists (yes, he invented that pilot's routine) for each child. He was alert to the utility of things. Reeve records a hilarious (to read, that is) lecture on "punk design":

> He also had a normal-looking flashlight with an ugly hexagonal head, to which feature he drew our attention every time he put the flashlight down on a flat surface.
>
> "You see that?" He would point. "It doesn't move." We saw. The flashlight lay there on the shelf, or the table, or the floor, exactly as he had placed it. It didn't move a bit. Nor did we, as he fixed us with his penetrating, instructive blue eyes.
>
> "It doesn't roll off the table," he would say, looking at us searchingly, challenging someone to contradict him. Nobody did.
>
> "Why aren't all flashlights made like this one?" he wondered aloud. None of us would hazard a guess.
>
> "Cylinders!" He explained irritably. "You buy a flashlight, nine times out of ten it comes in a cylindrical shape. Now, a cylinder will always roll. A cylinder was made to roll. And rolling is fine, for a rolling pin. But you put down a cylindrical flashlight in the dark, near a place where you're

working, so you can use two hands, and what's it going to do? It's going to roll away from you, of course! Off the shelf, under the car, what good is that?"

No good at all, we knew. And we knew what he would say next, too.

"All they would have to do is change the shape of the head. Not the whole flashlight, just the head. The whole problem would be solved. What's the matter with these people? Pentagonal, hexagonal, even a square, for heaven's sake. Just the head. . . ."

As one surveys his life, one sees him move from phase to phase, much as the human race itself has done. The boy on the farm, fascinated by husbandry. By eugenics, a pseudoscience of the day. By nature. By medical science to improve life. By machinery. By flight. By the next step after the propeller, jet propulsion—as early as the late 1920s. Fascinated by the old civilizations that he had flown over throughout his life, he now saw how precarious they were in the face of the instrument that he had helped perfect, the aircraft. He saw the necessity for the avoidance of war, while establishing an equilibrium between the planet's resources and human population. By the need to understand ancient tribal patterns, in order to undo or mitigate what science is doing to modern man. He lived among primitive tribes; tried to understand their ancient adaptabilities. He literally thought himself, doggedly, from one level to the next.

Towards the end, he had come to dislike the world that he had done so much to create. First, he noticed the standardization of air bases everywhere. The sameness of food, even landscape. The boredom of air travel in jet liners. The fun was gone. A key word in his early works was "adventure." He stops using it. Finally, there is his lifelong vein of mysticism. Many of the early flyers had a curious sense of hyperreality when contemplating their own relationship with earth and sky, not to mention with the tiny human beings whom they passed over, swiftly, like gods. Much of the magic of air power at the beginning was the image of a silver ship-bird coming out of the blue, like a sky-god returning to the ground people.

The early fliers were literally extraterrestrial as they came in for their landings, for their rebirth as earthlings. On this subject, Lindbergh was amused by the great myth-maker himself, Carl Jung. The Lindberghs sat with the "old wizard" on the Zurichsee's north bank. "Conversation turned to 'flying saucers.' Jung had written a book about them. . . . I had expected him to discuss the psychological and psychiatric aspects of people's fantasizing. . . . I was amazed to find that he believed in their reality. . . . When I mentioned a discussion I had had with General Carl Spaatz, the chief of staff of the Air Force . . . Jung said, 'There are many things taking place upon earth that you and General Spaatz do not know about.' " Lindbergh reflects upon superstition as a constant in human affairs:

> I know myself as mortal, but this raises the question "What is I?" Am I an individual, or am I an evolving life stream composed of countless selves? . . . As one identity, I was born in A.D. 1902. But as twentieth-century man, I am billions of years old. The life I consider as myself has existed through past eons with unbroken continuity. Individuals are custodians of the life stream—temporal manifestations of far greater being, forming from and returning to their essence like so many dreams. . . . I recall standing on the edge of a deep valley in the Hawaiian island of Maui, thinking that a life stream is like a mountain river—springing from hidden sources, born out of the earth, touched by stars, merging, blending, evolving in the shape momentarily seen.

By thinking ahead from what he had observed, Lindbergh had been able to think himself back to Lucretius: *Nil posse creari de nilo,* "Nothing can be created out of nothing." Or, "The sum of things is ever being replenished and mortals live one and all by give and take.

Some races wax and others wane, and in a short space the tribes of living things are changed, and like runners hand on the torch of life." Lindbergh sums up: "I am form and I am formless. I am life and I am matter, mortal and immortal. I am one and many—myself and humanity in flux. . . . After my death, the molecules of my being will return to the earth and sky. They came from the stars. I am of the stars."

Disraeli, born a Jew, christened an Anglican, avoided church. A character in one of his novels was asked what his religion was. The character responded, "All wise men have the same religion." When asked what that was, he said, "Wise men never say." It is the most perfect irony that Roosevelt and Lindbergh, heroic antagonists, shared, at the end, the same religion. Each wanted to be buried so that his atoms would get back into circulation as quickly as possible, one with a missing side to his coffin in a rose garden, the other in a biodegradable wooden box on a Pacific island. Thus, each meant to rejoin the life stream, and the genitive stars. Meanwhile, it might be a pleasant gift to the new century and the new millennium to replace the pejorative 1812 caricature of a sly treacherous Uncle Sam with that of Lindbergh, the best that we are ever apt to produce in the hero line, American style.

The Times Literary Supplement
30 October 1998

At least two generations of Americans were conceived to the sound of Sinatra's voice on record or radio. Conception in cinema houses was not unknown but considered flashy. There were several Sinatras in the six or seven decades of his career. There was the wartime idol of the young. He was skinny, gaunt-faced with a floppy bow tie and a left profile like that of a Donatello bronze. At New York's Paramount Theater pubescent girls howled like Bacchae at the sight and sound of him and fainted like dowagers in tight stays.

I met him first while I was in the army, just before going overseas. We were at a Hollywood party where everyone was a star and I was a private to whom no one spoke except Sinatra, who singled me out and charmed me for life. In person and in art. That was the hero Sinatra whose populism was to bring him soon to ruin.

The story, a selective part of it, is well known. Born in New Jersey, Francis Sinatra had a formidable mother, active in Democratic city ward politics. He knew at first hand the politics of immigrant Italians, of the urban working class. He was one of them.

He began his career singing wherever he could; he became famous singing with the big bands of the day. "His grace notes are like Bach," said Virgil Thomson, our leading music critic. Everyone thought Virgil was joking but he wasn't. Sinatra's voice was like no other. But I leave that to music critics. What interests me is the rise and fall of a political hero whose apotheosis, or, to be precise, hell, was to become a neutered creature of the American right wing, crooning in Nancy Reagan's ear at the White House. An Italo-American Faust.

At the height of Sinatra's popular fame as a singer he made a short documentary called *The House I Live in*. This was 1947; he won an Academy Award for the song, whose lyrics—The people that I work with. The workers that I meet. . . . The right to speak my mind. That is America to me—were a straightforward plea for tolerance that neither cloyed nor bored.

Jon Wiener in *Professors, Politics and Pop* (Verso) has given a moving account of how Sinatra then fell foul of the FBI and the professional patriots and the then powerful Hearst press. In the course of the next eight years, Congress's Un-American Activities Committee, in its *Index* "of Communists," named *The House I Live In* twelve times while the *New York Times*, forever up to no good, in its *Index* for 1949 published a cross-reference: "Sinatra, Frank: See U.S.—Espionage." That was all the news fit to print about our greatest popular singer.

To add to the demonization, one Harry Anslinger, head of the Federal Narcotics Bureau, and the FBI's ineffable J. Edgar Hoover (who lived long enough to keep a file on the subversions and perversions of John Lennon), were out to get Sinatra not only as a crypto-Communist but as a mafioso. Since any nightclub singer must work in a nightclub or a casino and since the mob controlled these glittering venues, every entertainer was obliged to traffic with them.

In 1947 Sinatra was smeared as a mafioso by a right-wing Hearst columnist, Lee Mortimer. Sinatra, notoriously short-tempered and not unfamiliar with fiery waters, knocked Mortimer down in a nightclub. Press ink flowed like Niagara Falls. Sinatra was transformed by the right-wing press "overnight," as Wiener wrote, "from the crooning idol of bobby-soxers into violent, left-wing mafioso."

Roman Catholic organs, respectful of their co-religionist's fame, tried to downplay the attacks, maintaining he was a mere "pawn." But he wasn't. Sinatra had indeed been active in left-wing (by American standards) activities. In 1946 he blasted Franco, a favorite of America's High Command. That same year he became vice-president of the Hollywood Independent Citizens Committee of the

Arts, Sciences and Professions, along with many other stars and Thomas Mann.

In 1948 he supported Henry Wallace for President against the proto-McCarthyite Harry S Truman. Undeterred by the harm to his career, Sinatra wrote an open letter to the then liberal *New Republic* imploring Henry Wallace, as heir to Roosevelt, "to take up the fight we like to think of as ours—the fight for tolerance, which is the basis of any fight for peace." Wiener reports that three months later he was publicly branded a Communist and sacked from his radio show; by 1949 Columbia Records had broken with him and by 1950 MGM dismissed him from his film contract. A has-been at thirty-four.

After a time of trouble with his wife, Ava Gardner, and the loss of his voice due to alcohol and stress, he made his astonishing comeback in the film *From Here to Eternity*, for which he was obliged to take a minimal salary. He also developed a brand-new voice, grace notes like Mabel Mercer.

By 1960 Sinatra was again political. He had been a playmate of Jack Kennedy in his senatorial days; he was also gung-ho to help out his conservative but attractive Catholic friend. But some Kennedy advisers thought the Red Mafioso should be avoided at all costs, others wanted to use him for a voter drive in Harlem "where he is recognised as a hero of the cause of the Negro," something that Kennedy was not, to say the least.

Although, at times, Sinatra seemed to be ranging between megalomania and just plain hard drinking, he was still a major singer, also a movie star, famous for doing scenes in only one take—known in the trade as "walking through." Kennedy's candidacy revved him up. But for those who have wondered what dinner might have been like for Falstaff when Prince Hal—now King—snubbed him, I can report that after Kennedy was nominated in Los Angeles at the convention where I was a delegate, Tony Curtis and Janet Lee gave a movie-star party for the nominee. I was placed, along with Sinatra, at the table where Kennedy would sit. We waited. And waited. Sinatra looked edgy; started to drink heavily. Dinner began. Then one of the toothy sisters of the nominee said, casually, "Oh, Jack's sorry. He can't come. He's gone to the movies." Opposite me, Falstaff deflated and spoke no more that evening.

Once Kennedy was elected, Sinatra organized the inaugural ball. But the President's father and brother Robert said no more Sinatra and there was no more Sinatra.

When President Kennedy came to stay in Palm Springs, he stayed not with Sinatra, as announced, but with his rival Bing Crosby. Insult to injury. From then on, in public and private, he often behaved boorishly (to riot in understatement).

In due course, he was called before a Congressional committee on the Mafia. They got nowhere. Nowhere to go. Nowhere for him, either. He became a Reagan Republican. But then no Democratic President asked him to perform at the White House. It was sly old Nixon, whose House committee had smeared him, who asked Sinatra to sing *The House I Live In*.

"At the end of the program," Wiener writes, "for the first time in his public career, Sinatra was in tears." It is not easy to be good, much less a tribune of the people, in the land of milk and money once your house is gone.

The Observer
17 May 1998

C. P. CAVAFY

Forty years ago, in a more than usually run-down quarter of Athens, there was a bar called the Nea Zoe. The brightly lit raw-wood interior smelled of pinecones and liquorice—retsina wine and ouzo. A jukebox played Greek music—minor key with a strong martial beat—to which soldiers from a nearby barracks gravely danced with one another or in groups or alone. Women were not encouraged to join in. The Nea Zoe was a sanctuary where Greek men performed pre-Christian dances taught them by their fathers, who in turn had learned them from their fathers all the way back to the start of history if not before. The dances celebrated the deeds of gods and heroes. I recall one astonishing—dizzying—solo where a soldier arrived on the dance floor with a great leap and then began a series of rapid turns while striking the floor with the flat of his hand.

"He is doing the dance of Antaeus," said the old Greek colonel who had brought me to the bar. "Antaeus was son of the sea god Poseidon out of Gaia, mother earth. Antaeus is the world's strongest wrestler but he can only remain strong by touching earth, his mother." The colonel knew all the ancient dances and he could tell from the way a boy danced where he came from: the islands, the Peloponnese, Thessaly. "There used to be a dozen of these places here in Athens but since that movie . . ." He sighed. *That* movie was the recently released *Never on Sunday*; it had charmed the world but it had also inspired many American tourists to come to places like the Nea Zoe to laugh at the fairies dancing. Since ancient Greek has no word for such a made-up category as fairy, the soldiers were at first bewildered by so much weird attention. Then, when they realized how insulting the fat Americans were, they would gravely take them outside and beat them up. Unfortunately, tourism is more important to governments than two-thousand-year-old dances; the bars were shut down.

Nea Zoe means new life. "That was also the name of the magazine where Cavafy published many of his best poems." I should note that my first visit to Athens took place in 1961, the year that *The Complete Poems of C.P. Cavafy* was published by the Hogarth Press with an introduction by W. H. Auden. We were all reading Cavafy that season, in Rae Dalven's translation from the Greek. Now, forty years on, Theoharis Constantine Theoharis has given us what is, at last, all the poems that he could find.

Constantine P. Cavafy was born at Constantinople, April 17, 1863, not too long after Walt Whitman added Calamus to *Leaves of Grass*. Constantinople had been built to be the capital of the Eastern—and largely Greek—Roman empire. For several generations the Cavafys were successful manufacturers and exporters. But by the time of the death of Cavafy's father, there was almost no money left. After a time in London, the widow Cavafy and six sons moved on to the other ancient Greek city, Alexandria, in Egypt. Although Cavafy's formal education was classical, he was a bookish young man who largely educated himself while being supported by a family network until, on March 1, 1892, not quite twenty-nine—a shadow-line for the young men he writes of in his poems—he became provisional clerk in the Ministry of Irrigation. Since he had chosen to be a Greek citizen, he remained for thirty years "provisional," a permanently temporary clerk of the Egyptian government. Thanks to his knowledge of English, French, Italian, Greek, and Arabic, he sometimes moonlighted as a broker. In 1895 he acquired a civilized friend, Pericles Anastasiades, who would be for him the other self that Etienne de la Boëtie had been for Montaigne. This was also the year Cavafy began to write "seriously." By 1903 he was being published in the Athenian magazine *Panatheneum*. A year later he published his first book, containing fourteen poems; he was now forty-one. From 1908 to 1918 he published frequently in *Nea Zoe*;

he became known throughout the Greek world: then came translations in English, French, Italian. From 1908 to 1933—the year of his death—Cavafy lived alone at 10 Lepsius Street, Alexandria, today a modest shrine. There is a long hallway lined with books and a living room that contains a large sofa and what is described as "Arab furniture"; his study was also his bedroom.

E. M. Forster famously described him at the time of the First War: ". . . A Greek gentleman in a straw hat standing absolutely motionless at a slight angle to the universe. His arms are extended, possibly. 'Oh, Cavafy . . . !' Yes, it is Mr. Cavafy, and he is going either from his flat to the office, or from his office to the flat. If the former, he vanishes when seen, with a slight gesture of despair. If the latter, he may be prevailed upon to begin a sentence—an immense complicated yet shapely sentence, full of parentheses that never get mixed and of reservations that really do reserve; a sentence that moves with logic to its foreseen end, yet to an end that is always more vivid and thrilling than one foresaw. And despite its intellectual richness and human outlook, despite the matured charity of its judgments, one feels that it too stands at a slight angle to the universe."

Although Cavafy himself appears to have been a conventional Greek Orthodox Christian, as poet he inhabits the pagan Greco-Roman world of legend as well as the everyday world of Alexandria in which he might be called the Pindar of the one-night stand between males. A troubled, sometime Christian puritan, W. H. Auden, suspects that the passionate encounters he describes are largely one-sided because the poet no doubt paid: It is true that the grave soldiers at the Nea Zoe expected a small payment for their company but the business transacted was always mutual and the double nimbus of accomplished lust can be spectacularly bright in a shadowy room full of Arabian furniture not to mention ghosts and even gods.

Yes, the gods themselves, always youthful, eternal, still appear to men. "When an August morning dawns over you, / your scented space gleams with their life; / and sometimes a young man's etherial [sic] form, / vanishing, passing quickly, crosses the tops of your hills." *In One of Their Gods,* Cavafy observes: "When one of them passed through Selefkia's market, / at the hour when darkness first comes on, / as would a tall, and consummately handsome youth / with the joy of invulnerability in his eyes . . . headed for the quarter that only lives at night, with orgies and debaucheries / with every type of frenzy and abandon, / they speculated about which of Them he was, and for which of his suspicious entertainments / he'd descended to the streets of Selefkia / from his Worshipped, his most Venerated Halls."

Here is a standard exercise given students in classical times: imagine that you are Julius Caesar, you have just crossed the river Rubicon; you are at war with your own republic. Now, as Caesar, write what you are thinking and feeling. A canny exercise because to put yourself in the place of another encourages empathy and understanding. J. G. Herder even invented the German word *Einfühlen* to describe those, like Cavafy, who have the capacity to enter and inhabit other-time. Some of his best poems are soliloquies that he invents for those who once lived and died in history or, more intimately, for those whom he has known and loved in his own story.

The history that he most draws upon is the world of Alexander the Great, whose heirs created Greek kingdoms in Egypt and Asia Minor, sovereignties that, in less than three centuries, were powerless Roman dependencies. Marc Antony's loss of the Roman world to Octavian Augustus particularly fascinates him. "Suddenly, at midnight, when an invisible troupe / is heard passing, / with exquisite players, with voices— / do not lament your luck, now utterly exhausted / your acts that failed . . . / listen, taking your final pleasure, / to the sounds, to that mystic troupe's rare playing, / and say your last farewell to her, to that Alexandria you are losing." For Cavafy, Alexandria, not Cleopatra, is the heroine of the hero's tragedy.

Despite Cavafy's sense that the old gods have never forsaken us, he shows no sympathy at all for the Emperor Julian, who, vainly, tried to restore the worship of the gods in the fourth century. Admittedly, Julian could be a grinding bore, but even so, the essentially pagan Cavafy should have admired him. But he doesn't. Why not? I think one pronoun shows us what Cavafy is up to. "In Antioch we were perplexed on hearing / about Julian's latest behavior." There it is. *We.* Cavafy is writing as a Christian citizen of Antioch, a city which disdained the emperor and all his works. *Einfühlen* at work. Cavafy is like an actor here, in character—or like Shakespeare when he imagines himself heir to a murdered king even though, according to one of Cavafy's most ingenious poems, it is Claudius who is the good king and Hamlet, the student prince, the villain, the youth, "was nervous in the extreme, / while he was studying in Wittenberg many of his fellow students thought him a maniac."

Cavafy once analyzed his own temperament and talent. "To me, the immediate impression is never a starting point for work. The impression has got to age, has got to falsify itself with time, without my having to falsify it.

"I have two capacities: to write Poetry or to write History. I haven't written history and it's too late now. Now, you'll say, how do I know that I could write History? I feel it. I make the experiment, and ask myself: Cavafy, could you write fiction? Ten voices cry No. I ask the question again: Cavafy, could you write a play? Twenty-five voices again cry No. Then I ask again: Cavafy, could you write History? A hundred and twenty-five voices tell me you could." The critic Robert Liddell thought Cavafy could have been a master of historical fiction. Luckily, he chose to be himself, a unique poet at an odd angle to our culture.

It was noted at the death of America's tragic twentieth-century empress—the one who died with a Greek name as well as fate—that her favorite poem was Cavafy's *Ithaca*. One can see why. Cavafy has gone back to Homer: the origin of Greek narrative. Odysseus, returning from Troy to his home island of Ithaca, is endlessly delayed by the malice of the sea god Poseidon. Cavafy appears to be addressing Odysseus himself but it could be anyone on a life's journey. "As you set out toward Ithaca, / hope the way is long, full of reversals, full of knowing." He advises the traveler not to brood too much on the malice of those who want to destroy him, to keep him from his goal. If you don't take them to heart, they cannot defeat you. The poet also advises the traveler to enjoy the exotic cities along the way; he even favors selective shopping, something that also appealed to our nineteenth-century tragic empress, Mrs. Abraham Lincoln. Why not take advantage of a visit to Egypt for wisdom? "Keep Ithaca always in your mind. / Arriving there is what has been ordained for you. / But do not hurry the journey at all. Better if it lasts many years: and you dock an old man on the island, rich with all that you have gained on the way, not expecting Ithaca to give you wealth / Ithaca gave you the beautiful journey. / Without her you would not have set out. / She has nothing more to give you." Then the final insight; acceptance of a life now lived. "And if you find her poor, Ithaca has not fooled you. / Having become so wise, with so much experience, / you will have understood, by then, what these Ithacas mean." One does not need to be a tragic empress to be impressed by Cavafy's practical wisdom.

PART II

PART II

GEORGE

I grew up in Washington, D.C. Did I—or anyone so situated—give much thought to the man for whom our city was named? Hardly. The Washington Monument, even for me at the age of ten, was of world-class boredom. Mount Vernon on the Potomac was interesting—particularly George's clothes, lovingly displayed. He was a giant, with large hands and feet and a huge rump; also a formidable poitrine due to some sort of syndrome which rendered him Amazonian in appearance and childless—mulelike—for life. But he was a man of great dignity and strength and once when he ordered two soldiers to stop a fight and they went right on, he picked each up by the scruff of the neck and banged the two heads together. Very satisfying. Plainly a dominatrix of the old-fashioned sort.

A condition of my admission to St. Albans, a local school, was that I read a biography of Washington. I, who could, even then, read almost anything, was desolate. George Washington. The syllables of that name had the same effect on me that Gerald Ford now does. But I finally got through what was a standard hagiography of the sort that every nation inflicts upon its young in order to make them so patriotic that they will go fight in wars not of their choosing while paying taxes for the privilege. Pre-Watergate, to get people to do such things it used to be necessary to convince the innocent that only good and wise men (no women then) governed us, plaster-of-Paris demigods given to booming out, at intervals, awful one-liners like "Give me liberty or give me death." Thus were we given the liberty to pay our taxes, though it might have been nice to have had the freedom to use for the public good some of the money taken from us.

A long time has passed since my school days and my first encounter with George. Currently, incomes are down. Taxes are up. Empire has worn us out and left the people at large broke. In the process, we ceased to have a representative government. In 1996, 51 percent of those qualified to vote chose not to vote for president. President Clinton was reelected by 49 percent of the voters, a minus mandate to put it mildly. And so, George, where are you now when we need you? To which the answer is, which George do you have in mind? Bush or . . .

The real George Washington, to the extent that we can reconstruct him, was born in 1732 and died in 1799, younger at death than the crotchety Bob Dole was in the late election. When George was eleven, his father died, and he was brought up by his half brother, Lawrence, who had married into the Fairfax family, one of the richest in Virginia. It was Lawrence who owned that fine estate on the Potomac River, Mount Vernon. As George was not much of one for books and school, he became a surveyor at fifteen; he was also land-mad and so, while surveying vast properties, he started investing every penny he could get his hands on in land. Some of it, crucially, along the Ohio River. Meanwhile, the Grim Reaper was looking out for George. Lawrence and his daughter both died when George was twenty, making him the master of Mount Vernon. Now very rich—but never rich enough—he took up soldiering. The colonial governor of Virginia sent him to the Ohio Valley (near today's Pittsburgh) with orders to drive the French from "American" territory. And so, in 1754, the first of George's numerous military defeats was inflicted upon him by the French. With characteristic Gallic panache, they sent him back home, where he was promptly promoted to colonel. But then anyone destined to have his likeness carved on a mountainside can only fall upward. In 1758, George was elected to the Virginia legislature, the House of Burgesses; the next year he married a very rich widow, Martha Dandridge Custis. George was now, reputedly, the first American millionaire.

George and Revolution. As George looked like a general—the unpleasantness near Pittsburgh was overlooked—the Second Continental Congress, in a compromise between Massachusetts and Virginia, chose him to be commander in chief of the new Continental Army, whose task it was to free the thirteen American colonies from England. "No taxation without representation" was the war cry of the rebelling colonists just as it is of the Reverend Jesse Jackson and close to a million disenfranchised blacks in George's city today.

A far less accomplished general than Ethan Allen or Benedict Arnold, George did know how to use *them* well. In 1775, although Boston and New York were in British hands, George sent an army north to conquer Canada—Canada has always been very much on the minds of those Americans inclined to symmetry. When the White House and Capitol were put to the torch in 1814 and President Madison fled into the neighboring woods, where was the American army? Invading Canada yet again. The dream. The impossible dream.

George moved south to New York, where he managed to lose both Long Island and Manhattan to the British, who remained comfortably in residence until the French fleet came to George's aid in October 1781 and the British, now bored, bad-tempered, and broke, gave up the colonies. In a moving ceremony, George took over New York City, and as the British flag came down and our flag went up, there was not a dry eye to be seen, particularly when the American soldier shimmying up the flagpole to hoist New Glory suddenly fell with a crash at George's feet. The treacherous Brits had greased the pole.

George went home. He was a world figure. The loose confederation of independent states was now beacon to the world. George farmed. He also invented a plow so heavy that no ox could pull it; he was grimly competing with crafty fellow farmer Jefferson, who had invented the dumbwaiter. Never an idle moment for the Founding Dads. Then Something Happened.

Captain Daniel Shays of Massachusetts, a brave officer in the Revolution, had fallen on hard times. Indeed most of the veterans of the war were suffering from too little income and too many taxes. They had been better off before independence, they declared, and so Shays and his neighbors, in effect, declared war on Massachusetts in 1786 when Shays and several hundred armed veterans marched on the state arsenal at Springfield. Although this impromptu army was soon defeated, Shays' Rebellion scared George to death. He sent agonized letters to various magnates in different states. To Harry Lee: "You talk . . . of employing influence to appease the present tumults in Massachusetts. I know not where that influence is to be found, or if attainable, that it would be a proper remedy for the disorders. *Influence* is no *government*. Let us have one by which our lives, liberties and properties will be secured, or let us know the worst at once." There it is. The principle upon which the actual American republic was founded, erasing in the process Thomas Jefferson's astonishing and radical proposal that, along with life and liberty, the citizen has the right to pursue happiness and even—with rare luck—overtake it. George was too hardheaded for that sort of sentimentality. George knew that property must always come first and so, in due course, he got the republic that he wanted, a stern contraption set in place to ensure the safety and property of the prosperous few.

After two terms as president (with Alexander Hamilton acting as prime minister), George went home to Mount Vernon in 1796, mission accomplished. Although Madison and Mason (with Jefferson back of them) came up with the mitigating Bill of Rights, that Bill has never won many American hearts. After the Civil War the Fourteenth Amendment made it clear that the rights for United Statespersons also applied to each citizen as a resident within his home state. The Supreme Court, always Georgian save for the Earl Warren lapse in the Sixties, promptly interpreted those rights as essentially applicable to corporations. And so, in death, George won again.

The man? George was dignity personified. The impish Gouverneur Morris was bet ten dollars that he wouldn't dare go up to Washington at one of Lady (they called her that) Washington's lev-

ees and put his hand on George's shoulder. Morris did; collected his
bet; then said, "I don't think that I shall do this a second time." In
his last address as president, George warned against foreign adventures and also *permanent* alliances with foreign nations while, as
rarely as possible, trusting to "*temporary* alliances for extraordinary
emergencies." In his worst nightmares, George could never have
dreamed of just how many "extraordinary emergencies" his forty-
odd successors would be able to cook up.

George and posterity? He is ever present in our decaying institutions. Iconography? The movies have generally ignored him while
his biographies tend to be dull because the biographers are too busy
defending his principles while pretending that we live—or are supposed to live—in a democracy, an absolute nonstarter from the
beginning.

George today? A year or two ago a wealthy friend (so rich that
he never handles actual cash) picked up a dollar bill that someone
had left on a table and said, with wonder, "When did George Bush
put Barbara's picture on the money?" Barbara Bush and George are
lookalikes. In the end, as it was at the beginning, it *is* all about
money as George knew from the start.

In December, coming to a theater near you: Steven Spielberg's *Amistad*. The explicator of the Holocaust turns his compassionate gaze upon the peculiar institution of slavery, deferring yet again the high hopes of Armenians that their tragic story will be screened by the *conscience de nos jours*. Meanwhile, a press release from the Lyric Opera of Chicago tells us that, "by remarkable coincidence," November 29th will see the world première of an opera, *Amistad*, by Anthony Davis, with libretto by Thulani Davis. What, then, is the *Amistad* affair that we now have so much of it?

In early 1839, Portuguese slavers kidnapped several hundred West Africans for shipment to the slave markets of Cuba. Among them was twenty-five-year-old Joseph Cinqué, from Sierra Leone, a British colony where slavery had been abolished. Cinqué's wife and three children had no idea what happened to him: he simply vanished one day from the rice fields where he worked. During the two months that it took for the slave ship to sail to Cuba, a third of the captives died. But Cinqué survived the trip, with every intention of freeing himself or dying in the attempt.

Although the Spanish king had outlawed the slave trade in 1817, his Cuban governors continued to sell the services of Africans to local planters, while a mere ninety miles to the north of Cuba slavery was not only legal but a triumphant way of life in the Southern states of a republic whose most eloquent founder had proclaimed that "all men are created equal"—except, as is so often the case in an imperfect world, those who are not. But by 1839 organized opposition to slavery was mounting in the North of the

United States, to such an extent that, in twenty years, there would be a fiery disunion of South from North, and civil war. The case of the young rice farmer from Sierra Leone proved to be the first significant shot in that war.

In Havana, two Spaniards, José Ruiz and Pedro Montes, bought fifty-three slaves, paying four hundred and fifty dollars apiece for the adult males, among them Cinqué. The captives were then herded aboard the schooner *Amistad* to be transported to Puerto Príncipe, the Cuban town where they would be sold. Below deck, Cinqué found a nail and broke the lock on his iron collar. Then he freed the others. Mutiny on the *Amistad* had begun. Captain and cook were killed, and two sailors leaped overboard. Ruiz and Montes were taken captive. Cinqué spoke no Spanish; he also knew nothing about navigation. But he did know that when they came from Africa they had sailed into the setting sun, so now, to return home, he wanted the course set into the rising sun. Through sign language, he instructed Montes, who took the helm. But Montes tricked him. In the daytime, he would let the sails flap, making little headway; then, at night, he headed north to the Mecca of slavery, the United States. After two months, the ship ran out of food and water off the coast of Long Island.

When Cinqué and several men went ashore to forage, they were met by the local inhabitants. Once Cinqué was convinced that these white men were not Spaniards, he offered them doubloons to take them all home to Sierra Leone. But by then an American man-of-war was on the scene, and the *Amistad*, with its human cargo, was taken not to a port in New York, where slavery had been abolished, but to New London, Connecticut, where slavery was still legal.

At first, Cinqué and his comrades got a predictably bad press. They were pirates—*black* pirates—who had murdered captain and crew. (Happily, personality and appearance have always meant more to Americans than deeds, good or bad, and Cinqué was unmistakably handsome, "son of an African chief," the press sighed—a young Sidney Poitier.) A Connecticut judge promptly put the new arrivals in the clink and bound them over to the next grand jury of Hartford's United States Circuit Court.

At this point I said to Jean-Jacques Annaud, the director with whom I was discussing how to film *Mutiny on the Amistad*, in 1993, "What do we do with the dialogue? For almost half the picture Cinqué and the Africans don't talk in English, while Montes and Ruiz speak Spanish. That means an awful lot of subtitles." He was unperturbed. As it turned out, Annaud and I did not make the picture, but now Spielberg has, and I'm curious to see how he handles dialogue in the "action" sequences. The opera in Chicago, one reads in the press release, will be "sung in English with projected English titles," a somewhat inspired solution.

It was the last half of the *Amistad* story that most intrigued me, although the sympathetic Cinqué hasn't much to do at this point. The story turns into a titanic legal struggle at whose heart is the explosive question: Can slavery be permissible in a nation ostensibly founded on the notion that all men are created equal? More to the point, the United States was the last among civilized "white" nations to maintain the institution rightly called peculiar. That is the real story back of the *Mutiny on the "Amistad,"* the title of a first-rate study by Howard Jones (Oxford, 1987). Coincidentally, I should mention that there is also a new book called *Amistad*, the work of a journalist named David Pesci (Marlowe; $22.95). The publishers refer to it as "a page-turning novel," a true novelty for the Internet's jaded readers; and it comes to us with high praise from one Roberta Flack, the "singer, songwriter, and entertainer." Apparently, Spielberg has not used Mr. Pesci's book as a source for his movie.

Why bother now with this long-forgotten incident? Because it shows a black man who wins—a rarity in the age of slavery. Cinqué gets to go home, as he intended all along. He outsmarts the government of the United States, and in this enterprise he is aided by one of the most remarkable men in our history, the sixth President, John Quincy Adams. After one unhappy term (1824–28), Adams was defeated by Andrew Jackson, who is best remembered for driving Eastern Indian tribes to "reservations" west of the Mississippi and for his wild destruction of the Bank of the United States, which led to several years of financial chaos. But Adams was destined for greater things than the Presidency. He became the permanent scourge of what he called the "slaveocracy."

Of all our forgotten Presidents . . . As I write that line, I recall what the wife of a film director once said to a journalist who was writing yet another in-shallow study of the late Grace Kelly. Inevitable question: "How many of her leading men did she go to bed with?" Gracious response: "It might save us both time if I were simply to skip to the ones that she did *not*." Now, in a somewhat similar context, when I speak of forgotten Presidents I refer to just about the whole line. Although the names of the four on Mount Rushmore are not entirely unknown to Anglophone Americans, the rest of the cavalcade is very dim indeed. At the time of John F. Kennedy's assassination, it was discovered that 10 percent of the American people had never heard of him. It was not until the televising of his proto-Dianesque funeral that they were put, at last, in the picture. Of course, we're now up to forty-two Presidents, and more than two centuries have passed since the first one. Even an attentive, politically minded person would have trouble keeping them all straight. Nevertheless, with a history as murderously fascinating as ours, it is truly a marvel that, year after year, History is found to be the least popular subject taught in high schools. Certainly, it is the least well absorbed.

Adams. *Amistad.* Spielberg. If the film—an action thriller, I suspect—works, people will, for a few months, learn of J. Q. Adams and his fierce brilliance in the matter of race. Since there is no longer any possibility of actual American history ever being taught in the public schools—and not all that much penetrates the private ones— the only way our history will get to us is through movies and television. Unfortunately, on the rare occasion filmmakers put a horny Jurassic toe, as it were, into controversial waters, the result is muddied. Some years ago, television made a fine mess of the Adams family, turning four generations of our most interesting family into costumed dummies. Lately, the estimable Ken Burns turned his attention to the mind and landscape of Thomas Jefferson. Despite the presence of several fine historians onscreen, the result was chloroform. Any attempts (at least mine) to note significant flaws and contradictions in Jefferson's character were carefully removed. In regard to Jefferson, J. Q. Adams himself might have been called as witness. He found dining with Jefferson exasperating, because of what Adams called his "prodigies," a polite word for lies of a Munchausen splendor. When Jefferson was in France, he claimed that the thermometer remained below zero for six weeks; then he shyly confided that on a trip to Europe he had taught himself Spanish. "He knows better," J.Q.A. groaned, "but he wants to excite wonder." And admiration, something no Puritan Adams could ever do.

Currently, *John Quincy Adams: A Public Life, a Private Life,* by Paul C. Nagel (Knopf; $30), is being published—the first biography of J.Q.A. in a quarter century, according to the publisher, and the first "that draws upon Adams' massive manuscript diary." That journal is now available on microfilm; it is unlikely ever to be published in its entirety. But then four generations of the Adams family probably produced more words than any other family in American history, starting in 1755, when John Adams began *his* diary, and ending only with the death, in 1927, of his great-grandson Brooks, whose sketch of the intellectual tradition of the Adams family forms a preface to his late brother Henry's *The Degradation of the Democratic Dogma* (1919)—a title that suggests a not entirely sanguine view of our national development. Mr. Nagel feels that there is a mystery at the core of J.Q.A.'s life. It is true that family and contemporaries found him "enigmatic," a necessity for a hard-minded politician not about to give away the game. He was often accused of "disagreeableness." But *anyone* who takes on unpopular causes is bound not to agree with those millions who supported slavery, say, or who find risible the spending of government money to educate the people; Adams was much mocked by congressional yahoos when he called for astronomical observatories, which he poetically called "lighthouses of the sky."

Adams was the first President to be photographed—fourteen years after he left office. He was five feet seven, bald and stout, like most of his family—his father, John, the second President, was known as His Rotundity. Now I read that Adams is to be impersonated in *Amistad* by Anthony Hopkins, a solid, workmanlike English repertory actor, often excellent with a good English script like *The Remains of the Day*, often not so good if miscast, as in *Nixon*. But then it is always dispiriting that whenever a somewhat tony highbrow sort is to be impersonated, American producers, as vague about American class accents as about English ones, seize on British actors. I am sure that there are American actors more than capable of re-creating that sharp-tongued total New Englander J.Q.A. As Joe Pesci said when I joined the cast of a picture in which he starred, "I saw this list of all these English actors for the part of this Harvard professor you're playing and I said, 'Why do we always have to take an English asshole when we have one of our own?'"

Although the occasional screening of our history is probably the last chance we shall ever have to know something about who we were, a moving picture, because it moves, is the one form of narrative that cannot convey an idea of any kind, as opposed to a generalized emotion. Mary McCarthy used to counter dedicated *cinéastes* with "All right. In *Battleship Potemkin*, what does that abandoned baby carriage bouncing down the steps *mean?*"

Worse, our writers and directors tend to know as little about the country's history as the audience, so when they set a story in the past the characters are just like us except they're in costume. But the past is another country, and to bring it to some sort of dramatic life takes a capacity for which there is no English word. It was not until the eighteenth century that a German, J. G. Herder, coined *Einfühlen*—the act of feeling one's way into the past not by holding up a mirror but by stepping *through* the mirror into the alien world.

For instance, we keep death out of sight, and out of mind, too. But the world of the Adamses was saturated with death: infants dead at birth; their mothers, too. Plagues took off whole families—

memento mori on every side gave a dark resonance to their days. Words were also different for them. They looked upon words as deeds. Words defined the republic that the Adamses helped create. Words defined the role that the Adams family wanted our Union to play in the world. But convincing words are the one commodity that Hollywood cannot supply our predecessors, as American vocabularies shrink with each generation. "I don't do grammar," an expensive screenwriter said to a director friend of mine who had suggested that perhaps a highly educated English teacher in a film wouldn't keep saying "between you and I." Now that the action film's clattering machinery and vivid flames have crowded so much else off the screen, dialogue is more and more used as captions to pictures, to explain to slow members of the audience what they are looking at. Yet spoken language is not only the sum of a dramatized character; it is just as much action as a car crash.

John Quincy Adams spoke as follows on the Fourth of July, 1821: the true America "goes not abroad in search of monsters to destroy. . . . She well knows that by once enlisting under other banners than her own, were they even the banners of foreign independence, she would involve herself, beyond the powers of extrication, in all the wars of interest and intrigue, of individual avarice, envy, and ambition which assume the colors and usurp the standard of freedom. . . . She might become the dictatress of the world; she would no longer be the ruler of her own spirit." This is a terrible truth that can still, I think, rock an American soul—if such there be, of course. It is also language that, chauvinistically, I would rather hear from Newman or Pacino or Hoffman than from an actor, no matter how gifted, not implicated in our curious enterprise.

The standard life of J.Q.A. remains that of Samuel Flagg Bemis (personally I prefer Marie B. Hecht's *John Quincy Adams*, 1972). Mr. Nagel now gives us the inner man, based on the diaries that J.Q.A.'s son Charles Francis once cut down and edited to twelve volumes. Of his father, he said, wearily, "He took to diary writing early, and he took to it bad."

J.Q.A. was always something of a prodigy with words and ideas and concepts. When John Adams was made American minister to France, and then Holland, he took his son with him. An aptitude for languages combined with a natural eloquence made J.Q.A. a formidable diplomat. At fourteen, he was sent to St. Petersburg as secretary to an American diplomat. After John Adams was posted to England, in 1785, J.Q.A. glumly gave up his exciting life to enter Harvard and prepare to be a lawyer. Even before we had a country, we had lawyers, who, in due course, gave us the Revolution and the Constitution, under which, in succession to George Washington, John Adams became President and moved to the village in the Southern wilderness named after his predecessor, where he and his wife, Abigail, camped out in the unfinished White House.

Although J.Q.A.'s mother is one of the first brilliant women recorded in our history, she was not at her best as a mother. She was cold, domineering, and insensitive. J.Q.A. had a good deal to put up with. She also proved to be the carrier of an alcoholic gene: J.Q.A.'s two brothers and, later, his two sons were all to die of acute alcoholism. J.Q.A. himself often confided to his diary that he had talked "overmuch" the night before and felt somewhat despondent the next day. Much of his famous depression (Nagel's "Rosebud" is that J.Q.A.'s irritable nature was due to manic depression) sounds to me like serial hangovers. Luckily, Adams married Louisa Johnson, a woman as intelligent as Abigail and far more amiable.

After Harvard, J.Q.A. listlessly tried the law. But he found his true métier as a polemicist. Under various newspaper pseudonyms, he supported George Washington's general policy of neutrality in regard to other nations. Washington's celebrated—and long ignored—farewell to the nation, warning against passionate friendships and enmities with foreign powers, was influenced by letters that he (and Alexander Hamilton) had read from J.Q.A., whom he had made minister to The Hague.

In 1802, J.Q.A. was elected to the Massachusetts legislature, and then to the United States Senate, where he proved to be disastrously independent. Though President Jefferson's personality got on his nerves—throughout Jefferson's career, Adams found his perfidy "worthy of Tiberius Caesar"—Adams supported Jefferson whenever he thought him right, particularly in regard to the 1807 embargo on American products to England and France, a retaliation for their wartime restrictions on United States trade. Since New England lived by trade with Europe, J.Q.A.'s support of the embargo so infuriated Massachusetts that he was forced out of the Senate before his term was up. But Jefferson's successor, Madison, made him the first U.S. minister to Russia, and then sent him to Ghent to negotiate the end of the War of 1812, and on to London as minister, where he stayed until he became Secretary of State to the new President, Monroe, for whom he drafted what is still known (even if it is no longer in force) as the Monroe Doctrine.

In those days, Secretaries of State tended to succeed their Presidents, and so J.Q.A. made, many thought, "a corrupt bargain" with Henry Clay. Although Andrew Jackson had got the most votes for President in 1824, he failed of a majority, and the election was decided in the House of Representatives, where the Speaker, Clay, gave Adams his votes. J.Q.A. began his Presidency under a cloud that got even darker when he made Clay Secretary of State. Four years later, when Adams was thoroughly defeated by the triumphant Jackson, he claimed to see a silver lining to this darkest cloud: at last he could go home, write poetry, plant trees, be a wise essayist, like Cicero. Instead, after a year of retirement he was so bored that he did what no other former President had—or has—done: he was elected to Congress. It was Ralph Waldo Emerson who got his number when he wrote: "Mr. Adams chose wisely and according to his constitution, when, on leaving the presidency, he went into Congress. He is no literary old gentleman, but a bruiser, and he loves the *mêlée*. . . . He is an old roué who cannot live on slops, but must have sulphuric acid in his tea."

Paradoxically, as a lowly member of the House, J.Q.A. had now entered upon the major phase of his political career: ineffectual President became impassioned tribune of the people. To make sure that slavery could not be debated, the Southern members had put in place a so-called "gag rule." For eight years, J.Q.A. fought the rule with all his wit and eloquence. Finally, in 1844, he got the House to rescind the gag rule. Of Jackson's 1837 removal of the Indians to the West, he noted, "We have done more harm to the Indians since our Revolution than had been done to them by the French and English nations before. . . . These are crying sins for which we are answerable before a higher Jurisdiction." As for slavery, he thought it "an outrage upon the goodness of God." One difference between then— so foreign to us—and now is the extent to which Christians actually believed in the Christian God. Where our politicians oscillate between hypocrisy and bigoted religiosity, they had, for better or worse, religion, something that takes a lot of *Einfühlen* for us to grasp. Needless to say, in 1846 J.Q.A. found morally reprehensible the American invasion of Mexico that would give us the Southwest and California.

Finally, the mutiny on the *Amistad*. The noble Lewis Tappan, a founder of the American Anti-Slavery Society, persuaded J.Q.A. to join forces with the lawyer Roger S. Baldwin to defend the by now thirty-nine Africans before the Supreme Court. A federal judge had agreed that the Africans were not slaves; rather, they were free men who had been kidnapped in order to be turned into slaves by Spanish Cubans, and their mutiny had forestalled enslavement. Thus far, the case was clear-cut. But, as so often happens in our affairs, a Presidential election had intervened, and Jackson's heir, Martin Van Buren, a smooth New Yorker who was eager to be reelected with Southern votes, filled the air with arcane talk of laws of the sea and the complexities of international treaties, effectively stalling the release of the Africans. He also came up with a plan that would have sent them to Cuba for trial. What pleasure this might have given the voters of the South was insufficient to reelect Matty Van, as he was known; he went down to defeat in November 1840.

In February 1841, the Supreme Court met to decide what should be done with the mutineers from the *Amistad*. J.Q.A. had not appeared before the Court in many years; had not, indeed, appeared in courts at all during his long periods of public service. He was nervous. He was also less and less master of a temper that was growing more terrible with age as he denounced equally intemperate Southerners in the House. Many thought his eruptions were not so much righteous as mad; and he himself prayed, in his diary, for "firmness to rule my own spirit."

Baldwin opened for the defense. The next day, a somewhat jittery J.Q.A. closed the defense. Over the years, despite a shrill voice, he had become a great orator; thousands came to hear him wherever he spoke—for seldom less than three hours. Now, in the dank subterranean Supreme Court, beneath the Capitol's Senate chamber, he faced a packed house, always an encouragement to a performer.

Five members of the Court, including Chief Justice Roger B. Taney, were Southerners. It was thought that they were inclined to send the Africans back to Cuba, in their double capacity as merchandise and murderers. Happily, one Southerner was too ill to sit upon the case and another died of a heart attack the evening of the day J.Q.A. finished his four-and-a-half-hour defense. Baldwin had already questioned the jurisdiction of the Court in determining the fate of men who, even had they been slaves, were free in New York State; also, had not our finest and greatest Chief Justice, John Marshall, ruled at the beginning of the Republic, "The Courts of no country execute the penal laws of another"? One wonders if Noriega's American lawyer quoted Marshall in that travesty of a trial where, after murdering a number of Panamanians in Panama during peacetime, George Bush ordered the kidnapping of the Panamanian leader, Noriega, so that he could be tried in an American court, which had no jurisdiction over him, on charges that should have been brought, if at all, in Panama, an allegedly foreign nation.

J.Q.A. took much the same tack as Baldwin, but he was out for blood, specifically that of former President Van Buren, whose interference in the case he found intolerable. On March 9th, Associate Justice Joseph Story, of Massachusetts, gave the majority opinion. Apropos J.Q.A.'s defense, he wrote his wife that it was an "extraordinary argument . . . extraordinary . . . for its power, for its bitter sarcasm, and its dealing with topics far beyond the record and points of discussion." Wisely, Story ignored the possible culpability of Van Buren and kept to the issue: Were these free men who had been unlawfully seized and, in self-defense, had freed themselves, a natural right, "the ultimate right of all human beings in extreme cases: to resist oppression, and to apply force against ruinous injustice"? Since it seemed unlikely to the Court that they had intended "to import themselves here as slaves, or for sale as slaves," the mutineers were declared free to go home to Sierra Leone. And so, nearly three years after Cinqué left Africa, he finally achieved this season's wonderful TV word, "closure," which is so akin to death. And now, a hundred and fifty-five years later, he is enjoying posthumous closure, so like resurrection, The Movie.

John Quincy Adams ended his days as a beloved national hero. The son of a Founding Father, he must have seemed to his contemporaries as an ever-bright link to the first days of the Republic. He loved a good fight and fought the noblest one on offer in his time, earning himself what he regarded as the supreme accolade from a Virginia congressman, who found him "the acutest, the astutest, the archest enemy of Southern slavery."

Adams's last days were very much like the last days of anyone old. He suffered a stroke. He weakened. But he continued to go to the House. On February 21, 1848, he cast his last vote, a "no" in regard to the war upon Mexico. He motioned to the chair that he would like to speak. As he rose, he staggered. Another member caught him before he hit the floor. He was carried into the Speaker's private chamber. For two days, he drifted in and out of consciousness. Then, on February 23rd: "This is the last of earth," he was heard to murmur. "I am composed." Final words. Articulate to the end.

There is, of course, no place for such a man in American politics today—and only through the exercise of a powerful will did Adams make himself so high a place in his own time. Nevertheless, instead of today's whites emptily apologizing for their ancestors' enslavement of the ancestors of black Americans, Congress would be better advised to hire some sculptors with sandblasters and let them loose on Mount Rushmore so that they can turn the likeness of the war lover Theodore Roosevelt into that of a true hero, John Quincy Adams. The only American historian of the last half century who can safely be called great, William Appleman Williams, particularly revered Adams because, among other things, "he challenged America to become truly unique by mastering its fears. It was Jefferson and his followers who did not face up to the tension that freedom involved. They denied it was possible to be free *and* disciplined. Adams insisted that was the only meaningful definition of freedom. . . . 'The great object of civil government,' Adams declared in his first annual message to the Congress, 'is the improvement of the conditions of those who are parties to the social compact.' "

The New Yorker
10 November 1997

For nearly twenty years I lived at Barrytown on the east bank of the Hudson, upriver from the villages of Hyde Park, Rhinebeck, and Rhinecliff. Technically, I was a River person, since I lived in a River house built in 1820 for a Livingston daughter; actually, I was an outsider from nowhere—my home city of Washington, D.C., being as close to nowhere as any place could be, at least in the minds of the River people. *The* Mrs. Astor, born Caroline Schermerhorn, boasted of having never been west of the Hudson—or was it her drawing room at Ferncliff which *looked* west upon the wide Hudson and the Catskill Mountains beyond? The River road meandered from some spot near Poughkeepsie up to the old whaling port of Hudson. Much of it had been part of the original Albany Post Road, not much of a post road, they used to say, because it was easier to take mail and passengers by boat from New York City to Albany. Even in my day, the Hudson River was still a splendidly convenient boulevard.

The area entered our American history when the Dutch patroons, centered upon New Amsterdam, began to build neat stone houses north of their island city. Of the Dutch families, the grandest was called Beekman. Then, in war, the Dutch gave way to the English, some of whom were actually gentry though most were not. But the river proved to be a common leveler—or raiser up. The newcomers were headed by one Robert Livingston, who had received from James II the "Livingston Manor" grant that included most of today's Dutchess and Columbia counties. Other wealthy families began to build great houses on the east bank of the river, making sure that their Greek Revival porticoes or mock Gothic towers would make a fine impression on those traveling up or down river. The Dutch coexisted phlegmatically with the new masters of what was no longer New Amsterdam but New York; they also intermarried with the new Anglo ascendancy.

By the middle of the last century, all in a row from Staatsburg north to the Livingston manor, Clermont, there were the houses of Roosevelts, Vanderbilts, Astors, Delanos, Millses (theirs was Mrs. Wharton's House of Mirth), Chanlers, Aldriches, Montgomerys. The Dutch Roosevelts of Hyde Park were fifth cousins to President Theodore Roosevelt (of Long Island). They had also intermarried not only with the Beekmans but with the Delanos. In fact, for Franklin Delano Roosevelt, his Beekman heritage was a matter of great pride, rather like an Englishman with a connection to the Plantagenets, the one true legitimate, if fallen, dynasty. So it was with Franklin's cousin Margaret (known as Daisy) Suckley; although a member of a good River family she, too, exulted in her Beekman blood and now in Geoffrey C. Ward's engrossing study, *Closest Companion*, of the two cousins and their . . . love affair? the joy that they take in their common Beekman heritage is absolute proof that although President Roosevelt wanted to inaugurate "the age of the common man," it was quietly understood from the very beginning that a Beekman connection made one a good deal more common than any other man and, thus, democracy had been kept at bay.

I remember Daisy well. She was a small, pleasant-looking woman in her sixties, with a charming, rather secretive smile. She had a soft voice; spoke very little. Unmarried, she lived in her family house, Wilderstein, having sold off an adjacent River house, Wildercliff, to the critic and Columbia professor F. W. Dupee. I would see her at the Dupees' and at Mrs. Tracy Dows's but only once at Eleanor Roosevelt's Hyde Park cottage (the ladies did not really get on); I knew that she was the President's cousin (Eleanor's too) and that she had been with Franklin the day he died in Georgia. One thought of her as a poor relation, a useful near-servant, no more. By and large, there was not much mingling of the River cousinage. As the Astor family chieftain, Vincent, put it, "No Visititis on the Hudson." Even though—or because—they were all related, most seemed to be on amiably bad terms with the rest. Only Daisy, wraithlike, moved from River house to River house, a benign presence. Now Ward has read her letters to Franklin as well as Franklin's letters to her, and Daisy has become suddenly very interesting as Ward, politely but firmly, leads us onto history's stage.

Did Daisy and Franklin have an affair? This is the vulgar question that Ward is obliged to entertain if not answer. But what he is able to demonstrate, through their letters and diaries, is the closest friendship of our complex mysterious President, who kept people in different compartments, often for life, never committing too much of his privacy to anyone, except his Beekman cousin and neighbor, quiet Daisy.

It is no secret that Ward has already written by far the best study* of Franklin Roosevelt that we are ever apt to get. Along with his scholarship and wit, the last rather rare in American biography, Ward shared with Roosevelt the same misfortune, polio—he, too, spent time at Warm Springs, Georgia, a spa that Roosevelt had founded for himself and others so struck. Polio was the central fact of Roosevelt's mature years. He could not walk and, towards the end, could no longer even fake a steel-braced upright step or two where useless leg muscles were compensated for by strong arms and whitened knuckles, as he clutched at the arm of a son or aide.

The first fact of Franklin's entire life was his adoring mother, Sara Delano Roosevelt, known to the River as Mrs. James. She adored him, he adored her. He always lived in *her* house on the River where she was chatelaine, not his wife and cousin, Eleanor. By 1917, the Franklin Roosevelt marriage effectively ended when Eleanor discovered that he was having an affair with her social secretary, Lucy Mercer. Eleanor's ultimatum was swift; give up Lucy or Eleanor will not only divorce Franklin but allow Lucy the added joy of bringing

* *A First-Class Temperament: The Emergence of Franklin Roosevelt.*

up *his* five children. Since Franklin already had the presidency on his mind, he gave up Lucy while Eleanor, with relief, gave up their sexual life together. Gradually, husband and wife became like two law partners. He did strategy and major courtroom argument; she went on circuit. I never detected the slightest affection—as opposed to admiration—for Franklin in the talks that I had with Mrs. Roosevelt during the last years of her life. She had been profoundly shaken to find that Lucy was present that day at Warm Springs when he had his terminal stroke. Worse, she discovered that he had been seeing her for years, often with the connivance of Daisy. Eleanor at the graveside was more Medea than grieving widow.

A number of "new" aspects of Franklin's character emerge from those previously unpublished letters and diaries, many not even known of until now. One is his almost desperate need for affection from a woman (or amiable company from a man like Harry Hopkins) and how little he got of either. Until his mother's death, he relied on her for comfort. When she was gone he was either alone and depressed in the White House or surrounded by people for whom, despite his failing strength, he had to be unrelievedly "on" or, as he put it, "Exhibit A."

Most Rooseveltians are either Franklinites or Eleanorites. Since I never knew him, I saw him largely through my family's eyes—that is to say, as a sinister, rather treacherous, figure who maneuvered us into war—while I got to know Eleanor as a neighbor and, later, as a political ally when I ran for Congress in the District. Now I begin to see how Eleanor must have looked to Daisy and, perhaps, to Franklin, too. The portrait is forbidding. She is forever on the move, on the firm's behalf, of course, but there are hints that she would rather be anywhere than at his side. Daisy is almost always careful to praise Eleanor's good works. But there are times when Daisy grows exasperated with a wife who is never there to look after an invalid husband who, by 1944, is visibly dying before their eyes. On February 8, 1944, Daisy notes in her diary: "I said he should either take a rest or a short drive, every afternoon. He said he hated to drive alone. I said he should ask Mrs. R. He laughed: 'I would have to make an appointment a week ahead!' "

Eleanor also saw to it that Franklin would never have a decent meal in the White House:

> The P. [President] & all the men came back about 7.45; all enthusiastic about their supper. The P. told them at supper that in W. H. he never had such good beef stew, carrots, macaroni, home baked bread, butter, & coffee! Poor Mrs. [Henrietta] Nesbitt, the W. H. housekeeper!

Ward comments:

> Mrs. Nesbitt was a Hyde Park caterer whom Eleanor Roosevelt had hired to manage the White House kitchens. FDR disliked her and detested her pallid cooking, but was unable to get rid of her. She was evidently as imperious as she was inept; when the President sent her a memorandum detailing his dislike of broccoli, she ordered the chefs to serve it to him, anyway. "It's good for him," she said. "He *should* like it."

Daisy concedes, "His wife is a wonderful person, but she lacks the ability to give him the things his mother gave him. She is away so much, and when she is here she has so many people around—the splendid people who are trying to do good and improve the world, 'uplifters' the P. calls them—that he cannot relax and really rest." But then, confronted with the disastrous news of his first thorough medical checkup in the spring of 1944—enlarged heart, congestive heart failure, hypertension—Eleanor said that she was not "interested in physiology." Like Mary Baker Eddy, she felt such things were weaknesses of the mind.

The Beekman cousins began their close relationship when he invited her to his first inauguration as president. Daisy was enthralled and wrote her cousin; thus, the long correspondence began; later, they would travel together. Daisy was what used to be called, without opprobrium, a spinster. Of the two boys and four girls at Wilderstein only one girl was to marry. Their mother, still alive in the Thirties, loathed sex and, as Ward puts it, "invariably wept at weddings at the thought of the awful things awaiting the bride." Daisy showed no interest in marriage and, presumably, none in sex. By 1933 the Suckley fortunes were at a low ebb; the eldest brother had invested badly but then matters stabilized and she had her small income and could still live at home. In due course, she was put in charge of the Roosevelt Library at Hyde Park. She was intelligent but not clever; drawn to quack doctors, numerologists, astrologists; she also *knew* that the ghost of Abraham Lincoln was constantly aprowl in the White House.

Daisy's first "date" with Franklin was in September 1934. He took her for a drive to Eleanor's getaway cottage, Val-Kill. There is rather a lot in her diaries of *little* me and the President *himself* at the wheel.

By November Franklin is writing, "You added several years to my life & much to my happiness." By early 1935, when the New Deal is in crisis with Huey Long, the Supreme Court, Dr. Townsend, Franklin writes her, "I need either to swear at somebody or to have a long suffering ear like yours to tell it to quietly!"

For the remaining ten years of Franklin's life, Daisy provided that ear. The letters to her have not all survived but hers to him are complete as well as her diary. She came to know many secrets. She was on hand when Churchill came to Hyde Park. Daisy was not quite temperance but Churchill's constant whisky drinking awed her. When they visited Franklin's blue-haired cousin, Laura Delano, something of a card, the Prime Minister asked for his usual whisky while the willful Laura, a devotee of complex sugary drinks, gave him a daiquiri to drink. Not noticing what was in the glass, Churchill took a sip and then, to Laura's horror, spat it out at her feet. Even in my day, a decade later, Laura would look very stern at the mention of Churchill's name. Interestingly, for those clan-minded River families, so like the American South, Daisy was closer to Eleanor in blood than to Franklin—fourth cousin to her, sixth to him.

If anything "happened," it would have begun during August 1933 when they took shelter from a storm on what they called Our Hill. The spinster and the sickly polio victim seem unlikely as lovers, though, a year earlier at Warm Springs, Elliot Roosevelt assured my father that the President was very active sexually, particularly with his secretary Missy LeHand. But that Franklin and Daisy were in love is in no doubt and that, of course, is the point. They were already discussing a cottage atop Our Hill for after the presidency, or even before, if possible. It should be noted that Missy LeHand's family thought that the house on Our Hill was to be for Missy and Franklin and I suspect that he might even have mentioned it as a getaway to his last love, Crown Princess Martha of Norway, who came to stay during the war, causing Missy to retire (and promptly die) and Daisy to note with benign malice, "The Crown Princess hasn't much to say, but as the P. talks all the time anyway it didn't make much difference. It is strange, however, that a person in her position, & with so much natural charm, has no *manner*! Even in her own home . . . she leaves the guests to take care of themselves. . . ."

Daisy reads Beverly Nichols for hints on how to do up the house-to-be. Franklin thinks his own tastes are too simple for "B. Nichols" (how thrilled that silly-billy would have been to know that he was read and reread by the Leader of the Free World). Meanwhile, history kept moving. Reelection in 1936. Again in 1940. The Allied armies are finally beginning to win, and the President's body is gradually shutting down. It is poignant to observe Daisy observing her friend in his decline. She tries to feed him minerals from one of her cranks. (Analysts found nothing harmful in them, and nothing beneficial either.) She puts a masseur on to him who tells him he'll soon be walking. So eager is Franklin for good news that he claims to have been able to move a little toe.

Daisy never forgets that she is River, not Village. But Franklin the politician must speak for Village, too. She applauds his efforts at educating the national Village folk "because so many people in our class still object to more than the minimum of education for the mass of the people" as "they lose the sense of subservience to—shall I say?—us." It is plain that neither Beekman cousin ever had much direct experience with Villagers.

Daisy records a very odd conversation with the President's eldest son, James, on January 26, 1944 (the war is ending):

> At lunch, Jimmy talked about the young, uneducated boys who are learning that you kill or get killed, etc., etc., and may prove to be a real menace if, at the end of the war, they are suddenly given a bonus, and let loose on the country— He thinks they should be kept in the army, or in C.C.C. camps or something like that, until jobs are found for them, or unless they are put back to school—He says many are almost illiterate.

Fear of class war is never far from the River mind. Happily, Franklin was ready with the GI Bill of Rights, which sent many Villagers to school, while his heir, Harry Truman, compassionately put the country on a permanent wartime footing, thus avoiding great unemployment. Curiously, River's fear of Village was to come true after Vietnam when the Village boys came home to find that they had been well and royally screwed by a Village, not a River, government. The rest is—today.

At the time of the 1944 election, the infamous fourth term (decried by many Roosevelt supporters), Franklin was dying. But he pulled himself together for one last hurrah; submitting to heavy makeup, he drove in the rain in triumph through Manhattan. He was now sleeping much of the day. Harry Hopkins, his closest man friend, was also dying and so, in effect, the war was running itself to conclusion. It was Daisy's view that Franklin wanted to stay in office long enough to set up some sort of League of Nations and then resign and go home to the River. Incidentally, in all the correspondence and diaries there is not one reference to Vice-President Truman.

Daisy's last entries are sad, and often sharp, particularly about Eleanor's abandonment of her husband. After some logistic confusion at the White House, she writes, "Mrs. R. should be here to attend to all this sort of thing. The P. shouldn't have to—and it has to be done."

Apparently, Franklin was always prone to nightmares. (Like Lincoln in a similar context?) One night he called for help with "blood curdling sounds." He thought a man was coming "through the transom," and was going to kill him. He asked to see a screening of *Wilson*, a fairly good film of obvious interest to Franklin as Woodrow Wilson's heir and fellow Caesar; by the picture's end, and Wilson's physical crack-up, the President's blood pressure was perilously high; and there were no beta blockers then.

The Yalta meeting wore him out and both Churchill and Stalin noted that their colleague was not long for this world. But he knew what he was doing at the meeting. Eleanor told me that when he got home—they met briefly before he went to Warm Springs—she chided him for making no fuss over leaving Latvia, Lithuania, and Estonia in Russia's hands. The *Realpolitik* member of the firm told her that Stalin would not give them up without a war. "Do you think the American people, after all they've gone through, would fight for those small countries?" Eleanor sighed, "I had to agree that he was right again."

The deviousness of Franklin, the politician, was a necessity, increased no doubt by whatever psychic effect his immobility had on him. One of the reasons he tossed his head this way and that was not only for emphasis but to command attention—after all, he could never get up and walk out of a room—and his constant chattering was also a means to disguise what he was up to while holding everyone's attention. Of the two, Eleanor was more apt to be brutal. It was a disagreeable surprise to me, an Eleanorite, to read:

> Mrs. R. brought up the subject of the American fliers who came down in Arabia, & were mutilated & left to die in the desert. She insisted that we should bomb all Arabia, to stop such things. The P. said it was an impossible thing to do, in the first place, as the tribes are nomadic, & hide in secret places etc. Also, Arabia is a huge desert etc. Besides, it would be acting like the Japanese, to go & bomb a lot of people, who don't know any better. . . . I put in one word, to the effect that we have lynching in this country still, but we don't go & bomb the town where the lynching occurs— Harry Hopkins joined Mrs. R.—but their point seemed to me so completely illogical that I restrained myself, & kept silent!

One is struck by what such awesome power does to people and how it is the "compassionate" Eleanor who wants to kill at random and the Artful Dodger President who does not.

Finally, Franklin's obsessive stamp collecting pays off. He knows his geography. Unlike subsequent presidents, he knows where all the countries are and who lives in them. He is also aware that the war with Japan is essentially a race war. Who will dominate the Pacific and Asia, the white or the yellow race? As of June 1944, race hatred was the fuel to our war against Japan, as I witnessed firsthand in the Pacific. Yet Franklin, Daisy reports, is already looking ahead:

> In regard to the Far East in general which means the yellow race, which is far more numerous than the white, it will be to the advantage of the white race to be friends with them & work in cooperation with them, rather than make enemies of them & have them eventually use all the machines of western civilization to overrun & conquer the white race.

Today, such a statement would be denounced as racist if not, indeed, an invocation of the Yellow Peril.

———

Last speech to Congress to report on Yalta. I saw the newsreel at an army hospital in Alaska. The President spoke, seated; apologized for not standing but he said the weight of his metal braces was now too much. Never before had he publicly referred to his paralysis. The voice was thick, somewhat slurred. It was plain that he had had a stroke of some sort. Then Franklin and Daisy were off to Warm Springs, where they were joined by Lucy Mercer Rutherfurd and a painter friend. Laura Delano was also on hand. The River was rallying around him. Then, while being painted, he slumped and said, "I have a terrific pain in the back of my head." As he was carried into the bedroom, Laura alone heard him say, "Be careful." After fire, he most feared being dropped. Eleanor came and history resumed its course, and Mr. Truman does get a mention, when he is sworn in as president.

Toward the end Daisy was always there—closest companion—to feed him and watch him as he dozed off, to talk of the River and, doubtless, of Our Hill, though it had been plain for some time that he would never live there. I should note she signed her letters to him "M" for Margaret, her real name, or simply "YM," "Your Margaret." He signed his letters "F." All in all, an unexpectedly sweet story in a terrible time, when, along with wars and depressions and dust bowls, Villages became cities and the River polluted and one Beekman cousin petrified into history while the other Daisy simply faded, smiling, away. Ward has made FDR's story something no one else has managed to do, poignant, sad.

The New York Review of Books
11 May 1995

It all began in the heat of the summer of 1940. Hitler was at his peak in Europe. France had been defeated. Operation Sealion, the invasion of Britain, would be launched once the aerial bombardment of England had, presumably, broken the spirit of the island's residents. Although Franklin Delano Roosevelt, twice elected President of the United States, was doing his best to aid the British, who were flat broke, 88 percent of the American people wanted no part of a war in Europe, while the isolationists in Congress were uncommonly eloquent. But Roosevelt was a sly and devious man (and I mean those adjectives, as Nixon once said when applying them to Eisenhower, "in the best sense of those words"). Some time that summer, probably in June, FDR decided to run for a third term, something no President had done before. But slyness and deviousness were very much the order of the day, particularly when, after a closed session with Congressional leaders, FDR was promptly quoted as having said that the border of the United States was the Rhine River; this was a dangerous misquotation. What to do?

Into history strode one Henry Kannee—a mere walk-on, an under-five-lines player, as they say in movies. But remember that name. This under-five changed history, permanently. Why not, he said, bug the Oval Office? FDR was delighted. David Sarnoff, the head of RCA, was sent for, presumably with his drills and wires and toolbox, as well as a Kiel Sound Recorder, the ancestor of today's tape recorder.

William Doyle has written *Inside the Oval Office*, an entertaining study of "The White House Tapes from FDR to Clinton." This subtitle is something of a misnomer, since not all the presidents taped themselves and their visitors. Ronald Reagan, as befitted a bona fide movie star, was not about to be demoted to what, in effect, was a mere radio performer. He occasionally called in video recorders to show him in full majestic crisis-control as well as in full color to emphasize those curious bright red clown spots on his cheekbones. (It should be noted that Doyle is partial to our very conservative presidents, as opposed to the standard conservative models we are usually permitted.)

In 1988 Doyle made a fascinating documentary for television. Apparently, from August to November 1940, FDR was haphazardly taped (the microphone was in his desk lamp). The tapes were not discovered until 1978. One FDR admirer has remarked how similar his private speaking voice was to his high ecclesiastical speechifying. What is fascinating is how *un*-bishoplike the New York politician is in private. The voice is dry; vowels short; consonants clipped at the end like every other farmer in the Dutchess County of those days. He was something of a chatterbox and often filibustered to make sure that he wasn't told what he didn't want to hear. He also, as Harry Truman sternly noted, "lies." Associates of Truman have noted the same thing of Truman and, indeed, shocking though it must be to contemporary members of the House of Representatives, presidents, when not outright telling lies, feel obliged to shade the truth most of the time. This is called politics; when a President lies successfully, he is called a statesman.

FDR's tapes provide little of interest. He does wonder how best to smear his opponent in the 1940 election, Wendell Willkie, who was having a fairly open affair with "the gal," Irita Van Doren, editor of the *New York Herald Tribune Book Review* (imagine George W. Bush even knowing the name of Michiko Kakutani). They were intellectual giants then. FDR tells civil rights leaders that he's been integrating blacks into the armed services; this is a real whopper. When challenged, he forlornly notes that the innate musicality of Negroes might pep up the military bands and so could lead, with luck, to an indigo band leader. Doyle affects shock that FDR refers to black men as "boys," particularly in front of black civil rights leaders. It is sickening, of course, to be exposed even fifty-nine years after the fact to such a horror at a time when our sensibilities have never been so delicately attuned to the feelings of others. But I suppose this is a small flaw in the man who gave us the entire world. Doyle sadly quotes Dean Acheson, an Assistant Secretary of State at the time, on how FDR "condescended [to people]. . . . it was patronizing and humiliating." Doyle neglects to note that Acheson was bounced by FDR in 1933 only to be rehired in a lesser capacity eight years later. I don't think Doyle likes FDR; if he does, why does he note gratuitously that FDR "laughed at his own jokes"?

Potentially, the most interesting tape is the Cabinet meeting after our fleet was sunk at Pearl Harbor. Although FDR knew that his ultimatum of November 26, 1941, would oblige the Japanese to attack us somewhere, it now seems clear that, thanks to our breaking of many of the twenty-nine Japanese naval codes the previous year, we had at least several days' warning that Pearl Harbor would be hit; yet, mysteriously, the American commanders in Hawaii were given no alert. It was commented upon at the time that the President was less astonished than others by what had happened; in any case, it would be interesting to reinterpret the talk in the Oval Office on December 8, in light of the revelations about to be made in *Day of Deceit* (The Free Press, December), where Robert Stinnett, after years of studying those coded naval intercepts, shows that FDR was complicitous in the attack since, otherwise, he could not have got the American people into the virtuous war against Hitler. With this latest information, one might be able to . . . well, *de*code the cryptic White House conversations about the—expected?—attack that brought us into the Second World War.

Except for a brief tryout of FDR's recording apparatus, Harry Truman did not record himself or others for history or even blackmail. Doyle is now obliged to slog his way through the management styles of various presidents. While Truman presented us with a militarized economy and government, Eisenhower brought the skills of a military politician to the Oval Office. He regarded the taping of conversations as a "management tool," and in his memoir *Crusade in Europe* he duly notes that he was a recorder of talk from early days. Of course, "I made it a habit to inform visitors of the system that we used so that each would understand its purpose was merely to facilitate the execution of business." This shows a noble concern but such candor was not, perhaps, the best way to get interesting information out of people who didn't want their secrets put on the record.

Most Presidents tend to have a low view of their immediate predecessors. Eisenhower, the methodical staff officer executive, disliked FDR's chaotic, secretive style, and he was disgusted by Truman's use of cronies. It was Ike who switched off the British Empire for good at the time of Suez. In "secret," Britain, France, and Israel attacked Egypt, ostensibly to recover the Suez Canal, which Nasser had rudely seized. Ike and Prime Minister Anthony Eden (recorded by a "dead key"—someone listening in on the telephone) provided a poignant last post for Eden, Suez and the ghost of the Raj. The beginning of their talk is superb and sets the tone. Eisenhower: "This is a very clear connection." Eden: "I can just hear you." Was it not ever thus between slave and master? Ike has ordered a cease-fire at Suez. An edgy Eden sounds as if he has to go to the bathroom; actually, he is due in "my" Parliament in five minutes. Eden takes down his orders; then Ike says, "Now that we know connections are so good, you can call me anytime you please." Eden: "If I survive here tonight I will call you tomorrow." Three months later Eden was, as they say nowadays, toast.

Kennedy was the least prepared of the presidents whom Doyle deals with. He quickly demonstrated his inability to execute a coherent policy at the Bay of Pigs, a misadventure cooked up by his predecessor that he had then made his very own, with disastrous results. Although Kennedy had a sharp mind, he was not used to hard work of any sort other than the haphazard barnstorming of politics. After the Cuban disaster, McGeorge Bundy wrote him a memo, placing the blame firmly, if tactfully, on Kennedy's management style, to the extent that he could be said to have one. "We can't get you to sit still. . . . Truman and Eisenhower did their daily dozen in foreign affairs the first thing in the morning, and a couple of weeks ago you asked me to begin to meet you on this basis. I have succeeded in catching you on three mornings, for a total of about eight minutes, and I conclude this is not really how you like to begin the day." Although the Kennedy promiscuity has been much discussed, far more important for the state was his bad health. He was in bed a good deal of the time, and the cortisone injections he was obliged to take did not concentrate his mind.

In the summer of 1962 Kennedy installed the most thorough recording system of all, wiring the Oval Office, Cabinet room, parts of the living quarters. In his office, a button controlled the recording switch. When it was on, others did most of the talking while the self-conscious President was laconic, grave, noncommittal. Doyle gives us the dialogue with the Governor of Mississippi when the university was being integrated and civil war seemed a possibility, at least in Oxford, Mississippi. Kennedy expertly maneuvers the Governor into place. He's learning.

On October 16, 1962, McGeorge Bundy informs the President that the Soviets have placed missiles in Cuba. Crucially, military intelligence is certain that the missiles do *not* have nuclear warheads. Oddly, no one really questions the absolute certainty of the team that brought us the Bay of Pigs. It was only a few years ago that we learned that the missiles were indeed so equipped and that if Cuba was attacked, the Russians were willing to take out a number of American cities as far north as Seattle. The dialogue is chilling in light of what we now know. Shall the missiles be taken out with an airstrike, promptly followed by invasion? General Taylor notes that the United States is vulnerable from the south. Ambassador Thompson comes up with a compromise—a blockade. But Air Force Chief of Staff Curtis LeMay ("Bomb 'em back to the Stone Age") is all for some serious bombing. It has been reported that LeMay's presence at any meeting with Kennedy was sufficient to give the President "fits." LeMay is ready for an all-out war over Cuba; Berlin, too, if we're not chicken. This does not play well in the Oval Office. In the end, Kennedy's political instinct was classic: When in doubt, *do nothing*, particularly if the something that you do could end life on the planet. When Khrushchev helped Kennedy end the crisis, JFK was heard to say: "If they want this job, fuck 'em. They can have it—it's no great joy to me."

President Johnson started installing recording devices his first day in office. Johnson is perhaps the only great comic figure to have occupied the White House. He was not only a master of Lincolnian outhouse humor but he was a deadly mimic. He recorded, between November 1963 and 1968, some 700 hours of White House meetings and phone calls: well worth a CD of his very own. When Johnson names the venerable Senator Richard Russell to the Warren Commission investigating Kennedy's murder, they meet. Russell is furious.

> *Russell:* Well, Mr. President, you ought to have told me you were going to name me.
> *LBJ:* I told you. I told you the other day I was going to name the chief justice. I called you.
> *Russell:* You did not. You talked about getting somebody from Supreme Court. You didn't tell me you were going to name [both Warren and me]. . . . Mr. President, please now. . . .

> *LBJ:* I just want to counsel with you and I just want your judgment and your wisdom, 'cause I haven't got any Daddy and you're going to be it. . . .

> *Russell:* Well, I'm not going to say anything more, Mr. President. I'm at your command.
> *LBJ:* You damned sure going to be at my command. You're going to be at my command as long as I'm here.

The most startling revelation is how clearly—and early—LBJ understood that the Vietnam War was unwinnable. As of 1964, he is again confiding in Russell.

LBJ: What do you think of this Vietnam thing?
Russell: I don't see how we're ever going to get out of it, without getting in a major war with the Chinese and all of them down there in those rice paddies and jungles. I just don't see it. It's—I—I—just don't know what to do.
LBJ: Well, that's the way I've been feeling for six months. . . . I spend all my days with Rusk and McNamara and Bundy and Harriman and Vance and all those folks that are dealing with it and I would say that it pretty well adds up to them now that we've got to show some force. . . . I don't think that the American people are for it. . . . You don't have any doubt that if we go in there, and get them up against a wall, the Chinese Communists are going to come in?
Russell: No doubt at all.
LBJ: That's my judgment, and my people don't think so. . . .
Russell: I guess going in there with all the troops, I tell you it'll be the most expensive adventure that this country ever went into.

Doyle quotes C. Douglas Dillon to the effect that LBJ so frightened everybody that no one dared tell him the truth about the extent of defeats until the Tet Offensive. But it is clear from what's on record that he had a perfectly clear view of how he had been trapped by his inherited Kennedy advisers, to a man vain and blinkered, and by his own innate cowardice, which allowed him to be turned into a disastrous war-President instead of what he was born to be, the completer of the New Deal.

Where Kennedy never forgot that he was being recorded, Nixon seems never to have remembered. He is being immortalized. Despite intermittent political skills, Nixon seems, on the evidence of the tapes, to have had no conscious mind. He is all flowing unconscious. Remembered slights, grudges, conspiracies. "We are surrounded by enemies," he declared after his reelection by one of the greatest majorities in history. Two years into his first term Nixon joined the taping club. Along with the normal presidential desire to get something on others before they get it on him, Nixon had Kissinger. Nixon knew, everyone knew, that Kissinger would say one thing to the President and then just the opposite to journalists in order to build himself up in the eyes of the public. All in all, it would have been cheaper—and less bloody—for Nixon to have got a new foreign policy adviser, but, as Dick liked to say, jowls aquiver, that would be the *easy* way. Along with tracking enemies, Nixon used the tapes simply to rant against the Ivy League, Georgetown set as well as Jews, the Pentagon, the CIA. Regularly, he ordered crimes to be committed that his staff promptly forgot about. Doyle quotes Bob Haldeman as observing, "Nixon was the weirdest man ever to live in the White House." The great Gen. Alexander Haig said, "My God, if I had done everything Richard Nixon told me to do, I'd probably be in Leavenworth today!" In any case, at the end, Nixon's own talk did him in. He obstructed justice, suborned witnesses, and, most horrifying, talked dirty and even *blasphemed* in the Oval Office, the pure heart of our empire. So—California, here I come.

Doyle accepts the generous view that Nixon was a master of foreign affairs who brought to an end the Vietnam War. That is one way of looking at it. But the war that he pretended to have a plan to end in 1968 kept right on going through 1972 and almost up to his own political end.

Nixon's appointed Vice President, Gerald Ford, vowed that he would not record. Doyle has found an authorized telephone tape between Ford and Kissinger. They appear to think the world of each other. Doyle also pads things out with the minutes of the tense national security meetings over the seizure of an American merchant ship by the Cambodian Khmer Rouge Communists. Thus Gerald Ford underwent *his* baptism of fire as, yet again, the resolve and will and credibility of the United States, the earth's only *good* nation, were being tested by crafty Asian Communists. One senses the tension in those meetings. Also the playacting. Even Doyle recognizes that the "participants seem to be as concerned with bellicose posturing and inflicting punitive damage on Cambodia as much as with the actual rescue. Kissinger advised: 'Let's look ferocious.' " The United States has now entered its Cowardly Lion phase. The appointed Vice President, Nelson Rockefeller, has a presentiment of what is to come when he warns: "Many are watching us, in Korea and elsewhere. The big question is whether or not we look silly."

Carter did not record. He was also ill suited for the presidency because his virtues—an engineer's convergent mind—were of no use in a job that requires almost surreal divergency. Engineers want to connect everything up and make sense. Politicians—and artists—realize that nothing really makes sense and nothing ever hooks up. As Carter's Vice President, Walter Mondale, sadly noted, "Carter thought politics was sinful." Happily, he was born to be a *former* President, a phantom office that he has since enhanced. Two years after Ronald Reagan replaced Carter, he too was faced with a crisis. The free world was at risk, yet again, thanks to ruthless Commies at work on the small island of Grenada, where 1,000 Americans, many of them medical students, might possibly be at risk from a Mr. Bishop, the local point man for the evil men in the Kremlin. Well, Ron stood tall; he hit his mark. An actor's got to do what an actor's got to do—so we invaded, 'cause if we hadn't we'd reveal to the world "that when the chips were down, we backed away." This is a great scenario only slightly spoiled by mean old General Haig, who observed that "the Provincetown police force could have conquered Grenada."

I feel that Doyle is somewhat dazzled by the Great Communicator, who slept more on the job than any other President since his idol Calvin Coolidge, who wisely stayed in bed every chance he got. Reagan did attend to his occasional acting chores but, as in his movie career, he almost never had a good script. Sample: Reagan is being videotaped as he tries to sell some senators on his pro-*contra* line: "I think what is at issue today is whether we're voting for or against a plan, we're really voting are we going to have another Cuba, a Marxist-Leninist totalitarian country as we have now in Nicaragua, on the mainland of the Americas, or are we going to hold out for people who want democracy." Well, it probably played better than it reads. It was Reagan's astonishing luck to have, in Gorbachev, a Soviet leader who was willing to switch off the cold war (and the Soviet Union in the process, presumably by accident), and a wife, Nancy, who finally took U.S. policy in hand and made peace with the Russians while not missing a single lunch with Betsy Bloomingdale. Tapes of *their* telephone conversations would indeed be the stuff of history.

On to Bush. We are faced by even more Enemy of the Month Club choices now that the Soviet Union is flying apart. Qaddafi, Noriega (invasion of Panama, hooray!), Saddam Hussein (light show over Baghdad!). Next—Clinton. Bit soon for a useful summing up. Doyle does think that the White House should be wired for the record, but with the tapes sealed for twenty years unless otherwise needed. He seems aware of the dangers of absolute surveillance over everyone, today's trend. He quotes Frank Church's warning of a quarter-century ago. The Senator realized how, with modern technology, we now have the capacity "to make tyranny total in America, and we must see to it that this agency [the National Security Agency] and all agencies that possess this technology operate within the law and under proper supervision, so that we can never cross over that abyss. That is the abyss from which there is no return."

Doyle seems to think that there is nothing wrong with the American political system that a few honest guys and gals in high office couldn't cure. But to obtain high office those guys and gals have to raise millions and millions of dollars first and this can only be done dishonestly, even by our Rube Goldberg rules, the ever-shifting campaign financing laws. As for intellectual honesty, the consumer society in which we glory is based on advertising which is at best hype and at worst plain lying. Thus even the most virtuous candidate is sold, with a merry spin. It has been a long time since any public figure has openly said anything useful, much less true, even in the relative privacy of the Oval Office. Up to a point, this is the nature of our society and kind of fun. When the wise Frank Church heard the virtuous Jimmy Carter promise the American people that he would never lie to them if elected president, Church said, with morose delight, "He would deny the very nature of politics." But when, as must happen, all sense of social reality is lost, the rulers and the ruled then plunge into the churchly abyss where nothing at all is ever real again and even the ghost of the Republic is gone while the first, and probably last, global *nuclear* empire reels from crisis to crisis, involving ever weaker enemies, led by ever more off-the-wall rulers.

The overall impression that *Inside the Oval Office* gives is that the Second Law of Thermodynamics is now in serious play: Everything is running down. From our Augustus, FDR, who never worried about his place in history because he knew that he was supremely history, to the present day one notes the increasing second-rateness of our Oval Ones. I suggest that this has nothing to do so much with the caliber of the individuals as it does with an overextended military industrial political complex that wrings tax money from Congress to fight drugs, terrorism and bad guys who use eyeliner like Qaddafi. Money for "defense" (*sic*) should be spent repairing our rotted home base. But it won't be. Meanwhile, the Ovoids do their best to please the corporations that house them so nicely. They also talk, as politicians always have, in code. FDR was accused of making different agreements with different people. Wearily, Eleanor Roosevelt, if she remembered, would warn those about to approach FDR in his office: "When Franklin says yes, yes, yes, he isn't agreeing with you. He's just listening to you." So when polls show that the American people over a weekend rate highly this or that President, they are really only saying yes, yes, yes because there's not much point in saying no, no, no until we can find a new way of selecting what, after all, are essentially powerless figureheads—except in wartime, which is why . . . You complete the sentence. I feel their pain.

The Nation
27 September 1999

In the summer of 1967, I wrote my father from Venice about a ball given at the Palazzo Rezzonico. Guests arrived by gondola. Hundreds of torches lit up the facade of the palace on the Grand Canal, while inside thousands of candles burned in the great chandeliers as liveried footmen offered champagne to what looked to be every Perhapsburg in Europe. I had arrived with my assigned date, Clare Boothe Luce, the recent widow of the founder of *Time*, in whose giggly pages both my father and I had so often been fictionalized. *Time* was founded as a news magazine in 1923; actually it was an opinion magazine that presented real people as if they were characters in an ongoing melodrama where Christ and Capitalism were forever at risk. *Time* set, alas, the tone for most journalism since. The malice was unremitting, the humor merry as an open grave.

As our gilded barge docked, Clare and I stood, rather like Antony—well, Octavian—and Cleopatra, while the flashbulbs of paparazzi douched us in that blinding icy white light—limelight— each found so nourishing. At the ball, by candlelight, the sixty-four-year-old Clare was a perfect silvery moon set among the zircon stars.

I had known her slightly most of my life. Our relationship is pretty much summed up in the note I sent to my father:

I said I felt novels were finished. She said, "Yes, but there's still a kind of fiction people love!" "Yes," I said, "*Time* magazine." "No," she said, "I meant fiction." "I know," I said, "I meant *Time*." "Don't be naughty," she said. "I meant detective stories." Then she insisted we be photographed in the room where Browning died (enclosed).

The picture is lost. But I recall that as we stood beside a round table (that he wrote at?) Clare, in a melting voice, misquoted "My Last Duchess." Gently, I corrected her. Then I misquoted Elizabeth Barrett Browning's "I shall but love thee better after death" sonnet, and she radiantly corrected me. One-upmanship was how we passed the rare times we saw each other.

The last time I saw Clare Boothe Luce was in 1985, on her final trip to Rome, where, from 1953 to 1956, she had been Eisenhower's turbulent ambassador, single-handedly saving Italy from Communism, blissfully unaware that Italian Communists had little interest in leveling the classes—her great fear—and little sympathy for the *ci-devant* Soviet Union. No matter. Clare was a fierce professional warrior for God and the deserving rich and, at one point, for Trieste to rejoin Italy—or was it the other way around?

The American Ambassador gave a dinner for her, which Imelda Marcos excitingly crashed. A ten-year-old godchild of mine was put next to Clare. She spent most of her time at table amusing the wide-eyed girl, who could not believe that an interesting and witty grown-up would want to talk to her when there were so many fascinating folk at hand to dazzle. Clare was endlessly seductive. She was also a great many other things, as Sylvia Jukes Morris points out in *Rage for Fame: The Ascent of Clare Boothe Luce* (Random House; $30), which takes her life up to 1942, when, after three hit plays on Broadway and the power marriage to Henry R. Luce, she got elected to Congress from Connecticut; here Morris ends her first volume.

This is a biography of the sort that only real writers—as opposed, say, to professional scholars or journalists—can write. Morris has done serious research; yet she writes in short, sharp, dramatic bursts. Like her subject, she has a gift for aphorism: Clare became, in later life, "more conservative now that she had so much to conserve."

This sort of book does make one wonder what will become

of the mallsters' novelists. Clare's life has every staple of pop fiction: illegitimacy (hers), poverty, a mother who advanced from lowly call girl to kept woman; then Clare's marriage to and divorce from a rich alcoholic by whom she had a daughter, later tragically killed. Once divorced, she goes to work, rises from caption writer at *Vogue* to managing editor of *Vanity Fair* while being herself somewhat kept by that busy financier and world-class bore, Bernard Baruch. Then on to the heights: the marriage to Luce in 1935; the hit plays; the elections won. . . . The Collins sisters are left far behind in the gold dust of fact.

Everyone turns up in Clare's story, in or out of bed. One can only hope that Morris does not belong to the coitus-interruptus school of biography so starkly personified by her husband, Edmund Morris (after a splendid first volume on Theodore Roosevelt's life, he has kept us waiting for eighteen years for the next shoe to drop) and by sly Arthur Schlesinger, Jr., who put aside *in medias res* his distinguished multivolume life of FDR to grind out fictional narratives about the wayward residents of Riverdale, New York's, house of Atreus.

What was Clare like to know? I've used the word "seductive." Most people do. She was five feet five and slender, and she was often compared to a Dresden doll because of her yellow hair, blue eyes, and chiseled features—chiseled first by Noguchi in marble and then by a plastic surgeon, obliging Clare to call Noguchi in for an emergency session to make her marble nose conform to "Nature." Noguchi denies that he made the change, but he did. In any case, "Dresden doll" suggests a delicate figurine easily broken. Clare was not breakable. In her senior years, she swam, snorkeled, water-skied; and outlived most of her detractors, while occasionally dropping a bit of acid.

The day after the Embassy party, we had lunch at Vecchia Roma, near my apartment in Largo Argentina. Clare was accompanied by her biographer, Ms. Morris. I remember wondering, How is *this* going to turn out? Because if they become friends . . . ? A further complication for an honest biographer: Clare enjoyed lying about herself. But then there had been a great deal for her to lie about, starting with a failed-musician father, who never married her mother; and a mother who married a country doctor but was kept to the end by one Joel Jacobs (she wouldn't marry *him* because he was a Jew); and, finally, Clare's syphilitic brother, who failed at everything, including embezzlement (he got caught).

But I did note, at lunch, that she was being candid about most things. Also, for once, she and I did not row about politics. Instead memory lane beckoned. My stepfather, Hugh D. Auchincloss (known as Hughdie), awash with Standard Oil money, befriended an impoverished Yale classmate, one Harry Luce, son of a missionary in China, awash with Jesus and raw ambition. Hughdie paid for Harry's first trip to Europe. In reflective mood, Hughdie would observe, "You know, wherever we went in Europe, Harry managed to make new enemies for the United States." Later, Hughdie put up a part of the eighty-six thousand dollars with which Harry started *Time*; when the magazine was profitable, he was repaid, without interest. Later still, Harry, no doubt in sentimental mood, tried to take Hughdie's wife away from him. I think that is why my mother was one of the few women of Clare's generation who did not hate her on principle. After all, she could afford to be generous: she had, as they used to say, put the horns on Clare. "Poor Clare," she would sigh, after she turned down Harry's offer of marriage in the spring of 1942. (I was in the next room and heard him say, "Clare doesn't understand me. We don't share the same interests. We're getting a divorce.") As it turned out, my mother did divorce Hughdie in order to marry not Luce but an Air Force general, while the Luces, now seriously incorporated as business partners, continued their manifold good works to the end of his life. She had her affairs. He had his. Understanding, finally, had everything to do with it.

At that last lunch, Clare mentioned the one story that most enraged her. A zealous convert to Catholicism, she is supposed to have been observed in the Vatican, haranguing the Pope, who kept saying, over and over again, ever more desperately, "But, Madam, I *am* Catholic."

"The story was invented by . . ." She named a name I've forgotten. "It's not like me at all, anyway." But, of course, it was. Once, when we were both going at each other in a political quarrel, she said, grimly, "I see you have a didactic side, too."

"Anyway, I had a talk with Punch Sulzberger"—the *Times'* publisher. "And I said I know that that story is going to be the lead in my obituary and it's absolutely untrue and you must do something about it."

"Did he?" The *Times'* little treacheries were almost in a class with Harry's own *Time* magazine.

"Well, you'll know before I will." I did, in 1987. The story was repeated widely.

After Eleanor Roosevelt, Clare was easily the most hated woman of her time—she was too beautiful, too successful in the theater, in politics, in marriage. Feminism as we now know it was a minor eccentricity in those days. Otherwise, she might have been admired as what she was, a very tough woman who had so perfectly made it in a man's world. But then, as one thinks of Hillary Clinton, perhaps not—of course, Hillary-haters are mostly men, and the men of long ago were generally fetched by Clare. It was the women who wanted to do her in. She had her revenge.

Clare had a savage tongue as well as the dangerous gift of phrase. In her ascent from poverty and from a life on the wrong side of just about every track the country had to offer, she educated herself, and became rich through a society marriage to one George Brokaw and then the union with Luce. She also maintained a long relationship with Bernard Baruch, thirty-two years her senior, with whom she had, she records sadly in her diary, "half-sex." "He gave her millions," my mother would say with wonder. But Clare would say that he only invested money for her, and, as a popular playwright, she earned a great deal.

With Clare's second Broadway play, she let the girls have it. *The*

Women, with its all-female cast, was a great success in the theater and on the screen. The women struck back as best they could: Clare could not have written the play all by herself; it was actually the work of George Kaufman and Moss Hart, together or separately. Finally, Kaufman made a public statement: If he had written *The Women,* "why should I sign it Clare Boothe?" No one seems to have had any more than an editorial hand in a comedy whose bubbling misogyny was Clare at her purest.

But, from that moment on, practically everything she wrote was supposedly the work of a man, including her wartime reportage for *Life.* Rather like Hillary Clinton, today, Clare could not be allowed to win.

At lunch: "Do you realize that because of Harry I was never on the cover of *Time?*"

"He kept you off?"

"No, *they* kept me off. The editors." I should note that for almost a half century to appear on the cover of *Time* meant that its subject was a permanent, for good or ill, member of the world's grandest vanity fair.

Even Dawn Powell, our best mid-century novelist, had it in for Clare. Dawn herself had enjoyed almost no success from her novels and plays; then along comes what she regards as a dilettante beauty who takes Broadway—and all the other ways save the strait and narrow—by the proverbial storm. Dawn parodies the Luces as Julian and Amanda in *A Time to Be Born.* Like everyone else, Dawn takes it for granted that Amanda doesn't bother to do her own writing. Amanda believes that "the tragedy of the Attic poets, Keats, Shelley, Burns, was not that they died young but that they were obliged by poverty to do all their own writing."

Dawn also reflects another generally held theory about Clare: that a woman so attractive to men must be, at heart, cold and calculating and . . . yes, the ultimate putdown in sexist times, frigid. "She knew," writes Dawn, "exactly what she wanted from life, which was, in a word, everything. . . . She had a genuine distaste for sexual intimacy . . . but there were so many things to be gained by trading on sex and she thought so little of the process that she itched to use it as currency once again."

Morris has read Clare's diaries; and candid they are. Apparently, she liked sex very much. At eighteen she fell in love with a young Army lieutenant who then married an older woman with money, proving to Clare that man is "only a sublimated anthropoid ape." But the iron—or should one say the bright gold?—had entered her soul. "I'll marry for money," she confided to a girlfriend. "Lots of it. . . . Damned if I'll ever love any mere man. Money! I need it and the power it brings, and someday you shall hear my name spoken of as famous." This was fifteen years before Scarlett O'Hara sprang, full-bosomed, from the pages of *Gone With the Wind*.

In 1922, Clare's mother and Clare were taken to Europe by her step-father, Dr. Austin. In the shabby streets of defeated Berlin, Clare had a vastation. Newspapers were sailing along the sidewalk. One wrapped itself around her leg, she told me in 1970 over lunch at her beachside pleasure dome in Hawaii. "My mother had a sententious side to her—which I've inherited, they tell me." Clare gave me a quick look to cut me off at the pass. "Anyway, when she saw that newspaper she said, 'This is the sort of thing that happens when a society grows decadent and no longer keeps itself up.' I was deeply impressed. Now you ask me why I gave up New York. Well, one day not long after Harry died, I came out of the Sherry Netherland and a newspaper suddenly wrapped itself around my leg. I heard my mother's voice, saw a street even worse than that dusty Berlin street, realized the Weimar Republic had arrived in New York, and so I went off to live in Hawaii, happily beneath the American flag."

In youth, Clare tried silent-movie acting, without success. Later she worked briefly for that passionate women's-rights activist Alva Vanderbilt Belmont. But Clare was not made for distributing pam-phlets. She was sexually experienced by the time she married money in the form of George Brokaw, who was an alcoholic then in his mid-forties. Although Clare claimed to have brought a virginal body to the bridal suite at the Plaza Hotel, she also claimed that she wanted to jump out the window on their wedding night. When her new husband didn't simply pass out, the mustard remained largely uncut, or, as she later put it, with hardly a virginal tentativeness, "The Bill of Fare is neither varied nor sufficient." Eventually, a daughter was born, followed by a friendly divorce.

The restless Mrs. Brokaw wanted a job at *Vogue*. When nothing seemed available, she simply arrived one day, took over a desk, and soon was put to work writing picture captions. No one ever actually hired her. But everyone was delighted that she was there. She was now twenty-six. What next on the Bill of Fare? Why not Fame? As she wrote in her school yearbook, "What rage for fame attends both great and small." This aphorism is perhaps not airtight—the small are too busy trying to survive ever to daydream of a ride in triumph through the streets of Persepolis.

From *Vogue* she moved to Condé Nast's *Vanity Fair*, where she wrote a great deal of lively copy. Condé Nast's wife, Leslie, was a daughter of Bilitis, in those days the most secretive cult in the United States. Clare, ever experimental, allowed Leslie to seduce her, commenting afterward on the prodigious length and sharpness of Leslie's fingernails. But the central affair in Clare's life was with Donald Freeman, a young, brilliant, unbeautiful editor who taught her a good deal about writing. When Freeman killed himself in a car crash, Clare was consoled by the fact that she was his successor as managing editor of *Vanity Fair*; she also got her hands on his journals, and kept them. In his last letter to her he wrote, "It is only human nature that I should be discarded—what with . . . men of affairs like Mr. Baruch sighing for your time. . . . It has been only in the past few days that the cloud of my three years' love for you has been gradually lifting from the brain of one who has almost been a madman for the whole time." She was now twenty-nine.

Two years later, at a dinner, Fame arrived in the shape of "a tall sandy-haired man whose copious eyebrows arched over narrow eyes." Apparently, she teased Henry R. Luce about the flaws in his latest magazine, *Fortune*, and suggested he publish a picture magazine.

(She had given Condé Nast the same advice, but he lacked the money.) Luce did his usual social number, firing dozens of questions at her, like a prosecuting attorney; then he looked at his watch, said he was late, left. Clare thought him the rudest man she had ever met and was, of course, hooked.

They next met at an Elsa Maxwell ball at the Waldorf-Astoria. After a drink together, he said that he had something he wanted to tell her. They found as private a spot as they could. Clare expected a job offer. Instead she had a Luce offer: "The French call it *coup de foudre*. I know you are the one woman in my life." Clare was astonished: she had been in his life, thus far, less than an hour. Luce also said, according to Morris, that "whether or not romance developed between them . . . he had decided to end his marriage of eleven years. For at least the last two, he had felt a need for a different kind of companionship. His wife did not share his interests." Six years later, I heard him make the exact same speech to my mother—only by then Clare was the wife.

In Miami, while the *foudre* was still electrifying him, they became as one sexually; and this proved to be an ominous failure. Although no man can become a daughter of Bilitis, Morris tells us that "in old age, Clare painfully recalled Harry's strong hands and long fingers. 'If he touched you it was like he was tearing you apart. I suppose today I would have given him a handbook of sex, but in those days women were expected to keep quiet.' " I must say it is hard to imagine Clare not lecturing him on the spot, but then her clumsy partner meant not only money but Fame. He was, periodically, impotent with Clare, unlike his first wife, with whom "he simply did it and then rolled over and thought about *Time*."

Whatever their incompatibilities, each needed the idea of the other. What failed them in the sack sustained them on the page, and they wrote each other interesting analyses of themselves. Clare: "A badly burnt child I am so afraid of happiness, that let a perfect moment begin to unfold like a rose in my hands, and I instantly try to crush it." Harry: "Happiness, I thought until recently, had nothing whatever to do with my life. . . . Now I think otherwise. . . . There are those who can always hear, beneath the rumble of traffic, the stars singing." One must not forget that he was the indulgent employer of the dread poet Archibald MacLeish. Clare: "Most everyone that knew me casually preferred to think of me as a cold, remote, shrewd and ambitious woman: I have always contrived to behave so in their company." Others thought her a sexpot, but, "until I met you I never knew anyone who challenged enough of the real heart and mind of me, to interrupt me in my emotional juggling." Thus Lioness to Lion.

The first Mrs. Luce took Harry to the cleaners; as a result, he became a resident of Connecticut, where there was no state income tax. Clare returned to playwriting, but, as Morris points out, "reluctant to be totally honest about her experiences, she was at the same time so self-obsessed that she was unable to write well about anyone or anything else." Two days after her play *Abide with Me* failed on Broadway, she married Luce. *Time*'s play reviewer was in a bind. He drafted a favorable review. Luce, in his role as God, said, "Show isn't that good. Write what you thought." He did. Later she beat Harry at golf; he never played with her again. Also, her attempts to be helpful with the magazines were sternly rebuffed, particularly when she expected to have a hand in what she always claimed was her original idea, a photo magazine that became the highly popular *Life*. Soon Lion was more or less permanently impotent with Lioness, not perhaps the best situation for a man of a romantic if narrow temperament to find himself in. But they had by then been more or less permanently incorporated, with him as the highly potent senior partner. With no role to play in his magazines, Clare was obliged to make her own fame, in what was then, after movie stardom, the showiest place of all, Broadway.

In three days in 1936 Clare wrote the first draft of *The Women*, par for the Noel Coward course, to which she brought her . . . what is it? a mashie? Anyway, commercially the play was a hole in one, and the all-star film that George Cukor made of it still amuses audiences. At the time, this hymn to misogyny rather shocked the gentlemen while, perversely, the ladies were delighted with Clare's witty send-ups of *other* ladies. Meanwhile, 1936 was also a year of triumph for Harry. *Life* appeared, and was a success. Harry was now having Presidential daydreams. Then *The New Yorker*'s Wolcott Gibbs did a Profile of him, in which *Time*'s awful phony Homeric style was parodied: "Prone he to wave aside pleasures . . . argues still that 'names make news,' that he would not hesitate to print a scandal involving his best friend"—or get off with his wife. When Harry complained to *The New Yorker*'s editor, Harold Ross, he was told that the Luce periodicals had a reputation for "crassness in description, for cruelty and scandal-mongering and insult." That was the upside. As for Harry himself, he was held to be "mean," even "scurrilous" at times, and was "in a hell of a position to ask anything." What price glory?

In 1938, the Luces decided to check out Hitler's Germany. It was Harry who missed the point, and Clare, possibly because of her long affair with Baruch and her mother's affair with Jacobs, who quickly saw the dangerous rise in anti-Semitism. (Incidentally, it is now the custom to establish that anyone worthy of an "intimate" biography must be revealed not only as a homosexual but as an anti-Semite: plainly the two most dreadful "preferences" of all. Clare did have at least one fling with a daughter of Bilitis, but she was no anti-Semite.) Where Harry noted, approvingly, that Hitler had "suspended the class system," whatever that meant, Clare saw a close analogy between the Nazis and our own Ku Klux Klan: "Indeed the swastika never burns more brightly or savagely in the Schwarzwald than the Fiery Cross of the Klan once burned in the bayous and cypress swamps of Dixie." This was from the introduction to her next Broadway hit, *Kiss the Boys Good-Bye,* set in the South. Meanwhile, her friend Baruch was trying to get Roosevelt to rearm. "The nation is not ready," said the President, who, himself, was.

Like so many successful commercialites, Clare had immortal longings. Would she—could she—reach Shaw's level? George Bernard, not Irwin (who had rebuffed her advances). Eleanor Roosevelt wrote that Miss Boothe might indeed be a first-class playwright, "when the bitterness of the experiences which she has evidently had are completely out of her system." Clare thanked her for the kind thought but said that the cold "stupidity" of this world had done her in, she feared, as a potential builder of another, "sweeter place."

Back to Europe in the crucial year 1939. Clare flirted with Gertrude Stein. Then, in two weeks, she wrote her anti-Nazi play, *Margin for Error,* a somewhat confused melodrama with quite a few sharp, funny lines: "The Third Reich allows no margin for error."

Clare was now turning more and more political. In September 1939, she marched into the office of *Life*'s editor and said that she wanted to be a war correspondent. She was no longer just the boss's interfering wife. She was a famous writer and, as such, she was hired, though Harry worried about their being separated for so long, even though they had not been getting on. So, as was her habit, Clare wrote him a position paper, noting that for him "to conjure up some dominant discontent or misery out of such good fortune as ours is positively wanton." Then:

> There are times when a man or woman does better to act with sense than to react with sensibility. This seems to me to be one of them. . . . I would like to show more sympathy to you in this matter, but . . . if I did, I should not be acting with as much love as I feel for you. You see, I not only love you . . . but I like you, and admire you far more than you think. Indeed, you always seem to be afraid that if I didn't love you blindly, I would dislike you openly. That is not the case. . . . Now darling, to bed. I do not like to go to bed without you. But somehow, lately, even when I'm with you, I seem to go to bed without you.

Had Broadway been less sternly lowbrow, Clare might have been our Congreve.

Harry's response was hardly in the same class. In short, he said he feared Time's winged wastebasket. By February 1940, they were discussing divorce. Meanwhile, war correspondent Clare was having a splendid time in Europe. Lecherous Ambassador to Britain Joe Kennedy had designs on her as well as a good deal of pro-Nazi propaganda to pour into her ear. Clare was at the Ritz Hotel in Paris when the Germans swept through France. She wanted to stay until the very end, but on May 30th the concierge told her that she must leave the now deserted hotel, because "the Germans are coming." When Clare asked him how he knew, he said, "Because they have reservations."

Clare's reports were well written and became a successful book, *Europe in the Spring*. Dorothy Parker's review was headed "All Clare on the Western Front." "While it is never said," Parker notes, "that the teller is the bravest of all those present, it comes through."

Clare and Harry were both interventionists by now, and they spent a night at the White House, working over President Roosevelt, who was all smiling amiability. Clare thought he looked old, with trembling hands. Yet it was fairly certain that in November he would run for a third term—and why not? A fourth one if the country should be at war.

Although politically minded, Clare could not be said to have any proper politics. She was basically a vulgar Darwinist. The rich were better than the poor; otherwise they would not be rich. She could mock the *idle* rich, but the self-made must be untaxed by such do-gooders as the Roosevelts. Harry was much the same, except for one great bee in his bonnet: he believed, fervently, that it was the task of the United States in the twentieth century to Christianize China, the job that his dad, the missionary, had so signally failed to do. The damage that this one bee did to our politics is still with us, as the Christian right now beats its jungle drums in the chigger belt, calling for war with China.

Clare became a kingmaker. She would elect as President Wendell Willkie, Roosevelt's Republican challenger. Morris describes her appearance at Madison Square Garden: "She wore a plain black dress, and as she stepped forward on the platform, a powerful spotlight beamed down from distant rafters onto her glossy blond hair. The crowd responded with wild enthusiasm even before she opened her mouth. None of her experiences on a movie set or theater stage had equaled this moment. It was the giant arena she had sought since adolescence." Even H. L. Mencken was impressed. "Slim, beautiful and charming . . . when she began to unload her speech, it appeared at once that she was also a fluent and effective talker." *Don't cry for me, Dun & Bradstreet.*

Two years later, she would be elected to Congress from a Connecticut district; she served two terms. The team of Luce would continue until his death, in 1967.

At our last meeting, in my Roman flat, the sirocco was blowing and the shutters were banging. An Italian woman who occasionally did typing for me unexpectedly arrived. When she saw the former Ambassador, she nearly fainted. She had worked for Clare at the Embassy. Clare was amiable. The woman left. I think it was Morris who asked what her function had been. "Actually," Clare said, "she worked for my consort. She was traffic coordinator for Harry's countesses."

Morris heads her long list of acknowledgments with "Above all, I wish to thank the late Clare Boothe Luce for cooperating with me on this biography during the last six years of her life. From the age of fifteen . . . she had kept letters, diaries, scrapbooks and masses of other documents, all of which she courageously allowed me to see." Courageously? Oh, dear. Could that knowing smile in the middle distance belong to the inexorable Janet Malcolm, brooding upon yet another example of her iron law, the necessary betrayal of subject by observer-writer?

> She also submitted to countless hours of interviews and let me stay and work with her in her Washington apartments, her Honolulu house, and a rented mansion one summer in Newport. We spent time together in New York City, her birthplace, in Connecticut, her main residence for most of

her life, and at Mepkin Abbey, the former Luce plantation in South Carolina, where she would be buried. We traveled to Canada and London for semi-centennial productions of *The Women*, and to Rome to see the villa and embassy where she had lived and worked as United States Ambassador to Italy. The fruits of that last research, as well as details of our complex personal relationship, will appear in the second volume of this biography.

Complex? All about Eve? The Lady or the Tiger? Rosebud?

Whatever wonders are yet to come, Sylvia Jukes Morris has written a model biography of a woman who, if born a man, could easily have been a president, for what that's worth these days: a cool billion, I believe. As it is, if nothing else, Clare Boothe Luce certainly enlivened the dull—when not downright dangerous—century her husband so pompously hailed as "the American." Now we are more modest or, as the current president somewhat edgily put it, we are the one "indispensable"—or was it "undisposable"?—nation, while *Time* no longer sets the pace for partisan ad hominem malice. Although Harry's poisonous gift to American journalism is still widely imitated, the "fame" of the Luces themselves has been erased as century ends. Of their once proud monuments, nothing beside remains in the lone and level sands except the logo of a dull, incoherent conglomerate, Time Warner.

The New Yorker
26 May 1997

★ TRUMAN

An English paper asked a number of writers to meditate, briefly, on their heroes or villains. My villain, I wrote, is a perfectly nice little man called Harry S. (for nothing) Truman. A worthy senator, he had been casually chosen by our Augustus, Franklin D. Roosevelt, to be vice-president in 1944. Some months later, Augustus joined his imperial ancestors Jefferson, Polk, Lincoln, and cousin Theodore in Valhalla (just above Mount Rushmore). Truman was now master of the earth, a strange experience for a failed farmer, haberdasher, and machine politician from Missouri.

Roosevelt, the late conqueror, had not bothered to tell his heir that we were developing an atomic bomb or what agreements he had made about the postwar world with the barbarian chieftain and ally, Stalin. Truman had to play it by ear. The whole world was now his: what to do with it?

Lately, as the American empire bumps to an end—too many debts, insufficient military enemies—Truman and the empire are being mythologized at an astonishing rate. A recent biography of Truman emphasized his grit, and his miraculous reelection against terrible odds.

At no point in the hagiographies of Truman does anyone mention what he actually did to the United States and the world. First, he created the National Security State. He institutionalized the Cold War. He placed us on a permanent wartime footing. He started that vast hemorrhage of debt which now is more than $4 trillion and growing by $1 billion each day. Why did he do this? First, the good reason. When the Japanese, much provoked by us, attacked, we had not got out of the Depression that followed the crash of 1929. The Roosevelt New Deal of the Thirties had been palliative, but not a solution. There was still great unemployment and the specter of violent social change. War gave us full employment. War removed our commercial rivals and put an end to the colonial empires of our allies, empires we quietly took over in the name of "self-determination," democracy, and Grandma Moses, an icon of the day.

Truman and his advisers from both political parties decided that they would, in effect, declare war on a vile religion known as Communism and its homeland, the Soviet Union. The demonization of the Soviet Union started in 1947, when they were no threat to the American empire and its clients. They were indeed unpleasant masters to their own people and to those buffer states that we allowed them to keep after the war. We thought they were unduly paranoid about being invaded, but a nation that has been three times invaded from the west might be forgiven a bit of nervousness.

Although the United States has not been invaded since the British burned down Washington, D.C., in 1814, Truman and company deliberately created a siege mentality. The Russians were coming, they proclaimed. To protect us, the National Security Act was passed in 1947. Thus, government was able to regiment the American people, keep the allies on a tight leash, and lock the Russians up in their northern cage. In 1950 the American republic was quietly retired and its place taken by the National Security State, set up secretly and outlined in a document not to be made public for twenty-five years, the National Security Council Memorandum 68. War and Navy Departments were combined into a single "Defense" Department while the CIA, an unconstitutional secret police, was invented. The NSC-68 established the imperial blueprint that governed the world until the recent crack-up of the Soviet Union, which happened *not* as a result of our tactics of ongoing wars, and an arms race that they could not afford, but was due to the internal fragility of an artificial state which was, in a sense, a crude mirror of our own, now falling apart, as well, through debt and internal ethnic wars.

Truman's blueprint made seven points. First, we were never to negotiate with the Soviet Union in any honest way. Two, we were to develop the hydrogen bomb. Three, build up conventional forces and reinstate the draft. Four, increase taxes to pay for this—in 1954 I earned $100,000 and paid $90,000 to the peacetime government of the U.S. This is the only thing that Ronald Reagan, equally hit in the same town, Hollywood, and I ever had in common. Five, mobilize through the media all Americans to fight Communism— Truman instituted "loyalty oaths," a nice totalitarian gimmick that Joseph McCarthy would have a lot of fun with. Six, control the Allies with NATO, hence our military presence to this day in Europe. Seven, propagandize the Russians through misinformation, and so on. Since 1950 the U.S. has been compulsively at war (hot) in Korea and Vietnam and Iraq; (tepid) Panama, Nicaragua, El Salvador, Guatemala; and (cold) Iran, Angola, Chile, Grenada. Also, the interference through our secret police in European elections, starting with April 1, 1948, when the CIA ensured the election of the Christian Democrats in Italy, through the harassment of Harold Wilson's Labour government in the Sixties, to various crimes in every continent. . . .

I shall stop here. Deliberately, the thirty-third president of the United States set in train an imperial expansion that has cost the lives of many millions of people all over the world. Now we are relatively poor, unloved, and isolated, with a sullen polity ready for internal adventures. Thanks a lot, Harry.

The Independent Magazine
3 October 1992

Early spring, 1959. Dutchess County, New York. My telephone rang. "Senator Kennedy is calling." It was Evelyn Lincoln, Jack's secretary. (Her employer hadn't yet metamorphosed into the imperial acronym JFK.) Years later, Mrs. Lincoln wrote a fairly unrevealing memoir of her years with Kennedy—a pity, since she knew a great deal about him, including the subject of his call to me. Jack came on the line. No hello. No how are you. "That friend of yours up there, Dick Rovere. He's writing a piece for *Esquire* about 'Kennedy's last chance to be President' or something. Well, it's not true. Get to him. Tell him I don't have Addison's disease. If I did, how could I keep up the schedule I do?" Many more staccato sentences. No time to lose. Primaries were coming up; then the Convention. Before I went down the road to see Rovere, I looked up Addison's disease: a deterioration of the adrenal function that can lead to early death. No wonder Jack was panicky. Even a hint that he was mortally ill . . .

Background: In 1953, Jack married Jacqueline Bouvier, whose stepfather, H. D. Auchincloss, had been my stepfather until, in a fit of generosity, my mother passed him, like a well-stuffed safety-deposit box, on to Jackie's needy mother. Through Jackie, I got to know Jack; delighted in his darkly sardonic humor, not unlike my own—or Jackie's, for that matter. In due course, I shifted from the noble—that is, Adlai Stevensonian—side of the Democratic Party to the raffish gang of new kids from Massachusetts, by way of Riverdale, N.Y. Then I, too, went into active politics; by 1960 I would be the Democratic-Liberal candidate for Congress from New

York's highly conservative Twenty-ninth District, and our party's Presidential candidate was a matter of poignant interest to me. When Jack rang me—the first and last time—I was eager for him to be nominated, even though I had already seen a poll that indicated that his Roman Catholicism could cost our district the election. In the end, I was to get 43.3 percent of the vote to his 38 percent; this was very satisfying to me. Unfortunately, the Republican incumbent congressman got 56.7 percent. This was less satisfying. "Your loss," Jack grinned afterward, "was a real tragedy for our nation." Whatever else, he was funny.

Richard H. Rovere wrote the much read and admired Letter from Washington for *The New Yorker*. "The Washington Letter as mailed from vital Rhinebeck, New York," Jack used to chuckle. "That shows real dedication. Endless tracking down of sources. In-depth analyses on the spot . . ." But Dick was now on to something that could cost Jack the nomination.

Rovere lived in a gingerbread frame house on a tree-lined street in Rhinebeck. He had a large, nearly bald head with patchy red skin and a scarred neck. Jack had asked me if he was a drinker. I said no, I thought it was eczema. Thick glasses so magnified his eyes that he seemed like some rare aquatic specimen peering back at you through aquarium glass. In youth, Rovere had been a Communist. Later, when he saw that the Marxist god had failed, he left the Party; he also must have made some sort of inner vow that never again would he be taken in by anyone or anything that required mindless loyalty. As of spring 1959, Rovere was inclined to support Stevenson, who had not yet made up his mind about running for a third time.

I began, to the point, "Kennedy does not have Addison's disease."

Rovere insisted that he did. He had acquired the journalist's habit of always being, no matter what the subject, more knowledge-able than anyone else in the room. I asked him how *he* knew. "A friend's wife has Addison's, and they took her to the Lahey Clinic in Boston where they have all the latest procedures, including one that was cooked up for Kennedy. They put a pellet under your skin and it's supposed to drip adrenaline into you for a week or so and then you get another pellet."

I used Jack's arguments. How explain his tremendous energy? How could he have been campaigning so furiously ever since 1956 if he was ill, etc.? Dick was unimpressed. He had the doctor's name; he had a lot of clinical data. He was already writing the piece. *Esquire* had been advertising it. No turning back.

Question for today: Did I suspect that the story was true? I suppose, in court, I'd say I'm not a pathologist and so how could I know? Jack had had, all his life, numerous mysterious illnesses. Four times, he had been given the last rites. The yellow-gold complexion (typical of Addison's) was explained as the result of wartime malaria. I suppose now, with hindsight, I had already made up my mind that if he thought he could survive four years of the Presidency "vigorously"— his key word that season—as well as he had survived four years of campaigning, then whatever was wrong with him was under control. Thus one embraces, so painlessly, falsity.

Dick's piece duly appeared with no mention of Addison's disease. I did bet him a hundred dollars, even money, that Jack would be nominated and elected. Dick was cheerfully condescending. "At those odds, I can get you a lot more bets." In November, he paid off. Oddly—well, not so oddly—Dick and I never again alluded to our business.

Point to story: How easily so many people—best and brightest as well as worst and dullest—got caught up in the Kennedy bandwagon. The amount of lying that went on in that era was, the ineffable Nixon to one side, unique in our homely history.

Three years later, Rovere and I had a row that pretty much put an end to our friendship. Again the subject was Kennedy lying. The Cuban missile crisis of October 1962 was resolved between Kennedy and Khrushchev with a secret deal: we would remove our missiles from Turkey if the Soviets withdrew theirs from Cuba. Neither side would give the game away. No gloating. No publicity. But, as always, there was a leak. To plug it, Jack got his old friend the journalist Charles Bartlett to write a *Saturday Evening Post* article declaring that the bold macho leader of the free world could never have backed down on anything. JFK had simply ordered the Russians off the premises, and they had slunk away. In a fit of thoughtful malice, Jack decided that this would be a good moment to knife his ambassador to the United Nations, Adlai Stevenson, and he added that "that old woman Adlai" had wanted the President to make a deal. Bartlett wrote that the resolute Jack never made deals with darkness.

I learned what had happened from Bartlett's assistant: my half sister, Jackie's stepsister, who had heard Bartlett discussing details of the article with Kennedy over the telephone. I repeated the matter to Rovere. "No!" he said, which was his response to whatever anyone said. Dick got very red. A heavy smoker, he almost vanished in a blue-white cloud. To my amazement, he was, by now, so much a Kennedy loyalist that not only could he not believe so vicious a tale but if it was by any chance even remotely true he was done with Kennedy forever, presumably as he had finished with that other god that failed him.

Now I read in *One Hell of a Gamble*, a fascinatingly detailed narrative of the Cuban missile crisis (by Aleksandr Fursenko and Timothy Naftali; Norton; $27.50), that an aide to McGeorge Bundy was sent round to Bartlett to tell him that Stevenson "had angered the President by suggesting that the United States pull out its missiles in Turkey in an exchange for the Soviet missiles in Cuba. . . . Poor Adlai Stevenson, the two-time failed Democratic Presidential nominee . . . was being hung out to dry." Later, "Bartlett had a private dinner with the President. He handed over the draft of the article. . . . As Bartlett recalls today, the President 'marked it up.'"

"I told you so," I muttered to myself, in lieu of the now dead Rovere, when I read the confirmation of Jack's lively malice.

This is a deliberately roundabout way of getting to Seymour Hersh (*The Dark Side of Camelot*, Little, Brown; $26.95) and his current collision with what I have just been describing: the great disinformation apparatus put in place forty years ago, a monster that even now continues to metastasize within academe and the media to such a degree that myth threatens to overthrow history. Spin is all. Spin of past as well as present.

For some reason, Hersh's "revelations" are offensive to many journalists, most of whom are quick to assure us that although there is absolutely nothing new in the book (what a lot they've kept to themselves!), Hersh has "proved" nothing. Of course, there is really no way for anyone ever to prove much of anything, short of having confessions from participants, like the four Secret Service men who told Hersh about getting girls in and out of Jack's bed. But when confronted with these smoking guns the monkeys clap their hands over their eyes and ears and chatter, "Foul allegations by soreheads." The responses to Hersh's book made me feel as if I were in a deranged time warp. Since there is not, in any foreseeable future, a Kennedy candidate for President, why is there so much fury and fuss at Hersh's attempt to let daylight in on old, old black magic? Sufficient, surely, to the day is the blessed martyr Paula Jones, small potatoes, perhaps, but our very own tuber rose.

Incidentally, how our masters the synergists must be tied in knots. Remember, back in the Eighties: wouldn't it be wonderful if you could own a network *and* a studio that made films to show on it as well as magazines and newspapers to praise them in *and* a publishing house for source material *and* . . . ? Well, now we have the marvelous comedy of Hersh's book being published by Little, Brown, which is owned by Time Warner, and reviewed negatively-nervously, nervously-negatively by *Time* (same ownership), while *Newsweek* (owned by the Washington Post Company and still, perhaps, influenced by Kennedy's old friend Ben Bradlee) denounces Hersh, while ABC (owned by Disney) prepares a TV documentary that is tied in with . . . Many years ago, there used to be something called "conflict of interest." No longer, I'm afraid. Today, we all bathe in the same river. It will be a relief when Bill Gates finally owns everything and there will be just the one story.

Now let me declare my interest. I got a second telephone call thirty-six years after the one from Jack. This was from Seymour

Hersh, whom I'd never met. He told me about the book he was writing and why he was ringing me. He had just read my memoirs, *Palimpsest.* "You have some new stuff on Kennedy in your book," he said, "and I wondered why I hadn't heard about it before. I got curious. I got a researcher to check your American reviews, and I found that not one mentioned all the new things you'd come up with. Why did nobody write about you spending a couple days with Kennedy at Hyannis Port during the Berlin crisis and keeping notes?" I gave him my theory. Few American reviewers actually read an entire book, particularly if the author is known to hold opinions that are not those of the conglomerate for which the reviewer is writing. Also, since I'm a novelist, my books are given to English teachers to review, rather than to history teachers, say—which is possibly no great improvement if they serve the empire too well or, worse, grow misty-eyed when they hear "If Ever I Would Leave You."

"Well," said Hersh, "I'm glad I got to you." Hersh is brisk and bumptious. "I got some questions for you. That detail in your book about how he was having sex in the tub with this girl on top of him and then, as he's about to come, he pushes her head underwater. Why?"

Now, I think that I am one of the few Americans who honestly don't want to know about the sex lives of real people as opposed to fictional ones, as in pornography. Like Kennedy, I came out of the Second World War, where a great promiscuous time was had by just about all who could hack it sexually. Most of us were not into warm, mature, meaningful relationships. We were cool, "immature," meaningless. Getting laid as often as possible was the name of our game, and I don't regret a moment so spent. Neither, I am sure, does Jack's ghost. But this is hardly the right attitude at century's end, when the dull heirs and heiresses of Cotton Mather are like Seventh-Day Adventists with St. Vitus' dance, darting about with scarlet "A"s in one hand and, in the other, emblematic rosy curved cocks as big around as a—*quarter?*

I explained to Sy that the shock of the head being shoved underwater would cause vaginal contractions, thus increasing the pleasure of a man's own orgasm. "Crazy," he said. "So how do you know this?" I said I'd been told the story years ago by an actress Jack and I both knew. Sy was exuberant. "Well, I got four retired Secret Service men—serious guys—and one of them told me how he would bring the President a hooker when he was lying on his back in the tub and then she'd get on top of him and then when he was ready the Secret Service guy standing behind her would shove her head underwater. Well, I couldn't really believe this. But now you tell the same story. You both can't be making it up." A bit irritated, I said not only did I have no reason to make the story up, I could never have thought it up.

Predictably, the press frenzy over Hersh's book has centered on JFK's promiscuity. This is believed to sell newspapers. But then no other country, save our edgy adjunct the U.K., bothers with the sexual lives of its public men, on the ground that their official lives are sufficiently dispiriting, when not downright dangerous, to occupy what small attention the average citizen of the average country can force himself to give to political figures.

This was the case in the United States before mid-century. Private lives were dealt with by gossip columnists, often in what were called "blind" items (principals unnamed), while public matters were kept to the news columns. The blurring of the two began when vast amounts of money were suddenly required to fight the Second World War and then, immediately after, to pay for our ever-expanding and still ongoing empire, set in place in 1950. The empire requires huge expenditures for more and more bombers that do not fly in the rain, as well as the maintenance, with secret bribes and threats, of our NATO-ASEAN axis, which girdles the thick rotundity of the globe itself. With that much money being wrung from the taxpayer, the last thing that those who govern us want is any serious discussion of what is actually happening to all "our" money.

Put bluntly, who collects what money from whom in order to spend on what is all there is to politics, and in a serious country should be the central preoccupation of the media. It is also a very in-

teresting subject, at least to those who pay taxes, which in this country means the folks at home, not the conglomerates that own everything. (Taxes on corporate profits once provided the government
with more than 40 percent of its revenues—almost as much as the
personal income tax provided—but taxes on corporate profits today
contribute barely 12 percent.) During Kennedy's three-year Administration, he increased the defense budget of the Eisenhower years by
seventeen billion dollars. This was one of the biggest, quickest increases in our history. That was—is—the story that ought to have
been covered. Unfortunately, politics is the last thing a government
like ours wants us to know about. So how do they divert us from the
delicate subject?

Until recently, anyone who questioned the Pentagon budget,
say, was apt to be labeled a Communist, and that would be that: he
could lose his job; become unemployable. This is diversionary politics at its crudest. When Communism went away, sex came into its
lurid own as the diversionary smear of choice—a peculiarly American specialty, by the way. Once the imaginary teams, straight and
fag, had been established at the start of our century, the fag smear
was an irresistible means of destruction. It was used, unsuccessfully,
against Adlai Stevenson, while Jack and Bobby would giggle as they
argued over which of them first thought to call James Baldwin "Martin Luther Queen."

Basically, misuse of tax money is the interesting scandal. Much
of the expensive imperial changeover started by Truman was institutionalized by Kennedy's policy of constant overt and covert
foreign confrontation. But Hersh, aware that this is pretty much
a nonsubject for mass media and most academics, must first get
the folks into his sideshow tent. Hence the highlighting of Jack's
sexual shenanigans. Later, Hersh does get around to politics—Cuba,
Vietnam—and though he has new insights and information, his
critics generally fail to respond coherently. They rehash such weighty
matters as whether or not JFK briefly married a Palm Beach girl
and did his friend Chuck Spalding remove the records from the
Palm Beach courthouse. A Camelot court joke circa 1961: Anyone

married in Palm Beach in the year 1947 is now no longer married, since Joe Kennedy, while destroying Jack's records, tore out a whole year's worth of marriage registrations.

Typical of the critics is Evan Thomas, in *Newsweek*, who notes skeptically that Hersh's sources include a "mob lawyer" who allegedly brokered a meeting in Chicago between Sam Giancana and Joe Kennedy at which Joe is supposed to have enlisted organized-crime support within Chicago's labor unions, providing much of the hundred-and-nineteen-thousand-vote margin by which Jack won the 1960 election. Another Hersh source is "Tina Sinatra, who says her father Frank acted as a go-between for the Kennedys and Giancana." Although daughters are not taken too seriously, by and large, in the still sexist shady cellars of public life, let me attest that Tina Sinatra is a most intelligent woman who knows a great deal about what went on in those days. The writer does concede that: "All [this is] possible—but Hersh never stops to ask why the Kennedys needed Giancana to fix the Chicago election when they had Mayor Richard Daley's machine to stuff the ballot box." "What's still missing," he writes more in anger than in sorrow, "is the kind of solid proof that would rewrite history." Well, it would be nice, but where would you find such proof? Truman's National Security State, still in place as of this morning, has seen to it that miles of our history, archives, and "secrets" have been shredded, deep-sixed, made over into frog princes, for the delectation of the dummies we are, collectively, taken to be.

In the tangled weave of human events, there is no *solid* proof. Particularly when governments, with everything to hide or distort, can do so with electronic ease, scattering their misinformation like confetti all over, as well as under, the Internet. At best, what we get are self-serving tales from survivors, not to mention the odd forger of genius. And spin.

Predictably, one of Hersh's chief attackers is Arthur M. Schlesinger, Jr. (*sic*—the Jr., that is). Ever eager for distinction like that of his father, the historian Arthur Schlesinger, young Arthur bestowed on himself his father's middle name so that he could call himself "Junior," thus identifying himself with an already famous brand name in academe. Later, his infatuation with the Kennedys earned him the sobriquet "the tenth Kennedy," the brilliant if pudgy child that Joe and Rose Kennedy had never had.

"I *worked* at the White House," Junior told *The New York Times*. "No doubt, some things happened, but Hersh's capacity to exaggerate is unparalleled." This is curiously and carefully phrased. In a sense, as the weight of the evidence mounts, it is already quite plain to all but the most enthralled that Hersh's case, slapdash as it often is, is essentially true, if not Truth. Although "I worked at the White House" sounds as if Schlesinger were in on everything, he was not; he was neither a policymaker nor an intimate. Kennedy made a cold division between the help and his friends—"his white-trash friends," as Schlesinger observed bitterly and, I fear, accurately to me. Schlesinger amused Jack, who liked to call him "the film critic from *Show* magazine," his other job. But should Arthur ever say that he had no idea about the Kennedy brothers' dalliance, let us say, with Marilyn Monroe, one has only to look at the photograph from the night of the birthday gala for the President. The two Kennedy lads are leaving Monroe, while off to one side stands swinger Arthur, glass in hand, beaming like Emil Jannings in *The Blue Angel*, only he has two male Marlene Dietrichs, the Kennedy brothers, to be demoralized by.

Not all of the press has been trash. In *Slate*, a mysterious apparition of a paper edited by "On the left, I'm Michael Kinsley," as he used to say on the wondrously silly program *Crossfire*, Jacob Weisberg zeroes in on one of the most interesting bits of news Hersh has brought us, demonstrating the power—and corruption—of the fabled military-industrial complex that Kennedy did so well by.

In August 1962, the Los Angeles apartment of a beautiful young woman, Judith Campbell Exner, was broken into. She had been having the usual off-and-on couplings with JFK, as well as with Sam Giancana, and there was an FBI stakeout on her apartment. The break-in was observed by the agents on watch, and they identified the perpetrators as the two sons of the head of security for General Dynamics, which a few months later received an "otherwise inexplicable" six-and-a-half-billion-dollar defense contract. Hersh concludes that General Dynamics used the information about Exner to blackmail Kennedy into giving it the contract. Hersh admits that he can't *prove* this: despite five years' effort, the two intruders into Exner's apartment would not talk to him. Hugh Sidey, once *Time*'s White House correspondent, said on Larry King's television program that Hersh, in effect, is making it all up for his "evil book." But then the good Sidey never met a President he couldn't worship. On the other hand, I tend to believe this story. First, it is the way our world works. Second, it is the way the Kennedys operated. Third, defense contractors will do anything when billions of dollars are at stake, and, finally, in a well-run world the President involved should have been found out, impeached, and tried.

Weisberg is confused by "minor inconsistencies": "Hersh relates one anecdote about a Secret Service agent having to prevent the first lady from finding out for herself what she suspected was going on in the White House swimming pool. Later in the book, Hersh describes Jackie Kennedy's strenuous efforts to *avoid* catching JFK in action" (my italics). But this is not a contradiction, only sloppy writing. Jackie knew all about Jack's sex life in the White House and before. What she did not want was any sort of confrontation with his playmates. The Kennedys were an eighteenth-century "amoral" couple, together for convenience. They would have fitted, with ease, into *Les Liaisons Dangereuses*. I mean this very much as praise, though others affect shock. Paradoxically, toward the end of their marriage they actually established something very like a friendship. She said to me, as early as their first year in the White House, "We never actually got to know each other before the election. He was always off somewhere campaigning. Then, when we did get to this awful place, there we were, finally, just the two of us." His sexual partners were to her simply anonymous physical therapists. I suspect that's what they were to him, too.

In December 1959, Jackie asked me to a charity costume ball at the Plaza. "I'll put you at Jack's table, so he'll have someone to talk to. Just ignore what I'm placing between you. She's very beautiful. Very stupid. She's also just arrived from England, so Jack will have first crack at it." "It," not "her."

We sat at a round table with eight or so other guests. Jack's costume was a holster with two six-shooters and a bandanna around his neck. He puffed a cigar and gazed intently at the blond girl between us. She was very beautiful. "You're in politics, aren't you?" Thus she broke the ice. I was curious to see Jack in action. "Uh . . . well, yes, I am. I'm . . . uh, running for President."

"That's so fascinating!" she exclaimed. "And will you win?"

"Well, it won't be easy . . ."

"Why not?"

"Well, you see, I'm . . . uh, Catholic . . ."

"But what's that got to do with anything?"

"Oh, Gore, *you* tell her." I did, and then he and I talked politics across her: not a woman's court, Camelot.

To this day, Kennedy loyalists point to the missile crisis as a sign of JFK's superb statesmanship, when it is obvious that even to have got oneself into such a situation was hardly something you'd want to write mother, much less Rose, about. Certainly you don't prepare invasions of Cuba and repeatedly try to kill Castro without encouraging Castro to egg on the Soviets to what proved to be a mad adventure.

Incidentally, those Kennedy apologists who deny that JFK knew anything about the various CIA-Mafia plots to murder Castro are nicely taken care of by Robert Scheer in the *Los Angeles Times*. "The entire nefarious business is documented in excruciating detail," he writes, "in 'Report on Plots to Assassinate Fidel Castro,' a 133 page memorandum prepared in 1967 by CIA Inspector General J. S. Earman for Director Richard Helms." The report was so hot that all copies were destroyed except one "ribbon copy," which was declassified in 1993. Scheer also notes "that Giancana was a key player in the effort to overthrow Castro and that the President's brother, the country's top law-enforcement official, knew all about it."

The Kennedy brothers put a lot of pressure on the CIA to take care of Castro. When—and how—these callow young men got it into their heads that to them belonged the power of life and death over others is more of a metaphysical than a political question. We all know by heart their story: crook pro-Nazi father makes fortune; drives boys to a political peak unavailable to him. But there was always something curiously brittle about the two murdered sons. They were physically fragile. Hence, the effort of will to drive themselves hard, politically and sexually. As their nonadmirer Eugene McCarthy, former senator and forever poet, observed, "Isn't it curious that they always played touch football and never football."

Currently, the heirs to Camelot are pointing to the just released tapes that JFK made of himself during October of 1962. When he was ready to address his council, he would secretly switch on a recording machine. The others did not know they were being immortalized, and the nuke-'em-all military men are chilling. JFK is cautious: on the record. Robert Manning, in the international edition of *Newsweek*, gently made fun of the way the whole situation is now being depicted. "As one who sat in on some of those White House deliberations in the President's cabinet room, I believe that the case can be made that the dangers of that 13-day interlude in October 1962 have been greatly exaggerated." Manning was an assistant secretary of state; later the *Atlantic Monthly* editor. His case is simple. Whatever Khrushchev might want to do in extremis, we had five thousand nuclear warheads ready to erase the Soviet Union; and they had only between seventy-five and three hundred. "All those factors dictated a peaceful settlement." The Russian general who recently said that Moscow had given the commanders in Cuba permission to use nuclear weapons *at will* "was a pompous windbag, and his claim proved to be patently untrue." So much for the iron nerve, cool wisdom of Sidey's hero.

To further undo JFK's delicate physical balance, along with the cortisone that he took regularly, there was his reliance on—addiction to, in fact—the amphetamines that the shady drug dispenser Dr. Max Jacobson regularly injected him with. It was through Chuck Spalding that Max entered JFK's life. Max made more than thirty recorded visits to the White House; traveled with the President; provided him with shots that he could give himself. So, in addition to cortisone, which can have dangerous side effects—a sense of misplaced, as it were, euphoria—the President was now hooked on speed. According to Jacobson's memoirs, Bobby was sufficiently concerned to want the medicine analyzed. " 'I don't care if it's horse piss,' " Jacobson quoted Kennedy as saying. " 'It's the only thing that works.' " In 1975, Max's license to practice medicine was revoked.

In Hersh's interviews with the Secret Service men, sex and drugs to one side, one is struck by how little actual work Jack got done. There were many days when Kennedy "didn't work at all. He'd come down late, go to his office. There were meetings—the usual things— and then he had pool time before his nap and lunch. . . . We didn't know what to think." My own impression, reading this, was how lucky we were that he wasn't busy all the time, because when he did set his hand to the plow Cuba got invaded and Castro was set up for assassination, while American troops were sent to fight in Vietnam, and the Diem brothers, our unsatisfactory viceroys in that unhappy country, were put to death in a coup, with White House blessing if not direct connivance.

In a way, the voices of the Secret Service men are the most damning of all, and I was prepared for what I call the Historians' Herndon Maneuver. William Herndon was for seventeen years Lincoln's law partner and shared an office with him. Herndon is the principal historical source for those years, except when Lincoln told Herndon that he had contracted syphilis in youth and had a hard time getting rid of it. Herndon wrote this after the President's death. The Lincoln priesthood's response to the syphilis charge is Pavlovian: Herndon was a disreputable drunk and not to be relied on— except when he is. As I read Hersh, I knew that the Kennedy zealots would say the same about the Secret Service man who mentions Jack's nongonorrheal urethritis and all the rest of it. On Larry King, a professor appeared along with Hugh Sidey. He conceded that JFK had a "squalid covert life." Then, when one of the Secret Service men was named, it was Sidey who executed the Herndon Maneuver: the agent later had a problem with "alcohol."

I think Hersh comes to some wrong conclusions, inevitable considering his task. Incidentally, it is ridiculous to accuse him of not being a serious, sober historian, careful to footnote his way through a past that very few American academics could even begin to deal with. After all, if they were competent to do the job, what effect would it have on those powerful entities and personages who endow universities? Hersh is an old-style muckraker. The fact that he's found more muck in this particular Augean stable than most people want to acknowledge is hardly his fault.

I don't believe, however, that Lyndon Johnson blackmailed Jack into taking him as Vice-President, which is what Hersh suspects. Although I certainly was not in the allegedly uncrowded room when the decision was made, I was a member of the New York State delegation, and I was present in Los Angeles as the candidates came around, one by one, to work us over. (Tammany Hall had already committed us to Kennedy—the highest form of democracy.) Johnson entered the room in a blaze of TV lights. He was no more manic than usual. Very tall, with a huge head, and a gift for colorful invective, he had taken to calling Kennedy, more or less in private, "that spavined hunchback." He discussed his own recent heart attack—before any of us could. He was good as new now. But in the hospital he *had* wondered if he should go ahead and buy this blue suit he had ordered just before the attack. "Finally, I told Lady Bird, O.K., go buy it. Either way, I'll be using it." As he was leaving, he stopped to speak to several delegates. I was too far away to hear him. Later, I was told that he had mentioned something about Jack's "illness." He had been vague, but by evening Addison's disease was being talked about. If Johnson had gone there to take second place, he would certainly not have mentioned Jack's health. In any case, none of us could imagine why the omnipotent majority leader of the Senate would want to be a powerless Vice-President. Certainly, in the normal actuarial course of things, Jack was bound to outlive him. In those matters, it is wise to strop Occam's razor. Jack had to carry Texas to win and with Johnson on the ticket he did, barely.

Finally, a correction for Hersh and his readers: He writes, "There was some talk from inside the family of having a Kennedy-Kennedy ticket in 1964"—Robert to replace Lyndon as Vice-President—"most of it, Gore Vidal told me in an interview, coming from Ethel Kennedy, Bobby's wife." Actually, it was Hersh who told me this story last year. As for Ethel Kennedy, I've only met her once. She wanted to know if I was writing a new dirty play, like Edward Albee.

Hersh does not take his book where it is logically headed from the beginning, the murder in Dallas, and what looks to be a Mob killing. Too many lunatics have already checked in on that subject; and Hersh is wise to leave it alone. But it is also frustrating, since the inventors of our official history are forever fetched by that lone mad killer, eaten up with resentment and envy, the two principal American emotions, if our chroniclers are to be believed. Yet the gunning down in public view with wife to one side and all the panoply of state fore and aft is purest Palermo sendoff. Some years ago, the head of the Italian national police, General dalla Chiesa, was similarly killed—at the center of a cortège of police as he drove triumphantly down the main street of Palermo shortly after taking command of the "war" against the Sicilian Mafia.

What, then, as movie producers like to say, is the "take-away" of Hersh's book? This means, what is the audience supposed to think at the end? First, for me, the dangerous inadequacy of the American press. We are seldom, if ever, told what we need to know about how Presidents get elected and then, once in office, what they do of a secret and often unconstitutional nature, particularly abroad. That the political system doesn't work is no news. Whoever can raise the most corporate money by providing services once in office will be elected, or at least get to be on offer. Clinton and Dole spent, it is said, more than half a billion dollars on the last Presidential election. The press accepts all this as just the way things are. On the rare occasions when a journalist does have a specific smoking-gun complaint, he will find few outlets available to him. Soreheads need not apply for space in the mainline press, much less hope for a moment on the Koppel hour of charm.

In retrospect, it has always been incredible that someone as thoroughly disreputable as Joe Kennedy should have been allowed to buy his sons major political careers. So—could that happen today? Yes. It is even worse now, as anyone can attest who has so much as gazed disbelievingly upon Steve Forbes or Michael Huffington, empty suits with full wallets. We all agree, monotonously, that a change in the campaign-financing laws would be helpful, but no Congress or President elected under the present corrupt system could bear to kick over the ladder that got him and his tools to the second floor.

Quite as serious is the danger of electing someone totally dependent on all sorts of mind-altering drugs to enhance mood, not to mention simply stay alive. Curiously, on April 9, 1961, I published a piece about Jack in the London *Sunday Telegraph*. Rereading it, I can see that, subliminally at least, my knowledge of his Addison's disease was bothering me then, just as not having gone public with it in 1959 bothers me now. I wrote that because of the "killing" job of the Presidency, "despite his youth, Kennedy may very well not survive." This is a pretty peculiar thing to write of a "vigorous" man of forty-three. I go on: "Like himself, the men Kennedy has chosen to advise him have not reached any great height until *now*. They must prove themselves now. Government service will be the high point of their lives." Alas, this turned out to be true. Between the second-rate cronies who made up the Irish Mafia—only Larry O'Brien was outstanding—and the "efficient" managers, like McNamara, with no conception of the world they had been set loose in, one wishes that he had taken on a few more aides and advisers who had made their mark elsewhere. But, as he said, plaintively, at the time, "I don't know *anybody* except politicians. Who the hell is Dean

Rusk?" So it came to pass, and even now the photogenic charm of the couple at the center of so much corruption and incompetence still casts its spell, and no harsh Hersh? light let in upon them can ever quite dissolve their magic until time itself places Jack in history's oubliette, alongside another handsome assassinated President, James Abram Garfield.

The New Yorker
1 December 1997

NIXON R.I.P.

On April 23 I was awakened early in the morning by a call from BBC radio. Richard Milhous Nixon had met his terminal crisis peacefully in the night. Sternly the program's host told me that both former Prime Minister Edward Heath and Henry (never to be former, alas) Kissinger had referred to the thirty-seventh President as a "towering figure." I said to the host that the first would have had a fellow feeling for another leader driven from office, while Kissinger's only claim to our attention was his years in service as Nixon's foreign policy valet. Otherwise, Henry would now be just another retired schoolteacher, busy at work on *Son of Metternich*.

So John Kennedy and Richard Nixon (Congress, class of 1946) are now both gone—paladin and goblin, each put back in the theatrical box of discarded puppets and, to a future eye (or puppet-master), interchangeable. Why not a new drama starring Jack Goblin and Dick Paladin? In their political actions they were more alike than not if one takes the longest view and regards the national history of their day as simply a classic laboratory example of entropy doing its merry chilly thing. In any case, as I wrote in 1983, "We are Nixon; he is us."

Much is now being made, among the tears for a man whom only a handful of Americans of a certain age remember, of Nixon's foreign policy triumphs. He went to Moscow and then détente. He went to Beijing and then saw the Great Wall. Other Presidents could have done what he did, but none dared because of—Nixon. As pictures of Johnson and Mao come on the screen, one hears that solemn baritone: "I am not saying that President Johnson is a *card*-carrying

Communist. No. I am not even saying that his presence on that wall means that he *is* a Communist. No. But I question . . ." As Nixon had been assigned the part of *the* Nixon, there was no other Nixon to keep him from those two nice excursions, ostensibly in search of peace.

After I heard the trumpets and the drums, and watched our remaining Librarians—the high emeritus rank that we bestow on former Presidents (a witty one because now no one does a whole lot of reading)—I played a film clip of Nixon in his vice presidential days. For some reason the soundtrack is gone. A silent movie. An official banquet of some sort. Nixon remembers to smile the way people do. Then a waiter approaches him with a large, corruptly sticky dessert. At that moment, Nixon leans over to speak to his partner on the left, frustrating the waiter's effort to serve him. The waiter moves on. Nixon sits back; realizes that his dessert has been given to the man on his right. He waves to the waiter, who does not see him. Now the Nixon face is beginning to resemble that of the third English king of his name. Eyes—yes, mere slits—dart first left, then right. The coast is clear. Ruthless Plantagenet king, using his fork like a broadsword, scoops up half the dessert on his neighbor's plate and dumps it on his own. As he takes his first taste of the dessert, there is a radiance in his eyes that I have never seen before or since. He is happy. Pie in the sky on the plate at last. R.I.P., R.M.N.

The Nation
16 May 1994

As I write these lines, nothing less than earthly intervention (by Perot?) can prevent the Clinton–Gore team from assuming, as the Chinese say, the mandate of Heaven come November.

They are, at first glance, Huckleberry Finn and Tom Sawyer, and the sight of them in shorts, like a pair of ducks waddling down rustic lanes, reminds us that they are not natural athletes, like the ancient, long-limbed Bush. Also, attractive Huck seems to have Tom's conniving character, while Tom seems to have no specific character at all. But at least we will be rid of Ichabod Crane (Bush) and his little pal Penrod (Quayle), who can now go home to Indiana.

In many ways, this has been the most interesting election of my lifetime because, unexpectedly, the people at large have become aware that the political system functions no better than the economic one, and they are beginning to suspect, for the first time, that the two are the same. When this awful connection is made, we will be seeing many more Perots and Dukes and worse, if possible, crawling out from under the flat rocks of the republic as the tremors grow more violent.

Since what is wrong with us is no longer cyclic but systemic, I suspect that more than half the electorate won't vote in November [it was four years later that they didn't vote] even though, paradoxically, they are more than ever worried about the economy. Yet they are bitterly aware that if there are solutions, no candidate has mentioned even one. Certainly the record and rhetoric of such a highly conventional, professional team as Clinton–Gore do not suggest that there will be a new dawn. Worse, the potential Clinton Cabinet, as guessed at by the press, lacks all vitality, much less new ideas. [It proved to be a gorgeous ethnic-sexual mix or mess, a sinking Noah's Ark of correctness.]

Even so, for the next hundred or so days after the election, we shall be reading in the press about the vigorous new team in Washington. Hopeful notes will be struck. The Sunday electronic zoo will honk and twitter over who is the *real* number three at State; meanwhile, a tax bill will be sent to Congress. Slightly higher taxes will be requested for the rich (Congress will say no: too little too late, if not too much too early). There will be no increase in the tax rate on corporate profits because, for all practical purposes, corporations are tax-exempt. In 1950, 38 percent of federal revenues came from a tax on corporate profits. Today, corporations provide only 10 percent. Corporations will not be taxed because they don't want to be taxed, and so they are not taxed, thanks to the Congresses and presidents that their political contributions have bought. After all, 90,000 lawyers and lobbyists are in place in Washington, D.C., not only to exempt their corporate employers from taxation but also to make sure that they can "legally" avoid those frivolous federal regulations that might require them, let us say, to cease poisoning their customers. Meanwhile, the Vice-President is the head of something called the President's Council on Competitiveness, which sees to it that any corporation can evade any disagreeable governmental regulation or standard in the interest of "competitiveness."

The new president will be applauded when he attacks waste at the Pentagon. Everyone is praised for attacking waste. But no one ever does anything about it because no one ever can. Although there have been no declared wars since 1945 (except those of our own undeclared intervention) the United States has a total war economy, and we shall go right on building aircraft carriers and Seawolf submarines until all the money's gone. Over the years, the Pentagon has seen to it that there is a significant "defense" plant in each congressional district; that is why most congressmen will always say no to cutbacks because of the Effect on the Economy.

In any case, Clinton–Gore, as southern conservatives, are wedded from birth to the military. Partly this is due to the hawkish nature of the southern states. During Reconstruction, politics and the army were about the only careers open to the ambitious southerner. Even for the unambitious, military service was often the only way out of poverty. The fact that southerners traditionally keep their congressional representatives in office longer than other regions means that they end up with those committee chairmanships that deal with the military, and so the South's great source of revenue has always come from "defense." Since expenditure on war is what got us into our present mess, one would think that the military budget—and its ominous twin, the interest that we must pay on $4 trillion of debt—should have been the centerpiece of the campaign.

But Clinton–Gore never got close to the subject, and they will not address it in office. Bush himself wisely kept the campaign focused on the sacredness of the fetus, hard to upstage in a country where, according to the good Dr. Gallup, 47 percent think that God created Man one afternoon out of some convenient mud, while 40 percent think that God may have taken a bit longer to put the finishing touch on what, after all, is His self-portrait. Only 9 percent believe in Darwinian evolution and science. So with folks like that out there, perhaps it is better to talk about abortion and adultery and who spells Jennifer with a *G* and who spells it with a *J*, and what can this *mean*?

In foreign affairs, we have one great opportunity, which only crafty Dick Nixon ever truly grasped—Russia. Although we don't have much money left to give them, a lively president and a few corporate magnates with no more than average IQs could start making deals to develop Russian oil and other resources. This would generate the money for the Russians to buy our consumer goods, which, in turn, would make us prosperous again. Naturally, this will require intelligence and planning, two things our corporate governing class has not been capable of since 1945. But the opportunity is superb. Until two years ago, it looked as if West Germany had landed the Russian account, but then their union with East Germany threw them off course. That leaves us and Canada as Russia's friendly industrialized neighbors in the Northern Hemisphere. H. L. Mencken noted many years ago that the "Russians were like the Americans. They, too, were naturally religious and confiding; they, too, were below the civilized average in intelligence; and they, too, believed in democracy, and were trying to give it a trial." The time has come for an economic union.

Our allies are deeply disturbed by the intensity of the sick religiosity that the United States is currently experiencing (due more to television preachers than to the Good Book). Obviously, a people who cannot deal with the natural sciences is not going to do very well in the twenty-first century, when religion will play hardly any part, at least in Western Europe and Asia, our competition.

Of course, it's not considered nice to criticize someone else's religion; yet this particular election has been based almost entirely on religion, and it is now clear just how our single-party system (with two right wings, one called Democratic, one called Republican) will end. The country is now splitting into the Party of God, whose standard-bearer the godless Bush so ironically tried to be, and the Party of Man, which represents, in theory, observance of religion-free laws and a limitation of the state's control of the private lives of the citizenry. In the primaries, only Jerry Brown grasped the necessity of a party of the people at large, while only Pat Buchanan grasped the true potency of God's Party.

Although Clinton—Gore are essentially Party of God politicians, they moderated their views and did not too piously defend the sacred fetus on the sensible ground that most women, even Godly ones, resent God's ministers' regulating their gynecologic works. After all, the reproductive system that God devised for both men and women is ridiculous enough as it is—certainly, any competent plumber could have done a better job; yet to pretend that the Great Baron Frankenstein in the Sky's sexual handiwork is evil (as in

original sin) is truly evil; and that is where the present conflict between the two evolving parties is taking place, and the ultimate confrontation, as ol' Ross Perot would say, ain't gonna be pretty.

Meanwhile, we have numerous elections but no politics. Each
candidate must hustle corporate money and then put together as
many groups as he can to win. After all, once elected, he does not
have to serve any voters, on the ground that if he pleases one group
he'll alienate another, so why rock the boat? But he does have to
serve Lockheed or Boeing or Exxon or the American Israel Public
Affairs Committee and all the other corporations or lobbies that pay
for him.

The office of vice-president is now the preserve of the Israeli
lobby, and Gore will continue the Quayle tradition. After all, in the
1988 presidential primaries, Gore's campaign was largely paid for by
the lobby, whose point man was the ineffable *New Republic* publisher, Marty Peretz (who boasted in *Spy* magazine that he'd written
"Al's" speech at the Democratic Convention). The alliance between
a Pentagon-oriented southern politician (Gore has never voted
against any appropriation for war) and the Israeli lobby was a not-
unnatural one in the days of the Cold War. But no longer. Imagine
if a Roman Catholic lobby were in place to siphon off billions of federal dollars to bail out the truly broke Vatican, while covertly supporting the terrorism of, let us say, the Irish Republican Army. I
don't think the Godly (non-Catholic) would like this, while the
Manly would be in court. Once selected by Clinton, Gore made his
first speech to AIPAC, where he groveled without shame. He was
there to get money for services rendered; and on offer. Happily, the
new Israeli prime minister, Rabin, has just given the American Israeli
lobby hell on the ground that their crude buying of senators in order to pit the legislative against the executive branch might start a
backlash among even the densest goyim. Henceforth, the Israeli
command post will be not the Senate but the vice-president's office.

What to do? The logical and intelligent solution would be to
go back to Philadelphia and make a new Constitution with a
stronger Bill of Rights, a weaker executive, a disciplined Supreme

Court (the original court mucked about with admiralty suits rather than trimesters, and they were much, much happier in their modest work). A parliamentary system might be more workable than our current—that word again—gridlock. Yes, I am quite aware that no ruling class has ever abolished or even reformed itself, so there is not much chance for us to invoke the great powers invested in We the People, who are ultimately sovereign, if we could ever again meet in Congress assembled and make a new charter. But if the times get too bad and a dictator does not take over, I suggest exercising the Philadelphia Option, not only in memory of Benjamin Franklin but of W. C. Fields, Philadelphia's other great son, whose screen performance as Mr. Micawber in *David Copperfield* was a prescient impersonation of Uncle Sam today.

In a sense, the great cancer of our system, the defense budget, will go into remission when the Japanese and the Germans are no longer buying our Treasury notes. But what then? Here, Clinton is making a bit of sense. Public works of the Rooseveltian sort could stave off revolution, which was exactly what the United States was facing in 1933, as I observed firsthand. Then came the New Deal. People got jobs. Roads. Conservation. Dams. When Roosevelt was told that he might well be the most popular president in American history, he said, "If I'm not, I will be the last."

For the present, in the pursuit of the Numero Uno job, Clinton has worked himself into a number of contradictory binds. But then so did Roosevelt, who promised, in Philadelphia (again), that if elected president he would balance the budget. In 1936, up for reelection and on his way back to Philadelphia, he turned to Sam Rosenman, his speechwriter, and said, "Well, what do I say now about the deficit?" Rosenman was serene: "Deny you were ever in Philadelphia."

Although no public jobs can be created and no bridges repaired as long as all that money goes for unworkable Rube Goldberg Star Wars systems, not to mention cost overruns and plain corruption, Clinton will have to overcome his natural southern affinity for all things military. Conversion is the name of the only game we have left. Conversion from war to peace. Instead of Seawolf submarines, he must build bullet trains (my advice to Jerry Brown, who dramatized it on television and won the Connecticut primary). The same workforce that now builds submarines has the same technology to build trains. This would not reduce the deficit, but then nothing ever will.

Clinton has a chance to take a deep breath and start building and repairing the country. If this is done rapidly and intensely—the way Roosevelt did in the Thirties, with fair success; and in the Second War, with great success—then we shall start generating that famous cash base Perot keeps nattering on about.

In any event, the only alternative to such a program is social chaos. Clinton's greatest asset is a perfect lack of principle. With a bit of luck, he will be capable, out of simple starry-eyed opportunism, to postpone our collapse. After all, Franklin Delano Roosevelt was equally unprincipled. On the other hand, he had the aristocrat's self-confidence, and he was a master of manipulation. Clinton's nervous eagerness to serve his numerous betters is not reassuring because, as he tries to manipulate them, they often, cold-bloodedly, manipulate him. But as Huck Finn with Tom's cunning, he may get himself—and us—through. Like Roosevelt, Clinton has a lot of energy, and an eye on the main chance: If he has only a bit of FDR's luck, we may ride out the storm. But "fasten your seat belts," as Bette Davis so memorably warned. It is going to take real slickness to get us past the deadly reef of true faith up ahead, so dangerously set in that sea of debt created by the few who could not resist ripping off the many in the name of Freedom, Democracy and a Supreme Being as personally revealed to good Dr. Gallup. We must wish Clinton luck. After all, if he fails, *he* will be the last president.*

*As the G. W. Bush presidency begins, it looks as if Clinton *was* the last president, while his successor is more in the imperial Japanese mode, feeble Mikado to Cheney's all-powerful shogunate rooted in the Pentagon.

All's fair. Presumably in love and war, not to mention in the American electoral process as it becomes more and more surreal. For those who laughed all the way through Bob Woodward's situation comedy *The Agenda*, *All's Fair* will give even greater delight. For one thing, this is a him-and-her comedy, worthy of early Hepburn and Tracy. *She* is Mary Matalin, a darkly handsome Croatian from Chicago, with a sense of humor. *He* is James Carville, a Louisiana Cajun, with a sense of humor. Picture Susan Sarandon and John Malkovich together for the first time.

No expense must be spared in this production, any more than any expense was spared in the great election of 1992 that pitted George Bush against Bill Clinton and then, for comic relief, added Pat Buchanan and Ross Perot, two choleric below-the-title character actors, good for cutaways when the stars needed a rest. Director? Preston Sturges, if alive, might have had too much gravitas. The Zucker brothers *et al.*, who gave us *Airplane!* and *Naked Gun*, are a bit too much on the nose. If I were the producer now I'm just spit-balling, this is early on—but I'd like to turn *All's Fair* over to Oliver Stone and tell him to make the hardest-hitting *serious* film that he can about the degradation of the democratic dogma. The result, I promise you, will be not only hilarious but good citizenship in spades.

This is the story of Mary Matalin, political director of George Bush's campaign for re-election to the Presidency that he so much adorned ("Read my lips, no capital gains taxes"), and James Carville, who acted in the same capacity for Bill Clinton, the Comeback

Kid. Love interest? This is the beauty part, as S. J. Perelman would say: Mary and James are in love before the campaign begins; then, after the election, they get married and settle down on television, where each now glows, he a "liberal" star, she a "conservative" one. Conflict? How can two professional politicians maintain their personal relationship in a campaign that grows more and more dirty as those magical days until November's first Tuesday fly by? It is not easy.

This is a political *Pillow Talk*, with alternating points of view. First, *James*. He gives his view of an event. Then *Mary*. She gives hers. They are often fascinating—sometimes deliberately, sometimes inadvertently—as they discuss the mechanics of election. James and Mary? There is something numinously biblical about their names: James, brother of our Lord, Bill, and Mary Magdalene . . . Matalin, who has a star-struck crush on George Bush, surely a unique condition.

Each was already a successful political operator when they met in 1991. She had worked on Bush's winning Presidential campaign. He had worked on a number of senatorial and gubernatorial campaigns, mostly successful after he teamed up with Paul Begala, now of the White House. Each is intrigued by what he's heard about the other. "I like to know people who do politics for a living," says Mary, upfront as always. He is equally curious about her, although she notes, dryly, that according to James's sisters, until he met Mary he had not been seen in the company of a female more than eighteen years of age. On their first date they quarrel about politics. Not to worry. Like most professionals who "do" politics, neither is an ideologue. She lashes out at lefties like Albert Gore (known to Bush as Ozone Man) for having written such Marxist nonsense as: the automobile is damaging the environment. Politically, James the populist openly prefers Bob Casey, the son of a coal miner in Pennsylvania, as governor, to a patrician like William Scranton; and that's about it for deep political thoughts.

Mary's first impression of James: "I took a look at him . . . a squinty-eyed, bald-headed skinny guy. He was wearing skin-tight jeans and a little muscle-man shirt with a green turtleneck collar. I'll bet any amount of money that he doesn't remember what I was wearing." *James:* "I know she had her hair the way I don't like it."

In the spring of 1991, Bush of Mesopotamia looks to be unbeatable. Such Democratic powerhouses as Lloyd Bentsen decide that it is impossible to beat him and choose not to run. Then two things happen. First, John Heinz, Senator from Pennsylvania, is killed in a plane crash. Next, Governor Casey, in violation of every law of American politics, appoints the man best qualified to be a senator, Harris Wofford. A special election is called. Enter James, campaign director. A long shot, Wofford is elected on universal health care. An issue is born. Also a political star: James is now in a position to audition Democratic candidates for the 1992 election. He turns down Senators Bob Kerrey and Tom Harkin. He takes on Clinton. He meets Mary, who has a strong sense of professional hierarchy. James is strictly a statewide operator while she is Presidential. When she learns that James has leapt above his humble station, she goes, as they say in the book, ballistic. How can what is now a couple be on opposing sides in a Presidential election? Grimly, Mary thinks, "If I didn't get [the job] because of Carville I'd have to kill him." But she gets it.

The media are mildly bemused by the situation. But then, like Wall to Pyramus and Thisbe, the media, which now keep them physically apart, bring them together. They are forever waking up in the morning—each in his own bed far from the other—to see the face of the beloved on the morning news. They are all over television, and thus two media stars are born. He is effective but she is splendid, with her dark cobra eyes and her secret smile to camera that tells us: I can't believe what I'm hearing. Give me a break.

There is a new vocabulary in play. James and Mary are professional "spin masters." James gives the press credit for this resonant phrase: "The word 'spin,' I think, means what political strategists do when we go out and put our candidate in the most favorable light. That's what spin is. Well, la-di-da, guess what? They're right. . . . Why don't the media just admit the truth about themselves that

they're way more into self-justification than information?" There is
a lot of talk about "body language" (Woodward likes this phrase,
too) though no explanation of what is meant, other than Gerald
Ford falling down. Needless to say, James and Mary are cautious on
the subject of the media (a plural noun becomes disagreeably singular as it means, paradoxically, more and more outlets). They must
live with media; exploit media; die with media.

James: "No one understands the power of the media in this
country. I went into this campaign believing they were powerful. I
didn't know. The power they have is staggering. . . . They like to
think of themselves as learned and insightful and thoughtful and
considered. They claim the mantle of truth. Hell, truth is they make
initial snap judgments and after that all of their time . . . is spent on
nothing but validating their original judgment." Also noted is the
media's fragmentation, best demonstrated by "the emerging power
of CNN . . . a very, very important player in Presidential campaigns. . . . It used to be that the Associated Press had the real effect on campaign coverage. *The New York Times, The Washington
Post* and the other majors are all morning papers, while the AP ser-
viced afternoon papers with the first take on breaking campaign
events. . . . But there are fewer and fewer afternoon papers in the
country, and CNN is on all day, every day. . . . They don't have a lot
of viewers but, hell, as long as you have a hundred reporters looking
at you and they are filing stories, you don't need to have numbers to
have influence."

Finally, there is the actual election of 1992. James steers Clinton
through primaries fraught with drama. Events from the past keep
slowing down what Bush used to call the Big Mo (momentum). All
our old friends make a final (presumably) appearance.

Gennifer Flowers (*Mary:* "God, if that's Clinton's taste in
women . . ."). Clinton plays golf at an unintegrated club (*James:*
"Someone close to the body" should have checked out the club. The
Body is the phrase for the Candidate, like the central puzzle in a
murder mystery). Interesting odd facts like: Why does television

spend so much time photographing Clinton when he jogs? In case he has a heart attack. Remember Jimmy Carter's eyes rolling upward during a marathon?

James dismisses Jerry Brown as "a nut" who is far too pessimistic for a happy people. He also glosses over Brown's primary victory in Connecticut where, for the first and last time, the defense budget was challenged with a brand-new thought—conversion from a militarized to a peacetime economy: make bullet trains in the same factories where submarines are made. Kerrey is a war hero, attractive in every way, but he has no "message." The others don't matter. The nomination is won. En route, Jesse Jackson is sandbagged, ostensibly because of a black singer rapping about killing whites, but largely because the Jackson image is still too radical for the sacred center where the votes are.

Incidentally, words like "liberal" and "conservative" and "radical" mean absolutely nothing in this text, any more than they do in American politics. The only radical note struck in the campaign was by Pat Buchanan when he prescribed a religious war for us. This certainly promises to liven up future elections—should any be held, of course. If *All's Fair* has a subtext, it is that the cost of electing one of two—or even three—essentially interchangeable candidates is not only too high but potentially divisive when Cross confronts Satanic condom.

Mary has a harder time than James. An incumbent President does not expect to have to fight in primaries, but suddenly there is Crossfire Pro-Cross Pat Buchanan, with his lullaby of hate and his 20 percent of the Republican vote. As if that were not enough bother, Ross Perot pays for a series of budget lectures on prime time. Not since Robert Benchley's "Treasurer's Report" has anyone given so much pleasure to so many with sheer numbers galore.

Mary, who has not only been there but knows a thing or two, does have one enthusiasm that passeth all understanding. *Mary:* "I picked up the phone and heard the unmistakable voice. Honest to God, my mouth went dry and my palms got sweaty. . . . No one, myself included, could believe it was actually him." The Pope? Who on earth—or in heaven—could that voice belong to? "He was incredibly deferential and respectful. Didn't want to bother me, but was wondering, if it wasn't too much trouble, could he get a copy of the 'hypocritical Democrats' fax. . . . To my even greater amazement and pleasure, he did a whole monologue to my notorious fax." Did you guess who? Rush Limbaugh. (Tim Robbins is interested.)

Rush had got interested in the campaign as it started to go very "negative." Apparently, Clinton had gone to Moscow as a student and the KGB had turned him into the Manchurian Candidate. He had also written a letter explaining why he disapproved of the Vietnam War, easily the *most* distinguished and honest statement of his career thus far. But as Bush drops in the polls, the decision is made to play dirty, school of Lee Atwater, Mary's guru, whose recent death had left the campaign singularly lacking in Willie Horton–style ads. Little Miss Mary Mischief is thrilled: "No one had really been happy with the option of just doing positive Bush because we didn't think we'd break through. And besides, going negative puts everybody in a mischievously productive and creative mood." All sorts of tricks and treats are then offered an electorate that, according to James, has no real grasp of any political issue other than the economy and how it directly affects them. In fact, James concludes that, between the knee-jerk party-line voters and the indifferent majority, elections are decided by between 3 and 7 percent of the electorate. Get *their* attention and approval and you win.

Neither hero nor heroine quite agrees on what happened at the end. The dull look of the economy should have been enough to eject an incumbent President, but Mary thinks that Bush was done in, ultimately, by Lawrence E. Walsh, the independent counsel, who, on October 30, 1992, produced sufficient smoking revolvers to convince 3 to 7 percent of American voters that Bush was up to his ears in the Iran-contra capers of the Reagan era. If, as the Bush campaign kept chattering, the election was based on "trust" (I think the word they meant was "plausibility"), then Bush lost on October 30. A *Time* magazine poll reported that 40 percent thought Clinton was lying about his draft status, but 63 percent thought Bush was lying about Iran-contra. That did it, somewhat helped by the debates, where Clinton came through as "caring" while Bush looked at his watch (Mary is angry that the public thought this was a sign of boredom at the debates, when it was really a signal to the questioner to cut off a long-winded Clinton answer), and the small but imperfectly formed Perot failed to get onto the high stool assigned him: he managed the first rung but not the second and so ended up leaning, oddly, against—what else? the impossible dream. Of such stuff is our little history made.

Mary is shattered by Bush's defeat. James is more thrilled at not losing than winning, although "I always fall in love with my candidate." A last meeting with the Clintons. Falstaff with Henry the King. Everything is changed. Prince Hal is no more. James will not serve in the Administration. There is a fond farewell, then James goes home to Mary.

James still checks in at the White House, as Woodward reports. Mary is now prime-time, big-time television. Mr. and Mrs. Clinton are currently suffering the trials of Job. George Bush is alone with his memories, of which, perhaps, the most vivid he describes to Mary: They are aboard his campaign train through Ohio and Michigan.

"He called me into the back car, had something he wanted to tell me.

" 'I've been mooned. I've been mooned!'

" 'Oh, my God.'

"He thought this was incredibly funny. 'Yes, an entire family. Mother, father and children. Can you imagine?' "

One can imagine very easily. But it was not the good man from Kennebunkport, Texas, who was being so honored. Rather, it was the system that he and Bill and James and Mary represent. Moonie power is bound to prevail in the end—or so we optimists believe as we wait, impatiently, for the James and Mary film, *The Mooning of the President.*

The New York Times Book Review
18 September 1994

Four years ago, I wrote that "nothing less than earthly intervention (by Perot?) can prevent the Clinton–Gore team from assuming, as the Chinese say, the mandate of Heaven." Now history seems ready to repeat itself: Clinton will defeat Dole, whose original choice for a vice-presidential running mate, I can now reveal, was God. Why not? God has expressed no preference for either party, and on abortion, not even Pat Buchanan can instruct Him in those uterine mysteries the far right so furiously celebrate in the eldritch caverns of Eleusis, Mississippi. But God had other fish to fry.

In 1992 I compared Arkansas Clinton and Tennessee Gore to Huck Finn and Tom Sawyer, which was how they were presenting themselves to the folks. Actually, Clinton (Yale Law School) is plainly avatar to the Artful Dodger, while Gore (Harvard) is wealthy heir to a dour political dynasty. But each presents himself as an old-style southern moderate, while each has that haunted look of the southern lad who knows, as he enters middle age, that no amount of jogging and dieting will prevent him from one day becoming unelectably fat.

Usual question: What are the Clintons really like? Here is William Jefferson Clinton (né Blythe) on the subject recently: "Hillary was born forty, and she'll always be forty. . . . I was born sixteen, and I'll always be sixteen." So he has engagingly remained. There is a famous picture of him at about that age, shaking President Kennedy's hand at the White House. The boy Clinton is radiant. "How," one can imagine him thinking, if not daring to ask, "do you get laid around here?" In a candid mood, the thirty-fifth president could have had a lot of tips for the forty-second. After all, at heart, Kennedy was a sophisticated nineteen-year-old with a ravenous sexual appetite, while Jackie was as old as Mother Nile. For some, power is quite enough. For Mrs. Thatcher, to be alone with her boxes was, surely, world enough and time. But Clinton seems almost in the Kennedy class of innumerable brief encounters with that majority of the electorate which, appreciatively, favors him by an astonishing 24 percent over Dole, while with the male minority he barely holds his own. Women like men who like women, no matter how exasperating. When there was a rumor that Hillary had flung a lamp at her husband, a White House aide solemnly acknowledged that this was true. "Not only did she throw it," he said, "she hit him with it, and we have buried him in the Rose Garden. We never thought you people would notice."

Clinton's disposition is also highly mercurial. One of Clinton's most useful aides is the small but exquisitely formed George Stephanopoulos. When the First Magistrate is in a rage, he seizes his youthful adjutant and begins to hurl him around the room. As the stoic youth ricochets off the wall like Buster Keaton, he gamely serves his president until the storm is passed and they can move more serenely on to some seminar, at which they will eat lots of fried things together.

As Clinton moves—majestically now—through his campaigning, he seems sure of his reelection. Certainly, this time around, the earthly Perot poses no threat to anyone except perhaps the Dole–God dream ticket, and even then, a well aimed thunderbolt could send him scurrying back to his home planet, Texas.

Thunderbolts of human rather than divine construction are on all our minds these days. Foreigners find mystifying the amount of mayhem permitted in the United States despite ever more draconian laws against something loosely called terrorism. There is now one gun for each of the country's quarter billion citizens. As yet, each man, woman, and child has not got his gun, but that day of perfect equality is bound to come. After all, according to one of the most powerful buyers of politicians, the National Rifle Association, "Guns don't kill people, people kill people." Meanwhile, the gun lovers have now learned how to blow up federal buildings with only farm detritus, while easily manufactured pipe bombs can cause a good bit of havoc in a public park. Clinton, after choking up on television at the thought of terrorism's innocent victims, rushes to join Congress in making laws intended to remove the protecting shield of the Bill of Rights from any citizen tagged as a potential "terrorist." But no candidate dares explain to the American people *why* the country is apparently spinning into chaos, because to do so would be to confess that there are, in effect, two governments of the United States. There is the visible (official) one, which is powerless to do anything about the economy short of waging—but never declaring—a war, preferably on a very small country, like Panama. Then there is the invisible government, the actual ownership of the country—currently (and uncharacteristically) at sea almost as much as its employees in Congress. Could it be that times *have* changed?

Our traditional panacea, the undeclared war, is less profitable than it used to be, and the wartime economy that Harry Truman and company imposed on the United States in 1950 is now some $5 trillion in debt—which does not stop 77 percent of the country's before-tax income from going to the 1 percent that owns most of the wealth. Some 39 million Americans now live in poverty of a sort unknown to other First World countries; and despite happy cries from the Clinton administration at each job created by the fast-food emporia, the median income of the famous middle class (some 65 percent of the whole) has dropped 13 percent since 1973, when the wives of workers were first obliged to take jobs just to maintain the family budget. As one woman happily observed on television the other day, "Oh, Clinton's right when he says there are plenty of jobs out there. Fact, my husband and I have four jobs between us, and we're still broke."

Although the stunning increase in the wealth of the few—the core of the invisible government—and the increase in the poverty of the unrepresented many have been precisely noted by the Congressional Budget Office, no politician will explain *how* we mislaid what was once a fairly egalitarian, highly prosperous society. As the people at large are instinctively aware that their visible government neither represents them nor regards them benignly, they have pretty much stopped voting.

The American takes it for granted that his moral fiber is never to be weakened by health care, education of the people at large or, indeed, anything at all except Social Security, a moderately profitable independent trust fund set up in 1935. Unfortunately for the American, thanks to the expense of the all-out cold-hot war on the Great Satan of the North Pole, the fund is for all practical purposes empty. Dolorous representatives of the Pentagon now tell us that it was wasteful "people programs" that used up the money—even though, in the interest of an arcane rite called "balancing the budget," what small amounts that did go to the poor in the way of job training and welfare have just been cut back by Clinton, always one step ahead of a Congress that has, since 1992, been in the hands of zealous reactionaries in thrall to the fetus and the flag as well as at angry war with those who do not have money. It does not take the ghost of a Marie Antoinette to realize that when the few declare war on the many, the millinery business is headed for bad times.

Does Clinton know what he's doing? (Even the invisible government's chief media spokesman, *The New York Times*, termed the reduction-of-welfare bill that he signed "odious.") As the most intelligent politician on the American scene, yes, he knows pretty much what is wrong, but he is not about to do anything that might cost him a single vote.

Clinton has learned to play the dull, reactive media like the virtuoso he is, and Dole, if not God, can't think what to do about him. No matter what new bêtise the Right comes up with, Clinton has got there at least a day early and has made their issue his. Currently, everyone hates (when not raping or corrupting on the Internet) teenagers. What is to be done with these layabouts? This is a crucial Republican–family values issue, the result of all that money (practically none, in fact) *thrown* at the poor, who, by nature, are lawless, drugged, sexy, violent. But before the Doleful could get around to a death penalty for pubescent vagrants, Clinton struck. Curfews for teenagers, he proclaimed. Whoever said "freedom to assemble" applied to anyone with acne? Uniforms to be worn at school, particularly those whose students come from families with not enough money to buy ordinary clothes, much less brown or beige shirts. Then, before Dole had picked himself up off the greensward, Clinton called for a national registry of sex offenders *and* a crackdown on fathers who do not pay for their children, two groups that could well overlap. All Dole could gasp was, "Character. Integrity. Or whatever. That's what it's about. America."

Clinton struck again. No more violence on television (the freedom to censor is the hallmark of a democracy). No teenage sex, much less smoking. Since there isn't any public money left (military procurement still burns up about $250 billion a year for that big war with China—gotta be ready), Clinton is now turning to the states and cities to help him with his programs in a joint crusade to go "roaring into the twenty-first century, united and strong." Meanwhile, Dole is on his knees, communing with Him, who might have been his copilot.

On the Friday before the Democratic Black Tuesday of 1994 that saw the election of Republican majorities in both houses of Congress, I had dinner with Hillary Clinton, her aide Maggie Williams, and three other guests. We had been invited to the White House (I'd met Mrs. Clinton when she visited Ravello, an Italian town where I live part-time), but as I have no fond memories of the *Executive Mansion*, I proposed a hotel across the street. Mrs. Clinton was delighted to come out. Maggie Williams was grimly funny about the hazards of life in the White House. A few weeks earlier, a small plane had been crashed—deliberately?—into the building. "So just as soon as I had finished explaining for the hundredth time to my mother that an airplane can fall on top of you just about anywhere, and she was getting to believe me, this man comes along and sprays the front of the White House with a machine gun."

"You should apply for combat pay," I said to Mrs. Clinton.

"What about pay? I've never worked so hard in my life."

We all knew that the Tuesday vote was going to be bad for the Democrats, so we avoided the subject. Talked about Washington in general. About Eleanor Roosevelt, whom I'd known and she was fascinated by. Then I began to probe, tactfully, I hope: How well did the Clintons understand just what they were up against? Did they know who actually owns and is rather idly ruling the United States—a very small class into which Bush had been born and trained and they had not? So, Who? What? How? I gave an example of poignant concern. In 1992 the country, by a clear majority, wanted a national health service. But insurance companies, in tandem with the medical-pharmaceutical axis, have always denounced any such scheme as Communist, and so the media, reflecting as it must the will of the ownership, had decreed that such a system is not only unworkable but un-American. As our people are never allowed more than one view of anything, Mrs. Clinton failed to get the administration's health plan through Congress. But worse was to befall her and the president. The always touchy ownership of the United States felt that it had been challenged by what were, after all—despite such lofty "visible" titles as "president"—mere employees. If the Clintons could not be got rid of in an election, they could at least be so blackened personally and politically that they would no longer be taken seriously. So, to this punitive end, the ownership spent hundreds of millions of dollars on television advertisements "proving" that under the Clinton plan each citizen would lose his own doctor and become a cipher in a computer (which he is pretty much anyway, thanks to the FBI, etc.), while its authors were guilty of everything from murder to ill-grooming.

As an old Washingtonian, I mentioned some of the ways in which great corporate entities destroy politicians. "It will never be on the issues. It will always be something unexpected. Something personal. Irrelevant. From long ago. Then they will worry it to death."

"That's certainly true." Mrs. Clinton was grim. "No story *ever* ends around here. Even when it's over."

I was about to suggest that if there was to be a war (as there is) between hated insurance companies and a popular plan, why not target the insurance companies publicly as the enemy and go on the attack? But Paul Newman, another guest, saved Mrs. Clinton from the golden treasury of my hindsight: "Get Gore to tell you about the day the horse ran away with Eartha Kitt. . . ."

Like a pair of dusty Ronald Reagans, we told Hollywood stories of the Fifties. She brightened considerably. "I wish I'd been there. Back in those days. You make it sound so interesting." She has beautiful manners. She asked about the Roosevelt years, and I told her how Mrs. Roosevelt delicately one-upped those who attacked her. "No, I'm not angry," she would say with her gentle half smile. "Only a little . . . sad." I told her, too, that until the war there was practically no security. The president would drive himself along nearby country roads.

Mrs. Clinton shook her head, amazed. "I was talking to one of the Secret Service men about security the other day, and he said that as far as they were concerned, they'd be happier if we lived in a bunker and traveled the streets in a tank."

I, amazed in turn, asked, "Was he joking?"

She gave us her dazzling blue-eyed smile, said, "Good night," and made her way back to the White House, where painters had been hard at work hiding the machine gun's bullet marks.

Meanwhile, whither the republic? The election: Should the various inept business dealings of the Clintons back in Arkansas become a serious issue, the many millions of dollars that Dole has acquired over the years while serving the great corporations in the Senate will suddenly become an issue so large that even the highly conservative media will be forced, as in the case of Watergate, to report who paid how much to which campaign for what favor in return. But this sort of thing usually ends in a stalemate. In 1960 Kennedy's sex life and an allegedly annulled first marriage could not be used by the Nixonites because the Kennedyites would then bring up all the money that the billionaire plane maker Howard Hughes had funneled to the Nixonites. "It's so funny," Jackie Kennedy once said, "all the money we—and they—spend digging up all this dirt, and then no one ever uses any of it." She sounded a bit wistful at the thought of so much frivolously wasted money that she might have liked.

The financial state of the union will never, in 1996, be addressed. In 1992 Clinton vowed he would cut back the Pentagon budget. He did get rid of a lot of manpower, but the real government promptly set him straight on weapons procurement; yet even they must have been mildly embarrassed when their members of Congress insisted on giving the Pentagon a billion or two more dollars than the bottomless pit had actually asked for. Clinton spoke nobly of a reform of the way that the few can buy elections under the current rules. Now, as a beneficiary of the ownership's largesse, he is silent. They may fear and loathe him, but they always hedge their bets and always pay for both candidates; later, at the dark of the moon, they collect their ton of flesh from the winner.

Although much of the election will be about Important Moral Issues like abortion, prayer in school, and the status of "gays," *terrorists* will be the word most sounded in the land from now until November. Until recently, *terrorist* has been a code word for the Muslim world, which does not love Israel, whose lobby in Washington controls Democratic presidents on Middle East matters. Republican presidents are less vulnerable, but even they must placate the lobby. More worrisome, *terrorist* has now become a word used to describe those lumpen Americans who have come to hate a government that builds more prisons than schools, intrudes on their private lives through wiretaps and other forms of surveillance, and puts in prison for life young people caught a third time with marijuana.

Death sentences for terrorists is the current cry. Public executions are being mooted. Autos-da-fé! "Tonight we have who Mr. Dole hoped would be the Republican vice-presidential candidate on our program. Welcome, Governor God."

"Actually, Larry, just God will do. Or Ms. God. As you know, I have never sought public office."

"That's very interesting. Now, *briefly*, please, what is your informed view of the autos-da-fé, the public burning of heretics?"

"Well, Larry, in our private capacity, we always felt—"

"I'm sorry, our time is up."

Speaking of God—and who does not, often, in what we call God's country?—as part of the predeath plea bargain with the Almighty, R. M. Nixon has been allowed to give us his views on the candidates from beyond the grave through the medium of a former assistant, Monica Crowley, writing in the pages of *The New Yorker*. The undead Nixon is in great form. He describes a number of chats he had with Clinton just before Nixon moved his office to the sky, accompanied by a Secret Service detail glumly immolated on a ghat covered with ghee in order to guard him upstairs.

Nixon thinks the world of Dole. As of 1992, he thought him "the only one who can lead . . . by far the smartest politician—and Republican—in the country today." Nixon was thinking then of how to defeat the Fetus Folk with a sensible candidate. Nixon finds Clinton intriguing. He is touched—and relieved—when Clinton rings him and chats at length. Later they meet. Clinton is worried about the economy. Nixon—who learned in 1974 all about the invisible government when one of its members, Katharine Graham of *The Washington Post*, deftly flushed his presidency—notes that "history will not remember him for *anything* he does domestically. The economy will recover; it's all short-term and, let's face it, very boring." The old trickster knows that economic power is kept forever out of the reach of the corporate ownership's chosen officeholders. Leave the economy alone and they'll leave the president alone to have the most fun a president can ever have, which is to fight a big war, as Lincoln or the Roosevelt cousins did.

According to Crowley, Nixon thinks Clinton's main fault is "mistaking conversation for leadership, and personal interaction for decision making." Nixon himself preferred making state visits abroad to doing just about anything at all at home. What he ever did on these trips, beyond photo ops with Mao and company, is vague. He does admit, a bit sadly, about Clinton, "He loves himself,

though, and that comes across." Finally, "He could be a great president. . . . But I doubt it. It's clear that this guy can be pushed
around. . . ." Two years later, it would appear that it is the Artful
Dodger who is doing the pushing and the dodging and the joyous
stealing of any and every policy his opponents might favor.

I shall give myself the last word here, as I did in 1992 when I
predicted that Clinton would beat Bush, as he will beat Dole in
1996, barring the detonation of some rustic honey wagon in his
path. "Clinton's greatest asset," I wrote then, "is a perfect lack of
principle. With a bit of luck, he will be capable, out of a simple
starry-eyed opportunism, to postpone our collapse. After all, Franklin Delano Roosevelt was equally unprincipled." My ironic compli-
ments were, of course, misunderstood in media-land, where I was
accused of calling both FDR and Clinton crooks, which they were—
and are—but no more than any other politicians in a society whose
elections are as corrupt as ours. Actually, I was paying each the high
compliment of being a nonideological pragmatist, unlike the true
believer, who will destroy the world or, failing that, brings us
Auschwitz or the Great Depression. What is needed in a time of class
and race wars is a quick-witted, devious, soothing leader, always sufficiently nimble to stay a step or two ahead of a polity that, if it is
going anywhere, is heading down the economic scale, jettisoning, in
its dizzy progress, our sacred "inalienable rights."

Finally, no matter how great Clinton's plurality or majority, *he*
now knows, even if we don't, that he will not be allowed to do much
of anything at home. He doesn't find economics as boring as Nixon
did, because he knows more about such things. But Clinton might
find it wise, once reelected, to reverse some of the astonishing
notions that he has recently put forward in order to preempt reactionary opponents.

I ended my piece in 1992 with "We must wish Clinton luck.
After all, if he fails, *he* will be the last president." Many thought this
melodramatic—the office will go on, even if the country should find
its eventual niche somewhere between Argentina and Brazil. But I
meant "last" in the sense that if the half of the people who now don't

vote are joined by too many more, then the high office is itself irrelevant, something that Clinton sensed when he declared, in a fit of pique, that despite the new Republican Congress of 1994, the president is *not* irrelevant, which means the thought is very much in his mind.

Meanwhile, let us give Clinton his proper due. Lincoln to one side, he does better funerals than any American president in our increasingly murderous history. This is no small thing. After all, who would care about Pericles today had he not given a sublime funeral oration—as reported by General Thucydides, Retired—in which he reminded the Athenians that an empire like theirs, no matter how larcenously acquired, is a very dangerous thing to let go? Ditto now, as Perot would say.

GQ
October 1996

Like so many southerners or half-southerners, I have never much cared for the fictions of William Faulkner. But where others find shocking, and I find life-enhancing, his use of that emblematic corncob in *Sanctuary*, I am put off by the *familiarity* of his work. I seem to know all his stories in advance, twice-told tales, you might say. I also dislike the ornate imprecision, to put it mildly, of his style, which involves the misuse of gorgeous-sounding words—"euphemistic" for "euphonious" and vice versa, while the Bible's "Suffer the little children" Faulkner takes to be Bronze Age child abuse and not seventeenth-century "Allow the little children." But I am not his editor and stylist, as Suzanne Pleshette so vividly introduced herself to the great American author Youngblood Hawke in that great, eponymous—or was it euphemistic?—film of yesteryear.

But, personally, I liked Faulkner, and we had a true connection. He came from Oxford, Mississippi, and his mythical Yoknapatawpha County takes in parts of Chickasaw and Webster counties, founded by the Gore family, among others, in the 1840s. Faulkner knew many of the Gores of his time and spoke fondly of my great-aunt Mary Gore Wyatt, who taught him—or was it Stark Young?—Latin. In 1954 I adapted two Faulkner short stories for live TV. After *Smoke* and *Barn Burning* were aired, Faulkner congratulated me in the lobby of the Algonquin Hotel. "I don't have the television," he said, "but relations do, and they liked those shows very much." We chatted about kin. What else sustains individuals in a somewhat wild part of the world, never entirely benign to the human? Hence the importance of kin, family, clan. The clans have always been the integuments that hold together southern communities. They are often vast in numbers and intricate in their workings.

Once a year, the Gore clan gathers, often in a town like Calhoun City (founded by T. T. Gore, born 1776). In 1990 I attended Gore Day in the town of Houston, not far from Elvis Presley's capital city of Tupelo, where I arrived by plane from New York via Nashville with a BBC TV crew: A documentary was being done on my life and times, and as I had never visited Mississippi, where my mother's father, who had brought me up, was born, it was thought that . . . Well, I'm not sure I had any idea what to expect.

I stayed with a cousin, Dr. Ed Gore, a fourth-generation M.D. who heads a large clinic. He is younger than I, with a grown son by his first wife and a bright blond ten- or eleven-year-old son, Blake, by a second wife. The TV crew noted that Blake looked like me at ten. But then the Gore genes are strong, making for large noses and ears and, in many, chinoiserie-style eyes, more gray than blue. Blake certainly had inherited the Gore sharpness of tongue. When one of my Brit companions made some remark about the recent film *Mississippi Burning*, not the most tactful allusion, the older Gores looked puzzled. Why, no, they hadn't seen it. . . . Blake roared with laughter: "You never heard so much fussin' going on round here as when that picture came out." If there is an uncomfortable truth to be told, at least one Gore can always be counted on to bear sardonic witness. The clan is far-flung now, from one end of the country to the other. Even so, two or three hundred saw fit to gather together to meet, with wives and kin, on a Sunday in Houston in Chickasaw County, which once belonged (all of it, they claim) to our ancestor T. T. Gore, who had bought a considerable chunk of land from the Chickasaw tribe in the 1840s. Earlier, the Indians had been driven west to Mississippi by Andrew Jackson, and then, later, they would, with a dozen other tribes, be transferred to their own territory in what is now Oklahoma, whose first senator proved to be my grandfather, brought up near Houston in nearby Webster County.

Ironies abound, historical and human, in the story of our clan.

One irony is that T. T. Gore, in a sense, dispossessed the Indians of their Mississippi land while his great-grandson, T. P. Gore, by establishing the state of Oklahoma in 1907, confined them to reservations on bad land that, when oil was discovered, inspired the federal government to dispossess them yet again. Late in life, T. P. Gore would try to make amends.

"We pick the cousins we want to acknowledge, and we sort of let the others drop," a Gore lady confided to me at the reunion. I was borderline acceptable. Word of my atheism (like that of my grandfather) had not spread too far. Many of the Gores I met in Houston are born-again; all are believers. For the most part they belong to the professional classes: lawyers, politicians, preachers, teachers, military men. Curiously, none was in trade. Back of them, of course, were generations of farmers and rude mechanicals from the British Isles who came to Maryland and Virginia in the seventeenth century (a "Thomas Gore, Gentleman" was a lost colonist at Jamestown). The eighteenth-century Gores, pursuing land, moved on to South Carolina, then to Pickens, Alabama, and, finally, to Mississippi, in the 1840s.

Faulkner, in his novels, dwells lovingly on the class divisions of his not-so-mythical county. There were the aristos, called Sartoris (naturally, he, in his Harris tweed jacket, was a Sartoris), while the educated professional class, the Stevenses, were the Gores. Finally, there was the white trash, the pullulating Snopeses, ever breeding, ever multiplying, ever, ah, inheriting all earth itself, so many little foxes forever chomping on the voluptuous vulpine sour grapes of Sartoris and Stevens. "Of course," said one old lady, "Bill himself wasn't so much. After all, this is redneck country. There aren't—never were—many negroes and certainly no great plantations like they have—or had—down in the Delta. *Those* were the folks who had the mansions with the columns and all the wealth, most of which got lost in the war. Bourbons, we call them. They ran the state for years through the Democratic Party, which our family started to oppose in the 1880s, when your great-grandfather and his people, over in Emory and Eupora and Walthall, helped organize the Party of the People—populists, they were called—and when T.P. ran for the legislature, he ran as a populist. He was in his early twenties and lost in a dirty election that was the making of him, because he skedaddled out of here for Corsicana, Texas, with his father and brothers, to practice law, and then on to the territories, where, practically single-handed, he invented Oklahoma as a state." I don't think that Governor "Alfalfa Bill" Murray would like so much credit to go to Senator Thomas Pryor Gore—but then we are in Gore country now.

When T. P. Gore left Mississippi on the last day of December, 1895, he was twenty-five, and he vowed he would never return until he was a U.S. senator. He kept his vow. Eighteen years later, Senator Gore was back in Mississippi, a national figure who had played a considerable part (to his everlasting regret) in the election of Woodrow Wilson as president in 1912 and again in 1916. I should note that due to two separate accidents, he was blind from the age of ten, yet got through law school with a cousin—yet again—who read to him.

Although the Gores have—and had—many of the usual prejudices typical of their time and region, the marked absence of slave owners in the family meant that when the Civil War came, they were what they called "patriots": They were against secession, as were their cousins across the nearby state line of Tennessee. This presented T.P.'s father, Thomas Madison Gore, age twenty-four in 1861, with a terrible choice. Should he go fight for his state against the union that the Gores had helped create in 1776, or should he turn his back on his immediate kin and go join like-minded cousins in nearby eastern Tennessee, which, most famously, did not secede?

With camera crew, I went to the Webster County courthouse, where Thomas Madison had spent all of one day agonizing on the steps. The building is large and imposing—and practically alone in the wilderness all about it. Nearby is the one-room schoolhouse where my grandfather had learned to read and write until his own light was switched off.

I sat on the steps where Thomas Madison had sat. Described to the camera how one can be torn between duty to the clan and to the nation. Described how, in the end, the clan usually wins. He chose to fight with his two brothers for Mississippi. One brother was killed, and Thomas Madison was wounded and taken captive not far from home at Shiloh. "As far as I know," he would say years later, when he had settled in as chancery clerk of Webster County (in the same building on whose steps he had agonized as a youth), "I am the only Confederate soldier who never rose above the rank of corporal. Somehow the others all got to be majors and colonels." It should be noted that one of his brothers, too young to fight, was Albert Cox Gore, who after the war graduated from the Memphis Medical College in Tennessee.

I have been told so many times how Thomas Pryor Gore and Albert Arnold Gore, Sr., are related that I have permanently forgotten and must again ask the cousinage or check various biographies (fifth cousins, I have just been told again). T. P. Gore was the clan's great man for the first half of the twentieth century. We never claimed our Tennessee relations as kin because we had hardly heard of them until Albert Sr. came to the House of Representatives in 1939, age 31. He had been born in 1907, the year T. P. Gore came to the Senate, age thirty-seven. I remember sometime around 1940 my grandfather's telling me that he had been sitting in the Senate cloakroom "and this young man comes up to me and says, 'You know, you look just like my father.' " It was the new congressman from Tennessee—and they did look alike. They also knew how they were related.

There was nothing sufficiently witty or unpleasant that Alice Roosevelt Longworth, daughter of President Theodore, did not have to say of her cousin President Franklin, who was, I believe, the same relation to President Theodore as the current vice president is to me. Once I teased her when she was going on about Franklin, whom she called "the Feather Duster"—"the sort of person you never asked to the dinner but only to come in after." "So," I asked, "why were you always so down on him?" Alice's gray-yellow eyes blinked as she revealed the huge, snaggled Roosevelt teeth in a thin-lipped smile. "We were the President Roosevelts, and then along comes these Hyde Park nobodies, and suddenly they were the President Roosevelts, forever and ever. The fact that Eleanor was my first cousin didn't help, either. And, oh, she was so noble! So sickeningly noble. But to tell the truth, I'm afraid that our feelings were nothing more than outraged vanity." This, in a milder way, was rather my family's view when Albert Sr. went to the Senate in 1952 and became *the* Senator Gore (T.P. had died in 1949).

I seem to have mislaid Gore Day. In honor of me, a dozen hymns were sung, and four Gore preachers spoke the Word, and I was duly drenched—drowned—in the Blood of the Lamb. A few days later, in Jackson, I asked Eudora Welty if this was usual. "Well," she said, "it was a Sunday, and there's not much else to do up there in the country. Of course, I'm from the city. But I did go to school with girls from all over the state, and you could spot where they were from just by the way they looked and talked. We always thought your upstate cousins were a bit on the simple side, while the Delta girls—oh my!—they were *fast*! Even though we all wore uniforms, they *did* things to theirs."

Significantly, Senator Albert Gore, Jr., due to come, as always, to the reunion of the cousinage, bowed out at the last minute, "because of a fund-raiser," he said. But, I was told, this too was in honor of me. I was not only a notorious radical in politics but I had recently written a book about a man still deeply resented in the state, Abraham Lincoln. Even so, the cousinage did not like being stood up for a fund-raiser, that central activity of *fin de siècle* American politics and, perhaps, young Albert's Achilles' heel. I have always avoided him on the ground that one day plausible deniability will be useful to each of us. But I had known Albert Sr. slightly. Once, at a convention, shortly after I'd run for Congress, we were interviewed together on television. When asked the usual questions about how we were related, Albert Sr. said, "Fourth cousins, I think, but if he'd been elected, it would have been a lot closer than that."

After Gore Day, I met the last of T.P.'s first cousins, Taffie Gore

Griffin. She was in her nineties. In 1951 she was the first woman to be elected to state office. As circuit clerk, she shocked many people by industriously registering blacks to vote. She remembers when T.P. was considered a sure thing as vice president in Woodrow Wilson's second term. Unfortunately, T.P. had opposed our entry into the First World War. When the Chamber of Commerce of Oklahoma City finally ordered him, by telegram, to vote for war, he wired them back: "How many of your members are of draft age?" Duly defeated in 1920, he returned to the Senate in 1930, where he promptly collided with FDR on monetary policy. Senator Carter Glass told me how he'd been present when T.P., in effect, called the president a liar: "Franklin turned gray and said nothing. Lucky your grandfather couldn't see his face, because there was this look that said 'Kill.' " And FDR saw to it that T.P. was defeated in the 1936 primary. Of his overprincipled approach to politics, my grandfather used to say, "When the Republicans are in, I'm a Democrat, and when the Democrats are in, I'm out of step."

As you can see, I am uneasily circling a subject that few writers nowadays ever touch upon, and that is character. Ordinarily, I steer clear of such matters, too, out of tact, but as Albert Jr. may be the forty-third president at a crucial time in the republic's life, we had better start finding out where he came from, who he is or if, relevant question, he is anyone at all.

In the matter of race, Albert Arnold Gore, Sr., behaved as well as a senator with a southern border constituency could. Although he voted against the Civil Rights Act of 1964 (a vote he later said he regretted), he refused to sign Senator Strom Thurmond's 1956 Southern Manifesto, a celebration of the joys and character-building aspects of slavery in the past and of harmonious inequality in the present. But when it comes to the matter of war and peace, Albert Sr. bears a comforting resemblance to T.P. in the previous generation. Alone, I believe, among the usually war-minded southern legislators, Albert Sr. spoke out against the long idiocy of the Vietnam War. Essentially, populists don't like foreign wars, particularly in lands that they know nothing of and for no demonstrable goals. For exercising good judgment, Albert Sr. was defeated in 1970 by an opponent who used the familiar line that he was "out of touch with the voters of Tennessee." If this was true, the voters, supremely misled by three administrations, were seriously out of touch with reality. Exactly fifty years after T. P. Gore departed the Senate because he had been against the First War, his cousin departed because of the Vietnam War. Curiously, the wives of each, though admiring their husbands' integrity, discerned a common tendency to masochism in the name of duty. Albert Sr.'s wife, Pauline, herself a lawyer and a canny politician, has contrasted her son (whom she quietly brought up to be president) with his father: "Al, by nature, is more of a pragmatist than his father. As am I. I tried to persuade Albert Sr. not to butt at a stone wall just for the sheer joy of butting." While Nina Kay Gore, wife to T.P., observed, "The Gores tend to be brilliant, but they've got no sense." She would sigh whenever confronted with her husband's implacability; as for my own, she used to warn, "Never stir up more snakes than you can kill with one stick." Plainly, Albert Jr., his mother's son, need never fear snakebite.

The three Gore senators were never much at money-making, as opposed to fund-raising, where Albert Jr. is willing to be smeared as a pro- or crypto-Buddhist in his Grail-like pursuit of campaign money. Ninety-one years ago, T. P. Gore spent $1,000 on his successful Senate campaign. Although he was later to write the legislation for the oil depletion of resources allowance that made some of his constituents as rich as Saudi Arabs, he was never paid off by them; but then his campaigns were inexpensive. By Albert Sr.'s time, the costs of electioneering were high indeed. In 1938 he was elected to the House of Representatives, on borrowed money. Well, "family" money, as we shall see.

Albert Jr. was brought up on his father's Carthage, Tennessee, farm as well as in Washington, D.C., where he attended St. Albans, an all-boys school that I had gone to twenty years earlier. The two Alberts had settled down on the eighth floor of our cousin Grady Gore's hotel, the Fairfax (later the Ritz Carlton), where they lived, the Cousins chant, for free. Grady's branch of the family had not gone west like the rest of us and so, staying on in Maryland, they had made a fortune, something the rest of us never quite managed to do. Grady's daughter Louise is a Republican who has inherited that damaged gene that impels some people to public office. Certainly, whenever the moon is full, cousin Louise can be counted on to run for governor of Maryland. Although she has never won, she did persuade Richard Nixon to take as his vice president Maryland's governor, Spiro Agnew, thus earning herself a merry footnote in history. Louise's sister Mary lost her first husband in a crash on Northeast Airlines, a company that my father had founded and owned, showing how our lives crisscross in Faulknerian tragedy as well as in Faulknerian comedy. Later she "kept company with" Nixon's attorney general John Mitchell, either just before or just after his time in prison. Plainly, we have our devil-may-care side.

I have often thought cousin Grady was the most interesting of the lot. In the 1930s, you could legally give as much as you liked to the candidate of your choice. Cousin Grady had always helped finance Tennessee's senior senator, Kenneth McKellar, until cousin Grady asked McKellar to take on Albert Sr. in his office as an intern, a position of decency in that far-off time. McKellar turned Albert Sr. down. Grady said, "Why?" "Don't like him," said McKellar. Now, there is a saying in the South that "if a snake bites a Gore, they all puff up." Grady puffed up. Told Albert Sr., "I was going to give that old bastard $40,000 for his reelection, but not now. I'm giving it to you. You're running for Congress." Thus Albert Sr. got to the House.

Later, in 1930, Albert Sr. went into business with one of the century's most gorgeous criminals, Armand Hammer. For those interested in Hammer's life as a Russian-American friend of Lenin's and a financial fixer for Stalin—a bridge, as he might have put it, between Communism and capitalism—I highly recommend Edward Jay Epstein's *Dossier: The Secret History of Armand Hammer*. As chairman of Occidental Petroleum, Hammer befriended (or, as the FBI might say, "bribed") many American politicians. At one point, he tried to get his hands on "a huge government-owned refinery in Morgantown, West Virginia," that the army was willing to lease to the highest bidder. Hammer went after it: "He had extended . . . largesse to both Republicans and Democrats," writes Epstein. "His principal contact among the Democrats in the House was Albert Gore of Tennessee. In 1950, Hammer had made Congressman Gore a partner in a cattle-breeding business, and Gore made a substantial profit." Hammer failed to get the lease, because of alarm in the government about his close relations with the Soviets. Later, during dé-tente, this connection worked to Hammer's benefit. On January 19, 1961, "Hammer was Senator Albert Gore's guest at one of the five black-tie inaugural balls." (JFK had just been inaugurated.) "He could count on Gore for such invitations. He had made him his partner in the cattle-breeding business—a partnership that had proved profitable—and he had given him each Christmas over the past five years a gift of antique silver." Gore also helped to get Ham-mer to Moscow later that winter, where Hammer did business suc-cessfully with Anastas Mikoyan and Khrushchev. Rogues have their uses. In 1970, when Albert Sr. was defeated for the Senate, Hammer made him chairman of his Island Creek Coal, the nation's third-largest coal producer.

Hammer had attended five presidential inaugurations as the guest of Albert Sr. He attended Ronald Reagan's 1981 inauguration as the guest of Albert Jr. Hammer not only reveled in reflected glory for its own sake but he had now a specific goal in mind, a presiden-tial pardon. Since 1938 the FBI had six times investigated him for the bribing and blackmailing of public officials. "Hammer had avoided prosecution," writes Epstein, "on a felony charge through a plea bargain." In 1984 he applied for a pardon for the "misde-meanors" he had admitted to in order that he might obtain, pre-sumably through a series of aurora borealis bribes, the Nobel Peace Prize (which Hammer actually deserved rather more than some of its recent recipients). But Reagan did not include him in the 1985 round of pardons. "In 1986, [Hammer] pledged $1 million to the Ronald Reagan Library. . . . This made Hammer the largest single pledger of funds for the project." Again, no pardon. Hammer upped the ante to $1.3 million. Still no pardon. By 1990 he was dead, at ninety-two, vindicated only by a last-chance pardon from George Bush. Happily, the Reagan Library never got a single pledged penny from Hammer's estate. Giants walked the earth in those days.

Albert Jr. The official story of his life makes curiously depressing reading. Certainly by the time he was enrolled at St. Albans, he was running for president, and the other boys knew it, as did several teachers from my era. Since many of the boys came from political families, ambition of a political nature was hardly a surprise if it surfaced in any boy, no matter how young. I, too, was haunted by my grandfather's failure to become vice president—and why not thane of Glamis and Cawdor and king to be? I, too, wanted to complete the family business. But after three years in the army in the Second War, I had become a novelist. I had also been infuriated by American attitudes to same-sexuality, and so, between a political career already mapped out and publishing a book that would, the more effective it was, end all hope of completing the family business, I chose virtue and published *The City and the Pillar*, butting my head against a stone wall that others in the next generation were to dent somewhat. The book was published in January 1948. In March 1948, the Heavenly Campaign Manager of the Gores, aware that I was now a political dud, gave birth to Albert Jr., right on cue. The clan was back on track. There has been a weird symmetry in all this, whose meaning I leave to the witches on the heath.

One of Albert's teachers marveled to me at his no-doubt hard-earned lack of spontaneity: "He forced himself to be good at sports and win school elections. But he was not a natural at anything except painting, where he was really first-rate." I asked what sort of paintings he did. "Miniatures. They were exquisite. The sort of things only someone capable of great concentration and hard work could do." A Mr. Hank Hillin, in the book *Al Gore Jr., His Life and Career*, thinks the other boys envied Al his hard-won school success and later career, but my impression is they were mocking him for the uncool obviousness of his ambition when they nicknamed him

Ozymandias, after Shelley's King of Kings, whose ruined colossal statue lies in the sands with the admonition "Look on my Works, ye Mighty, and despair!" Al's contemporaries were dealing in irony of a sort not available to Hank or to his subject, Al, who, in order to sound more down-home folksy, changed his name to the bleak, rather unsuitable "Al Gore," under the pretense he was just another sharecropper farm boy who had come to pick cotton in Washington's Cathedral Close.

One advantage of being brought up in Washington in a senator's house is that you very quickly get the point to how and why things work. Where someone from outside might come to politics in order to bring justice to the people or, at the very least, Frank Capra, those on the inside know that it is all an intricate game of personalities and what today is called spin. Who you really are is not as important as how you have been made to seem; hence, the universal paranoia about media. Issues that so enthrall the politically minded outside the magic circle of hereditary politicians mean very little to those who start life with a political name that will act as a minimal description of its bearer. A Gore will be—or, let us say, will be thought to be—a mild populist, interested in the welfare of farmers, no open friend to conglomerate America and so on. The classic Gores are against foreign military adventures. It was here that Al Jr. broke with tradition when he was one of only ten Democratic senators to support George Bush's Persian Gulf caper; before that he had approved Reagan's Grenada and Libyan strikes.

At Harvard, Al Jr. met his own eminence grise, Martin Peretz, a sometime schoolteacher who had married a considerable fortune, thus making it possible for him to buy *The New Republic*, a once respectable liberal paper belonging to my brother-in-law Michael Whitney Straight. Yes, our Washington world is astonishingly small, and lives cross and recross for generations. Peretz is a mega-Zionist, and Al Jr. has proved to be a good investment for his lobby—and vice versa, though in Al's 1988 bid for the presidency, the Peretz connection cost him New York's black vote and got him practically none of the Jewish vote, except, possibly, the one cast by Mayor Ed Koch. Peretz has been known to take credit for Al Jr.'s speeches.

In the matter of Vietnam, our hero played it perfectly. He knew that he could not stay out, even though, like his father, he was against the war; and he knew that a visit to Canada's cooler climes would be fatal in the eyes of his patriotic constituency. So he became a journalist for six months with an engineering unit outside Saigon. He never saw action, but he did see to it that, weapon in hand, he was photographed for the Al Gore, Jr., Library. Plainly, the nation had changed after the Second War. I can think of hardly anyone of my generation who dodged the draft, while many of us, especially those with an eye to politics, enlisted and even got killed, something the gung ho Vietnam generation never did as they found solace in neutral lands or hearkened to a call from God to join His ministry on earth.

Along the way, Al married an appropriate wife and had four appropriate children, all rather better-looking than is usual in the clan, but then they also had a mother as did he. Of Pauline Gore, one of his teachers at St. Albans said, "She was the driving force, not the father. She was the one who wanted him to be class president and so on." Where Albert Sr. saw himself as a voice for truth in the world, his wife and his son duly noted that he was not spending as much time at home with the folks as he should, and so number one on the checklist of what the son would *not* do when he began his ascent was neglect the home folks. He would, also, work hard to play down nonfolksy St. Albans and Harvard, as well as Vanderbilt, where he studied, briefly, for the ministry in order "to atone for the sins" in Vietnam, whatever the sins of a noncombatant might have been; then, once he had exorcised the trauma of man's inhumanity to man, he shifted over to the law school.

A five-year stint at the Nashville *Tennessean* taught him a great deal about how newspapers work, and about publicity. Meanwhile, he took part in his father's various livestock and tobacco dealings. Later he was to share, most publicly at a convention, the guilt he still felt because he had once grown and sold the poisonous leaf that had struck down a beloved sister in her youth. He ceased to traffic with the murderous weed, prayed for forgiveness. He promptly had to face what friends call the "Gore jinx." The speech—the work of Marty Peretz?—wetted every eye, including the speaker's. Actually, Al had somehow forced himself to continue in the tobacco business for quite some time after her death. Plainly, the cigarette burned more brightly than the bush on the hard road to Damascus.

The Gore jinx becomes operative whenever Al is inclined, as Sam Goldwyn used to say, to geld the lily. All politicians do this, of course. But Al's air of solemn righteousness sets him up every time for a pratfall, including the astonishing assertion that he and his bride had inspired Erich Segal to write *Love Story* in their common Harvard days. Segal is a brilliant classicist, whose *Roman Laughter*, a study of Plautus, I highly recommend; he sharply denied any connection. Pratfall. Al should have stayed in the family and said that *Myra Breckinridge* had been inspired by the magic couple.

Lily gelding is a harmless activity and, perhaps, a necessity for someone fearful of being thought too young for the presidency in 1988. Al also portrayed himself as a home builder, the developer of a subdivision; actually, others did the work, while he and his father were fairly inactive partners. But Al did make a packet by reselling some of his father's farm after he had first bought it with a Federal Farm Credit System low-interest loan of the sort usually made to finance farmers' crops. Profit to one side, he gelds lilies in order to create an image of himself as farmer, home builder, warrior, relentless crime reporter who sent to jail corrupt officials (they didn't go to jail), and so on. But then, as a member of the House who served with him observed, "Around here he's what we call a 'glory boy.' He gets to the House and starts running for the Senate. Gets to the Senate and starts running for the White House. There's no time left to do any of the real work the rest of us have to do."

Four terms in the House, then to the Senate in 1984. After four years of the Senate, at the age of thirty-nine, Al is ready for the presidency. During the primaries, family lines crossed. Senator David

Boren of Oklahoma told me that the more Al stumped T. P. Gore's state, the closer the family connection became: "By the end, you'd have thought he was your nephew." Save for the Peretz connection, a nephew to be proud of, by and large. In politics, credit is taken, if not given, for just about anything admirable or popular at the moment: anything that can't immediately be checked on, that is. The Al Gore résumé is wondrously virtuous, if slightly short on achieved specifics.

T. P. Gore used to say that the most fervent prayer of any politician was "Would that my opponent had written a book!" In 1992 Al did just that. *Earth in the Balance* was the ominous title of his hostage to fortune. *Ecology and the Human Spirit* was the subtitle, while, under that, " 'A powerful summons for the politics of life and hope'—Bill Moyers." In the introduction, the author says that he has for "more than twenty-five years . . . [been] in search of a true understanding of the global ecological crisis and how it can be resolved." All right, so it was not exactly twenty-five years. How about twenty-four? Certainly, the book is solidly researched; the prose as resolutely dull as its author's speeches; the conclusions obvious to nearly everyone who has given the matter thought, except, ironically, the great sources of pollution and warming, Corporate America, without whose money and media no one can be elected president. But then, when Al wrote the book, he had taken himself out of the '92 presidential race, never thinking that, within a year, he would be Clinton's vice president and that his "antibusiness" tract would outrage *The Wall Street Journal's* fellow polluter-travelers. Since no good deed goes unpunished, one suspects this will convince Al that his unique moment of reasonable altruism is not going to go unpunished and perhaps he'd better go back to endorsing such military-procurement programs as the MX, the Trident D-5, etc. Meanwhile, the Gore jinx again surfaced when the book's greatest fan proved to be the Unabomber.

Dick Morris, the political spin master whose sex life caused him to depart the as yet uncongenial Clinton White House, has written, thus far, the best account of how presidential politics work today. He is particularly intrigued by the Clinton-Gore relationship. "Gore is the single person in the world whose advice the president most values. He sees Gore as a junior president. . . . When he wants a clear-eyed assessment, he turns to Gore, as he does when he wants something really important handled really well." Yet it was Al who helped bring aboard Leon Panetta as chief of staff: a fatal choice, because when the hard times came, Panetta was one of the first to turn on Clinton. Was this a setup? One almost hopes, out of sheer dramatic imagination, that the deliberately colorless Gore may yet turn out to be Iago, secretly planting handkerchiefs all round the West Wing. Certainly, he has placed a number of his own people in places of power. But he has also, thus far, living up to his own book, done his best to preserve the environmental-protection programs.

About the 1995 battle over the budget, Morris makes an interesting observation: "A more subtle difference existed between Clinton and Gore. Both wanted a deal [with the congressional Republicans]. But Clinton wanted a compromise, whereas Gore wanted a deal that all but completely protected his priorities: the environment, technology, and so forth. Gore is more interested in specifics than in themes." This is an important distinction that goes to the heart of American practical politics. By and large, the great presidents have been thematic. FDR never mastered the specifics of anything. But he had a genius for getting across to the electorate his general view of where the country should be going and who should make what deal—New Deal, even—to get us all there. FDR possessed what Bush so memorably disdained as "the vision thing." But Al has a graduate student's need to pile up specifics for a good grade. Like Carter, he dotes on facts, figures, blueprints of how to build that tree house. Certainly, it is a sign of seriousness and goodwill that he works on environmental matters not only on TV but behind closed doors; yet it is also a sign of tactical weakness that he has Jimmy Carter's fascination with endless technical detail, more fitting for someone aspiring to a safe berth in Harvard's American Civilization department than the presidency. FDR was the first to admit that he often stumbled. I may not, he once said, always get a hit each time I come up to bat. . . . But he had a buoyancy that was contagious. When one thing failed, he'd quickly try another. An overattention to each tree and not to the forest that contains it could be the fatal flaw in the character of a miniaturist President Gore, whose mind is convergent—only connect things—while the great presidents know that nothing on earth or in politics really connects and that the quick, divergent mentality is the one that best adapts and moves ahead.

In order to be reelected in 1996, the Clinton-Gore administration adopted a series of right-wing Republican, even protofascist, programs, with lots more prisons, death penalties, harassment of the poor, cries of terrorism, and, implicitly, control by government over the citizenry, as the Unabomber duly noted. As one sees these politics evolve in Morris's narrative, one realizes that no one in the White House is thinking about much of anything other than, somehow, finessing the other party, which is slightly more in thrall to the Christian right and somewhat better funded by corporate America than are the Democrats. It is a somber narrative, particularly if one has been studying, as I have, the Bill of Rights lately. But we are now trapped in the rapid erosion of an ever more alien system, currently further skewed by all the atrocious law that Kenneth W. Starr has managed to squeeze from a brain-dead Supreme Court, where only its prince of darkness, Scalia, betrays an inkling of common sense about the harm being done our judicial system as lawyer-client and president-adviser protocols are overthrown in ill-written and worse-conceived judgments.

In 1883 Congress passed a law preventing city and courthouse machines from obliging those on the public payroll to kick back at election time—a sort of tithing to raise money for an election or, perhaps, just riotous living: an evening at Delmonico's with Boss Tweed. Virtue outlawed this practice, officially. Now Janet Reno of Waco ponders a special counsel to investigate Albert Jr., among others, for making calls to raise soft money from a public building, the White House, instead of from a cellular phone in the Lafayette Park convenience parlor. I consulted, in a vision, the Heavenly Campaign

Manager of the Gores. He was dismissive. "If they try making something of that, what about Dole and Gingrich telephoning from Capitol Hill?"

I wondered about the Buddhist fundraiser for Albert Jr. "Forget it. Even the Bush family's Heavenly Campaign Manager—dyslexic, by the way—says there's no mileage in it."

"What about Clinton and Monica? Will that rub off on Albert Jr.?"

"If Clinton goes before 2000—not much chance, I'd say—Al's in place to run as a sitting president. Anyway, once Bill's gone, end of sex story. You see, Al is sexproof. Designed never to lust in the Oval Office or even in his heart, and—the Beauty Part—no one lusts for him. Oh, we're looking after—really looking after—the family this time." As the vision started to fade, I was bemused to note that our family's Heavenly Campaign Manager is wearing a saffron robe. A *Buddhist* campaign manager? *Shantih shantih shantih.*

Since there is no earthly reason for Albert Jr. to be president, by the same happy logic there is no unearthly reason for him not to be. But should, by some mishap, the mandate of heaven not come to Albert A. Gore Jr., the next generation of Gores is bound to succeed, and I am now putting my money on the future president Blake Gore of Houston, Mississippi, who will initiate a golden age not too long after A.D. 2050.

GQ
December 1998

Most establishment American journalists tend to be like their writing, and so, duly warned by the tinkle of so many leper-bells, one avoids their company. On the other hand, after reading from beginning to end *The Thirty Years' Wars*, I realized why it was that I so liked Andrew Kopkind and always read his bulletins from the political front, which were also, endearingly, bulletins from his own life as well, which ended much too soon last October.

Born in 1935, Andy was a decade my junior. Since we were like-minded in so many ways that decade should not have made much difference, but it did in the sense that he was always somewhat exotic to me. The Sixties never meant much to me but they were everything to someone his age. I was—and am—the Forties–Fifties, shaped by the second war and Dr. Kinsey, "radicalized" by Korea and Joe McCarthy. Even so, the slight sense of strangeness I felt about him and his generation only made his take on matters of mutual interest attractively aslant.

To read what Kopkind calls *Dispatches and Diversions of a Radical Journalist 1965–1994* is to be given a deliberately eccentric tour of the American empire's slow deterioration as well as that of its mirror-image on the chilly steppes which so perversely cracked from side to side—seven years' bad luck (and maybe seven more) as my grandmother used to say. I say eccentric because I always thought that I had first met Andy at the Democratic convention in Chicago in 1968, but now I read that he had only touched base there for a moment or two. Then, before Mayor Daley could shout Sheeney! at Senator Ribicoff, Andy had gone to the real action: Czechoslovakia, where he observed the Russian invasion and Dubcek's fall. While I was anticipating with excited horror Nixon's coming victory, Andy was writing from Prague: "One of these days—when the 'German problem' is solved—the Czechs will find a new way out of the Soviet sphere and others will follow. Beyond that, Russia has discredited leftist parties and the left in general for years to come. And within the Warsaw Pact countries, and perhaps even in Russia, Czechoslovakia has already become an embryonic 'Vietnam.' " It took twenty years for Andy to be proved right, during which time he did his best to shore up "the left" in our own essentially apolitical land.

A generality about the sort of journalist Kopkind was. Unlike the overwhelming majority of the breed, he did not go in for Opinions, the daily ashen bread of the Sunday TV zoo and of those columnists who appear in such papers as *Time* and *Newsweek*, recycling the sort of mindless received opinion that dissolves before one's eyes into its original constituent parts—blurred ink, glossy paper. He had opinions, of course, but he didn't offer them until he had first proved, through detail, his reasons for holding them. Most American journalists who "do" politics cannot resist getting to know the Players. Walter Lippmann was typical of an earlier generation, the disinterested wise man who remained aloof, chiseling great thoughts on marble columns. Actually a casual trawl through FDR's library at Hyde Park shows how eager Walter was for White House invitations and interviews. At least today's media chorus are all openly bought as they rush to White House to help with a speech, then off to newsroom to praise their own work, then onto television where now they condescend—no doubt, rightly—to mere senators and Cabinet members. Who can forget, a few elections ago, the egregious Phil Donahue wagging a minatory finger in the faces of a clutch of presidential candidates? This is no way to keep separate first and fourth estate, but then, in so tight and collusive a system, it is to no one's real interest to draw a line.

Happily, Andy did not collude, he drew a line: kept his eye steadily on the obscure who might or might not be making a revolution in the national consciousness if not in the streets. How to explain him? He started life in conventional middle-class New Haven. Father, a Republican District Attorney. There was Yale nearby, the Vatican of reactionary politics not to mention nursing mother to OSS and CIA. But Andy had the good luck to have, as he put it, a "commie pinko rabbi." He avoided Yale; went to Cornell as a pre-med student. Like me, he was exposed young to the *New Statesman*, a paper that once had the power not only to enlighten but to convert the susceptible to socialism. Medicine was abandoned for writing; then two and a half years at the London School of Economics, trying to be a "classy" English journalist. Then home for a stint at *Time* magazine at the height of its "unleash Chiang" mania.

Unlike so many Jewish left-leaning journalists of that period, Kopkind never bought into Jewish nationalism, which means wholehearted support of Pentagon, Christian right, as well as of those legions of anti-Semites who support Israel in order to benefit, if not from Rapture at Armageddon, military procurement. He regarded Israel as any other polity.

After some police trouble in California (he had been caught practicing same-sexuality, which is an abomination not only in the eyes of the Lord but, rather more important, in those glazed mica-like orbs of Henry Luce), Kopkind was obliged to turn "straight" with the aid of a psychiatrist paid for by *Time*. Despite prayers to Freud as well as the numerous ritual dances and dietary observances necessary to achieve that state of heterosexual grace which has made the United States a thigh-slapping joke in the Western world, *he failed to Mature*. At twenty-nine, Kopkind left *Time*.

Time at Berkeley. Some writing for *The New Republic* before it became press office for the Israeli Embassy. Then, early 1965, the march on Selma in Alabama. This was the beginning of the latest but, alas, so far unconcluded phase of the black attempt to achieve parity in a society where whiteness is compulsory if one wants to be a full citizen. Suddenly, there was an eruption of radical political activity—SNCC, SDS—and Kopkind plunged in: "I was still the journalist, but I was part of the movement too. The genie was out of the bottle," and for the next thirty years the genie was on duty.

It is odd to note the change of words over the years; in 1965, Negro starts to change to black. The times really seemed to be changing with Jack Kennedy murdered and Martin Luther King moving, in triumph, to the same slaughterhouse that awaits all agents of change in our imperial history. Kopkind is more kindly than not with such enemies of change as the ADA liberals: "It is hard for liberals, traumatized by both Stalinism and McCarthyism, to understand the new left's attitudes about communism." That is to riot in understatement. The radical activist takes far more fire from the liberal establishment that so loyally upheld the right of the United States to be in Vietnam than ever it will from the likes of George Wallace.

In due course, after the April 17, 1965, March on Washington to End the War in Vietnam, the movement splintered and the war went on for another decade, making it possible for a radical movement to pick up the pieces. But no such movement has ever, thus far, been able to get through to—much less rationalize—our society. As for promoting economic justice . . . that's really un-American. To understand why it is not possible to do anything is the burden of Kopkind's genie-hood. Meanwhile, he hates the absurdities of official rhetoric: "The best that can be said about the domino theory is that it works in reverse. The deeper America's involvement in Vietnam becomes, the less effective is its deterrence value. It is one thing to lose a war with 17,000 advisers and quite another to lose it with 125,000 battle troops" (this was written in 1965); "to win it (whatever that means) with a land army of half a million would be worst of all. That kind of victory is the death of policy, not the foundation of it."

He quotes Carl Oglesby (president of SDS), who "accused the liberals of underpinning the elements of the very system that the New Left attacked: the military and industrial 'corporatism' that keeps . . . the poor alive but powerless and, in the end, still poor."

Plainly, we live under a malign star: thirty years later this analysis still describes our estate.

The genie hovers over the Watts riots and notes the obvious: there is more fire to come. In 1966 he was one of the few who thought that "mini-star" Reagan would beat Pat Brown and become governor of California because Reagan's "philosophical line is an entirely incomprehensible jumble of every myth and cliché in American life." But there are the odd small victories along the downward way: the House Un-American Activities Committee takes a well-earned hit. "The kids" were out in force, mocking the committee. Not only did no one take the Fifth, no one showed anything but contempt of Congress. One youth said, "I will not answer that question on the grounds that it nauseates me and I might vomit all over the table." Times a'changing? Well, they did change, in this instance. No more HUAC.

Kopkind's pieces for the *New Statesman* are brief but elegant. In *The New Republic* he is more thorough but not as lively. In *Ramparts* he now has an unmistakable voice; read a sentence or two and you know who wrote them. For a time, he pins his hopes on Senator Robert Kennedy, but even in *The New York Review of Books* (Bobby-enthralled as of 1967), Kopkind suspects that there is not much substance behind the rhetoric; that he is not an "insurgent," since the official liberal line was that Bobby is in place to "save" the system the way that the New Deal "saved" the system. But Kopkind sees that this wouldn't work even if there was a system worth saving. He has radically grasped the point: top-down reforms are bound to fail. "It is not Kennedy's fault that he can do no other; it is his situation." This is generous. He does not note Kennedy's presumably deep conviction "that we have every moral right to be in Vietnam."

There are crucial moments when Kopkind was not on the spot. The two Kennedy assassinations are not recorded, only referred to. The rise of Nixon happens in the margins of his prose. But he keeps a close eye on those in the ranks (down-top) who are for civil rights and an end to war and to the militarized state. Along the way he makes a disturbing sketch of Allard Lowenstein's politics and death, bringing together Kopkind's two central themes—radicalism of politics (we must go to the *roots* of our distress) and same-sexuality, which tormented Al, or so Kopkind thought. Al's first political campaign was, briefly, for me in 1960. I found him bright but consumed with a sort of ambition that I don't think Andy could have imagined, so alien was it to his own serenely balanced communal nature. Al realized that without a sacrifice of his true nature on the altar of Family, he could not be president or even an influence on one. He was not tortured by *who* he was but by *what* he had to do in order to rise. He married (happily, I am told) but continued to burn; and was burnt, as it were, to death. Also, there is the troubling possibility that overwrought ambition had made him a double agent, or, as Kopkind puts it, "Lowenstein was part of a cultural and ideological nexus that sanctioned covert operations and mounted public movements against radicalism at home and abroad." If so, his radical death was grimly ironic.

May 1968 finds Kopkind in North Vietnam. He is impressed by how well people are coping with enforced decentralization. He captures the differences: "Our questions often made no 'sense' to the Vietnamese because they assumed a context of issues in our own society, not theirs." If only McNamara had had the slightest of clues! He captures the spirit of the Republican convention at Miami Beach (it is here, I think, that we met). "The party found its perfect hero in Barry Goldwater because he expressed the inevitability of human defeat; now its choice of Miami Beach . . . completes the metaphor." He did not share my sudden vision, as the born again and yet again R. M. Nixon lurched forward to accept the nomination, that here was our thirty-seventh President and that we hadn't seen nothing yet. In the fall of that crucial year, Kopkind goes to Cleveland to visit white blue-collar Wallaceland. Again he zeroes in on the real people as opposed to the PR simulacra at Miami Beach. One worker muses aloud: "Humphrey—everything good . . . but he's too easy on race, that's a minus. (Boy, am I making myself out a racist?) Wallace—I only like him 40 percent . . . but the fact that he won, or got a lot of votes, would get people together. So I'm for Wallace. . . . But you know, sometimes I'm not sure why I vote for someone. Does that make sense?" It did to Henry Adams and it does to our current land-slide Republican Congress, elected by only one-third of the elec-torate: Two-thirds thought that it made sense to give up on a system from which they are excluded.

Here comes (and there goes) Gene McCarthy. "Are we in the middle of a revolution?" is the title of one of Andy's pieces from the front. "Those who hold steadfastly to the old values are true conser-vatives; those who only sense the new are worried liberals; those who see the whole pattern very clearly are radicals, and they don't know what to do about it." This is Sartre's *No Exit* Americanized. It was also Sartre who once observed that the bourgeois theater will put up with the most harshly accurate depiction of the human case, as long as there is no hint that a solution might exist. What is, is, and must ever be.

Americans land on the moon and the war goes on. Wood-stock . . . and the war goes on. Judge Julie Hoffman versus Abbie Hoffman *et al.*, at Chicago . . . and the war . . . Weathermen . . . *Sgt. Pepper* . . . Black Panthers murdered by the state. . . . But Andy is tiring now.

At the beginning of 1970 he withdraws to a sort of commune in Vermont. Where "I was taking a lot of acid." He also met John Scagliotti and, as they say, "came out," though I never suspected for a moment that he had ever been in, but then I've always been closet-blind. Andy and John remained together until the end. Happily, Andy did not retire, though, for a time, there was a hiatus "when I stopped writing and I stopped doing politics the same day. I couldn't figure any of this out. I couldn't figure out who I was, and what I was doing this for and this movement that seemed to have gone completely out of control, disappeared into a million crazy bits." Gradually, he started to "do" writing and politics again but in a less urgent style since the disparity between what the United States thinks it is and what it actually is is now too great to be reconciled. One can only chip away at the edges. "I was lucky, too: I learned enough to make myself permanently and constitutionally unable to accept America and its internal and external empires." So, at the end, he was to make not a separate peace with our evil empire but a separate war, the best that any of us can do in what Jack Kennedy used to croon, "this twilight time"—presumably before midnight comes up like thunder over D.C.'s Federal Theme Park.

In Andy's last years, he was much involved with sexual politics—as I write these words I cannot believe just how absurd a country has to be to insist on so categorizing its inmates. Cunnilingus over here . . . buggery to the right . . . frottage on the floor . . . keep moving. Bisexuals, stop it! Right now.

But Andy charges in. Present, as he puts it, "at the creation." "There were millions of homosexuals before Stonewall, of course, but there was no coherent, self-aware gay community." This is more or less true, but one wonders what sort of country needs a "gay community"? Although there are prohibited sexual acts (for everyone) in Catholic Mediterranean countries, no one is shocked or even interested in the fact that the shepherd Silvio likes to bugger young Mario (at least, when the ewes are menstruating) nor does Silvio's pleasure in Arcadia—young Mario's too—prevent either from being good or bad family men, something that the old culture expected them to be but did not fuss about if they decided not to breed. Anglo-Saxon attitudes were—and are—more crazed and punitive: particularly when sex becomes an exercise in control; hence, sexual politics, alas. Hence, some of Andy's best writing as he describes the lunatic bleatings of the Pentagon generals and psychically challenged Congresspersons, most of whom, as kids say nowadays, have "seen Dorothy," and given her a big kiss—in Oz if not Kansas.

The last time Andy rang me, officially—that is, as journalistic quarry—it was for a magazine piece that he was doing on Tim Robbins. Tim had produced and directed and starred in the film *Bob Roberts*, in which I appeared. He had also written the script and the lyrics for the songs and, as I recall, organized the catering for cast and crew. Andy's usual opening was always reassuring. "Don't worry. This interview's absolutely pointless," my favorite kind. "I'm doing this piece for one of these magazines . . . you know, they pay you all this money for stories about Mike Ovitz and they look like those giveaway magazines you get on airlines." We both went on journalistic autopilot. But suddenly, trying to explain what made the youthful Robbins tick, I heard myself say, "I suppose it's just natural *wu-wei*." Andy's voice became alert. "What's that?" I chided him for having read so little Lao Tzu. I then gave an English approximation: "passive achievement." The archer who isn't worried about going for the gold can pick up his bow and hit the bull's-eye easily. If he strains—is jittery—he will miss. "Tim has natural *wu-wei*." And so, I thought, as I hung up, do you. In due course *wu-wei* appeared, for the first and last time, in an airline-type magazine, two shriveled small words between the Gucci and the Lancôme ads.

Although the perhaps mythical sage Lao Tzu meant *wu-wei* as a goal for the individual, he does see its application to the state. In *The Way of Acceptance*, he observes: "The more the people are forbidden to do this and that, the poorer they will be. The more sharp weapons the people possess, the more will darkness and bewilderment spread through the land. The more craft and cunning men have, the more useless and pernicious contraptions will they invent." Even using homely fertilizer. "If I work through Non-action the people will transform themselves." So either Andy Kopkind *wu-wei* or—*Oklahoma OK*!

The Nation
12 June 1995

Shortly after the publication of David McCullough's prizewinning biography *Truman*, an ad hoc committee of concerned historians was formed to ponder how any historian, no matter how amiably "in the grain," could write at such length about so crucial a President and reveal absolutely nothing of his actual politics, whose effects still resonate in the permanent garrison state and economy he bequeathed us. Since this question has many answers, we continue to meet—in secrecy: Tenure is at stake in some cases, while prizes, grants, fellowships, hang in a balance that can go swiftly crashing if any of us dares question openly the image of America the beauteous on its hill, so envied by all that it is subject to attacks by terrorists who cannot bear so much sheer goodness to triumph in a world that belongs to *their* master, the son of morning himself, Satan.

As we discuss in increasing detail the various American history departments, a large portrait of Comer Vann Woodward beams down on us; he is the acknowledged premier conductor of that joyous, glory-bound gravy train. In due course, we plan to give a Vann Woodward Prize to the historian who has shown what biologists term "absolute maze-brightness," that is, the ability to get ahead of the pack to the scrumptious cheese at a complex labyrinth's end. Comer's own Pulitzer Prize (bestowed for his having edited the perhaps questionable diary of Mary Chesnut) was the result of a lifetime of successful maze-threading, which ended with a friend, John Blum, awarding him the prime cheddar for what is hardly history writing in our commitee's strict sense. To be fair, Comer did deserve an honorable mention back in 1955 for *The Strange Career of Jim*

Crow. Our committee tends to agree that prize-giving is largely a racket in which self-serving schoolteachers look after one another. We shall, in due course, address this interesting if ancillary subject.

Meanwhile, we debate whether or not to create a vulgar splash and give an annual prize to the worst American historian of the year. But the first nominations are coming in so thick and fast that none of us really can, in a single life, read all the evidence—and graduate students are forbidden to do our work for us. So we have tentatively abandoned that notion. Instead, we have been surveying current publications, applying our strict standards to the works of an eclectic group that has only one thing in common (badness aside): the public approbation of like-minded toilers in the field.

Our criteria: First, the book must be badly written. Since this is as true, alas, of some of our best historians, we do not dwell too much on aesthetics. Gibbon and Macaulay and Carlyle knew that history was an important aspect of literature and so made literature; but this secret seems to have got lost by the end of the last century. Even our own wise hero, Edmund Wilson, didn't really write all that good himself. Second, the book in question must be composed in perfect bad faith. This is much easier for us to judge than literary value and very satisfying, particularly when one can figure where the writer is, as they say, coming from. Naturally, our own tastes condition our responses. Most of us are not enthusiasts of the National Security State of 1950 *et seq.* And we suspect that the empire, now spinning out of control, was a bad idea. After all, the federal government must borrow heavily every single day to keep it humming along. But anyone who can make a good case for Truman's invention of the National Security State does not necessarily, on the ground of our own political incorrectness, earn a place in the crowded *galère.* Only if he or she denies that there is such a thing as an American empire (an act of bad faith, since that is the line those who endow universities want taken) will inclusion occur.

In the matter of race, the opportunities for bad faith are beyond mere counting. Even so, our committee has just voted *unanimously* that the worst of the books currently in print is *America in Black and White: One Nation, Indivisible, Race in America*, by Stephan Thernstrom and Abigail Thernstrom. The two nervous subtitles betray unease, just as rapid eye-blinking, behaviorists tell us, signifies a liar in full flood. In presenting the Thernstroms' work as the first of a series of bad histories we do not want to create in them a sense of pride or, indeed, of uniqueness. There are many, many others in their league and, from time to time, they too will be revealed in these pages.

The Thernstroms are a husband-and-wife team: He is a Harvard professor, she a self-proclaimed liberal because, she said to me, she wrote once for *The Economist*. The hearty laughter you now hear from across the Atlantic is that of Evelyn Rothschild, that splendid conservative paper's splendidly conservative proprietor.

The Thernstroms are crude writers, but then if they were not, they would not be so honored here. What they have perfected—much appreciated by their natural constituency, the anti-blacks—is what we call the Reverse Angle Shot in the matter of race. In the movies a reverse angle is exactly what it sounds like. You shoot a scene one way; then you switch about and shoot it from the exact opposite point of view. In debate, however, the Thernstrom Reverse Angle is supposed to take the place of the master shot: that is, the wide-angle look at the whole scene. Their argument is simple. Affirmative action for minorities is wrong, particularly in the case of African-Americans, because such action takes it for granted that they are by nature inferior to whites and so require more financial aid (and slacker educational standards) than canny whites or those eerily look-alike, overly numerate Asians. This is inspired. Now the Therns can maintain that the true racist is one who believes in affirmative action, because he is anti-black, while *Economist*-reading Therns believe that blacks can stand on their own two feet alongside the best of whites if only evil liberals, in their condescending racism, would not try to help them out of ghettos of their own feckless making.

To "prove" this, the Thernstroms have come up with a blizzard of statistics in order to make the case that blacks were really getting their act together from 1945 until the Sixties, when affirmative action, welfare, and other liberal deviltries so spoiled them that they took to drugs and murder while, most tragic of all, not living up to "our" SAT norms.

One of the hallmarks of the truly bad historian is not so much the routine manipulation of the stats as the glee with which it is done, sad and sober though he tries to appear, crocodile tear forever clinging to nose-tip. The Therns' Introduction is high comedy. Quotations routinely turn reality upside down. A state court strikes down a blacks-only scholarship program at the University of Maryland: " 'Of all the criteria by which men and women can be judged,' the court intoned, 'the most pernicious is that of race.' " Therefore, special blacks-only scholarships are racist.

But like so many zealots, the Therns cannot control that Strangelovian arm forever going rigid with a life of its own as it rises in salute. A few lines after establishing the overt racism of affirmative action, they up the rhetoric: "What do we owe those who arrived on our shores in 1619 and remained members of an oppressed caste for more than three centuries?" I like that "our shores." After three centuries surely these are African-American shores, too, not to mention the shores of the indigenous Mongol population, which needs quite as much affirmative action these days as do "our" involuntary African visitors. Certainly the Therns themselves are hardly in the "our" business; they did not, as idle gossip has it, hit shore with Leif Ericson. Rather, theirs is the disdain, even rage, of recent arrivals against those who preceded them but did less well. Racism, after all, is a complex matter beyond the competence of a pair of publicists for the shrinking white majority and its institutions, among them the Manhattan Institute, where Abigail is "a senior fellow," as well as the John M. Olin Foundation and the Bradley, Richardson, Earhart, and Carthage generators of light, fueled by corporate money. Joel Pulliam, one of the Therns' undergraduate helots, "worked for us part-time throughout his college career." The Pulliam family are—or were—newspaper proprietors of great malignity. (Our committee is now taking cognizance of these un-American covens and shall, in due course, work to remove their tax exemptions on the ground that they are political activists.)

Now the argument again: Everything was getting better for the blacks until *Brown v. Board of Education*, affirmative action, etc. destroyed their moral fiber. Result: "Today's typical black twelfth-grader scores no better on a reading test than the average white in the eighth grade, and is 5.4 years behind the typical white in science." Our committee is still examining all Thernstrom figures that "prove" blacks have never been better off than now, or were better off before anyone did anything to be of use to them, or aren't really worth bothering with as they are demonstrably inferior. After all, "the proportion of blacks in poverty is still triple that of whites. The unemployment rate for black males is double the white rate, the rate of death from homicide . . ." and so on. Then the horror, the horror: "Blacks from families earning over $70,000 a year have lower average SAT scores than whites from families taking in less than $10,000." So even if they make money (dealing drugs, entertaining, or playing games), they are still awfully dumb. Curiously, no Thern has questioned the value of the SAT score or, indeed, the value of the curriculum that is taught in "our" high schools or available in universities. "G.V." was so bored at one of the country's best prep schools (prewar) that he made no effort to do more than pass dull courses. Could it be that African-American culture might not be satisfied with what passes for education today? Even—or especially, when one considers the Therns' polemics—at Harvard?

For the Therns, the political activism of the Sixties is the wrong road taken. Apparently, "three of four Southern whites . . . were ready to concede that racial integration was bound to come," presumably when the bird of dawning singeth all night long. But Americans rightly deplored "brutal tactics"—i.e., demonstrations. The Therns produce an ancient cold war gloss on the matter of race: "Surveys disclosed a pervasive and bizarre skepticism about whether the civil rights movement reflected the true feelings of typical African-

Americans." As of a 1963 poll, a quarter of the white population suspected the Commies of egging on listless African-Americans. The
FBI bugging of Martin Luther King, Jr., on the suspicion that he
was in with the Commies is justified "in the context of the deadly
struggle between the United States and Soviet totalitarianism." Thus
the Great Red Herring once again makes an obligatory appearance,
in a footnote.

"G.V." must now confess that he met the Therns in 1991. He
had come to Harvard to deliver the Massey lectures, which are sponsored by a small, suitably obscure department known, he recalls, as
"American Civilization," then headed by Professor Thern. "G.V."
met them at a dinner, which was, he now realizes, a day of apotheosis, particularly for Mrs. Thern, an adorable elfin minx. The Los Angeles Police Department had just beaten Rodney King to a pulp and
a video of cops clobbering his fallen figure had been playing on television all day. Abigail was firmly on the side of the police. "Their
work is so dangerous, so unappreciated." Her panegyric to the
LAPD stunned the dinner party. She speculated on Rodney King's
as yet unrevealed crimes and shuddered at the thought of his ebon-
dark associates, lying in wait for pink porker cops. Professor Thern
gave a secret smile as his helpmeet's aria grew more and more rich
and strange.

Now, somewhat sated by numbing stats, the Therns go on attacking
blacks in what they appear to think is a sound and sympathetic way.
They quote angry citizens like the young black man who says, after
King's attackers were let off by a Simi Valley jury, "Is there a conspiracy to allow and condone the destruction of black people?"
Needless to say, there is nothing a Thern likes as much as a conspiracy theory to pooh-pooh. "That these charges have been repeated so often and so vehemently does not make them true. The
issue is complicated." The Therns conclude that blacks are locked up
more often than whites because they commit more crimes, and to
try to help them is useless, as the Sixties proved.

As one reads this curiously insistent racist tract, one begins to sense that there is some sort of demonic spirit on the scene, unacknowledged but ever-present, as the Therns make their endless case. Reading Thern-prose, somewhat more demure than Abby's table-rant, I was put in uneasy mind of kindly old Dr. Maimonides. In Book III, chapter 51 of his *Guide for the Perplexed* (copyright 1190 C.E.), the revered codifier of the Talmud lists those who cannot begin to acknowledge, much less worship, the true God. Among those nonhumans are "some of the Turks [he means Mongols] and the nomads in the North and the Blacks and the nomads in the South, and those who resemble them in our climates. And their nature is like the nature of mute animals, and according to my opinion they are not on the level of human beings, and their level among existing things is below that of a man and above that of a monkey, because they have the image and the resemblance of a man more than a monkey does." When this celebrated book was translated into English early this century, the translators were embarrassed, as well they should have been, by the racism. So instead of using the word "black" or "Negro," they went back to the Hebrew word for blacks—Kushim, which they transliterated as Kushites—a previously unknown and unidentifiable tribe for Anglophones and so easily despised.

There was an eccentric English duke who, according to legend, spoke only once a year. His remarks were treasured. At the time of the abdication of Edward VIII, he suddenly said at a Sunday dinner, "If there is any trouble anywhere, look for an archbishop." Change "archbishop" to "monotheist" and one understands the powerful engine that drives Therns to write bad history. Also, in fairness, it must be noted that Judaism's two dreary spinoffs, Christianity and Islam, have given even wider range to the notion of the true godless folk as "white man's burden," "cursed infidels" and "lesser breeds" so much less human than those whipped up in the true God's bookish image.

Finally, a bad historian is one who dares not say what he means. He must count on his "evidence"—those stats—to bring us round to his often hidden-in-plain-sight point of view. At the conclusion of their screed, the Therns produce such tautologies as "the issue of group differences is actually enormously complicated." This extraordinary insight appears as late as page 541. "The complexities of the matter become evident when we notice that the socioeconomic gap between Jews and Christians today is greater than the gap between blacks and whites. Jewish per capita incomes are nearly double those of non-Jews, a bigger difference than the black-white income gap. Although Jews make up less than 3 percent of the population, they constitute more than a quarter of the people on the *Forbes* magazine list of the richest four hundred Americans. . . . Asian Americans similarly outrank whites on most measures." We are also told that Scots are highly educated but don't make all that much money, because they are drawn to "the ministry and teaching." Cajuns? Forget it. "What explains why some of these groups have done so much better than others is very hard to say." Actually, it is quite easy for a Thern to say, but perhaps a bit dangerous. So at the end of their long book, the matter of race is both a reality and a chimera. In short, *complicated*; yet, to the Therns' credit, we know exactly what they mean.

Perhaps the only literary form perfected by late-twentieth-century United Statespersons is the blurb for the dust jacket. It is for us what the haiku was for the medieval Japanese. Of all the varieties of blurb, the Academic Courtesy is the most exquisite in its balances and reticences and encodements. Now, there was one blurb that the Therns knew that they dare not publish without: that of the chairman of Harvard's Department of Afro-American Studies. Would this elusive, allusive—illusive?—figure misread their text as hoped or, worse for them, would he actually read it for what it is? Great risk either way. One can picture the Therns agonizing over how best to rope him in. He was their White Whale, nay, their Cinque of Sierra Leone. Night after night, Therns and their ilk flitted about Harvard Yard, suitably hooded against the night air. Meanwhile, the beleaguered chairman, quite aware of their plot, was careful to take the Underground Railroad when crossing the Yard. But in the end, he broke. He gathered loved ones around him. "I can no longer live like this, in terror of the Therns. I'm going out." Loved ones keened, "But not *tonight*. The moon's full. *This is Thern weather*."

But the chairman said, "I fear not. My blurb will protect me from all harm." Blurb? Had he perjured himself? No, he had not, he declared; and so, casting aside fear, he entered the Yard, where a posse of howling Therns promptly held him for ransom in the form of what proved to be the very paradigm of all Harvard blurbs: "This book is essential reading for anyone wishing to understand the state of race relations at the end of the great American century." Thus, he tricked his pursuers and freed graduate students as yet unborn from, at the very least, a hoisting by the Thern petard.

The Nation
20 April 1998

★ BLAIR

In 1964 I watched the election returns in a ballroom at London's Savoy Hotel. The room had been taken by Pamela Berry, whose husband owned *The Daily Telegraph*. As one would expect, considering our hostess's powerful political views, the guests were largely Conservative, though the odd transatlantic visitor could stare at the vast screen which, historically, the first British "television" election was filling with faces and numbers. Whenever Labour won a seat, there were boos and hisses. When a Tory prevailed, applause. Then the moment of awful truth: Labour had won and the next Prime Minister would be Harold Wilson. Lives and sacred honor, not to mention fortunes, were now at risk as universal darkness buried all.

Gladwyn Jebb, former ambassador to the United Nations, said to me, "Parish pump politics. Let's go watch the real news." He led me into a side room where, on a small screen, the fall of Khrushchev was being gloated over. Jebb: "Now *this* is the real thing."

A third of a century later I was again in London at the start of the election just concluded. BBC television had hired me to chat about it. Most of the surviving Tories from the Savoy—or their children and grandchildren—were voting for something called New Labor, headed by Tony Blair, while the Conservatives were led by John Major, a Prime Minister who made much of the fact that he was a lower-middle-class Everyman pitted against a posh elitist who had gone to public school. The startling difference between 1964 and 1997 was that where Labour once represented the working classes and poor (today's "disadvantaged"), it is now a home for prosperous suburbanites on the go as well as disaffected Scots and Welsh. In the end, the Tories did not win a single seat in Scotland or Wales, something that has not happened in a century.

The only real issue was, Should the British, if they ever meet the required standards, join a common European currency? But no politician was about to stick his neck out on that one. Another big issue that the local press was fretting over: Are British elections becoming Americanized? Presidentialized? Devoid of relevant content? The answer is, more or less, yes. The tabloids have created a terrible Clintonian atmosphere. "Sleaze" is the principal word one sees in every headline. Since Rupert Murdoch, a devotee of honest government, has abandoned the Tories for New Labour, and as this Australian-turned-American is allowed to own Britain's most popular daily paper (*The Sun*) as well as the weekend *News of the World*, Tory politicians are being wildly smeared as sexual degenerates and crooks.

With a BBC crew I made the rounds of the three parties. Each presented its program to the nation. Liberal Democrat Paddy Ashdown received the press in a small crowded ecclesiastical room. "To make it look like a great crowd," a journalist whispered in my ear. Pamphlets were distributed. Ashdown is blond, athletic-looking; also quick-witted by American standards, but then any public schoolboy in England speaks more articulately than any American politician except for the great Oval One.

Ashdown played the honesty card, something of a novelty. He wants better education for everyone. He admits that this will cost money. The two other parties swear they will never raise taxes, which, of course, they will. . . .

I go to the Royal Albert Hall. Major points out Tony Blair's contradictions and evasions. I suspect a few ancient heads in the audience were at the Savoy that night so many years ago when Harold Wilson won and socialism would level all. (Once in Downing Street, Wilson quickly said that, actually, he had never read Marx.) As the hall filled with the gorgeousness of Elgar, I intoned for the camera: "Land of hope and glory, of Drake and Nelson, of Clive and Crippen."

The fascinating kickoff was Mr. Blair's. We were in an early-nineteenth-century building with a dome, dedicated to engineers. Press milled about in the rotunda downstairs, where stood a tall dark man, Peter Mandelson, reputedly Blair's Rasputin. He gave solemn audience to the journalists of the lobby. Words murmured to one, hand held over his mouth. TV cameras, including ours, avoided. He had the insolent manner of one born to the top rung but three. The mood of the Labourites was paranoid, particularly the handsome blond girls in black suits with curled lips and flashing eyes. Blair's lead was so great in the polls that only a blunder on his part could stop his irresistible rise. So one could not be made. Although the BBC and I had been cleared by the press party office, I suddenly looked like a possible blunder.

We take our seats. Blair enters, followed by what will be much of his Cabinet. He has been told not to smile. The smile has been criticized by the press. Too loopy. Too youthful. He is forty-three, JFK's age in 1960. He is slender with a beaky, mini-Bonaparte sort of nose. The dark hair does not entirely convince. He holds up the party manifesto with his own face, smiling on the cover. I am close enough to him to realize that he does much of his breathing through his mouth. Lips pressed tight together cause his nostrils to flare as he tries to get enough air in. The speech, his program, was written, we have been told—as if it were from the hand of St. John of Patmos—in his own garden in his own longhand. As it turns out, he has no program. But things will be better, he tells us. Afterward, to every question he says simply, "Trust me." He departs

The press, seeing that I'm all that's left in the room, surround me. The blondes try to shoo them away. Question: "Are we becoming more Americanized?" Answer: "Well, you do resemble us in that you now have a single party with two right wings."

Question: "Which wing is more to the right?"

Answer (in my gravest and most reverential voice): "One does not bring a measuring rod to Lilliput."

Then we were all thrown out. Labour complained to the BBC that I had preempted their affair to "slag Blair."

In the next six weeks, Blair makes no errors. He now has a huge majority in the House of Commons. Although he has no plans, I am sure that whatever it was that Mr. Murdoch wanted him to do, he will do. I talked to a Scots MP who knows Blair well. "He's another Thatcher. Authoritarian. Hands-on control freak." I go to my splendid ancient friend and former head of the Labour Party, Michael Foot: "Blair is excellent. Really excellent." I ask, "Whatever happened to socialism?" At this Mrs. Foot looked grim. "Yes," she asked her husband. "What did?" He smiles. "Socialism? Oh, social-ism! Yes! Yes! . . . Well, there's time. . . ." I move on. "The young, even in America," I said, "are reading Gramsci." Foot was delighted. "Good. Good. While you and I are reading Montaigne."

Question I never got answered by anyone: You are an offshore island. But off whose shore? Europe's or ours?

The Nation
26 May 1997

PART III

Duke Ellington on the jukebox: "Missed the Saturday dance, heard they crowded the floor, duh duh duh-duh. . . ." I can almost carry a tune but I can't remember the words to any song, including the inspired lyrics of our national anthem. But this song, and those notes, have been sounding in my head for over half a century, ever since I heard them at a dance hall near the army camp where I was stationed.

Just out of Exeter, I had enlisted in the army at seventeen. That was a year after George Bush, just out of Andover, enlisted in the navy. Most important, my best friend from a Washington, D.C., school enlisted in the Marine Corps. He had been "safe" at Duke: he had a contract to be a professional baseball player when the war was over. But he thought that he should go fight too. He became a scout and observer for the Third Marine Division in the Pacific. He saw action at Guam. He was assigned to "Operation Detachment" and shipped out to Iwo Jima, where the Japanese were entrenched in tunnels beneath that bleak island's surface.

On February 19, 1945, the Marines landed on Iwo Jima, after a long, fairly futile aerial bombardment. The Japanese were out of reach belowground. On D-Day plus nine, elements of the Third Division landed on the already crowded island, eight square miles of volcanic ash and rock. Like the skull of some prehistoric brontosaurus, Mount Suribachi looms over the five-and-a-half-mile-long island. Lately, I have been watching closely each frame of an old newsreel that now seems so long ago that it might as well be a series of Brady stills from Antietam except for the fact that it is still as immediate to me as yesterday, even though I was not there but on another Pacific island, far to the north in the Bering Sea. It took a month to win the island. Twenty thousand Japanese were killed; 6,821 American troops, mostly marines, were killed. On D-Day plus ten, 1 March, 1945, at 4:15 a.m., Pvt. James Trimble was killed instantly by a grenade. He was nineteen years old. Bush and I survived.

It is somehow fitting that our generation—*the* war generation, as we think, perhaps too proudly, of ourselves—should be officially as well as actuarially at an end with the replacement of George Bush by a man who could be his—our—son. I say fitting because our generation, which won in battle the American Empire, is somehow nicely epitomized by the career of Bush, who served with energetic mindlessness the empire, always managing, whenever confronted with a fork in the road of our imperial destiny, to take, as did his predecessors, the wrong turning.

Elsewhere, I have noted that the American Golden Age lasted only five years; from war's end, 1945, to 1950, the Korean War's start. During this interval the arts flourished and those of us who had missed our youth tried to catch up. Meanwhile, back at the White House, unknown to us, the managers of the new world empire were hard at work replacing the republic for which we had fought with a secret national security state, pledged to an eternal war with communism in general and the Soviet Union in particular. It is true that Harry Truman and our other managers feared that if we did not remain on a wartime footing we might drift back into the Great Depression that had not ended until the Japanese attacked us at Pearl Harbor, and everyone went to war or work. It is part of the national myth that the attack was unprovoked. Actually, we had been spoiling for a war with Japan since the beginning of the century. Was the Pacific—indeed Asia—to be theirs or ours? Initially, the Japanese preferred to conquer mainland Asia. But when it looked as if we might deny them access to Southeast Asian oil, they attacked. Had they not, we would never have gone to war, in the Pacific or in Europe.

I was born eight years after the end of the First World War. As I was growing up, it was well remembered that we had got nothing out of that war in Europe except an attack on the Bill of Rights at home and, of course, the noble experiment, Prohibition. Young people often ask me, with wonder, why so many of us *enlisted* in 1943. I tell them that since we had been attacked at Pearl Harbor, we were obliged to defend our country. But I should note that where, in 1917, millions of boys were eager to go fight the Hun, we were not eager. We were fatalistic. In the three years that I spent in the army, I heard no soldier express a patriotic sentiment, rather the reverse when we saw the likes of Errol Flynn on the screen winning freedom's war, or, even worse, John Wayne, known to us by his real name, Marion, the archetypal draft-dodging actor who, to rub it in, impersonated a Flying Tiger in the movies.

Although we were not enthusiastic warriors, there was a true hatred of the enemy. We were convinced that the "Japs" were subhuman; and our atrocities against them pretty much matched theirs against us. I was in the Pacific Theater of Operations, where the war was not only imperial but racial: the white race was fighting the yellow race, and the crown would go to us as we were the earth's supreme race, or so we had been taught. One of the ugliest aspects of that war was the racial stereotyping on both sides. In Europe we were respectful—even fearful—of the Germans. Since blacks and women were pretty much segregated in our military forces, World War II was, for us, literally, the white man's burden.

So while the Golden Age had its moment in the sun up on deck, down in the engine room the management was inventing the "Defense" Department and the National Security Council with its secret, unconstitutional decrees, and the equally unconstitutional CIA, modeled, Allen Dulles remarked blithely, on the Soviets' NKVD. We were then, without public debate, committed to a never-ending war, even though the management knew that the enemy was no match for us, economically or militarily. But, through relentless CIA "disinformation," they managed to convince us that what was weak was strong, and that the Russians were definitely coming. "Build backyard shelters against the coming atomic war!" A generation was well and truly traumatized.

The Korean War put an end to our title as invincible heavy-weight military champion of the world. We might have maintained our mystique by avoiding this eccentric war (we did call it a "police action"), but by then we had so exaggerated the power of the Soviet Union in tandem with China that we could do nothing but reel from one pointless military confrontation to another.

Unfortunately, Kennedy was less cynically practical than those who had presided over what Dean Acheson called "the creation" of the empire. Kennedy actually believed—or pretended to believe—their rhetoric. He liked the phrase "this twilight time." He believed in the domino theory. He believed in "bearing any burden." He invaded Cuba, and failed. He turned his attention to Asia, to "contain China" by interfering in a Vietnamese civil war where a majority had already voted for the communist Ho Chi Minh, who, quoting Jefferson, asked Eisenhower to make Vietnam an American protectorate. But, as Ike explained in his memoirs, this wasn't possible: they were *Communists.*

In June 1961 Kennedy began the fastest buildup militarily since Pearl Harbor; he also rearmed Germany, setting off alarm bells in the Soviet Union. They spoke of denying us land access to our section of Berlin. Kennedy responded with a warlike speech, invoking "the Berlin crisis" as a world crisis. In response, Khrushchev built the wall. It was as if we were, somehow, willing a war to turn sad twilight to incandescent nuclear high noon.

The missile crisis in Cuba was the next move, with us as the provocateurs. Then, with the Vietnam War, we not only took the wrong road, we went straight around the bend, fighting the longest war in our history in a region where we had no strategic interest unless we were to openly declare what the management, then and now, does truly believe: the United States is the master of the earth and anyone who defies us will be napalmed or blockaded or covertly overthrown. We are beyond law, which is not unusual for an empire; unfortunately, we are also beyond common sense.

The only subject, other than the deficit, that should have been discussed in the late election was the military budget. Neither Bush nor Clinton came anywhere close. Eventually, we shall be unable to borrow enough money to preen ourselves in ever weaker countries, but until then, thanks to the many suicidal moves made by that imperial generation forged in the Second World War, our country is now not so much divided as in pieces.

The latest managerial wit has been to encourage—by deploring—something called "political correctness," this decade's Silly Putty or Hula Hoop. Could anything be better calculated to divert everyone from what the management is up to in recently appropriating, say, $3.8 billion for SDI than to pit sex against sex, race against race, religion against religion? With everyone in arms against everyone else, no one will have the time to take arms against the ruinously expensive empire that Mr. Clinton and the unattractively named baby boomers have inherited. I wish them luck.

There are those who sentimentalize the Second World War. I don't. There can be no "good war." We set out to stop Germany and Japan from becoming hemispheric powers. Now, of course, they are economic world powers while we, with our $4 trillion of debt, look to be joining Argentina and Brazil on the outer edge. All in all, the famed good, great war that gave us the empire that we then proceeded to make a mess of was hardly worth the death of one Pvt. James Trimble USMCR, much less the death of millions of others.

I have just listened to the original Duke Ellington record. Here are those lyrics that I always forget.

"Missed the Saturday dance, heard they crowded the floor, couldn't bear it without you, don' get around much anymore." All in all, it's a good thing for the world that with Bush's departure *we* don't get around much anymore. Somalia-Bosnia could be the last of our hurrahs, produced by CNN and, so far, sponsorless. Maybe now, without us, Clinton's generation will make it to the Saturday dance that we missed. And let's hope that the floor won't prove to be too crowded with rivals in trade if not in love, death.

*It is wonderful indeed, ladies and gentlemen, to have all of you here between covers, as it were—here being the place old John Bunyan called "Vanity Fair, because the town where 'tis kept, is lighter than vanity." But these days the town is not so much London or New York as the global village itself, wherein you are this month's movers and shakers, as well as moved and shaken (I feel your pain, Yasser). In a number of ways I find it highly fitting that we meet on the old fairground as twentieth century and Second Christian Millennium are saying goodbye. Personally, I thought they'd never go without taking us with them. There are, of course, 791 days still to go. I also note that the photographers have immortalized a number of smiles. Joy? Or are those anthropologists right who say that the human baring of teeth signals aggression? Let's hope not before 2001 C.E.

Of course, centuries and millennia are just arbitrary markings, like bookkeeping at Paramount Pictures. But, symbolically, they mean a lot to those who are interested in why we are today what we are and doing what we are doing. This goes particularly for those movers and shakers who have spent a lot of this year in meetings, courtesy of the one indisposable—or did President Clinton say indispensable?—nation on earth and last self-styled global power, loaded down with nukes, bases, debts.

Denver and Madrid were two fairgrounds. Nothing much is ever accomplished when the managing world director calls in his

---

* The *Vanity Fair* issue of December 1999 featured photographs of all the leaders as well as this text.

regional directors for fun and frolic. But when Clinton chose a cow-
boy theme at Denver, with boots for all, some regional directors actually dared whine. But they are easily replaced and know it. Later
the Seven Leading Economic Powers (plus Russia) decided, at
Madrid, to extend the North American Atlantic Organization to include Poland, Czechland, Hungary. Jacques Chirac, the French director of the . . . well, let's be candid: American empire . . . wanted
several more Eastern countries to join, while the Russian director
wanted *no* Eastern extension of a military alliance that he still thinks,
mistakenly, was formed to protect Eastern Europe from the power-
mad Soviet Union. Actually, as we shall see, NATO was created so
that the United States could dominate *Western* Europe militarily, politically, and economically; any current extension means that more
nations and territories will come under American control while giving pleasure to such hyphenate American voters as Poles, Czechs,
Hungarians. The French director was heard to use the word *merde*
when the American emperor said that only three new countries are
to be allowed in this time. The Frenchman was ignored, but then he
had lost an election back home. In any case, the North Atlantic confederation of United States–Canada plus Western Europe can now
be called the North Atlantic Baltic Danubian Organization, to
which the Black Sea will no doubt soon be added.

I see that some of you are stirring impatiently. The United States is
an empire? The emperor's advisers chuckle at the notion. Are we not
a freedom-loving perfect democracy eager to exhibit our state-of-
the-art economy to old Europe as a model of what you can do in the
way of making money for the few by eliminating labor unions and
such decadent frills as public health and education? At Denver a
French spearcarrier—always those pesky French—wondered just
how reliable our unemployment figures were when one-tenth of the
male workforce is not counted, as they are either in prison or on probation or parole. The Canadian prime minister, even more tiresome
than the French, was heard to say to his Belgian counterpart (over
an open mike) that if the leaders of any other country took corpo-

rate money as openly as American leaders do, "we'd be in jail." Plainly, the natives are restive. But we are still in charge of the Vanity Fair.

I bring up all this not to be unkind. Rather, I should like to point out that those who live too long with unquestioned contradictions are not apt to be able to deal with reality when it eventually befalls them. I have lived through nearly three-quarters of this century. I enlisted in the army of the United States at seventeen; went to the Pacific; did nothing useful—I was just there, as Nixon used to say, WHEN THE BOMBS WERE FALLING. But, actually, the bombs were not really falling on either of us: he was a naval officer making a fortune playing poker, while I was an army first mate writing a novel.

Now, suddenly, it's 1997, and we are "celebrating" the fiftieth anniversary of the Truman Doctrine and the Marshall Plan. Also, more ominously, July 26 was the fiftieth anniversary of the National Security Act that, without national debate but very quiet bipartisan congressional support, replaced the old American Republic with a National Security State very much in the global-empire business, which explains . . .

But, first, into the Time Machine.

It is the Ides of August 1945. Germany and Japan have surrendered, and some 13 million Americans are headed home to enjoy—well, being alive was always the bottom line. Home turns out to be a sort of fairground where fireworks go off and the band plays "Don't Sit Under the Apple Tree," and an endlessly enticing fun house flings open its doors and we file through. We enjoy halls of mirrors where everyone is comically distorted, ride through all the various tunnels of love, and take scary tours of horror chambers where skeletons and cobwebs and bats brush past us until, suitably chilled and thrilled, we are ready for the exit and everyday life, but, to the consternation of some—and the apparent indifference of the rest—we were never allowed to leave the fun house entirely: it had become a part of our world, as were the goblins sitting under that apple tree.

Officially, the United States was at peace; much of Europe and most of Japan were in ruins, often literally, certainly economically. We alone had all our cities and a sort of booming economy—"sort of" because it depended on war production, and there was, as far as anyone could tell, no war in the offing. But the arts briefly flourished. *The Glass Menagerie* was staged, Copland's *Appalachian Spring* was played. A film called *The Lost Weekend*—not a bad title for what we had gone through—won an Academy Award, and the as yet unexiled Richard Wright published a much-admired novel, *Black Boy*, while Edmund Wilson's novel *Memoirs of Hecate County* was banned for obscenity in parts of the country. Quaintly, each city had at least three or four daily newspapers in those days, while New York, as befitted *the* world city, had seventeen newspapers. But a novelty, television, had begun to appear in household after household, its cold gray distorting eye relentlessly projecting a fun-house view of the world.

Those who followed the—ugly new-minted word—media began to note that while watching even Milton Berle we kept fading in and out of the Chamber of Horrors. Subliminal skeletons would suddenly flash onto the TV screen; our ally in the recent war "Uncle Joe Stalin," as the accidental president Harry S Truman had called him, was growing horns and fangs that dripped blood. On earth, we were the only great unruined power with atomic weapons; yet we were now—somehow—at terrible risk. Why? How?

The trouble appeared to be over Germany, which, on February 11, 1945, had been split at the Yalta summit meeting into four zones: American, Soviet, British, French. As the Russians had done the most fighting and suffered the greatest losses, it was agreed that they should have an early crack at reparations from Germany—to the extent of $20 billion. At a later Potsdam meeting the new president Truman, with Stalin and Churchill, reconfirmed Yalta and opted for the unification of Germany under the four victorious powers. But something had happened between the euphoria of Yalta and the edginess of Potsdam. As the meeting progressed, the atom bomb was tried out successfully in a New Mexico desert. We were now able to incinerate Japan—or the Soviet, for that matter—and so we no longer needed Russian help to defeat Japan. We started to renege on our agreements with Stalin, particularly reparations from Germany. We also quietly shelved the notion, agreed upon at Yalta, of a united Germany under four-power control. Our aim now was to unite the three Western zones of Germany and integrate them into *our* Western Europe, restoring, in the process, the German economy—hence, fewer reparations. Then, as of May 1946, we began to rearm Germany. Stalin went ape at this betrayal. The Cold War was on.

At home, the media were beginning to prepare the attentive few for Disappointment. Suddenly, we were faced with the highest personal income taxes in American history to pay for more and more weapons, among them the world-killer hydrogen bomb—all because *the Russians were coming*. No one knew quite why they were coming or with what. Weren't they still burying 20 million dead? Official explanations for all this made little sense, but then, as Truman's secretary of state, Dean Acheson, merrily observed, "In the State Department we used to discuss how much time that mythical 'average American citizen' put in each day listening, reading, and arguing about the world outside his own country. . . . It seemed to us that ten minutes a day would be a high average." So why bore the people? Secret "bipartisan" government is best for what, after all, is—or should be—a society of docile workers, enthusiastic consumers, obedient soldiers who will believe just about anything for at least ten minutes. The National Security State, the NATO alliance, the forty-year Cold War were all created without the consent, much less advice, of the American people. Of course, there were elections during this crucial time, but Truman-Dewey, Eisenhower-Stevenson, Kennedy-Nixon were of a single mind as to the desirability of inventing, first, a many-tentacled enemy, Communism, the star of the Chamber of Horrors; then, to combat so much evil, installing a permanent wartime state at home with loyalty oaths, a national "peacetime" draft, and secret police to keep watch over homegrown "traitors," as the few enemies of the National Security State were known. Then followed forty years of mindless wars which created a debt of $5 trillion that hugely benefited aerospace and firms like General Electric, whose longtime TV pitchman was Ronald Reagan, eventually retired to the White House.

Why go into all this now? Have we not done marvelously well as the United States of Amnesia? Our economy is the envy of the earth, the president proclaimed at Denver. No inflation. Jobs for all except the 3 percent of the population in prison and the 5 percent who no longer look for work and so are not counted, bringing our actual unemployment close to the glum European average of 11 percent. And all of this accomplished without ever once succumbing to the sick socialism of Europe. We have no health service or proper public education or, indeed, much of anything for the residents of the fun house. But there are lots of ill-paid work-hours for husband and wife with no care for the children while parents are away from home. Fortunately, Congress is now preparing legislation so that adult prisons can take in delinquent fourteen-year-olds. They, at least, will be taken care of, while, economically, it is only a matter of time before the great globe itself is green-spanned.

Certainly European bankers envy us our powerless labor unions (only 14 percent of the lucky funsters are privileged to belong to a labor union) and our industries—lean, mean, downsized, with no particular place for the redundant to go except into the hell of sizzle and fry and burn. Today we give orders to other countries. We tell them with whom to trade and to which of our courts they must show up for indictment should they disobey us. Meanwhile, FBI agents range the world looking for drug fiends and peddlers while the unconstitutional CIA (they don't submit their accounts to Congress as the Constitution requires) chases "terrorists" now that their onetime colleagues and sometime paymasters in the Russian KGB have gone out of business.

We have arrived at what Tennessee Williams once called A Moon of Pause. When I asked him what on earth the phrase meant, as spoken by an actress in one of his plays, "It is," he said loftily, "the actual Greek translation of menopause." I said that the word "moon" did not come from *menses* (Latin, not Greek, for "month"). "Then what," he asked suspiciously, "is the Latin for moon?" When I told him it was *luna* and what fun he might have with the word "lunatic," he sighed and cut. But at the time of the Madrid conference about the extension of NATO, a moon of pause seemed a nice dotty phrase for the change of life that our empire is now going through, with no enemy and no discernible function.

While we were at our busiest in the fun house, no one ever told us what the North Atlantic Treaty Alliance was really about. March 17, 1948, the Treaty of Brussels called for a military alliance of Britain, France, Benelux to be joined by the U.S. and Canada on March 23. The impetus behind NATO was the United States, whose principal foreign policy, since the administration of George Washington, was to avoid what Alexander Hamilton called "entangling alliances." Now, as the Russians were supposed to be coming, we replaced the old republic with the newborn National Security State and set up shop as the major *European* power west of the Elbe. We were now hell-bent on the permanent division of Germany between our western zone (plus the French and British zones) and the Soviet zone to the east. Serenely, we broke every agreement that we had made with our former ally, now horrendous Communist enemy. For those interested in the details, Carolyn Eisenberg's *Drawing the Line (The American Decision to Divide Germany 1944–49)* is a masterful survey of an empire—sometimes blindly, sometimes brilliantly—assembling itself by turning first its allies and then its enemies like Germany, Italy, Japan into client states, permanently subject to our military and economic diktat.

Although the Soviets still wanted to live by our original agreements at Yalta and even Potsdam, we had decided, unilaterally, to restore the German economy in order to enfold a rearmed Germany into Western Europe, thus isolating the Soviet, a nation which had not recovered from the Second World War and had no nuclear weapons. It was Acheson—again—who elegantly explained all the lies that he was obliged to tell Congress and the ten-minute-attention-spanned average American: "If we did make our points clearer than truth, we did not differ from most other educators and could hardly do otherwise. . . . Qualification must give way to simplicity of statement, nicety and nuance to bluntness, almost brutality, in carrying home a point." Thus were two generations of Americans treated by their overlords until, in the end, at the word "Communism," there is an orgasmic Pavlovian reflex just as the brain goes dead.

In regard to the "enemy," Ambassador Walter Bedell Smith—a former general with powerful simple views—wrote to his old boss General Eisenhower from Moscow in December 1947 apropos a conference to regularize European matters: "The difficulty under which we labor is that in spite of our announced position we really do not want nor intend to accept German unification in any terms the Russians might agree to, even though they seemed to meet most of our requirements." Hence, Stalin's frustration that led to the famous blockade of the Allied section of Berlin, overcome by General Lucius Clay's successful airlift. As Eisenberg writes, "With the inception of the Berlin blockade, President Truman articulated a simple story that featured the Russians, trampling the wartime agreements in their ruthless grab for the former German capital. The president did not explain that the United States had abandoned Yalta and Potsdam, that it was pushing the formation of a West German state against the misgivings of many Europeans, and that the Soviets had launched the blockade to prevent partition." This was fun-house politics at its most tragicomical.

The president, like a distorting mirror, reversed the truth. But then he was never on top of the German situation as opposed to the coming election (November 1948), an election of compelling personal interest to him but, in the great scheme of things, to no one else. He did realize that the few Americans who could identify George Washington might object to our NATO alliance, and so his secretary of state, Acheson, was told to wait until February 1949, *after* the election, to present to Congress our changeover from a

Western Hemisphere republic to an imperial European polity, symmetrically balanced by our Asian empire, centered on occupied Japan and, in due course, its tigerish pendant, the ASEAN alliance.

The case for an American world empire was never properly argued, since the debate—what little there was—centered on the alleged desire of the Soviet Union to conquer the whole world, just as Hitler and the Nazis were trying to do until stopped, in 1945, by the Soviet Union with (what Stalin regarded as suspiciously belated) aid from the U.S.

On March 12, 1947, Truman addressed Congress to proclaim what would be known as the Truman Doctrine, in which he targeted our ally of two years earlier as the enemy. The subject at hand was a civil war in Greece, supposedly directed by the Soviet. We could not tolerate this as, suddenly, "the policy of the United States [is] to support free peoples who are resisting attempted subjugation by armed minorities or by outside pressure." Thus, Truman made the entire world the specific business of the United States. Although the Greek insurgents were getting some help from Bulgaria and Yugoslavia, the Soviet stayed out. They still hoped that the British, whose business Greece had been, would keep order. But as Britain had neither the resources nor the will, she called on the U.S. to step in. Behind the usual closed doors, Acheson was stirring up Congress with Iago-like intensity: Russian pressure of some sort "had brought the Balkans to the point where a highly possible Soviet breakthrough might open three continents to Soviet penetration." Senators gasped; grew pale; wondered how to get more "defense" contracts into their states.

Of the major politicians, only former vice president Henry Wallace dared answer Truman's "clearer than truth" version of history: "Yesterday March 12, 1947, marked a turning point in American history, [for] it is not a Greek crisis that we face, it is an American crisis. Yesterday, President Truman . . . proposed, in effect, that America police Russia's every border. There is no regime too reactionary for us provided it stands in Russia's expansionist path. There is no country too remote to serve as the scene of a contest which may widen until it becomes a world war."

Nine days after Truman declared war on Communism, he installed a federal loyalty-oath program. All government employees must now swear allegiance to the new order. Wallace struck again: "The President's executive order creates a master index of public servants. From the janitor in the village post office to the Cabinet members, they are to be sifted, and tested and watched and appraised."

Truman was nervously aware that many regarded Wallace as true heir to Roosevelt's New Deal; Wallace was also likely to enter the presidential race of 1948. Truman now left truth behind in the dust. "The attempt of Lenin, Trotsky, Stalin, et al. to fool the world and the American Crackpots Association, represented by Jos. Davies, Henry Wallace, Claude Pepper, and the actors and artists in immoral Greenwich Village, is just like Hitler's and Mussolini's so-called socialist states." Give 'em hell, Harry.

In the wake of Truman's cuckoo-like emergence from the old-fashioned closet of the original American Republic, a new American state was being born in order to save the nation and the great globe itself from Communism. The nature of this militarized state was, from the beginning, beyond rational debate. Characteristically, Truman and Acheson insisted on closed hearings of the Senate Committee on Foreign Relations. These matters were too important to share with the people whose spare ten minutes was now more and more filling up with television. The committee's Republican leader, Arthur H. Vandenberg, the great goose of Grand Rapids, Michigan, was thrilled to be taken into the confidence of the creators of the new empire, but he did suggest that, practically speaking, if hell wasn't scared out of the American people, Congress would have a hard time raising the revenues to pay for a military buildup in what was still thought to be, inside the ever more isolated fun house, peacetime. The media spoke with a single voice. Time Inc. publisher Henry Luce said it loudest: "God had founded America as a global beacon of freedom." Dissenters, like Wallace, were labeled Communists and ceased to engage meaningfully in public life or, by 1950, even in debate. Like the voice of a ghost, an ancestral voice, he spoke on May 21, 1947: "Today in blind fear of communism, we are turning aside from the United Nations. We are approaching a century of fear." Thus far, he is proved to be half right.

On July 26, 1947, Congress enacted the National Security Act, which created the National Security Council, still going strong, and the Central Intelligence Agency, still apparently going over a cliff as the result of decades of bad intelligence, not to mention all those cheery traitors for whom the country club at Langley, Virginia, was once an impenetrable cover. Years later, a sadder, if not wiser, Truman told his biographer, Merle Miller, that the CIA had become a dangerous mess and ought not to have been set up as it was. But in 1947 the CIA's principal role in Europe was not to counter Soviet activities but to control the politics of NATO members. French and Italian trade unions and publications were subsidized, and a great deal of secret money was poured into Italy to ensure the victory of the Christian Democratic Party in the elections of April 1948.

Acheson, in *Present at the Creation*, a memoir that compensates in elegance what it lacks in candor, alludes delicately to National Security Council document 68 (the 1950 blueprint for our war against Communism). But in 1969, when he was writing, he sadly notes that the memo is still classified. Only in 1975 was it to be declassified. There are seven points. First, never negotiate with the Soviet Union. No wonder the rebuffed Stalin, ever touchy, kept reacting brutally in Mitteleuropa. Second, develop the hydrogen bomb so that when the Russians go atomic we will still be ahead of them. Third, rapidly build up conventional forces. Fourth, to pay for this, levy huge personal income taxes—as high as 90 percent. Fifth, mobilize everyone in the war against internal Communism through propaganda, loyalty oaths, and spy networks like the FBI, whose secret agent Ronald Reagan, president of the Screen Actors Guild, had come into his splendid own, fingering better actors. Sixth, set up a strong alliance system, directed by the United States–NATO. Seventh, make the people of Russia, through propaganda and CIA derring-do, our allies against their government, thus legitimizing, with this highly vague task, our numerous unaccountable secret agents.

So, after five years in the fun house, we partially emerged in January 1950, to find ourselves in a new sort of country. We were also, astonishingly, again at war: this time in Korea. But as Truman-Acheson were nervous about asking Congress for a declaration, the war was called a United Nations police action; and messily lost. Acheson did prepare a memo assuring Truman that, hitherto, eighty-seven presidential military adventures had been undertaken without a congressional declaration of war as required by the old Constitution. Since 1950 the United States has fought perhaps a hundred overt and covert wars. None was declared by the nominal representatives of the American People in Congress Assembled; they had meekly turned over to the executive their principal great power, to wage war. That was the end of that Constitution.

As it will take at least a decade for us to reinvent China as a new evil empire, the moon is in a state of pause over the old fairground. We are entering a phase undreamed of by those "present at the creation" of the empire. Although many still reflexively object to the word "empire," we have military bases in every continent, as well as ten aboard the aircraft carrier called the United Kingdom. For fifty years we have supported too many tyrants, overthrown too many democratic governments, wasted too much of our own money in other people's civil wars to pretend that we're just helping out all those poor little folks all round the world who love freedom and democracy just like we do. When the Russians stabbed us in the back by folding their empire in 1991, we were left with many misconceptions about ourselves and, rather worse, about the rest of the world.

The literature on what we did and why since 1945 is both copious and thin. There are some first-rate biographies of the various players. If one goes digging, there are interesting monographs like Walter LaFeber's "NATO and the Korean War: A Context." But the link between universities and imperial Washington has always been a strong one as Kissingers dart back and forth between classroom to high office to even higher, lucrative eminence, as lobbyists for foreign powers, often hostile to our interests. Now, with Carolyn Eisenberg's *Drawing the Line*, there is a step-by-step description of the years 1944–49, when we restored, rearmed, and reintegrated *our* German province into *our* Western Europe. For those who feel that Eisenberg dwells too much on American confusions and mendacities, there is always the elegant Robert H. Ferrell on "The Formation of the Alliance, 1948–1949." A court historian, as apologists for empire are known, Ferrell does his best with Harry Truman, reminding us of all the maniacs around him who wanted atomic war at the time of Korea, among them the first secretary of defense, the paranoid James Forrestal, who, while reading Sophocles' *Ajax* in hospital, suddenly defenestrated himself, a form of resignation that has never really caught on as it should.

At one point, Ferrell notes that Truman actually gave thought to the sufferings of women and children should we go nuclear in Korea. As for Truman's original decision to use two atomic bombs on Japan, most now agree that a single demonstration would have been quite enough to cause a Japanese surrender while making an attractive crater lake out of what had been Mount Fujiyama's peak. But Truman was in a bit of a daze at the time, as were the 13 million of us under arms who loudly applauded his abrupt ending of the first out-and-out race war, where the Japanese had taken to castrating Marines, alive as well as dead, while Marines, good brand-name-conscious Americans, would stick Coca-Cola bottles up living Japanese soldiers and then break them off. Welcome to some *pre*-fun house memories still vivid to ancient survivors. The story that Lieutenant R. M. Nixon tried to persuade the Marines to use Pepsi-Cola bottles has never been verified.

The climate of intimidation that began with the loyalty oath of 1947 remains with us even though two American generations have been born with no particular knowledge of what the weather was like before the great freeze and the dramatic change in our form of government. No thorough history of what actually happened to us and to the world 1945–97 has yet appeared. There are interesting glances at this or that detail. There are also far too many silly hagiographies of gallant little guy Truman and superstatesman George Marshall, who did admit to Acheson that he had no idea what on earth the plan in his name was really about. But aside from all the American and foreign dead from Korea to Vietnam, from Guatemala to the Persian Gulf, the destruction of our old republic's institutions has been the great hurt. Congress has surrendered to the executive not only the first of its great powers, but the second, the power of the purse, looks to be up for grabs as Congress is forcing more money on the Pentagon than even that black hole has asked for, obliging the executive to spend many hot hours in the vast kitchen where the books are forever being cooked in bright-red ink. As for our Ouija-board Supreme Court, it would be nice if they would take time off from holding séances with the long-dead founders, whose original intent so puzzles them, and actually examine what the founders wrought, the Constitution itself and the Bill of Rights.

Did anyone speak out during the half-century that got us $5 trillion into debt while reducing the median household income by 7 percent when . . . No. Sorry. Too boring. Or, as Edward S. Herman writes, "Paul Krugman admits, in *Age of Diminished Expectations*, that the worsening of the income distribution was 'the central fact about economic life in America in the 1980s,' but as an issue 'it has basically exhausted the patience of the American public' "—the ten-minute attention span, unlike the green-span, has snapped on that one—"and 'no policy change now under discussion seems likely to narrow the gap significantly.' "

It was *The New Yorker*'s literary and social critic Edmund Wilson who first sounded the alarm. In 1963 he published *The Cold War and the Income Tax*. Stupidly, he admits, he filed no income-tax returns between 1946 and 1955. As I've noted, one of the great events of our first year in the fun house was the publication in 1946 of Wilson's novel *Memoirs of Hecate County*. Wilson's income—never much—doubled. Then a system of justice, forever alert to sexual indecency, suppressed his book by court order. He was now broke with an expensively tangled marital life. Wilson describes being hounded by agents of the IRS; he also goes into the background of the federal income tax, which dates, as we know it, from 1913. Wilson also notes that, as of the 1960s, we were paying more taxes than we did during the Second World War. Since NSC-68 would remain a secret for another twelve years, he had no way of knowing that punitive income taxes must be borne by the American people in order to build up both nuclear and conventional forces to "protect" ourselves from a Second World country of, as yet, no danger to anyone except weak neighbors along its borders.

In my review of Wilson's polemic (*Book Week*, November 3, 1963) I wrote: "In public services, we lag behind all the industrialized nations of the West, preferring that the public money go not to the people but to big business. The result is a unique society in which we have free enterprise for the poor and socialism for the rich."

It should be noted—but seldom is—that the Depression did not end with the New Deal of 1933–40. In fact, it flared up again, worse than ever, in 1939 and 1940. Then, when FDR spent some $20 billion on defense (1941), the Depression was over and Lord Keynes was a hero. This relatively small injection of public money into the system reduced unemployment to 8 percent and, not unnaturally, impressed the country's postwar managers: if you want to avoid depression, spend money on war. No one told them that the same money spent on the country's infrastructure would have saved us debt, grief, blood.

What now seems to us as Wilson's rather dizzy otherworldly approach to paying taxes is, in the context of his lifetime, reasonable. In 1939, only four million tax returns were filed: less than 10 percent of the workforce. According to Richard Polenberg, "By the summer of 1943, nearly all Americans paid taxes out of their weekly earnings, and most were current in their payments. . . . [And thus] a foundation for the modern tax structure had been erected." Then some unsung genius thought up the withholding tax, and all the folks were well and truly locked in. Wilson knew none of this. But he had figured out the causal link between income tax and cold war.

The truth is that the people of the United States are at the present time dominated and driven by two kinds of officially propagated fear: fear of the Soviet Union and fear of the income tax. These two terrors have been adjusted so as to complement one another and thus to keep the citizen of our free society under the strain of a double pressure from which he finds himself unable to escape—like the man in the old Western story, who, chased into a narrow ravine by a buffalo, is confronted with a grizzly bear. If we fail to accept the tax, the Russian buffalo will butt and trample us, and if we try to defy the tax, the federal bear will crush us.

At the time the original North American Treaty Organization was created, only the Augustus *manqué* de Gaulle got the point to what we were doing; he took France out of our Cosa Nostra and developed his own atomic bomb. But France was still very much linked to the imperium. Through the CIA and other secret forces, political control was exerted within the empire, not only driving the British Labour prime minister Harold Wilson around a bend too far but preventing Italy from ever having a cohesive government by not allowing the "historic compromise"—a government of Christian Democrats and Communists—to take place. The Soviet, always reactive, promptly cracked down on their client states Czechoslovakia, Hungary, East Germany; and a wall went up in Berlin, to spite their face. From 1950 to 1990, Europe was dangerously divided; and armed to the teeth. But as American producers of weapons were never richer, all was well with their world.

At Yalta, Roosevelt wanted to break up the European colonial empires, particularly that of the French. Of Indochina he said, "France has milked it for a hundred years." For the time being, he proposed a UN trusteeship. Then he died. Unlike Roosevelt, Truman was not a philatelist. Had he been a stamp collector, he might have known where the various countries in the world were and who lived in them.

But like every good American, Truman knew he hated Communism. He also hated socialism, which may or may not have been the same thing. No one seemed quite sure. Yet as early as the American election of 1848, socialism—imported by comical German immigrants with noses always in books—was an ominous specter, calculated to derange a raw capitalist society with labor unions, health care, and other Devil's work still being fiercely resisted a century and a half later. In 1946, when Ho Chi Minh asked the United States to take Indochina under its wing, Truman said, No way. You're some kind of Fu Manchu Communist—the worst. In August 1945, Truman told de Gaulle that the French could return to Indochina: we were no longer FDR anti-imperialists. As Ho had his northern republic, the French installed Bao Dai in the South. February 1, 1950, the State Department reported, "The choice confronting the United States is to support the French in Indochina or face the extension of Communism over the remainder of the continental area of Southeast Asia and, possibly, further westward." Thus, without shepherds or even a napalm star, the domino theory was born in a humble State Department manger. On May 8, 1950, Acheson recommended economic and military aid to the French in Vietnam. By 1955, the U.S. was paying 40 percent of the French cost of war. For a quarter-century, the United States was to fight in Vietnam because our ignorant leaders and their sharp-eyed financiers never realized that the game, at best, is always chess and never dominoes.

But nothing ever stays the same. During the last days of the waning moon, a haphazard Western European economic union was cobbled together; then, as the Soviet abruptly let go its empire, the two Germanys that we had so painstakingly kept apart reunited. Washington was suddenly adrift, and in the sky the moon of empire paused. Neither Reagan nor Bush had much knowledge of history or geography. Nevertheless, orders still kept coming from the White House. But they were less and less heeded because everyone knows that the Oval One has a bank overdraft of $5 trillion and he can no longer give presents to good clients or wage war without first passing the hat to the Germans and Japanese, as he was obliged to do when it came time to sponsor CNN's light show in the Persian Gulf. Gradually, it is now becoming evident to even the most distracted funster that there is no longer any need for NATO, because there is no enemy. One might say there never really was one when NATO was started, but, over the years, we did succeed in creating a pretty dangerous Soviet, a fun-house-mirror version of ourselves. Although the United States may yet, in support of Israel, declare war on one billion Muslims, the Europeans will stay out. They recall 1529, when the Turks besieged Vienna not as obliging guest workers but as world conquerors. Never again.

In the wake of the Madrid NATO summit, it is time for the United States to step away from Europe—gracefully. Certainly the Europeans think it is time for us to go, as their disdainful remarks at Denver betrayed, particularly when they were warned not to walk more than a block or two from their hotels for fear of being robbed, maimed, murdered. Yet why do we persist in holding on to empire? *Cherchez la monnaie*, as the clever French say. Ever since 1941, when Roosevelt got us out of the Depression by pumping federal money into rearming, war or the threat of war has been the principal engine to our society. Now the war is over. Or is it? Can we *afford* to give up our—well, cozy unremitting war? Why not—ah, the brilliance, the simplicity!—instead of shrinking, *expand* our phantom empire in Europe by popping everyone into NATO? No reason to have any particular enemy, though, who knows, if sufficiently goaded, Russia might again be persuaded to play Great Satan in our somewhat dusty chamber of horrors.

With an expanded NATO, our armsmakers—if not workers— are in for a bonanza. As it is, our sales of weapons were up 23 percent last year, to $11.3 billion in orders; meanwhile, restrictions on sales to Latin America are now being lifted. Chile, ever menaced by Ecuador, may soon buy as many as twenty-four American-made F-16 jet fighters. But an expanded NATO is the beauty part. Upon joining NATO, the lucky new club member is obliged to buy expensive weapons from the likes of Lockheed Martin, recently merged with Northrop Grumman. Since the new members have precarious economies—and the old ones are not exactly booming—the American taxpayer, a wan goose that lays few eggs, will have to borrow ever more money to foot the bill, which the Congressional Budget Office says should come to $125 billion over fifteen years with the U.S. paying $19 billion. Yeltsin correctly sees this as a hostile move against Russia, not to mention an expensive renewal of the Cold War, while our very own Delphic oracle, the ancient Janus-like mandarin George Kennan, has said that such an expansion could "inflame nationalistic anti-Western and militaristic tendencies in Russian opinion."

Where once we were told it was better to be dead than Red, now we will be told that it is better to be broke than—what?—slaves of the Knights of Malta? Meanwhile, conservative think tanks (their salaries paid directly or indirectly by interested conglomerates) are issuing miles of boilerplate about the necessity of securing the Free World from enemies; and Lockheed Martin lobbies individual senators, having spent (officially) $2.3 million for congressional and presidential candidates in the 1996 election.

For those interested in just how ruinous NATO membership will be for the new members, there is the special report *NATO Expansion: Time to Reconsider*, by the British American Security Information Council and the Centre for European Security and Disarmament. Jointly published 25 November 1996, the authors regard the remilitarization of the region between Berlin and Moscow as lunacy geopolitically and disastrous economically. Hungary is now aiming at a 22 percent increase in military spending this year. The Czechs and the Poles mean to double their defense spending. The world is again at risk as our "bipartisan" rulers continue loyally to serve those who actually elect them—Lockheed Martin Northrop Grumman, Boeing, McDonnell Douglas, General Electric, Mickey Mouse, and on and on. Meanwhile, as I write, the U.S. is secretly building a new generation of nuclear weapons like the W-88 Trident missile. Cost: $4 billion a year.

There comes a moment when empires cease to exert energy and become symbolic—or existential, as we used to say back in the Forties.

The current wrangling over NATO demonstrates what a quandary a symbolic empire is in when it lacks the mind, much less the resources, to impose its hegemony upon former client states. At the end, entropy gets us all. Fun house falls down. Fairground's a parking lot. "So I awoke, and behold it was a dream." *Pilgrim's Progress* again. But not quite yet.

It is a truism that generals are always ready to fight the last war. The anachronistic rhetoric at Madrid in July, if ever acted upon, would certainly bring on the next—last?—big war, if only because, in Francis Bacon's words, "Upon the breaking and shivering of a great state and empire, you may be sure to have wars."

Happily, in the absence of money and common will nothing much will probably happen. Meanwhile, there is a new better world ready to be born. The optimum economic unit in the world is now the city-state. Thanks to technology, everyone knows or can know something about everyone else on the planet. The message now pounding over the Internet is the irrelevancy, not to mention sheer danger, of the traditional nation-state, much less empire. Despite currency confusions, Southeast Asia leads the way while the warlords at Peking not only are tolerating vigorous industrial semi-autonomies like Shanghai but also may have an ongoing paradigm in Hong Kong. We do not like the way Singapore is run (hardly our business), but it is, relatively speaking, a greater commercial success than the United States, which might prosper, once the empire's put out of its misery, in smaller units on the Swiss cantonal model: Spanish-speaking Catholic regions, Asian Confucian regions, consensually united mixed regions with, here and there, city-states like New York–Boston or Silicon Valley.

In the next century, barring accident, the common market in Europe will evolve not so much into a union of ancient bloodstained states as a mosaic of homogenous regions and city-states like Milan, say, each loosely linked in trade with a clearinghouse information center at Brussels to orchestrate finance and trade and the policing of cartels. Basques, Bretons, Walloons, Scots who want to be rid of

onerous nation-states should be let go in order to pursue and even—
why not?—overtake happiness, the goal, or so we Americans have always pretended to believe, of the human enterprise.

On that predictably sententious American note, O movers and
shakers of the month, let us return to "the wilderness of this world,"
recalling the Hippocratic oath, which enjoins doctors: "Above all do
no harm." Hippocrates also wrote, O moved and shaken, "Life is
short, but the art is long, the opportunity fleeting, the experiment
perilous, the judgment difficult."

Vanity Fair
November 1997

IN THE LAIR OF THE OCTOPUS

In "Murder as Policy" (April 24), Allan Nairn notes, accurately, that the "real role . . . of all U.S. ambassadors [to Guatemala] since 1954 [has been] to cover for and, in many ways, facilitate American support for a killer army." Nairn's report on the capers of one Thomas Stroock, a recent viceroy, is just another horror story in a long sequence which it was my . . . privilege? to see begin not in 1954 but even earlier, in 1946, when, at twenty, a first novel just published, I headed south of the border, ending up in Antigua, Guatemala, where I bought a ruined convent for $2,000 (the convent had been ruined, let me say in all fairness, by earthquake and not by the Guatemalan military or even by the U.S. embassy).

Guatemala was beginning to flourish. The old dictator, Ubico, an American client, had been driven out. A philosophy professor named Arévalo had been elected president in a free election. A democratic socialist or social democrat or whatever, he had brought young people into government, tamed the army, and behaved tactfully with the largest employer in the country, the American company United Fruit.

Easily the most interesting person in—and out—of the town was Mario Monteforte Toledo. Under thirty, he was a thin, energetic intellectual who wrote poetry. He had a wife in the capital and an Indian girlfriend in Antigua, and when he came to visit, he and I would meet and talk, and talk.

Mario was President of the Guatemalan Congress and was regarded by everyone as a future president of the republic. In politics he was vaguely socialist. I, of course, reflecting my family's politics, was fiercely Tory. We had splendid rows.

Scene: patio of my house. Overhanging it the high wall of the adjacent church of El Carmen. Under a pepper tree, near an ugly square fountain like a horse trough, we would sit and drink beer. He told me the gossip. Then, after a ritual denunciation of the rich and the indifferent, Mario started to talk politics. "We may not last much longer."

"We . . . who?"

"Our government. At some point we're going to have to raise revenue. The only place where there is any money to be raised is *el pulpo.*" *El pulpo* meant the Octopus, also known as the United Fruit Company, whose annual revenues were twice that of the Guatemalan state. Recently workers had gone on strike; selfishly, they had wanted to be paid $1.50 a day for their interesting work.

"What's going to stop you from taxing them?" I was naive. This was long ago and the United States had just become the Leader of the Lucky Free World.

"Your government. Who else? They kept Ubico in power all those years. Now they're getting ready to replace us."

I was astonished. I had known vaguely about our numerous past interventions in Central America. But that was past. Why should we bother now? We controlled most of the world. "Why should we care what happens in a small country like this?"

Mario gave me a compassionate look—compassion for my stupidity. "Businessmen. Like the owners of United Fruit. They care. They used to pay for our politicians. They still pay for yours. Why, one of your big senators is on the board of *el pulpo.*"

I knew something about senators. Which one? Mario was vague. "He has three names. He's from Boston, I think. . . ."

"Henry Cabot Lodge? I don't believe it." Lodge was a family friend; as a boy I had discussed poetry with him—he was a poet's son. Years later, as Kennedy's Ambassador to Vietnam, he would preside over the murder of the Diem brothers.

As we drank beer and the light faded, Mario described the trap that a small country like Guatemala was in. I can't say that I took him very seriously. With all the world, except the satanic Soviet Union, under our control it was hardly in our national interest to overthrow a democratic neighbor, no matter how much its government irritated the board of directors of United Fruit. But in those days I was not aware to what extent big business controlled the government of our own rapidly expiring Republic. Now, of course, everyone knows to what extent our subsequent empire, with its militarized economy, controls business. The end result is much the same for the rest of the world, only the killing fields are more vast than before and we make mischief not just with weak neighbors but on every continent.

Mario had given me the idea for a novel. A dictator (like Ubico) returns from an American exile as the Octopus's candidate to regain power. I would tell the story through the eyes of a young American war veteran (like myself) who joins the general out of friendship for his son. The more I brooded on the story, the more complexities were revealed. *Dark Green, Bright Red*. The Greens, father and son, were the Company, and dark figures indeed, haunting the green jungles. Bright Red was not only blood but the possibility of a communist taking power.

"No novel about—or from—Latin America has ever been a success in English." As of 1950, my publisher was right.

Four years after the book was published, Senator Lodge denounced Arévalo's popularly elected successor, Arbenz, as a communist because, in June 1952, Arévalo had ordered the expropriation of some of United Fruit's unused land, which he gave to 100,000 Guatemalan families. Arévalo paid the company what he thought was a fair price, their own evaluation of the land for tax purposes. The American Empire went into action, and through the CIA, it put together an army and bombed Guatemala City. U.S. Ambassador John Peurifoy behaved rather like Mr. Green in the novel. Arbenz resigned. Peurifoy wanted the Guatemalan Army's chief of staff to become president, and gave him a list of "communists" to be shot. The chief of staff declined: "It would be better," he said, "that *you* actually sit in the presidential chair and that the Stars and Stripes fly over the palace."

Puerifoy picked another military man to represent the interests of company and empire. Since then, Guatemala has been a slaughterground, very bright red indeed against the darkest imperial green. Later, it was discovered that Arbenz had no communist connections, but the "disinformation" had been so thorough that few Americans knew to what extent they had been lied to by a government that had now put itself above law and, rather worse, beyond reason.

Incidentally, I note that the disinformation still goes on. In the April 9 *New York Times* (a "recovering" newspaper in recent years), one Clifford Krauss airily says that Guatemala's Indians have been regularly screwed for 400 years, so what else is new? He gives a tendentious history of the country—purest Langley boilerplate, circa 1955—but omits the crucial 1931–44 dictatorship of Jorge Ubico.

I must say I find it disconcerting to read in 1995 that "by surrounding himself with Communist Party advisers, accepting arms from Czechoslovakia and building a port to compete with United Fruit's facilities, Arbenz challenged the United States at the height of the cold war." God, to think that such evil ever walked the Central American night! "President Eisenhower's CIA organized a Guatemalan [*sic*] invasion force and bombed Guatemala City in 1954."

Dark Green, Bright Red was just reissued in England. Reviewing it in the *Evening Standard*, the journalist Patrick Skene Catling writes, "I wish I had read this prophetic work of fiction before my first visit to Guatemala in 1954. Gore Vidal would have helped me to understand how John Peurifoy . . . was able to take me up to the roof of his embassy to watch . . . the air raids without anxiety, because he and the CIA knew exactly where the bombs were going to fall."

A final note—of bemusement, I suppose. I was at school with Nathaniel Davis, who was our Ambassador in Chile at the time of Allende's overthrow. A couple of years later Davis was Ambassador to Switzerland and we had lunch at the Berne embassy. I expressed outrage at our country's role in the matter of Chile. Davis "explained" *his* role. Then he asked, "Do you take the line that the United States should never intervene in the affairs of another country?" I said that unless an invasion was being mounted against us in Mexico, no, we should never intervene. Davis, a thoughtful man, thought; then he said, "Well, it would be nice in diplomacy, or in life, if one could ever start from a point of innocence." To which I suppose the only answer is to say—Go! Plunge ever deeper, commit more crimes to erase those already committed, and repeat with Macbeth, "I am in blood / Stepped in so far that, should I wade no more, / Returning were as tedious as go o'er."

The Nation
5 June 1995

Article I, Section 9 of the Constitution requires government agencies to submit their budgets at regular intervals to Congress for review. Neither the CIA nor the DIA does this.* Occasionally, at the dark of the moon, they will send someone up to the Hill to disinform Congress, and that's that. After all, to explain what they actually do with the money that they get would be a breach of national security, the overall rubric that protects so many of them from criminal indictments. Although most Americans now think that the CIA was created at Valley Forge by General Washington, this unaccountable spy service was invented less than half a century ago, and since that time we have been systematically misinformed about the rest of the world for domestic policy reasons (remember Russia's outstanding economic surge in 1980?). Intelligence is an empty concept unless directly related to action. In a war, knowledge of the enemy's troop movements is all-important. In peacetime, random intelligence-gathering is meaningless, when not sinister.

Since our rulers have figured that one out, they have done their best to make sure that we shall never be at peace; hence, the necessity of tracking enemies—mostly imaginary ones, as the Pentagon recently revealed in its wonderfully wild scenarios for future wars. Since Communism's ultimate crime against humanity was to go out of business, we now have no universal war to conduct except the one against drugs (more than $20 billion was wasted last year on this crusade). As there is now no longer sufficient money for any of these

* Central Intelligence Agency, Defense Intelligence Agency.

"wars," there is no longer a rationale for so many secret services unless the Feds really come out of the closet and declare war on the American people, the ultimate solution: after all, one contingency plan in Ollie North's notebook suggested that in a time of crisis, dusky-hued Americans should be sequestered.

I would suggest that the State Department return to its once-useful if dull task of supplying us with information about other countries so that we might know more about what they'd like to buy from us. The hysterical tracking down of nuclear weapons is useless. After all, we, or our treasured allies, have armed all the world to the teeth. We have neither the money nor the brains to monitor every country on earth, which means, alas, that if some evil dictator in Madagascar wants to nuke or biologically degrade Washington, D.C., there's not much we can do about it. Certainly, the CIA, as now constituted, would be the last to know of his intention, though perhaps the first to get the good of his foul plot. I would abandon all the military-related secret services and I would keep the FBI on a tight leash—no more dirty tricks against those who dislike the way that we are governed, and no more dossiers on those of us who might be able to find a way out of the mess we are in, best personified by the late J. Edgar Hoover and best memorialized by that Pennsylvania Avenue Babylonian fortress that still bears his infamous name.

The Nation
8 June 1992

November 18, 1991. Despite jet lag, I find myself half-asleep, making a speech in a nineteenth-century auditorium in Pittsburgh. I stand behind a lectern at stage left, blinded by film and television lights. At stage right stands the youthful "Bob Roberts," played by Tim Robbins, who is also the director and writer of this film (as yet untitled). We are fictional characters. I am the incumbent liberal Senator from Pennsylvania; he is the challenger. "Bob" is a self-made millionaire turned pop singer, now turned politician. He is a sort of David Duke but without the luggage of a lurid past. He will win the election.

I have a weird sense that I have done all this before. Certainly, the hall is familiar, even to the entire text of the Gettysburg Address in giant gold letters above the stage. Then I realize that "I" have been through all this some weeks earlier. Only I was Harris Wofford and "Bob Roberts" was Dick Thornburgh and they, too, spoke in the same hall. That time Wofford won: this time he—"I"—lose. Then as my peroration resounds, I realize that I have never actually been in Pittsburgh before and that my familiarity with the hall is because of CNN—or was it C-Span?

Once I had finished my work as supporting "actor," I moved on to Dartmouth, where I spent a week in Hanover, New Hampshire, chatting with faculty and students. But, again, unreality kept breaking in. My first morning in Hanover, I looked out the bedroom window and for a moment I thought I was back at my old school, Exeter, from which I had graduated a half-century earlier, unless a recurrent nightmare runs true to course, in which case I did *not* graduate but have spent fifty dusty years trying, unsuccessfully, to make up a failed math test. Once awake, I found that my old friend *déjà vu* was back in town as a half-dozen hopeless presidential candidates were going through their quadrennial paces. In 1982 I had run against one of them, Jerry Brown, in California and lost a Senate primary election. Now he was making my old speeches. Should I warn him not to? No. Meanwhile, New Hampshire is in deep depression—shops out of business, banks failed, real estate belly-up, and everywhere the newly unemployed, looking for work where there is none.

From Dartmouth to Miami, and a firsthand look at the collapse of Pan American in its capital city. Local television devoted a great deal of time to the 7,500 workers suddenly let go, while stunned passengers crowded the ticket counters in order to read the scribbled message: "All Pan Am flights canceled"—forever. I thought of the arrogant Juan Trippe, who had founded the airline at about the same time that my father was founding what was to become TWA, now also near bankruptcy. I am definitely dreaming, I decided, and drove on to Key West, which I had not seen since my last visit to Tennessee Williams, thirty years earlier. German and French families crowded Duval Street, taking advantage of the cheap (ever cheaper as I write) dollar. I felt like a ghost who has been granted a day's visit to the future. I split for limbo, my home city of Washington, D.C., where I am due to address the National Press Club.

The usual efforts had been made to block my appearance but, as usual, they had failed. Apparently I am "outrageous," a word never exactly defined, though—from what I can tell—it appears to mean that as I say what I think about our political system and as I think a lot more about it than any of our journalists who are paid to present an irreal picture of these bad times, I cause a degree of outrage if not, as I would hope, rage.

This is the third time in thirty years that I have talked to the press club. Before me, my father addressed the club; before him, my grandfather. In a way, this is a family affair, but lately the family's hometown seems to have fallen apart. That morning I had strolled from the Willard Hotel toward the Capitol. Burnt-out buildings were just off Pennsylvania Avenue; burnt-out people were on the avenue—and elsewhere, too. It was like the spring of 1932, when jobless veterans of World War I marched by the thousands on the capital and made a camp at the Anacostia Flats. They wanted a bonus. On June 17, I drove with my grandfather to the Senate. They stoned his car. Ever since, I have always known that the famous "it" which can't happen here will happen here, and last month as I walked through my home city, "it" seemed ever closer to hand, and we are now in a prerevolutionary time. Hence, the emphasis in the media on the breakup of the Soviet Union and Yugoslavia, or of anything other than the breakdown, if not breakup, of the United States and its economy. Just now, a month later, I watched on television as angry workers stormed through the streets of what I took to be Moscow until CNN identified the city as New York and the workers as members of one of our few labor unions—construction workers, I think, protesting lack of work, hope.

Like a ghost—but this time from the future—I tried to explain to the press club what it is they do that they don't know they do. I quote, yet again, David Hume: The Few are able to control the Many only through Opinion. In the eighteenth century, Opinion was dispensed from pulpit and schoolroom. Now the media are in place to give us Opinion that has been manufactured in the boardrooms of those corporations—once national, now international—that control our lives.

Naturally, this sounded to my audience like the old conspiracy theory. Later, I was asked if I actually thought that Kay Graham and Larry Tisch really told the news departments of *The Washington Post* and CBS what to tell us. I said, Yes, of course, they do on occasion, but in everyday practice they don't need to give instructions because everyone who works for them thinks exactly alike on those economic issues that truly matter. I even mentioned the unmentionable, the ruling class. I noted that those members who were not going to inherit money are sent like Bush to Andover and me to Exeter—two schools for the relatively brainy. Those who will inherit money (e.g., the late Nelson Rockefeller) go to Groton or St. Paul's, where, in order not to grow up to become dissolute wastrels, they will be taught useful hobbies, like stamp or people collecting. This sort of education ensures that everyone so educated will tend to think alike. The few who break ranks are—what else?—outrageous. In any case, the indoctrination of the prep schools alone is usually quite enough to create a uniformity of ruling-class opinion when it comes to the rights of property. Since our corporate state is cynically democratic, there are always jobs available to middle-class careerists willing to play the game.

Almost forty years ago, I heard Secretary of State John Foster Dulles say that of course our foreign policy (as outlined in the then-secret National Security Council Memorandum 68) would lead to an arms race with the Soviet Union but that, as we were richer, they would cave in first. Dulles was right. They did. But he had not taken into account the economic cost to us or, worse, that in the process we would lose the old Republic and its Constitution, so revered by its current destroyers. Political decadence occurs when the forms that a state pretends to observe are known to be empty of all meaning. Who does not publicly worship the Constitution? Who, in practice, observes it at all? Congress has only two great powers under the Constitution: the power to declare war and the power of the purse. The first has been relinquished to the Executive; the second has drowned in a red sea.

The Supreme Court is no longer the Executive's equal. Rather, it is the Executive's tool. The White House's open coaching of the unqualified Clarence Thomas for a place on the Court made it dramatically clear that the Court now acts as a nine-member legal council to the Executive, its principal function the validation of Executive decrees. The current Court has also displayed a startling dislike of the American people, and the joy with which the nine nullities chop away at our Bill of Rights is a marvel to behold. But then the hatred of those *inside* the fabled Beltway for those *outside* has now—what else?—created a true hatred on the part of the Many for the Few who govern them, or appear to govern, since the actual decision makers—and the paymasters—are beyond anyone's reach, out there in the boardrooms of the world.

In the absence of true political debate, we have what I think of as the Sunday menagerie on television. Here journalists and politicians gaze at one another through the bars of received Opinion and chatter about "process," a near-meaningless word in these parts. Recently I watched Richard Darman, the budget director, gabble to Messrs. Evans and Novak about the deficit. To my amazement, the defense budget was actually mentioned by Evans. Apparently the Brookings Institution had daringly suggested that if a few hundred dollars were cut, we would still be able to support with our swift nuclear sword the "democracy" of Tonga. But although the defense budget continues to be the cancer that is killing our body politic, it may not be dealt with at any length by the media, and Darman was swift to create the necessary diversion: "Entitlements!" he moaned right on cue. "If only we could get *them* on the table." He shook his head in despair at the trillions of dollars that we waste on free dentures and on the financing in luxury of profligate unwed mothers.

Now it is wonderfully ironic for anyone to complain about what the zoo calls "people programs" because, wasteful or not, there aren't any. But no one can point this out on television because both journalists and politicians are hired by the same people and behind those people is the corporate wealth of the country, which requires that the budget be faked. The famous entitlements consist largely of disbursements for Social Security, and although Social Security contributions are always counted as part of the federal revenue, they are not. Social Security is a separate trust fund whose income and outgo have *nothing* to do with the actual budget. So why does the government like to pretend that Social Security payments are part of its annual revenue? Because if you take those payments *out* of the budget, everyone would realize that perhaps three-quarters or more of the federal income, over the years, has been spent on "defense" or war-related matters or on servicing the debt on money borrowed for war.

If Social Security payments are not counted as revenue, Bush is currently spending $1.1 trillion a year, while taking in only $726 billion from taxes. The real national debt is about $4 trillion; in 1980 it was a mere $1 trillion. It is true that the Pentagon itself gets less money these days than it used to, but debt service, foreign aid, nuclear energy and payments to the true victims of our wars, the veterans, still account for most federal expenditures and deficits.

From time to time it is shyly suggested that taxes be raised— for individuals but never for corporations. To those who maintain that our political life is not controlled by corporations, let me offer a statistical proof of ownership—the smoking gun, in fact. In 1950, 44 percent of federal revenues came from individual taxpayers and 28 percent from a tax on corporate profits. Today, 37 percent comes from individuals and only 8 percent from the corporations (see John McDermott, "The Secret History of the Deficit," *The Nation,* August 21/28, 1982).* Once Bush's only fiscal notion becomes law and the capital gains tax is eliminated, the work of corporate America will be complete, and the ownership will have ceased to support the United States. Naturally, should a badly run company like Chrysler go bust, the American people will be expected to pay for managerial mistakes. In any case, let it be solemnly noted that during the forty years of the national security state, corporate America not only collected most of the federal revenue for "defense" but, in the process, reduced its share of federal taxes by twenty percentage points. Was this a conspiracy? No. They all think alike? Yes. They all think alike.

Since it is unlikely that Japan and Germany will forever continue to buy our Treasury bonds, how will the ownership pay for itself? Well, we could always renege on servicing the debt, but as Richard Nixon would say, *that would be the easy way* (and will, alas, be taken). The sublime way, which will be taken by the next administration, will be to sell off that 31 percent of the United States that

---

* Yes, there are different figures for 1992 and now for 2000 and 2001. But the trend is the same: taxes on corporate profits ever down, on individuals ever up. Now the shogunate of Cheney begins. Mikado Bush attends to the tea ceremony.

is held by the federal government in our name.* This fire sale will be highly popular with the buyers but it will be odd for Americans to have so little real estate to call their own.

When I was at the press club three years ago Opinion makers were mildly interested in overruns at the Defense Department. There was to be an investigation, and John Tower would be in place to make sure that nothing untoward was discovered. But Dick Cheney got the job instead, and there have been no meaningful investigations on his watch.

It is a commonplace that half of those qualified to vote for president don't vote; also that half the adult population never read a newspaper. No bad thing, all in all, assuming that they *could* read a newspaper, which is moot as our public schools are among the worst in the First World while our prison population, symmetrically, is the highest, surpassing the *ci-devant* Soviet Union. Naturally, we lead the First World in the execution of criminals or "criminals."

Every four years the naive half who do vote are encouraged to believe that if we can elect a really nice man or woman President everything will be all right. But it won't be. Any individual who is able to raise $25 million** to be considered presidential is not going to be much use to the people at large. He will represent oil, or aerospace, or banking, or whatever moneyed entities are paying for him. Certainly he will never represent the people of the country, and they know it. Hence, the sense of despair throughout the land as incomes fall, businesses fall and there is no redress.

Before the national security state was invented, we had something called "representative government." It did not work awfully well but at least there was some sense that, from time to time, something might be done about a depression—the sort of thing that cannot be done by a system in which most public revenues are earmarked for weaponry and war and secret police forces and, of course, the servicing of trillions of dollars' worth of debt.

* A good chunk of Utah oil land was sold off in 1996.
** In the election of 1996, a billion dollars apiece was spent by Clinton and Dole. In 2000, Gore and Bush spent nearly $3 billion between them.

"When we suffer, or are exposed to the same miseries *by a government*, which we might expect in a country *without government*, our calamities is [*sic*] heightened by reflecting that we furnish the means by which we suffer. Government, like dress, is the badge of lost innocence; the palaces of kings are built on the ruins of the bowers of paradise." I quote from *Common Sense*, by Thomas Paine. How do we get rid of this bad government? There is certainly no road back to Eden in any society. Even if we could return, our own Eden was a most serpentine affair, based as it was on the enslavement of Africans and the slaughter or deportation of an indigenous population.

But until 1950, when our ramshackle world empire was institutionalized as the national security state, we *were* improving ourselves, and the generality took part in government while Opinion was not so cynically and totally manipulated as now. Since we cannot pay for the empire any longer, we shall soon be coming home—but to what? Our "inalienable" rights are being systematically alienated. Never has an American government been so busy interfering with the private lives of its citizens, subjecting them to mandatory blood, urine, lie-detector tests. Yet the war on drugs has nothing at all to do with drugs. It is part of an all-out war on the American people by a government interested only in control. As this grows more evident, I suspect that we shall begin to see an organized resistance to so tyrannous a state. Meanwhile, as we have neither political parties nor, indeed, politics, only issueless elections, I see only one peaceful way out of this corpse of a Republic, this literally bankrupt national security state.

Article Five of the Constitution describes two methods whereby it may be amended or otherwise altered. One way, and so far the only way yet taken, is by a vote of two-thirds of both houses of Congress. The amendment is then sent for ratification by the state legislatures. The *second* procedure is very interesting indeed—in fact, one might almost call it democratic.

Two-thirds of the state legislatures can request a constitutional convention, which Congress must then convene. Unlike us, the founders did not worship their handiwork. Many thought the original Constitution was bound to fail. Thomas Jefferson wanted to hold a constitutional convention at least once a generation because, as he said, you cannot expect a man to wear a boy's jacket. As it turned out, the jacket has been so reshaped over the past two centuries that it is now a straitjacket for the people at large and satisfying to no one except those who gain election—and profits—from a most peculiar institution.

In recent years there have been several movements to convene a constitutional convention. These efforts have been the work of single-interest groups usually on the far right. One group wants to forbid abortion to every woman. Another wants a balanced budget embedded in the Constitution. What *is* interesting is that in the 1970s and 1980s thirty-two state legislatures voted in favor of such a convention; but many of them cautiously noted that no subject other than a balanced budget, say, could be discussed.

In 1967, Senator Sam Ervin was so intrigued by Article Five that he researched the subject and explained the mechanics of such a convention in S.2307. He came to the conclusion that, as *We the People* are the true *de jure* sovereign of these states, *We the People* cannot be held by anyone to any single issue once we convene *our* convention. If we so choose, the entire Constitution could be rewritten. At this point I part company with the American Civil Liberties Union, who, for once, are more pessimistic about the people than I. The first thing *they* will get rid of is the Bill of Rights, the liberals moan. To which the answer is, first, I don't think the people are suicidal and, second, what is the difference between losing those rights at an open convention as opposed to a gradual loss of them behind the closed doors of the current Supreme Court?

It is true that we are a less homogeneous and less educated people than the three million original inhabitants of the thirteen colonies. But I cannot believe that our convention would do away with our liberties while granting more power, say, to the Executive to fight wars that in the end harm only *us*. I am aware that the people at large have been kept ignorant by bad schools and by the dispensers of false Opinion. That is true. That is a problem. But ignorance is not stupidity. And self-interest, as both Hamilton and Madison agreed, is a great motor to the state, properly checked and balanced.

In any case, we are now faced with the fury of those who have been deprived for too long of decent lives. It takes no unusual power of prophecy to remark that they will not be apathetic forever. "If it be not now, yet it will come. The readiness is all." Rather than be *un*ready for anarchy, I submit that we must sit down and in an orderly way rethink our entire government as well as our place in the world.

The founders' last gift to us is the machinery to set things right. Article Five. Let us use it.

Thus, I ended my speech to the National Press Club—outrageously, of course.

The Nation
27 January 1992

Over the years I have written quite a lot about the state of the Union. Now, in the interest of novelty, I'd like to discuss the *Union* of the State. I have always tried to say something so obvious that no one else has noticed it. For instance, I once suggested that we criminalize most firearms, and legalize most drugs. This would put an end to the now eternal War on Crime that, we are told, is devastating our alabaster cities and not doing the amber waves of marijuana much good either. I realize, of course, that vested interests are now too great for us to do anything of an intelligent nature in this—or almost any—regard. The National Rifle Association will never wither away as long as there is a single Congressman left to be paid off or a child unarmed.

Our violence and murder rate are unique in the First World. This may be a negative uniqueness but it is all our own, and to be cherished; at least we are number one at something other than indebtedness. We now have over a million people in prison* and another couple of million on probation or parole; why not just lock up half the population and force the other half to guard them? That would solve crime; it might also entice Amnesty International to start whining here at home. After all, 58 percent of those in our federal prisons are there for drug offenses. Most are not dangerous to the public, and even though our overkindly government thinks they are dangerous to themselves, they should still be allowed to pursue

* As of 2000, *USA Today* reports on its front page that 6.6 million adults (3 percent of the adult population) are in prison or "correction." No other society has ever done so deadly a thing to its people and on such a scale.

their constitutional, if unhealthful, happiness in freedom. Certainly they do not deserve to be confined to a prison system that a Scandinavian commission recently reported to be barbarous for a supposedly First World country.

Unfortunately, the rulers of *any* system cannot maintain their power without the constant creation of prohibitions that then give the state the right to imprison—or otherwise intimidate—anyone who violates any of the state's often new-minted crimes. Without communism—once monolithic and on the march—our state lacks a Wizard of Oz to terrify all the people all the time. So the state looks inward, at the true enemy, who turns out to be—who else? the people of the United States. In the name of correctness, of good health, or even of God—a great harassment of the people-at-large is now going on. Although our state has not the power to intimidate any but small, weak countries, we can certainly throw most Americans in prison for violating the ever-increasing list of prohibitions. Will this change for the better with a change of Congress or President? No. Things are going to get a lot worse until we apply the state's new white hope to the state itself: Three strikes, you're out. How then to "strike out" the state? I have an idea.

Kevin Phillips recently attacked—in *Time*—Washington, D.C., a beautiful city, built, if not on a hill, at least on what, in 1800, was a quite attractive swamp. He quoted Jefferson's warning that when every aspect of government is drawn to Washington—he meant the city, not the general—Washington, in his words, would become "as venal and oppressive as the government from which we separated." (This was England, by the way, not the Disney studio so recently and bloodily thrown back at Bull Run.)

Phillips tacitly acknowledges that the people have no representation within the Beltway, unlike the banks or insurance companies. Consequently, officeholders and their shadow, the media, are equally disliked by a vast majority. Unfortunately, the people are without alternative. That is what makes the situation so volatile and potentially dangerous. Think what might have happened had Ross Perot possessed the oily charm of Charlton Heston. Certainly, it is plain that when a people comes to detest the political system in which it is entrapped, that system will not endure for long.

I've always been mystified at how obtuse politicians and the media are. Every politician of consequence, for the last quarter-century, has run against Washington, against lobbyists, against insiders, against Jefferson's "venal and oppressive" ruling class—or, to be precise, the representatives of our actual rulers, who circle the globe like Puck with all the swift anonymous speed of a fax laden with campaign money. It is very hard, one would think, to live with so total a contradiction. For instance, both Carter and Reagan campaigned against Washington, and both won. Neither understood why people voted for him. Neither made the slightest attempt, even cosmetically, to curb Jefferson's tyrannous capital. The two new employees forgot their speeches and went right on doing business as instructed by those huge economic forces that govern earth.

Can someone like Clinton make a change? I don't see how. We would like health care of the sort every civilized nation has but we can never have a rational system as long as insurance companies are allowed to benefit. The people may want affordable health care, but they are not going to get it in the United States of America as now constituted.

Phillips has come up with an old notion of mine: devolution, the dictionary word for breaking up the Union into smaller, more manageable units. He would move much of the government away from Washington, I suppose, to inconvenience the 800,000 lawyers who will then be able to deduct as legitimate travel expense the weary weekly journey from cozy Montgomery County to sky-topped Denver. He would move various departments permanently to other states and rotate the capital from this to that city. He would like an amendment to the Constitution "setting up a mechanism for holding nationwide referendums to permit the citizenry to supplant Congress and the President in making certain categories of national decisions." Like declarations of war? Could he be *that* radical? Along with this bit of major surgery on the body politic, he has some useful Band-Aids. But no more. Nevertheless, I am well pleased that what I've been proposing for so long has now gone mainline. So let me go a bit further out.

In 1992 I switched on CNN and heard Jerry Brown—in New Hampshire—giving pretty much a speech that I had given for the National Press Club [see "Time for a People's Convention"] on how to restore power to its only legitimate source, We the People. As Jerry and I had not spoken since I ran against him in the California Senate primary in 1982, I was pleasantly surprised and praised him publicly for his wisdom, while blessing him for his plagiarism, no matter how belated. He rang me in Italy. Yes, it was my speech. Unlike Joe Biden, he is an honest man. And did I have anything more? And would I come to New Hampshire? I said, yes, I had more, but, no, I would forgo the winter wonderland of New Hampshire, currently known as Dole Land.

However, thanks to CNN and the fax machine, I could monitor his campaign and send him my thoughts immediately. So a number of suggestions of mine entered the primary campaign. The principal notion was conversion from war to peace. Find a defense plant that's closing and say that it should be kept open but converted to peacetime, using the same workforce and technology. Brown did just that in Connecticut. He told the soon-to-be-dismissed makers of Seawolf submarines that if he became President, they would be making not submarines but bullet trains. At five in the morning I got a call from political operator Pat Caddell. "We won!" he said. "We won Connecticut." Then they—not we—lost New York.

Meanwhile, Perot grabbed my We the People as the strange device for his eccentric banner. I felt very odd, watching CNN in Italy, and hearing at least three candidates using my lines.

Jerry was headed for Pennsylvania after New York and, as the game was up, I said why not propose something really useful: launch a new idea that might take a few years to penetrate but when it does, might save us all.

Here is the gist of what I wrote him. I started with the eternal problem of what we do about income tax. As the people at large get nothing much back from the money that they give the government—Social Security is not federal income—why not just eliminate the federal income tax? How? Eliminate Washington, D.C. Allow the states and municipalities to keep what revenue they can raise. I know that tens if not hundreds of thousands of lobbyist-lawyers and hired media gurus will have a million objections. But let us pursue the notion.

Why not divide the country into several reasonably homogeneous sections, more or less on the Swiss cantonal system. Each region would tax its citizens and then provide the services those citizens wanted, particularly education and health. Washington would then become a ceremonial capital with certain functions. We shall always need some sort of modest defense system, a common currency, and a Supreme Court to adjudicate between the regions as well as to maintain the Bill of Rights—a novelty for the present Court.

How to pay for what's left of Washington? Each region will make its own treaty with the central government and send what it feels should be spent on painting the White House and on our common defense, which will, for lack of money, cease to be what it is now—all-out offense on everyone on earth. The result will be no money to waste either on pork or on those imperial pretensions that have left us $4.7 trillion in debt. Wasteful, venal, tyrannous Washington will be no more than a federal theme park administered by Michael Eisner.

Will the regions be corrupt, venal, etc.? Of course they will   we are Americans!—but they will be corrupt on an infinitesimal scale. Also, more to the point, in a smaller polity everyone knows who's up to no good and they can police themselves better than the federal government ever could—even if it had ever wanted to.

All over the world today centrifugal forces are at work. In a bloody war in the old Yugoslavia and parts of the old Soviet Union, and in a peaceful way in the old Czechoslovakia. Since history is nothing but the story of the migration of tribes, we must now note that the tribes are very much on the move again, and thanks to modern technology we can actually watch Bengals and Indians overflowing each other's borders.

Racially, the composition of Europe has changed more in the past fifty years than in the previous 500. Whether this is good or bad is irrelevant. It is. Now, here at home, people fret about invasions from the Hispanic world, from Haiti, from the boat people of Asia. But, like it or not, we are changing from a white, Protestant country, governed by males, to a mixed polity, and in this time of change there is bound to be conflict. The fragmentations that we see everywhere are the result of a *dislike* for the nation-state as we have known it since the bloody nation-building of Bismarck and Lincoln.

People want to be rid of arbitrary capitals and faraway rulers. So let the people go. If our southern tier is to be Spanish and Catholic, let it be. But also, simultaneously, as we see in Europe, while this centrifugal force is at work—a rushing away from the center—there is also a centripetal one, a coming-together of small polities in order to have better trade, defense, culture—so we are back, if by chance, to our original Articles of Confederation, a group of loosely confederated states rather than a *United* States, which has proved to be every bit as unwieldy and ultimately tyrannous as Jefferson warned. After all, to make so many of Many into only One of one you must use force, and this is a bad thing, as we experienced in the Civil War. So let us make new arrangements to conform with new realities.

I will not go so far as to say that we shall ever see anything like democracy at work in our section of North America—traditionally we have always been a republic entirely governed by money, but at least, within the regions, there will be more diversity than there is now and, best of all, the people will at last have the sensation that they are no longer victims of a far-off government but that they— and their tax money—are home at last.

The Nation
26 December 1994

On June 3, 1996, *The Nation* showed in a foldout chart how most of the U.S. media are now owned by a handful of corporations. Several attractive octopi decorated the usually chaste pages of this journal. The most impressive of these cephalopod molluscs was that headed by Disney-ABC, taking precedence over the lesser Time Warner, General Electric–NBC, and Westinghouse Corporation calamari, from which dangle innumerable tentacles representing television (network and cable), weapons factories (GE aircraft engines and nuclear turbines) and, of course, GNA and other insurance firms unfriendly to health care reform.

As I studied this beast, I felt a bit like Rip Van Winkle. When last I nodded off, there was something called the Sherman Antitrust Act. Whatever happened to it? How can any octopus control so much opinion without some objection from . . . from whom? That's the problem. Most members of Congress represent not states or people but corporations—and octopi. Had I simply dreamed John Sherman? Or had he been devoured by Dragon Synergy? Little did I suspect, as I sighed over this latest demonstration of how tightly censored we are by the few, that, presently, I would be caught in the tentacles of the great molluscs Disney-ABC and General Electric–NBC, as well as the Hearst Corporation, whose jointly owned cable enterprise Arts & Entertainment had spawned, in 1995, something called The History Channel.

"It all began in the cold," as Arthur Schlesinger so famously began his romantic historical novel *A Thousand Days*. Only my cold was London, where, for Channel Four, I wrote and narrated three half-hour programs on the American presidency, emphasizing the imperial aspects latent in the office from the beginning, and ending, currently, with our uneasy boast that we are the last great global power on the . . . well, globe.

The programs were well received in Britain. The History Channel bought the U.S. rights. In ninety-minute form my view of the imperial presidency was to be shown just before the 1996 political conventions. But then, from the tiny tentacle tip of The History Channel, synergy began to surge up the ownership arm, through NBC to its longtime master General Electric; then ever upward, to, presumably, the supreme mollusc, Mickey Mouse himself, Lord of Anaheim. *Great Mouse, this program attacks General Electric by name. Attacks American imperialism, which doesn't exist. Badmouths all that we hold sacred.* Oh, to have been a fly on the castle wall when word arrived! The easy solution, as Anaheim's hero-President, R. M. Nixon, might have said, would have been to kill the program. But craftier minds were at work. *We'll get some "experts" like we do for those crappy historical movies and let them take care of this Commie.*

So it came to pass that, unknown to me, a GE panel was assembled; it comprised two flyweight journalists from television's Jurassic Age (Roger Mudd, Sander Vanocur) and two professors, sure to be hostile (one was my old friend Arthur Schlesinger, about whose client, JFK, I am unkind; the other was someone called Richard Slotkin). I was not invited to defend myself, nor was anyone else. As a spokesperson for The History Channel put it, "Vidal is so *opinionated* that we had to have real experts on." *The Nation*'s recent warning about the danger of allowing the corporate few to make and control mass opinion was about to be dramatized at my expense.

Fade in: Roger Mudd. He is grim. He wears, as it were, not so much the black cap of the hanging judge as the symbol of his awful power, *Mickey Mouse ears.* He describes my career with distaste. Weirdly, he says I had "social ambitions at the Kennedy White House and [*non sequitur*] ran for Congress" but lost. Actually, I ran for Congress before Kennedy got to the White House. Also, in upstate New York, I got some 20,000 more votes than JFK did as head of the ticket. During my campaign, Bobby Kennedy came to see me at Saugerties Landing. It was, appropriately, Hallowe'en. "Why," he snarled, "don't you ever mention the ticket?" "Because I want to win," I said, imitating his awful accent. That started the feud.

Mudd reports that I am "acerbic, acid-tongued," don't live in the United States (except when I do), and the viewer is warned beforehand that this is only my "bilious look" at American history and our presidents, whom Mudd says that I describe variously as incompetent, avaricious warmongers. This is—warmongering to one side—slanderously untrue. Then, Mickey Mouse ears atremble with righteous indignation, he reassures us that, at program's end, *real* historians will set the record straight. And so, muddied but unbowed, I fade in.

I begin in a sort of mock-up of the White House TV room. I say a few mildly bilious words about current politics.

> He who can raise the most money to buy time on television
> is apt to be elected president by that half of the electorate
> that bothers to vote. Since the same corporations pay for
> our two-party, one-party system, there is little or no actual
> politics in these elections. But we do get a lot of sex. Also,
> he who subtly hates the blacks the most will always win a
> plurality of the lilywhite-hearted. The word "liberal" has
> been totally demonized, while "conservative," the condition
> of most income-challenged Americans, is being tarnished
> by godly pressure groups whose symbols are the fetus and
> the flag. As a result, today's candidates are now rushing
> toward a meaningless place called "the center," and he who
> can get to the center of the center, the dead center, as it
> were, will have a four-year lease on this studio.

I then trace the history of our expansionist presidents from Jefferson's Louisiana Purchase to Bush of Mesopotamia's Gulf War, produced by Ted Turner's CNN, a sort of in-house TV war. I end the program in front of the Vietnam Memorial. We have come a long way, I say, from Jefferson's Declaration of Independence to "the skies over Baghdad have been illuminated." Then Mudd, more than ever horrified by what he'd seen and heard, introduces a TV journalist called Vanocur, who introduces Professors Schlesinger and Slotkin. It's very clear, says Vanocur, that Vidal doesn't like America. Arthur's response is mild. Well, let's say he is disappointed in what's happened.

At the beginning of Mudd's first harangue, I must say I did wonder what on earth had caused such distress. It was clear that neither cue-card reader had any particular interest—much less competence—in American history; but then, I had forgotten the following aria:

> Our presidents, now prisoners of security, have been for a generation two-dimensional figures on a screen. In a sense, captives of the empire they created. Essentially, they are men hired to give the commercials for a state which more and more resembles a conglomerate like General Electric. In fact, one of our most popular recent presidents spent nearly twenty years actually doing commercials for General Electric, one of our greatest makers of weapons. Then Mr. Reagan came to work here [in the White House], and there was the same "Russians are coming" dialogue on the same Teleprompter, and the same makeup men.

The GE panel, carefully, made no reference to their fellow pitchman Reagan, but they found unbearable my suggestion that we have been surpassed, economically, by Asia. I noted that:

> As Japan takes its turn as world leader, *temporarily standing in for China*,* America becomes the Yellow Man's Burden,

* Italics added 2000.

and so we come full circle. Europe began as the relatively empty, uncivilized Wild West of Asia. Then the Americas became the Wild West of Europe. Now the sun, setting in our West, is rising once more in the East.

This really hurt Mudd, and he couldn't resist noting that Japan's standard of living is lower than ours, a factoid that, presumably, magically cancels our vast debt to them. He reminds us that we have also been hearing a lot of bad economic news about other countries; but then we always do, lest Americans ever feel that they are being short-changed by a government that gives its citizens nothing for their tax money and companies like General Electric billions for often useless weapons and cost overruns. Approvingly, Mudd tells us that "industrious immigrants" are rushing to our shores. Well, those we have helped to impoverish south of the Rio Grande do come looking for work, particularly from countries whose societies we have wrecked in the name, often, of corporate America (United Fruit in Guatemala, ITT in Chile), or they come from Southern Asia, where our interferences dislocated millions of people, some of whom unwisely boated to our shores, lured by our generous minimum wage, universal health care, and superb state educational system.

Mudd's mouse squeak becomes very grave indeed as he tells us how the defense budget has been slashed to a mere fraction of what it used to be and must be increased if we are ever to keep the peace of the world through war. Yet today we outspend the military budgets of Western Europe and Japan combined. Although there have been large cuts in personnel as military bases are turned over to the real estate lobby, outlays of the sort that benefit Mudd's employers still run to nearly $300 billion a year.

The two historians were less openly protective of General Electric and military procurement. Schlesinger doesn't find much in the way of historical distortion. But then what motive would I have had to neglect what Jefferson liked to call "true facts"? I am neither political publicist nor hagiographer, and I know the country's history as well as most people who have dedicated a generation to its study.

Schlesinger does say that I misquote Jefferson's Declaration of Independence. That must sound pretty serious to the average viewer. It also sounds pretty serious to me that Arthur doesn't realize I was quoting, accurately, the original preamble, not the one edited and published by Congress. Jefferson—and I—preferred his first version, of which only a fragment still exists but, luckily, later in life he re-created the original: "All men are created equal and independent." Congress cut the "and independent." Then: "From that equal creation, they derive rights inherent and inalienable." Congress (looking ahead to the Rev. Pat Robertson and all the other serpents in our Eden?) changed this to "They are endowed by their Creator with certain inalienable rights." The introduction of a Creator has done our independence no good.

Early on, I observe that "an adviser to President Truman announced, 'What is good for General Motors is good for America.' The adviser was president of General Motors, of course." Arthur correctly notes that Charles Wilson was not a member of Truman's Cabinet but of Eisenhower's. Nevertheless, he was a significant *adviser* to Truman. Unfortunately, his famous advice to Truman got edited out of my final program. Here it is. In 1944 Wilson gave his rationale for a permanent militarizing of the economy: "Instead of looking to disarmament and unpreparedness as a safeguard against war—a thoroughly discredited doctrine—let us try the opposite: full preparedness according to a continuing plan." This was to be the heart of the National Security Act of 1947, and the new nation in whose shabby confines we still rattle about.

It is a little late in the day to turn Lincoln into an abolitionist, but the GE panel saw an easy way of making points by piously declaring how much great-hearted Lincoln hated slavery. But I had already noted, "He disliked slavery but thought the federal government had no right to free other people's property. In this case, three million African-Americans at the South." It should be noted—

yet again—that American history departments are now bustling with propagandists revising Lincoln so that he will appear to be something quite other than the man who said that if he could preserve the Union by freeing all the slaves, he would do so, or freeing some and not others, he would do so, or freeing none at all he would free none for the Union's sake. But for General Electric, blushing bride of Mickey Mouse, the image of Lincoln cannot remain half Disney and half true.

At one point, Slotkin accuses me of dealing in hindsight. But that, dear professor, is what history is, and you and I and even Arthur are historians, aren't we? It is true that I refused election to the Society of American Historians; but I am no less a historian than those who are paid to keep the two essential facts of our condition from the people at large: the American class system (there is no such thing, we are flatly told) and the nature of the U.S. empire (no such thing, either). Apparently, it is perfectly natural for a freedom-loving democracy, addicted to elections, to have bases and spies and now FBI terrorist fighters and drug hounds in every country on earth. When Vanocur tries to get Theodore Roosevelt off the imperialist hook, Schlesinger does mutter that the great warmonger did believe in "a vigorous foreign policy." Then Arthur makes a slip: TR was really only interested in our "domination of the Western Hemisphere." Well, certainly half a globe is better than none. But then, as TR said, "No accomplishment of peace is half that of the glories of war."

Schlesinger notes that if Jefferson and John Quincy Adams were to return today, they would be surprised that we had not annexed Canada, Cuba, and other Western properties. For the GE panel such continence is proof that there is no such thing as a U.S. empire. Well, it is true that after two failed invasions, Canada escaped us; even so, we have a naval base on Canadian soil (at Argentia), and Canada plays its dutiful if irritable part in our imperium, economically as well as militarily. Cuba was, in effect, our brothel during the Batista years; now, for trying to be independent of us, it is embargoed while we maintain on the island, as always, the military base of Guantánamo.

Toward the end of their "discussion," one of the Mouseketeers mocks the notion that big business is in any way responsible for a U.S. empire that does not exist. The GE panel, to a man, then proceeds to ignore this key section of my script:

> TR's successor, Woodrow Wilson, invaded Mexico and Haiti in order to bring those poor people freedom and democracy and good government. But stripped of all the presidential rhetoric, the flag followed the banks.
>
> The President was simply chief enforcer for the great financial interests.
>
> Many years later, the commanding general of the U.S. Marine Corps, General Smedley Butler, blew, as it were, the whistle, not just on Wilson, but on the whole imperial racket.

I had showed some fine newsreel footage of Butler, of Marines in Haiti, Taiwan, the streets of Shanghai. I did an imitation of his voice as I spoke his actual words:

> "I spent most of my time being a high-class muscle man for big business, for Wall Street and for the bankers. In short, I was a racketeer, a gangster for capitalism. I helped make Mexico safe for American oil interests in 1914. Made in Haiti and Cuba a decent place for the National City Bank boys to collect revenues in."

In later years, Butler also set up shop in Nicaragua, the Dominican Republic, and China where, in 1927, the Marines protected Standard Oil's interests.

> *Vidal as Butler:* "The best Al Capone had was three districts. I operated on three continents."

Needless to say, General Butler is a permanent nonfigure in our imperial story.

Slotkin began to paraphrase exactly what I had been saying—modern empires are not like the old-fashioned sort where you raise your flag over the capitol of a foreign country. From 1950 on, I demonstrated how the domination of other countries is exercised through the economy (the Marshall Plan after World War II) and through a military presence, preferably low-key (like NATO in Western Europe) and politically through secret police like the CIA, the FBI, the DEA, the DIA, etc. Currently, the empire is ordering its vassal states not to deal with rogue nations (the Helms-Burton bill).

Although the Soviet Union went out of business five years ago, we still have bases in Belgium, Germany, Greece, Italy, the Netherlands, Portugal, Spain, Turkey. In Britain we have seven air force and three naval bases. In 1948, Secretary of Defense Forrestal installed two B-29 groups in the English countryside; it would be a good idea, he said, to accustom the English to a continuing U.S. military presence. To create and administer a modern empire you must first discover—or invent—a common enemy and then bring all the potential victims of this ogre under *your* domination, using your secret services to skew their politics as the CIA did, say, to Harold Wilson's Labour Party.

Today, elsewhere, we have military presences in Bermuda, Egypt, Iceland, Japan, Korea, Panama, the Philippines, Saudi Arabia, Kuwait, etc., not to mention all over the United States and our territories as well as two bases in Australia, one of which is a mysterious CIA unit at Alice Springs. If all this does not constitute an empire I don't know what does. Yet we must not use the word, for reasons that the GE panel never addressed. At one point, Vanocur pretended that I had said the American people were eager for conquest when I said the opposite. Our people tend to isolationism and it always takes a lot of corporate manipulation, as well as imperial presidential mischief, to get them into foreign wars. Sadly, Schlesinger confirmed that this was so.

Slotkin thought that I had been saying that the late-nineteenth-century presidents were creatures of big business when what I said was that big business was off on its rampage and that the presidents, between Lincoln and Theodore Roosevelt, were dimly accommodating.

Then the question of why I was so evil was gravely addressed. Mouse ears were now on the alert. Schlesinger noted that I had headed the America First chapter at Exeter in 1940 and that I still seemed to be an isolationist. Vanocur said isolationists were right-wingers. Schlesinger countered that many, like Norman Thomas (and me), were on the left. Mud, as it were, in hand, Vanocur said that isolationism is "tinged with anti-Semitism," but that did not play. Schlesinger did note, with a degree of wonder, that there are those who do not seem to understand how our future is inextricably bound up in the politics of all the other continents. This might have been a good place to start an enlightening debate. Had I been included, I might have said that unless the nation is in actual peril (or in need of loot—I am not angelic) there is never any reason for us to engage in foreign wars. Since George Washington, the isolationist has always had the best arguments. But since corporate money is forever on the side of foreign adventure, money has kept us on the move, at least until recently.

I said that Stalin drastically disarmed after the war. Arthur rightly pointed out that so did we: pressure from the isolationist masses forced the government to let go millions of GIs, including me. But two days after the announcement of Japan's surrender, Truman said (August 17, 1945) that he would ask Congress to approve a program of universal military training—in peacetime! He made the request, and got his wish. We rearmed as they disarmed. Briefly.

Between May and September 1946, Truman began the rearmament of our sector of Germany while encouraging the French in their recolonization of Indochina, as well as meddling militarily in China and South Korea. The great problem of living in a country where information and education are so tightly controlled is that very little news about our actual situation ever gets through to the consumers. Instead we are assured that we are so hated by those envious of our wealth and goodness that they commit terrorist acts against us simply out of spite. The damage our presidential and corporate imperialists have done to others in every quarter of the world is a nonsubject, as we saw in August, when my realistic overview accidentally appeared on an imperial network and a panel of four was rushed into place to glue mouse ears back on the eagle's head.

Vanocur then affects to be mystified by why I say so many terrible things about the Disneyland that pays him his small salary. But I thought I had made myself clear. I am a patriot of the old Republic that slowly unraveled during the expansionist years and quite vanished in 1950 when the National Security State took its place. Now I want us to convert from a wartime to a peacetime economy. But since the GE-style conglomerates that govern us will never convert, something will have to give, won't it?

When the egregious Vanocur wondered why I had done this program, Arthur said, "To entertain himself—and to entertain the audience." That was disappointing but worthy of the Dr. Faustus of Harvard Yard.

I did not report on my country's disastrous imperial activities with much amusement. All I wanted to do was tell a story never told before on our television—and never to be told again as long as the likes of GE and Disney are allowed to be media owners and manipulators of opinion.

What to do? Break up the conglomerates. That's a start. And then—well, why not go whole hog—what about a free press, representative government and . . . Well, you get the picture.

The Nation
30 September 1996

The first American Secretary of Defense, James V. Forrestal, on July 15, 1949, in the name of NATO, the Four Freedoms, and the pursuit of happiness, accomplished the first successful invasion of England since the Normans when he sent two groups of B-29s to the U.K., observing privately to President Truman that it would be a good idea "to accustom the English" to the ongoing presence of the American air force. Less than a year later, suffering from nervous exhaustion, he put down his copy of Sophocles' *Ajax* and jumped out of a hospital window, leaving behind not only his annotated *Ajax* but the outward visible sign of American occupation, our English bases.

A busy half-century now draws to a close. Along the way, in 1989, the Evil Soviet Empire surrendered to our goodness. Now, as the self-styled Sole Global Nuclear Power, we fire commands rapidly at friend and foe alike. President Clinton, responding gleefully to Congress's targeting of "terrorist nations," has warned the entire world that if any foe or ally dares do business with Libya and Iran and Iraq, much less leprous Cuba, we shall . . . well, like Lear, we'll do something or other. Don't worry. Are we not the SGNP?

Currently American conservatives (whatever that word now means) are calling for a *new* imperialism. In the pages of the latest *Foreign Affairs* William Kristol and Robert Kagan (aesthetically, one wants a third "K") tell us that "today's lukewarm consensus about America's reduced role in a post–Cold War world is wrong." They like simple declarative sentences. So here's one for them. The largest debtor nation on earth has no choice but to reduce its imperial role. No money. The Ks are Reaganites and see the former President as a sort of American Bismarck, although it was as General Custer that he made his mark in movie history, which seems to be their only history, too. The Ks are in the grip of a most unseemly megalomania. "American hegemony is the only reliable defense against a breakdown of peace and international order." Tell that to the Asians.

The Ks also say that as we have never been so well off, we can afford to spend an additional $60–80 billion a year on war. This is nonsense. (The style is contagious.) They want a Reaganesque military buildup of great profit to aerospace industries and no one else. Their high-minded line is that there are bound to be many, many more exciting wars for us to fight and win. They seem to believe that our Declaration of Independence was not just for us but a blueprint for the whole world, which is longing to be American. The truth seems otherwise. Hearken to the howls from our allies as the radiant Oval One, from his ever more Byzantine capital, tells others with whom they may not trade.

One must at least give the "conservatives," as represented by the Ks, a mark for trying to find something for the United States to do now that the world has settled down to its usual mess of tribal rivalries and trade wars. The British, after the Suez debacle, were given to quoting Dean Acheson—a creator of the Global Empire—to the effect that Britain had lost an empire but had yet to find a role. In answer, J. B. Priestley wrote a wise meditation on the royal coat-of-arms—suggesting that now that the days of the lion were done, why not turn to the unicorn, a mythical elegant beast suggestive of magic and art? And so a considerable flowering in the arts lasted for at least a generation. We have no comparable heraldic lineage, only the bald-headed American eagle, so reminiscent of General Eisenhower when he tried to give up smoking.

The Ks want the eagle to be brought back to life, claws clutching thunderbolts, the odd olive branch. Apparently, earth is American and we must govern all of it for the good of the human race. But the other nations did not elect us leader post-1989. Rather, Western Europe comes slowly together. Japan prepares for a new metamorphosis while China, "the sleeping giant" that Napoleon said only a fool would awaken, is already an American creditor. The old order is gone forever and the brief hegemony of the white race is drawing to an unmourned close.

The Ks seem to be living in a world that never really existed outside the movies or American political rhetoric. They find "the Europeans and the Japanese supportive of [our] world leadership role." Not this week nor, indeed, for some years now has the United States been looked to as an upholder of international law and order. When requested to go before the tribunal at The Hague to explain alleged crimes against Nicaragua, the U.S. refused to accept the jurisdiction of a court that we had helped set up. Also, whenever the fit is upon the Oval One, he feels perfectly free to bomb Gaddafi's family or invade Panama killing quite a few Panamanians as he kidnaps their leader and then puts him on trial in an American court that has no jurisdiction over him. Such a model of international roguery is hardly eligible to fill the Ks' notion of a benign world hegemon. What they actually hanker after is Caesarism, no bad option if you are really stronger militarily and economically than everyone else but, alas, aside from the power to nuclearize the planet, Uncle Sam, he dead.

The Declaration of Independence is sometimes thought by old-fashioned European conservatives to be a liberal document. Here, I think, they mix it up with the French Rights of Man, a truly radical and always—to some of us—heartening trumpet blast. Our own declaration was a more modest affair. Life, liberty, and the pursuit of happiness were the set goals. But liberty hardly means the leveling of classes to those rich white conservative men who fancifully called the forcible separation of colonies from British Crown a revolution when it was simply an inevitable devolution. England was too small and too far away to govern so many people, so much territory.

Pursuit of happiness was an exceptional thought and, like the Holy Ghost for serious Christians, something to brood upon. In any case, the American day has pretty much run out. The Ks speak for no one except energetic political hustlers within the Washington Beltway. But as the U.S. grows shakier at home and abroad, accidents can still happen. That is why, in the light of the current uproar over President Clinton's boycotting of entire countries, it might be a good idea to start, as tactfully as possible, the removal of the United Nations from the United States and then of the United States from the United Nations (unless, of course, a billion dollars of dues owing are paid).

This sign of world solidarity would clear the air, to riot in understatement, and serve notice that no house in such economic and domestic disarray as that of the very last global power can exercise hegemony over anything other than itself. Such was the intention of our truly conservative founders two centuries ago when they adjured us to follow our own course toward some more perfect—if ungrammatical—union, making true in the process Ajax's hope: "Ah, boy, may'st thou prove happier than thy sire." And not, dementedly, slaughter sheep.

The Sunday Telegraph
11 August 1996

Immigration, emigration. Race. Let them in. Keep them out. Should we do the jobs that they do that we don't want to do? Last month an American poll showed that for the first time immigration is the number one anxiety of our stout, sugar-fed people as they restlessly switch channels and ponder the fate of dinosaurs and the nation state.

Recently I toured seven German cities, and spoke at various meetings. The German press was full of anxious reports on the neo-Nazi racists in its midst. It was even more upset by the *non*-neo-Nazi racists. The unemployed in particular were attacking Turks and East Europeans and other foreigners. What did it all mean?

There is no longer enough work to go around. That is, proper work as opposed to part-time labor with no future, the sort of work that ill-paid foreigners now do. Every day we read how another great industry has let go yet another 30,000 or 40,000 workers. Automation and reduced demand have made them redundant. What will these people do? Is the state to support them? If so, how? This basic question is generally avoided, particularly by professional politicians, so I shall, for the moment, sidestep it too.

Racism. The fear of otherness is an unattractive but constant human trait, and one that we social meliorists like to say education and peaceful commingling will do away with in, as always, time. There is some truth in this. There is also some truth in the saying that all men are brothers, as Abel must have reminded Cain, who replied as he lifted his club, "Yes, and all brothers are men."

In Germany I used a line that I often use in the United States when I think that the audience is unaware of the world outside its own national and ethnic bubble. I noted that at the start of the next millennium the white race will make up about 13 percent of the world's population. This statistic makes white Americans look even whiter, while the dusky faces in the audience begin to beam. The German reaction was hysteria. Race, declared a tense young man, is a myth. I said, no, race is a fact, but the prejudices that people have about races are often mythical.

Also, even if everyone was all the same gray-pink shade, the myths of difference would still be invoked, and myths are very potent. For me, God is a myth, but I am quite aware that millions of people have died nonmythical deaths in his name. In Britain, cavaliers and roundheads went into battle, each side shouting "Kill for Jesus."

Always accommodating, I said that if I could not use the word "race"—an everyday sort of word in my country with no built-in resonance—would "tribalism" do? No, that was unacceptable. People who spoke of races and tribes in Germany were almost always neo-Nazis. What word *could* I use?

"Multiculturalism" was the consensus in Stuttgart. But, I said, an American white and an American black will often be prejudiced against one another, and each shares exactly the same culture, or its absence. We left the subject in the air. But I remember thinking that if one does not have the words to discuss a matter objectively, emotions will ensure that it then becomes dangerously subjective.

Due to poverty in other sections of the world and a declining standard of living for most people in our part of it, emotions are getting pretty raw. The time is overripe for dialogue as opposed to the monologues of demagogues. I see this, curiously, more in Europe today than in the United States. We have had a race war between black and white for over a century now. It is like a low-grade fever that, from time to time, flares up and puts the patient at risk. On the other hand, we are used to it. We take or give our quinine, which is known as welfare, a bribe that we pay to the black underclass in order to exclude them from white society. Meanwhile, we never cease to boast that we are a nation of immigrants.

Racial stereotypes are irresistible, particularly in wartime. I know. I was an American soldier in the great race war against Japan. I served in the Pacific. Our indoctrination was crude and hilarious. In early 1941 the government assured us that should war come, we would easily win it through air power. Apparently, because of the weird configuration of the Japanese eye, they could not see well enough to be able to manage modern aircraft. Not long after, they sank our fleet at Pearl Harbor.

Before I left to go to the Pacific—I was first mate of an army freight supply ship—we were given an indoctrination course on how to tell our exquisite allies, the Chinese, from our brutish enemy, the Japanese. On a stage there was a life-sized cutout of a naked Chinese youth and another one of a Japanese. The Chinese was tall, slim, and well proportioned. The Japanese was bandy-legged, buck-toothed, subhuman.

These details were shown to us by an information officer with a pointer. "But the principal difference," he announced, "is the pubic hair. The Japanese is thick and wiry while the Chinese is straight and silky." I fear that I alone raised my hand to ask what sly strategies we were to use to determine friend from foe.

Our war with Japan was deeply ideological. They had the idea that the Pacific Ocean should be theirs, while we had the idea that it should be ours. This is known as a *conflict* of ideologies. As it turned out, our war of conquest was more successful than theirs. In fact, our hegemony in the Pacific and over Japan was the last great military victory that the white race will probably ever know. Now *they* have the technology and the wealth. And *we* decline.

In the fifteenth century it was as if there was a sudden big bang. The white race in Western Europe—itself a sort of Wild West to the Asian landmass—burst its cage. Like a plague, we infected the western hemisphere, Africa, Asia. We were also, literally, a plague, carrying with us so many new diseases that indigenous populations often died out. Though our numbers were relatively few, we colonized. The great goal for our race was China: specifically the north-central Shansi province, the world's largest coalfield.

By the start of the century the European powers and the United States were already established on the China coast. But we now had a rival in Japan. They too wanted the Middle Kingdom. So the struggle between our two races over the division of China has been pretty much the history of the century now ending. Yet, through all this, China has endured and is now set to prevail while Japan is finally *a*—as opposed to *the*—master race.

The loss of identity—not to mention wealth, power, and empire—makes for melancholy, or worse. As Dean Acheson famously put it, Britain has lost an empire but not yet found a role. Fifty years later the United States is in much the same situation. So, too, is Western Europe. In the fourteenth century our race was more than decimated in Europe by the plague. In the fifteenth century population revived—too much so. What were we to do with so many people? We broke loose and conquered most of the world.

The wealth of the western hemisphere paid for the Renaissance in Europe. The wealth of India fueled the industrial revolution in England. We colonized almost every part of the world, imposing, in the process, our peculiar version of monotheism, one that is crude, savage, and hostile to life. For most of the world, particularly those with older and subtler civilizations, we were an unmitigated curse. But we never suspected that we were anything but good, as we went about stealing and converting others to our primitive ways.

What is human history but the migration of tribes? The so-called Aryans swept down into Europe and Persia and India in about 1500 B.C. They settled and were absorbed. Then came Huns, Mongols, Arabs. They seldom stayed for long, nor did they, by and large, colonize. By the time our race got busy, we had somehow moved ahead in the applied sciences, particularly those relating to warfare. Incas, Mayans, Hindus, Chinese were no match for us.

Now as the twentieth century draws to a close, we seem to have run out of petrol. We still have the power to atomize the globe but then, with a bit of hard work, so can the Pakistanis. We are no longer unique, even in our destructive powers. We have entered a period of uneasy stasis. What are we to do next, if indeed we still are "we" at all, rather than just an element in a rainbow mix as is the case in many parts of the United States and, here and there, in Britain.

At the moment "we" are defensive, even paranoid. Are we to lose what's left of our identity? Are we to lose our traditional countries to immigrants of different races? There is much moaning in the West.

Since we have our countries, the desire to keep them reasonably homogeneous is reflexive and hardly extraordinary. Yet minor immigration has been the rule ever since native whites discovered that poorly paid other-tinted people would do work that whites find untouchable. But now major population shifts threaten. Everywhere the tribes are on the move. From south and east they converge on Europe; from south and west on North America.

Meanwhile, internal pressures are building up in all the nation states. In fact, a case can be made that the nation state, as redesigned by Bismarck and Lincoln, is obsolete. Certainly no one likes an expensive bureaucratic centralism, indifferent to the needs of the ethnic components that make it up. You cannot, in the name of the Holy Roman Emperor or even the higher capitalism, shove together and try to standardize a number of tribes that do not want to be together. We witness daily the explosions in what were once the Soviet Union and Yugoslavia. Might it not be wise simply to go *with* the centrifugal forces now at work and not try to oppose them anywhere?

The European aim should be a mosaic of autonomous ethnic groups—each as much on its own as possible, whether it be Basques or Scots or Armenians. This distresses old-fashioned statesmen. They want as many people as possible under their control, not a mere fraction of a multitribal whole. We shall lose, they say, our power in the world if we are fragmented. This was the Bismarckian, the Lincolnian line. Well, they have little to fear in the long run because the newly independent neighbors will come back together again in new, less confining arrangements.

In February 1987 Gorbachev invited to the Kremlin some 700 non-Communist worthies in the arts, sciences and business, to discuss a nonnuclear world. It was the first unveiling of what, he told us, would be a revolution in the Soviet Union. I was called upon to improvise a speech. A Japanese Minister of Trade had just announced that in the next century Japan would still be number one, economically, in the world. "No one can surpass us," he said. Then, in an expansive mood, he said, "The United States will be our farm and Western Europe will be our boutique."

Something must be done in order for us to survive economically in what looks to be, irresistibly, an Asian world. I would propose that, as our numbers are so few relative to those of China and India, say, we come together in a northern confederacy of Europe, Russia, Canada, the United States. The fact that the small nation states of Western Europe are having difficulty federalizing their relatively small common market means that federalism, at this stage, is a mistake, while a loose confederation for the general economic good is a more achievable business.

It is also just as easy—or vexing—to include Russia and the heartland states of the old Soviet Union as it is to agree, let us say, about the price of milk at Brussels. In other words, much strain in the short run but, in the long run, the creation of a large prosperous entity based upon geographical latitude and the pale, lonely 13 percent of the world's population.

It does not matter whether a large goal will ever be achieved. Rather, it is the fact that such a goal exists in order to give shape and symmetry to policies; and meaning, perhaps, to societies that otherwise are adrift. Motivate your football louts, continental skinheads, overwrought white American racists.

I realize that the nation state has accustomed us to the idea of conquest by force. It is hard not to think along those lines. In Germany some critics actually thought that my proposal was a white declaration of war on Asia. It is no such suicidal thing. It is a means of economic survival through union. Without links to us, Russia will break up; Europe will decline; lonely little England will drift off along with Ireland and Greenland and Iceland and Newfoundland and all the other Arctic islands; while the United States will take its place somewhere between hypertense Brazil and lachrymose Argentina.

Alexander Hamilton was by far the cleverest of America's founding fathers; he was also the most realistic. Instead of going on about the brotherhood of man, he said, in effect, let us take into account man's essential greed and will to dominate, and let us allow for these traits in our constitution so that self-interest, reasonably harnessed, can become the engine of the state and thus contribute to the common good. So why not extend this insight to our present dilemma, and make new world arrangements?

I regard race as nonsense, but most of the world feels passionately otherwise. In the unlikely event that the human race survives another millennium, there will be no white or black races but combinations of the two, and of every other race as well. But for now, let us use this negative force for a positive end, and create a great northern peaceful economic alliance dedicated*—if I may end on a chauvinist American note—to life, liberty, and the pursuit of happiness.

The Sunday Telegraph
10 October 1993

---

* When this piece was published in Russia, a number of enthusiasts elected me honorary president of the north.

⭐ CHAOS

On November 4, 1994, three days before the election that produced a congressional majority for the duller half of the American single-party system, I addressed the National Press Club in Washington. I do this at least once a year not because writer-journalists are present, wise and fearless as they are, but because cable television carries one's speech without editing or editorializing. This useful service, known as C-Span, specializes in covering such eccentricities as myself and the British House of Commons.

I reflected upon the confusion that each of us is feeling as this unlamented century and failed millennium draw, simultaneously, to a close, and there is no hint of order in the world—and is *that* such a bad thing? As for my own country, I said that there is now a whiff of Weimar in the air. Three days later, to no one's surprise, only a third of the electorate bothered to vote. The two-thirds that abstained now realize that there is no longer a government which even pretends to represent them. The great—often international and so unaccountable—cartels that finance our peculiar political system are the only entities represented at Washington. Therefore, in lieu of representative government, we have call-in radio programs, where the unrepresented can feel that, for a minute or two, their voices are heard, if not heeded. In any case, a system like ours cannot last much longer and, quite plainly, *something is about to happen*. I should note that one Rush Limbaugh, a powerful radio demagogue, greeted November's Republican landslide as a final victory over what he called the age of Lenin and Gore Vidal. It was not clear whether he meant Moscow's Lenin or Liverpool's Lennon. Then, to my amazement,

The Wall Street Journal, where I lack admirers, took seriously my warning about Weimar, and "*What* is going to happen?" is a question now being asked among that 2 or 3 percent of the population who are interested in politics or indeed in anything other than personal survival in a deteriorating society.

Certainly, I have no idea what is going to happen, but as the ineffable Ross Perot likes to say, it won't be pretty.

I have now lived through more than two-thirds of the twentieth century, as well as through at least one-third of the life of the American Republic. I can't say that I am any wiser now than I was when I first began to look about me at the way things are, or rather at the way that things are made to look to be, but I am beginning to detect an odd sort of progression in world affairs. And I have noticed lately that I am not alone.

Recently, the literary critic Harold Bloom, in the somewhat quixotic course of establishing a Western literary canon, divided human history into phases that cyclically repeat. First, there is a theocratic age, next an aristocratic age, followed by a democratic age, which degenerates into chaos and out of which some new idea of divinity will emerge to unite us all in a brand-new theocratic age, and the cycle begins again. Bloom rather dreads the coming theocratic age but as he—and I—will never see it, we can settle comfortably into the current chaos where the meaning of meaning is an endlessly cozy subject, and Heisenberg's principle is undisputed law of the land, at least from where each of us is situated.

I shall not discuss Bloom's literary canon, which, like literature itself, is rapidly responding if not to chaos to entropy. But I do have some thoughts on the cyclic nature of the way human society evolves as originally posited by Plato in the eighth book of the *Republic* and further developed by Giovanni Battista Vico in his *Scienza Nuova*.

Professor Bloom skips Plato and goes straight to Vico, an early-eighteenth-century Neapolitan scholar who became interested in the origins of Roman law. The deeper Vico got into the subject, the further back in time he was obliged to go, specifically to Greece. Then he got interested in how it was that the human race was able to create an image of itself for itself. At the beginning there appears to have been an animistic belief in the magic of places and in the personification of the elements as gods. To Vico, these legends, rooted in prehistory, were *innate* wisdom. Plainly, he was something of a Jungian before that cloudy Swiss fact. But then the age of the gods was challenged by the rise of individual men. Suddenly, kings and heroes are on the scene. They in turn give birth to oligarchies, to an aristocratic society where patricians battle for the first place in the state. In time, the always exciting game of who will be king of the castle creates a tyranny that will inspire the people at large to rebel against the tyrants and establish republics that, thanks to man's nature, tend to imperial acquisitiveness and so, in due course, these empire-republics meet *their* natural terminus in, let us say, the jungles of Vietnam.

What happens next? Vico calls the next stage Chaos, to be followed by a new Theocratic Age. This process is, of course, pure Hinduism, which was never to stop leaking into Greek thought from Pythagoras to the neo-Platonists and even now into the alert mind of my friend Allen Ginsberg and of numerous California surfers and ceramists. Birth, death, chaos, then rebirth, and so—on and on and on.

But though Vico's mind was brilliant and intuitive, the history that he had to deal with necessarily left out science—as we know it and he did not—and we must now ponder how chaos may yet organize itself with the use of computers and faxes and the means to control all the people all the time. Will the next god be a computer? In which case, a *tyrant* god for those of us who dwell in computer-challenged darkness.

A characteristic of our present chaos is the dramatic migration of tribes. They are on the move from east to west, from south to north. Liberal tradition requires that borders must always be open for those in search of safety or even the pursuit of happiness. In the

case of the United States, the acquisition of new citizens from everywhere has always been thought to be a very good thing. But now
with so many billions of people on the move, even the great-hearted
are becoming edgy.

So, what is going to happen? Well, Norway is large enough and
empty enough to take in 40 or 50 million homeless Bengalis. If
the Norwegians say that, all in all, they would rather *not* take them
in, is this to be considered racism? I think not. It is simply self-
preservation, the first law of species. So even those of us usually to
be found on the liberal end of the political spectrum are quite aware
that the tribes must stay put and be helped to improve wherever it is
that they were placed by nature or by our dissolving empires, to
which all sorts of odd chickens are presently coming home to roost.

Now, as world climate changes and populations increase, the
tribes are on the move, and the racial composition of Europe, say,
has changed. As an American, I think that this is not such a bad
thing, but there does come a moment when there are simply too
many people on the move and not enough space or resources to ac-
commodate them in the old established societies.

As we start the third millennium of what we in our Western section of the globe are amused to call the Christian era, we should be
aware, of course, that most of the world's tribes are, happily for
them, not Christian at all. Also, most of us who are classified as
Christians and live in nations where this form of monotheism was
once all-powerful now live in a secular world. So chaos does have its
pleasures. But then as Christian presuppositions do not mean anything to others (recently Buddhists sternly reminded the pope of this
in Sri Lanka), so, too, finally, Plato and his perennially interesting
worldview don't make much sense when applied to societies such as
ours. I like his conceit of the political progression of societies, and a
case can be made for it, as Vico did. But Plato, as political thinker,
must be taken with Attic salt, which John Jay Chapman brilliantly
supplies in an essay recently discovered in his archives; he died in
1933. Although he was America's greatest essayist after Emerson he

is almost as little known in his native land as elsewhere. This is a pity, but then these are pitiful times, are they not?

Watch as Chapman plays around with the notion of chaos—and of order, too. First, he is not well pleased with what passes for democracy in the great republic. No Anglophile, he does have a nice word or two for the British, in an essay that begins: "All good writing is the result of an acquaintance with the best books." Chapman often feels obliged to invent the wheel each time he addresses his readers. He goes on: "But the mere reading of books will not suffice. Behind the books must lie the habit of unpremeditated, headlong conversation. We find that the great writers have been great talkers in every age." He cites Shakespeare, as reported by Ben Jonson, Lord Byron, and our own Mark Twain. He then generalizes about other tribes, something now forbidden in the free world. He writes:

> The English have never stopped talking since Chaucer's time. And the other Europeans are ready-tongued, vocal, imaginative people, whose very folklore and early dialects have been preserved by the ceaseless stream of talk on castled terraces and on village greens since Gothic times.
>
> But our democracy terrifies the individual, and our industrialism seals his lips. The punishment is very effective. It is simply this: "If you say such things as that, I won't play with you." Thus the average American goes about in quite a different humor from the average European, who is protected and fortified by his caste and clique, by his group and traditions, by manners and customs which are old and change slowly. The uniformity of the popular ideals and ambitions in America is at the bottom of most of our troubles. Industrialism has all but killed the English language among us, because every man is afraid to make a joke— unless it be a stock joke. We are all as careful as diplomats not to show our claws. We wear white cotton gloves like waiters—for fear of leaving a thumb mark on the subject.

Emerson's advice about this problem is covered by his apothegm "If you are afraid to do any thing, do it!"

Chapman on Plato:

Plato somewhere compares philosophy to a raft on which a shipwrecked sailor may perhaps reach home. Never was a simile more apt. Every man has his raft, which is generally large enough only for one. It is made up of things snatched from his cabin—a life preserver or two of psalm, proverb or fable; some planks held together by the oddest rope-ends of experience; and the whole shaky craft requires constant attention. How absurd, then, is it to think that any formal philosophy is possible—when the rag or old curtain that serves one man for a waistcoat is the next man's prayer-mat! To try to make a raft for one's neighbor, or try to get on to someone else's raft, these seem to be the besetting sins of philosophy and religion.

The raft itself is an illusion. We do not either make or possess our raft. We are not able to seize it or explain it, cannot summon it at will. It comes and goes like a phantom.

As for Plato:

He was primarily an entertainer, a great impresario and setter of scenes, and stager of romances great and small where fact and fiction, religion and fancy, custom and myth are blended by imaginative treatment into—no one knows exactly what the mixture should be called.

The aim of his most elaborate work, the *Republic*, is identical with the aim of the Book of Job, of Bunyan's *Pilgrim's Progress*, of Milton's *Paradise Lost*, and indeed of half the great poems, plays and novels of the world, namely to justify the moral instinct.

But Chapman is a literary critic as well as a moralist. He wrote:

As a work of art, the *Republic* is atrocious, but as a garretful of antiquity it is thrilling. It is so cracked and rambling that Plato himself hardly knows what is in it. While clearing out a bureau drawer one day, he finds a clever little harangue denouncing sumptuary laws as both useless and foolish . . . "There's a glint of genius in that," says he and throws the manuscript into a big Sarcophagus labeled *Republic*.

Which is where, Chapman notes, it plainly does *not* belong, since Plato's entire work is based on the *necessity* of sumptuary laws.

We see then what sort of a creature this Plato was—with his poetic gift, his inextinguishable moral enthusiasm, his enormous curiosity, his miscellaneous information, his pride of intellect and, as his greatest merit, his perception that spiritual truth must be conveyed indirectly and by allusions. In spite of certain clumsy dogmatisms to be found here and there in him, Plato knows that the assault upon truth cannot be carried by a frontal attack. It is the skirmishing of Plato which makes his thought carry; and all the labours of his expounders to reduce his ideas to a plain statement have failed. If the expounders could reduce Plato's meaning to a statement, Plato would be dead. He has had wit enough and vision enough to elude them all. His work is a province of romantic fiction, and his legitimate influence has been upon the romantic fiction and poetry of the world. Plato used Philosophy as a puppet on his stage and made her convey thoughts which she is powerless to tell upon her own platform. He saw that philosophy could live in the sea of moving fiction, but died on the dry land of formal statement. He was sustained in his art by the surrounding atmosphere of that Hellenic skepticism which adored elusiveness and hated affirmations. His age handed him his vehicle—to wit, *imaginary conversation.* Is there anything in the world that evaporates more quickly and naturally than conversation? But *imaginary* conversation! Certainly Plato has protected himself from cross-examination as well as ever man did. The cleverest pundits have been trying to edge him into the witness stand during sixty generations, but no one has ever cornered him. The street is his corner.

Of Plato, as a voice from somewhere at the far edge of a democratic age, Chapman notes, with quiet pleasure, that:

It has thus become impossible for anyone to read Plato's dialogues or any other creation of the Greek brain with real sympathy; for those creations speak from a wonderful, cruel, remote, witty age, and represent the amusements of a wonderful, cruel, remote, witty people, who lived for amusement, and for this reason perished. Let us enjoy the playthings of this clever man but let us, so far as in us lies, forbear to cloy them with our explanations.

Vico saw fit to systematize, if not to cloy, Plato in order to give us a useful overview of the evolution of human society, as glimpsed in the dark shadow of the cross of his day. It should be noted that Vico made far more of Plato's ideal theory than Plato did. But then, alas, Vico, like us, is serious and schematic.

Plato and Vico, Montesquieu and Jefferson, Margaret Thatcher and Ronald Reagan—the urge to devise model states is a constant and if chaos does not absolutely disintegrate us, we might yet endure as a race—if it is not a form of racism to suggest that human beings differ in *any* significant way from the mineral and the vegetable, two realms that we constantly victimize and are rude to.

Apropos of human political arrangements, I have been listening, lately, to a pair of voices from the century before ours; two voices often in harmony, more often in gentle dispute. I refer to Gustave Flaubert and George Sand. Put simply—too simply, I confess— George Sand was a nonromantic socialist while Flaubert was a romantic reactionary. Neither had much illusion about the perfectibility of man or too many notions as to the constitution of an ideal state. They wrote each other during the Franco-Prussian War, the collapse of the Second Empire, the rise of the Commune at Paris, and each wondered, "What next?"

Flaubert is glum: "Whatever happens, it will be a long time before we move forward again. Perhaps there's to be a recurrence of racial wars? Within a century we'll see millions of men kill each other at one go. All the East against all Europe, the old world against the new? Why not?"

Flaubert then teases George Sand:

The general reverence for universal suffrage revolts me more than the infallibility of the Pope. Do you think that if France, instead of being governed, in effect, by the mob, were to be ruled by the "Mandarins," we'd be where we are now? If only instead of wanting to enlighten the lower classes we had bothered to educate the upper classes!

Sand strikes back:

In my view, the vile experiment that Paris is undergoing in no way disproves the laws of eternal progress that govern both men and things, and if I have acquired any intellectual principles, good or bad, this business neither undermines nor alters them. A long time ago I accepted the necessity for patience in the same way as one accepts the weather, the long winter, old age, and failure in all its forms.

Flaubert comes to the point: "I hate democracy (at least as it is understood in France), because it is based on 'the morality of the Gospels,' which is immorality itself, whatever anyone may say: that is, the exaltation of Mercy at the expense of Justice, the negation of Right—the very opposite of social order."

Sand remains serene: "I've never been able to separate the ideal of justice that you speak of from love: for if a natural society is to survive, its first law must be mutual service, as with the ants and the bees. In animals we call this collaboration of all to achieve the same end, instinct. The name doesn't matter. But in man, instinct is love, and whoever omits love omits truth *and* justice.

"Tell me whether the tulip tree suffered from the frost this winter, and whether the peonies are doing well."

That tulip tree may symbolize a benign way out of the current chaos. In the interest of shutting holes in the atmosphere, the human race may yet cooperate to survive, though I doubt it. For a new center to hold we must understand why it is that things fall apart the way they do. I have spent my life trying to understand what it was that so many others appear to need that I don't—specifically, a sense of deity, preferably singular, anthropomorphic, and, to explain the general mess of life that he has made on earth, an inscrutable jealous off-the-wall sort of god. I do not doubt that something new in this line is on its way, but, meanwhile, there is something to be said for creative chaos. Certainly order, imposed from the top down, never holds for very long.

Like everyone else, as the millennium is now ending, I keep thinking of how it began in Europe. Does a day pass that one does not give at least a fleeting thought to the Emperor Otto III and to Pope Sylvester II? I should highly doubt it. After all, they are an attractive couple; a boy emperor and his old teacher, the intellectual pope. Together, at the start of our millennium, they decided to bring back the Christian empire that two centuries earlier Charlemagne had tried to recreate or—more precisely—to create among the warring tribes of Western Europe. If Charlemagne was the Jean Monnet of the 800s, Otto III was the Jacques Delors of the 900s. As you will recall, Otto was only fourteen when he became king of Germany. From boyhood, he took very seriously the idea of a united Christendom, a Holy Roman Empire. Like so many overactive, overeducated boys of that period he was a natural general, winning battles left and right in a Germany that rather resembled the China of Confucius's era—a time known as that of the warring duchies.

By sixteen, King Otto was crowned emperor of the West. An intellectual snob, he despised what he called "Saxon rusticity" and he favored what he termed Greek or Byzantine "subtlety." He even dreamed of sailing to Byzantium to bring together all Christendom under his rule, which was, in turn, under that of God. In all of this he was guided by his old tutor, a French scholar named Gerbert.

As a sign of solidarity—not to mention morbidity—Otto even opened up the tomb of Charlemagne and paid his great predecessor a visit. The dead emperor was seated on a throne. According to an eyewitness, only a bit of his nose had fallen off, but his fingernails had grown through his gloves and so, reverently, Otto pared them and otherwise tidied him up. Can one imagine Delors—or even Helmut Kohl—doing as much for the corpse of Monnet?

Now we approach the fateful year 999. Otto is nineteen. He is obsessed with Italy, with Rome, with empire. In that year he sees to it that Gerbert is elected pope, taking the name Sylvester. Now emperor and pope move south to the decaying small town of Rome, where Otto builds himself a palace on the Aventine—a bad luck hill, as Cicero could have testified.

Together, Otto and Sylvester lavished their love and their ambition upon the Romans, who hated both of them with a passion. In the year that our common millennium properly began, 1001, the Romans drove emperor and pope out of the city. Otto died at twenty-two near Viterbo, of smallpox. A year later, Sylvester was dead, having first, it is said, invented the organ. Thus, the dream of a European union ended in disaster for the two dreamers.

I will not go so far as to say that the thousand years since Otto's death have been a total waste of time. Certainly, other dreamers have had similar centripetal dreams. But those centrifugal forces that hold us in permanent thrall invariably undo the various confederacies, leagues, empires, thousand-year-old reichs that the centripetalists would impose upon us from the top down.

Some years ago I had a lively exchange at an Oxford political club. I had remarked that the nation state, as we know it, was the nineteenth-century invention of Bismarck when he united the German tribes in order to beat the Franks, and of Lincoln in North America when he deprived of all significant power our loosely federated states in favor of a mystical highly centralized union. A not so kindly don instructed me that, as *everyone* knows, the nation state was the result of the Thirty Years War and the Treaty of Westphalia. I said that I was aware that that was indeed the received opinion, which he had been hired to dispense, but it was plain to me that the forceful bringing together of disparate peoples against their will and imposing on them universal education—to make them like-minded and subservient—as well as military conscription, signified the end of one sort of democratic era, to advert to Vico's triad, and the beginning of our modern unwieldy and, for their unhappy residents, most onerous nation states.

What is happening today in the old Soviet Union and Yugoslavia—as well as the thousand-and-one rebellions of subject tribes against master tribes—seems to me a very good thing if we are able to draw the right lesson from all this turbulence. Thanks to CNN and other television networks, we follow, day by day, at least one or two of the thousand or so wars for "freedom" that are simultaneously being fought as worn-out centralized political structures collapse. Instead of wringing our hands and dreaming dreams of a peaceful world order centered upon Brussels or Strasburg, why not accept the fact that if people want to separate they should be allowed to? The sky will not fall in. In due course, the Muslim states of the southern tier of the old Soviet Union may want to come together in some sort of loose trade and cultural and, alas, religious federation. Why oppose them? Western Europe has already gone about as far as it needs to go toward unification. A common currency will mean a common tax collector, which will mean a common police force, which will mean tyranny in the long run and a lot of time wasted in the short run. Despite the Norwegians' insistence on giving peace prizes to the wrong people, they are not entirely stupid when it comes to their common good.

The dream of Otto and Sylvester, if ever made even partial reality, will hasten a new theocratic age, which will promptly become imperial thanks to modern technology. The world could then, most easily, become a prison for us all and with no world elsewhere to escape to.

Great centrifugal forces are at work all around the earth, and why resist them? For the centripetally minded—theocratic or imperial or both—the mosaic of different tribes that will occupy Europe from homely Bantry to glittering Vladivostok are bound to come together in the interest of mundane trade. Is not that quite enough? At least in the absence of a new god.

Certainly, there is greater safety for the individual in a multitude of states where the citizen is computerized, as it were, upon a tape, than there can possibly be in any vast centralized state. Although the United States is only a middling-size country, it is often at the so-called cutting edge when it comes to the very latest technologies of control. Recently a government spokesman noted that by the year 2008 there will be a central computer that will contain every American's financial dealings, including bank balances, use of credit cards, and so on. At the touch of a button, the Treasury will know who has what money and the Treasury will then be able to deduct what it thinks it may need in the way of tax. "The power to tax; the power to destroy," as Emerson is said to have said.

Meanwhile, total control over all of the people all of the time is the traditional aim of almost every government. In earlier times, this was only a tyrant's dream. Now it is technically possible. And has any technology ever *not* been put to use? We are told that democracy is a safeguard against misuse of power. I wouldn't know. I have never lived in a democracy. There are several near-democracies in Europe, small countries like Denmark, Holland, Switzerland, small relatively homogeneous—or, like Switzerland, ingeniously balanced heterogeneous—populations that are able to put important issues immediately to the people through referenda. Large states cannot or will not do this. Certainly no serious attempt to create a democracy has ever been made in the United States—and now it is far too late in the day for us.

John Adams proudly proclaimed that Americans would have a government not of men but of laws. We have; but *what* laws!

As you may gather, I hate the nation state as it has been evolving in my time and now looks to be metastasizing in all of Europe and, perhaps, parts of Asia. I am literally a grandchild of the American Civil War, and I belonged to the losing side. Had the issue of that war been the abolition of slavery, I could not have faulted our defeat—morally at least. But Mr. Lincoln—the first of the modern tyrants—chose to fight the war not on the issue of slavery but on the holiness and indivisibility of a union that he alone had any understanding of. With his centralizing of all power at Washington this "reborn" (*sic*) union was ready for a world empire that has done us as little good as it has done the world we have made so many messes in.

Europeans think, rather smugly, that they are not given to such primitive Christianity as Americans, but this is wishful thinking. In bad times who knows what terrible gods will emerge from under the flat rocks of this old continent that has given the world so much mindless savagery in the twentieth century alone.

Meanwhile, for better or for worse, and for as long as possible, let pluralism and diversity be our aim. There is already more than enough union, through international cartels, which pay no nation loyalty, much less tax, and through television, which is better off in the hands of numerous minor states that it can ever be as the "public" television of any great united state.

Should a theocratic age be upon us—and certainly fundamentalist Christians, Jews, and Muslims have never been busier—then the larger the political entity, the greater the danger for that administrative unit the citizen. Currently, in the United States, militant Jesus-Christers are organizing in order to take political control not only at the local level but at that of the Congress itself. This is disturbing.

In the last century a Speaker of the American House of Representatives was so reactionary that it was said of him that if God had consulted him about creation, he would have voted for chaos. Considering the alternatives, so would I.

Oxford Amnesty Lecture, 1995

PART IV

Most Americans of a certain age can recall exactly where they were and what they were doing on October 20, 1964, when word came that Herbert Hoover was dead. The heart and mind of a nation stopped. But how many recall when and how they first became aware that one or another of the Bill of Rights had expired? For me, it was sometime in 1960 at a party in Beverly Hills that I got the bad news from the constitutionally cheery actor Cary Grant. He had just flown in from New York. He had, he said, picked up his ticket at an airline counter in that magical old-world airport, Idlewild, whose very name reflected our condition. "There were these lovely girls behind the counter, and they were delighted to help me, or so they said. I signed some autographs. Then I asked one of them for my tickets. Suddenly she was very solemn. 'Do you have any identification?' she asked." (Worldly friends tell me that the "premise" of this story is now the basis of a series of TV commercials for Visa, unseen by me.) I would be exaggerating if I felt the chill in the air that long-ago Beverly Hills evening. Actually, we simply laughed. But I did, for just an instant, wonder if the future had tapped a dainty foot on our mass grave.

Curiously enough, it was Grant again who bore, as lightly as ever, the news that privacy itself hangs by a gossamer thread. "A friend in London rang me this morning," he said. This was June 4, 1963. "Usually we have code names, but this time he forgot. So after he asked for me I said into the receiver, 'All right. St. Louis, off the line. You, too, Milwaukee,' and so on. The operators love listening in. Anyway, after we talked business, he said, 'So what's the latest Hollywood gossip?' And I said, 'Well, Lana Turner is still having an affair with that black baseball pitcher.' One of the operators on the line gave a terrible cry, 'Oh, no!' "

Innocent days. Today, as media and Congress thunder their anthem, "Twinkle, twinkle, little Starr, how we wonder what you are," the current president is assumed to have no right at all to privacy because, you see, it's really about sex, not truth, a permanent nonstarter in political life. Where Grant's name assured him an admiring audience of telephone operators, the rest of us were usually ignored. That was then. Today, in the all-out, never-to-be-won twin wars on Drugs and Terrorism, two million telephone conversations a year are intercepted by law-enforcement officials. As for that famous "workplace" to which so many Americans are assigned by necessity, "the daily abuse of civil liberties . . . is a national disgrace," according to the American Civil Liberties Union in a 1996 report.

Among the report's findings, between 1990 and 1996, the number of workers under electronic surveillance increased from 8 million per year to more than 30 million. Simultaneously, employers eavesdrop on an estimated 400 million telephone conversations a year—something like 750 a minute. In 1990, major companies subjected 38 percent of their employees to urine tests for drugs. By 1996, more than 70 percent were thus interfered with. Recourse to law has not been encouraging. In fact, the California Supreme Court has upheld the right of public employers to drug-test not only those employees who have been entrusted with flying jet aircraft or protecting our borders from Panamanian imperialism but also those who simply mop the floors. The court also ruled that governments can screen applicants for drugs and alcohol. This was inspired by the actions of the city-state of Glendale, California, which wanted to test all employees due for promotion. Suit was brought against Glendale on the ground that it was violating the Fourth Amendment's protection against "unreasonable searches and seizures." Glendale's policy was upheld by the California Supreme Court, but Justice Stanley Mosk wrote a dissent: "Drug testing represents a significant additional invasion of those applicants' basic rights to privacy and dignity . . .

and the city has not carried its considerable burden of showing that such an invasion is justified in the case of all applicants offered employment."

In the last year or so I have had two Cary Grant–like revelations, considerably grimmer than what went on in the good old days of relative freedom from the state. A well-known acting couple and their two small children came to see me one summer. Photos were taken of their four-year-old and six-year-old cavorting bare in the sea. When the couple got home to Manhattan, the father dropped the negatives off at a drugstore to be printed. Later, a frantic call from his fortunately friendly druggist: "If I print these I've got to report you and you could get five years in the slammer for kiddie porn." The war on kiddie porn is now getting into high gear, though I was once assured by Wardell Pomeroy, Alfred Kinsey's colleague in sex research, that pedophilia was barely a blip on the statistical screen, somewhere down there with farm lads and their animal friends.

It has always been a mark of American freedom that unlike countries under constant Napoleonic surveillance, we are not obliged to carry identification to show to curious officials and pushy police. But now, due to Terrorism, every one of us is stopped at airports and obliged to show an ID which must include a mug shot (something, as Allah knows, no terrorist would ever dare fake). In Chicago after an interview with Studs Terkel, I complained that since I don't have a driver's license, I must carry a passport in my own country as if I were a citizen of the old Soviet Union. Terkel has had the same trouble. "I was asked for my ID—with photo—at this southern airport, and I said I didn't have anything except the local newspaper with a big picture of me on the front page, which I showed them, but they said that that was not an ID. Finally, they got tired of me and let me on the plane."

Lately, I have been going through statistics about terrorism (usually direct responses to crimes our government has committed against foreigners—although, recently, federal crimes against our own people are increasing). Only twice in twelve years has an American commercial plane been destroyed in flight by terrorists; neither originated in the United States. To prevent, however, a repetition of these two crimes, hundreds of millions of travelers must now be subjected to searches, seizures, delays.

The state of the art of citizen-harassment is still in its infancy. Nevertheless, new devices, at ever greater expense, are coming onto the market—and, soon, to an airport near you—including the dream machine of every horny schoolboy. The "Body Search" Contraband Detection System, created by American Science and Engineering, can "X-ray" through clothing to reveal the naked body, whose enlarged image can then be cast onto a screen for prurient analysis. The proud manufacturer boasts that the picture is so clear that even navels, unless packed with cocaine and taped over, can be seen winking at the voyeurs. The system also has what is called, according to an ACLU report, "a joystick-driven Zoom Option" that allows the operator to enlarge interesting portions of the image. During all this, the victim remains, as AS&E proudly notes, fully clothed. Orders for this machine should be addressed to the Reverend Pat Robertson and will be filled on a first-come, first-served basis, while the proud new owner of "Body Search" will be automatically included in the FBI's database of Sexual Degenerates—Class B. Meanwhile, in February 1997, the "Al" Gore Commission called for the acquisition of fifty-four high-tech bomb-detection machines known as the CTX 5000, a baggage scanner that is a bargain at a million dollars and will cost only $100,000 a year to service. Unfortunately, the CTX 5000 scans baggage at the rate of 250 per hour, which would mean perhaps a thousand are needed to "protect" passengers at major airports from those two putative terrorists who might—or might not—strike again in the next twelve years, as they twice did in the last twelve years. Since the present scanning system seems fairly effective, why subject passengers to hours of delay, not to mention more than $54 million worth of equipment?

Presently, somewhat confused guidelines exist so that airline personnel can recognize at a glance someone who fits the "profile" of a potential terrorist. Obviously, anyone of mildly dusky hue who is wearing a fez gets busted on the spot. For those terrorists who do not seem to fit the "profile," relevant government agencies have come up with the following behavioral tips that should quickly reveal the evil-doer. A devious drug smuggler is apt to be the very first person off the plane unless, of course, he is truly devious and chooses to be the last one off. Debonair master criminals often opt for a middle position. Single blond young women are often used, unwittingly, to carry bombs or drugs given them by Omar Sharif look-alikes in sinister Casbahs. Upon arrival in freedom's land, great drug-sniffing dogs will be turned loose on them; unfortunately, these canine detectives often mistakenly target as drug carriers women that are undergoing their menstrual period: the sort of icebreaker that often leads to merry laughter all around the customs area. Apparently one absolutely sure behavioral giveaway is undue nervousness on the part of a passenger though, again, the master criminal will sometimes appear to be too much at ease. In any case, whatever mad rule of thumb is applied, a customs official has every right to treat anyone as a criminal on no evidence at all; to seize and to search without, of course, due process of law.

Drugs. If they did not exist our governors would have invented them in order to prohibit them and so make much of the population vulnerable to arrest, imprisonment, seizure of property, and so on. In 1970, I wrote in *The New York Times*, of all uncongenial places,

> It is possible to stop most drug addiction in the United States within a very short time. Simply make all drugs available and sell them at cost. Label each drug with a precise description of what effect—good or bad—the drug will have on the taker. This will require heroic honesty. Don't say that marijuana is addictive or dangerous when it is neither, as millions of people know—unlike "speed," which kills most unpleasantly, or heroin, which can be addictive and difficult

to kick. Along with exhortation and warning, it might be good for our citizens to recall (or learn for the first time) that the United States was the creation of men who believed that each person has the right to do what he wants with his own life as long as he does not interfere with his neighbors' pursuit of happiness (that his neighbor's idea of happiness is persecuting others does confuse matters a bit).

I suspect that what I wrote twenty-eight years ago is every bit as unacceptable now as it was then, with the added problem of irritable ladies who object to my sexism in putting the case solely in masculine terms, as did the sexist founders.

I also noted the failure of the prohibition of alcohol from 1919 to 1933. And the crime wave that Prohibition set in motion so like the one today since "both the Bureau of Narcotics and the Mafia want strong laws against the sale and use of drugs because if drugs are sold at cost there would be no money in them for anyone." Will anything sensible be done? I wondered. "The American people are as devoted to the idea of sin and its punishment as they are to making money—and fighting drugs is nearly as big a business as pushing them. Since the combination of sin and money is irresistible (particularly to the professional politician), the situation will only grow worse." I suppose, if nothing else, I was a pretty good prophet.

The media constantly deplore the drug culture and, variously, blame foreign countries like Colombia for obeying that iron law of supply and demand to which we have, as a notion and as a nation, sworn eternal allegiance. We also revel in military metaphors. Czars lead our armies into wars against drug dealers and drug takers. So great is this permanent emergency that we can no longer afford such frills as habeas corpus and due process of law. In 1989 the former drug czar and TV talk-show fool, William Bennett, suggested de jure as well as de facto abolition of habeas corpus in "drug" cases as well as (I am not inventing this) public beheadings of drug dealers. A year later, Ayatollah Bennett declared, "I find no merit in the [drug] legalizers' case. The simple fact is that drug use is wrong. And the moral argument, in the end, is the most compelling argument." Of course, what this dangerous comedian thinks is moral James Madison and the Virginia statesman and Rights-man George Mason would have thought dangerous nonsense, particularly when his "morality" abolishes their gift to all of us, the Bill of Rights. But Bennett is not alone in his madness. A special assistant to the president on drug abuse declared, in 1984, "You cannot let one drug come in and say, 'Well, this drug is all right.' We've drawn the line. There's no such thing as a soft drug." There goes Tylenol-3, containing codeine. Who would have thought that age-old palliatives could, so easily, replace the only national religion that the United States has ever truly had, anti-Communism?

On June 10, 1998, a few brave heretical voices were raised in *The New York Times*, on an inner page. Under the heading BIG NAMES SIGN LETTER CRITICIZING WAR ON DRUGS. A billionaire named "George Soros has amassed signatures of hundreds of prominent people around the world on a letter asserting that the global war on drugs is causing more harm than drug abuse itself." Apparently, the Lindesmith Center in New York, funded by Soros, had taken out an ad in the *Times*, thereby, expensively, catching an editor's eye. The signatories included a former secretary of state and a couple of ex-senators, but though the ad was intended to coincide with a United Nations special session on Satanic Substances, it carried no weight with one General Barry McCaffrey, President Clinton's war director, who called the letter "a 1950s perception," whatever that may mean. After all, drug use in the Fifties was less than it is now after four decades of relentless warfare. Curiously, the *New York Times* story made the signatories seem to be few and eccentric while the Manchester *Guardian* in England reported that among the "international signatories are the former prime minister of the Netherlands . . . the former presidents of Bolivia and Colombia . . . three [U.S.] federal judges . . . senior clerics, former drugs squad officers . . ." But the *Times* always knows what's fit to print.

It is ironic—to use the limpest adjective—that a government as spontaneously tyrannous and callous as ours should, over the years, have come to care so much about our health as it endlessly tests and retests commercial drugs available in other lands while arresting those who take "hard" drugs on the parental ground that they are bad for the user's health. One is touched by their concern—touched and dubious. After all, these same compassionate guardians of our well-being have sternly, year in and year out, refused to allow us to have what every other First World country simply takes for granted, a national health service.

When Mr. and Mrs. Clinton came up to Washington, green as grass from the Arkansas hills and all pink and aglow from swift-running whitewater creeks, they tried to give the American people such a health system, a small token in exchange for all that tax money which had gone for "defense" against an enemy that had wickedly folded when our back was turned. At the first suggestion that it was time for us to join the civilized world, there began a vast conspiracy to stop any form of national health care. It was hardly just the "right wing," as Mrs. Clinton suggested. Rather, the insurance and pharmaceutical companies combined with elements of the American Medical Association to destroy forever any notion that we be a country that provides anything for its citizens in the way of health care.

One of the problems of a society as tightly controlled as ours is that we get so little information about what those of our fellow citizens whom we will never know or see are actually thinking and feeling. This seems a paradox when most politics today involves minute-by-minute polltaking on what looks to be every conceivable subject, but, as politicians and pollsters know, it's how the question is asked that determines the response. Also, there are vast areas, like rural America, that are an unmapped ultima Thule to those who own the corporations that own the media that spend billions of dollars to take polls in order to elect their lawyers to high office.

Ruby Ridge. Waco. Oklahoma City. Three warning bells from a heartland that most of us who are urban dwellers know little or nothing about. Cause of rural dwellers' rage? In 1996 there were 1,471 mergers of American corporations in the interest of "consolidation." This was the largest number of mergers in American history, and the peak of a trend that had been growing in the world of agriculture since the late 1970s. One thing shared by the victims at Ruby Ridge and Waco, and Timothy McVeigh, who may have committed mass murder in their name at Oklahoma City, was the conviction that the government of the United States is their implacable enemy and that they can only save themselves by hiding out in the wilderness, or by joining a commune centered on a messianic figure, or, as revenge for the cold-blooded federal murder of two members of the Weaver family at Ruby Ridge, blow up the building that contained the bureau responsible for the murders.

To give the media their due, they have been uncommonly generous with us on the subject of the religious and political beliefs of rural dissidents. There is a neo-Nazi "Aryan Nations." There are Christian fundamentalists called "Christian Identity," also known as "British Israelism." All of this biblically inspired nonsense has taken deepest root in those dispossessed of their farmland in the last generation. Needless to say, Christian demagogues fan the flames of race and sectarian hatred on television and, illegally, pour church money into political campaigns.

Conspiracy theories now blossom in the wilderness like night-blooming dementia praecox, and those in thrall to them are mocked invariably by the . . . by the actual conspirators. Joel Dyer, in *Harvest of Rage: Why Oklahoma City Is Only the Beginning*, has discovered some very real conspiracies out there, but the conspirators are old hands at deflecting attention from themselves. Into drugs? Well, didn't you know Queen Elizabeth II is overall director of the world drug trade (if only poor Lillibet had had the foresight in these republican times!). They tell us that the Trilateral Commission is a world-Communist conspiracy headed by the Rockefellers. Actually, the commission is excellent shorthand to show how the Rockefellers draw together politicians and academics-on-the-make to serve their business interests in government and out. Whoever it was who got somebody like Lyndon LaRouche to say that this Rockefeller Cosa Nostra is really a Communist front was truly inspired.

But Dyer has unearthed a genuine ongoing conspiracy that affects everyone in the United States. Currently, a handful of agro-conglomerates are working to drive America's remaining small farmers off their land by systematically paying them less for their produce than it costs to grow, thus forcing them to get loans from the conglomerates' banks, assume mortgages, undergo foreclosures and the sale of land to corporate-controlled agribusiness. But is this really a conspiracy or just the Darwinian workings of an efficient marketplace? There is, for once, a smoking gun in the form of a blueprint describing how best to rid the nation of small farmers. Dyer writes: "In 1962, the Committee for Economic Development comprised approximately seventy-five of the nation's most powerful corporate executives. They represented not only the food industry but also oil and gas, insurance, investment and retail industries. Almost all groups that stood to gain from consolidation were represented on that committee. Their report [*An Adaptive Program for Agriculture*] outlined a plan to eliminate farmers and farms. It was detailed and well thought out." Simultaneously, "as early as 1964, Congressmen were being told by industry giants like Pillsbury, Swift, General Foods, and Campbell Soup that the biggest problem in agriculture was too many farmers." Good psychologists, the CEO's had noted that farm children, if sent to college, seldom return to the family farm. Or as one famous economist said to a famous senator who was complaining about jet lag on a night flight from New York to London, "Well, it sure beats farming." The committee got the government to send farm children to college. Predictably, most did not come back. Government then offered to help farmers relocate in other lines of work, allowing their land to be consolidated in ever vaster combines owned by fewer and fewer corporations.

So a conspiracy had been set in motion to replace the Jeffersonian ideal of a nation whose backbone was the independent farm family with a series of agribusiness monopolies where, Dyer writes, "only five to eight multinational companies have, for all intents and purposes, been the sole purchasers and transporters not only of the American grain supply but that of the entire world." By 1982 "these companies controlled 96 percent of U.S. wheat exports, 95 percent of U.S. corn exports," and so on through the busy aisles of chic Gristedes, homely Ralph's, sympathetic Piggly Wigglys.

Has consolidation been good for the customers? By and large, no. Monopolies allow for no bargains, nor do they have to fuss too much about quality because we have no alternative to what they offer. Needless to say, they are hostile to labor unions and indifferent to working conditions for the once independent farmers, now ill-paid employees. For those of us who grew up in the prewar United States there was the genuine ham sandwich. Since consolidation, ham has been so rubberized that it tastes of nothing at all while its texture is like rosy plastic. Why? In the great hogariums a hog remains in one place, on its feet, for life. Since it does not root about—or even move—it builds up no natural resistance to disease. This means a great deal of drugs are pumped into the prisoner's body until its death and transfiguration as inedible ham.

By and large, the Sherman antitrust laws are long since gone. Today three companies control 80 percent of the total beef-packing market. How does this happen? Why do dispossessed farmers have no congressional representatives to turn to? Why do consumers get stuck with mysterious pricings of products that in themselves are inferior to those of an earlier time? Dyer's answer is simple but compelling. Through their lobbyists, the corporate executives who drew up the "adaptive program" for agriculture now own or rent or simply intimidate Congresses and presidents while the courts are presided over by their former lobbyists, an endless supply of white-collar servants since two-thirds of all the lawyers on our small planet are Americans. Finally, the people at large are not represented in government while corporations are, lavishly.

What is to be done? Only one thing will work, in Dyer's view: electoral finance reform. But those who benefit from the present system will never legislate themselves out of power. So towns and villages continue to decay between the Canadian and the Mexican borders, and the dispossessed rural population despairs or rages. Hence, the apocalyptic tone of a number of recent nonreligious works of journalism and analysis that currently record, with fascinated horror, the alienation of group after group within the United States.

Since the *Encyclopaedia Britannica* is Britannica and not America, it is not surprising that its entry for "Bill of Rights, United States" is a mere column in length, the same as its neighbor on the page "Bill of Sale," obviously a more poignant document to the island compilers. Even so, they do tell us that the roots of our Rights are in Magna Carta and that the genesis of the Bill of Rights that was added as ten amendments to our Constitution in 1791 was largely the handiwork of James Madison, who, in turn, echoed Virginia's 1776 Declaration of Rights. At first, these ten amendments were applicable to American citizens only as citizens of the entire United States and not as Virginians or as New Yorkers, where state laws could take precedence according to "states' rights," as acknowledged in the tenth and last of the original amendments. It was not until 1868 that the Fourteenth Amendment forbade the states to make laws counter to the original bill. Thus every United States person, in his home state, was guaranteed freedom of "speech and press, and the right to assembly and to petition as well as freedom from a national religion." Apparently, it was Charlton Heston who brought the Second Amendment, along with handguns and child-friendly Uzis, down from Mount DeMille. Originally, the right for citizen militias to bear arms was meant to discourage a standing federal or state army and all the mischief that an armed state might cause people who wanted to live not under the shadow of a gun but peaceably on their own atop some sylvan Ruby Ridge.

Currently, the Fourth Amendment is in the process of disintegration, out of "military necessity"—the constitutional language used by Lincoln to wage civil war, suspend habeas corpus, shut down newspapers, and free southern slaves. The Fourth Amendment guarantees "the right of the people to be secure in their persons, houses, papers, and effects, against unreasonable searches and seizures, shall not be violated, and no Warrants shall issue, but upon probable cause, supported by Oath or affirmation, and particularly describing the place to be searched, and the persons or things to be seized." The Fourth is the people's principal defense against totalitarian government; it is a defense that is now daily breached both by deed and law.

In James Bovard's 1994 book, *Lost Rights*, the author has assembled a great deal of material on just what our law enforcers are up to in the never-to-be-won wars against Drugs and Terrorism, as they do daily battle with the American people in their homes and cars, on buses and planes, indeed, wherever they can get at them, by hook or by crook or by sting. Military necessity is a bit too highbrow a concept for today's federal and local officials to justify their midnight smashing in of doors, usually without warning or warrant, in order to terrorize the unlucky residents. These unlawful attacks and seizures are often justified by the possible existence of a flush toilet on the fingered premises. (If the warriors against drugs don't take drug fiends absolutely by surprise, the fiends will flush away the evidence.) This is intolerable for those eager to keep us sin-free and obedient. So in the great sign of Sir Thomas Crapper's homely invention, they suspend the Fourth, and conquer.

Nineteen ninety-two. Bridgeport, Connecticut. *The Hartford Courant* reported that the local Tactical Narcotics Team routinely devastated homes and businesses they "searched." Plainclothes policemen burst in on a Jamaican grocer and restaurant owner with the cheery cry "Stick up, niggers. Don't move." Shelves were swept clear. Merchandise ruined. "They never identified themselves as police," the *Courant* noted. Although they found nothing but a registered gun, the owner was arrested and charged with "interfering with an arrest" and so booked. A judge later dismissed the case. Bovard reports, "In 1991, in Garland, Texas, police dressed in black and wearing black ski-masks burst into a trailer, waved guns in the air and kicked down the bedroom door where Kenneth Baulch had been sleeping next to his seventeen-month-old son. A policeman claimed that Baulch posed a deadly threat because he held an ashtray in his left hand, which explained why he shot Baulch in the back and killed him. (A police internal investigation found no wrongdoing by the officer.) In March 1992, a police SWAT team killed Robin Pratt, an Everett, Washington, mother, in a no-knock raid carrying out an arrest warrant for her husband. (Her husband was later released after the allegations upon which the arrest warrant were based turned out to be false.)" Incidentally, this KGB tactic—hold someone for a crime, but let him off if he then names someone else for a bigger crime, also known as Starr justice—often leads to false, even random allegations which ought not to be acted upon so murderously without a bit of homework first. *The Seattle Times* describes Robin Pratt's last moments. She was with her six-year-old daughter and five-year-old niece when the police broke in. As the bravest storm trooper, named Aston, approached her, gun drawn, the other police shouted, " 'Get down,' and she started to crouch onto her knees. She looked up at Aston and said, 'Please don't hurt my children. . . .' Aston had his gun pointed at her and fired, shooting her in the neck. According to [the Pratt family attorney John] Muenster, she was alive another one to two minutes but could not speak because her throat had been destroyed by the bullet. She was handcuffed, lying face down." Doubtless Aston was fearful of a divine resurrection; and vengeance. It is no secret that American police rarely observe the laws of the land when out wilding with each other, and as any candid criminal judge will tell you, perjury is often their native tongue in court.

The IRS has been under some scrutiny lately for violations not only of the Fourth but of the Fifth Amendment. The Fifth requires a grand-jury indictment in prosecutions for major crimes. It also provides that no person shall be compelled to testify against himself, forbids the taking of life, liberty, or property without due process of law, or the taking of private property for public use without compensation.

Over the years, however, the ever secretive IRS has been seizing property right and left without so much as a postcard to the nearest grand jury, while due process of law is not even a concept in their single-minded pursuit of loot. Bovard notes:

> Since 1980, the number of levies—IRS seizures of bank accounts and pay checks—has increased fourfold, reaching 3,253,000 in 1992. The General Accounting Office (GAO) estimated in 1990 that the IRS imposes over 50,000 incorrect or unjustified levies on citizens and businesses per year. The GAO estimated that almost 6 percent of IRS levies on business were incorrect. . . . The IRS also imposes almost one and a half million liens each year, an increase of over 200 percent since 1980. *Money* magazine conducted a survey in 1990 of 156 taxpayers who had IRS liens imposed on their property and found that 35 percent of the taxpayers had never received a thirty-day warning notice from the IRS of an intent to impose a lien and that some first learned of the liens when the magazine contacted them.

The current Supreme Court has shown little interest in curbing so powerful and clandestine a federal agency as it routinely disobeys the Fourth, Fifth, and Fourteenth Amendments. Of course, this particular court is essentially authoritarian and revels in the state's exercise of power while its livelier members show great wit when it comes to consulting Ouija boards in order to discern exactly what the founders originally had in mind, ignoring just how clearly Mason, Madison, and company spelled out such absolutes as you can't grab someone's property without first going to a grand jury and finding him guilty of a crime as law requires. In these matters, sacred original intent is so clear that the Court prefers to look elsewhere for its amusement. Lonely voices in Congress are sometimes heard on the subject. In 1993, Senator David Pryor thought it would be nice if the IRS were to notify credit agencies once proof was established that the agency wrongfully attached a lien on a taxpayer's property, destroying his future credit. The IRS got whiny. Such an onerous requirement would be too much work for its exhausted employees.

Since the U.S. statutes that deal with tax regulations comprise some 9,000 pages, even tax experts tend to foul up, and it is possible for any Inspector Javert at the IRS to find flawed just about any conclusion as to what Family X owes. But, in the end, it is not so much a rogue bureau that is at fault as it is the system of taxation as imposed by key members of Congress in order to exempt their friends and financial donors from taxation. Certainly, the IRS itself has legitimate cause for complaint against its nominal masters in Congress. The IRS's director of taxpayer services, Robert LeBaube, spoke out in 1989: "Since 1976 there have been 138 public laws modifying the Internal Revenue Code. Since the Tax Reform Act of 1986 there have been thirteen public laws changing the code, and in 1988 alone there were seven public laws affecting the code." As Bovard notes but does not explain, "Tax law is simply the latest creative interpretation by government officials of the mire of tax legislation Congress has enacted. IRS officials can take five, seven, or more years to write the regulations to implement a new tax law—yet Congress routinely changes the law before new regulations are promulgated. Almost all tax law is provisional—either waiting to be revised according to the last tax bill passed, or already proposed for change in the next tax bill."

What is this great busyness and confusion all about? Well, corporations send their lawyers to Congress to make special laws that will exempt their corporate profits from unseemly taxation: this is done by ever more complex—even impenetrable—tax laws which must always be provisional as there is always bound to be a new corporation requiring a special exemption in the form of a private bill tacked onto the Arbor Day Tribute. Senators who save corporations millions in tax money will not need to spend too much time on the telephone begging for contributions when it is time for him—or, yes, her—to run again. Unless—the impossible dream—the cost of elections is reduced by 90 percent, with no election lasting longer than eight weeks. Until national TV is provided free for national candidates and local TV for local candidates (the way civilized countries do it), there will never be tax reform. Meanwhile, the moles at the IRS, quite aware of the great untouchable corruption of their congressional masters, pursue helpless citizens and so demoralize the state.

It is nicely apt that the word "terrorist" (according to the *OED*) should have been coined during the French Revolution to describe "an adherent or supporter of the Jacobins, who advocated and practiced methods of partisan repression and bloodshed in the propagation of the principles of democracy and equality." Although our rulers have revived the word to describe violent enemies of the United States, most of today's actual terrorists can be found within our own governments, federal, state, municipal. The Bureau of Alcohol, Tobacco, and Firearms (known as ATF), the Drug Enforcement Agency, FBI, IRS, etc., are so many Jacobins at war against the lives, freedom, and property of our citizens. The FBI slaughter of the innocents at Waco was a model Jacobin enterprise. A mildly crazed religious leader called David Koresh had started a commune with several hundred followers—men, women, and children. Koresh preached world's end. Variously, ATF and FBI found him an ideal enemy to persecute. He was accused of numerous unsubstantiated crimes, including this decade's favorite, pedophilia, and was never given the benefit of due process to determine his guilt or innocence. David Kopel and Paul H. Blackman have now written the best and most detailed account of the American government's current war on its unhappy citizenry in *No More Wacos: What's Wrong with Federal Law Enforcement and How to Fix It.*

They describe, first, the harassment of Koresh and his religious group, the Branch Davidians, minding the Lord's business in their commune; second, the demonizing of him in the media; third, the February 28, 1993, attack on the commune: seventy-six agents stormed the communal buildings that contained 127 men, women, and children. Four ATF agents and six Branch Davidians died. Koresh had been accused of possessing illegal firearms even though he had previously invited law-enforcement agents into the commune to look at his weapons and their registrations. Under the Freedom of Information Act, Kopel and Blackman have now discovered that, from the beginning of what would become a siege and then a "dynamic entry" (military parlance for all-out firepower and slaughter), ATF had gone secretly to the U.S. Army for advanced training in terrorist attacks even though the Posse Comitatus Law of 1878 forbids the use of federal troops for civilian law enforcement. Like so many of our laws, in the interest of the war on Drugs, this law can be suspended if the army is requested by the Drug Law Enforcement Agency to fight sin. Koresh was secretly accused by ATF of producing methamphetamine that he was importing from nearby Mexico, 300 miles to the south. Mayday! The army must help out. They did, though the charges against drug-hating Koresh were untrue. The destruction of the Branch Davidians had now ceased to be a civil affair where the Constitution supposedly rules. Rather, it became a matter of grave military necessity: hence a CS-gas attack (a gas which the U.S. had just signed a treaty swearing never to use in war) on April 19, 1993, followed by tanks smashing holes in the buildings where twenty-seven children were at risk; and then a splendid fire that destroyed the commune and, in the process, the as yet uncharged, untried David Koresh. Attorney General Janet Reno took credit and "blame," comparing herself and the president to a pair of World War II generals who could not exercise constant oversight . . . the sort of statement World War II veterans recognize as covering your ass.

Anyway, Ms. Reno presided over the largest massacre of Americans by American Feds since 1890 and the fireworks at Wounded Knee. Eighty-two Branch Davidians died at Waco, including thirty women and twenty-five children. Will our Jacobins ever be defeated as the French ones were? Ah . . . The deliberate erasure of elements of the Bill of Rights (in law as opposed to in fact when the police choose to go on the rampage, breaking laws and heads) can be found in loony decisions by lower courts that the Supreme Court prefers not to conform with the Bill of Rights. It is well known that the Drug

Enforcement Agency and the IRS are inveterate thieves of private property without due process of law or redress or reimbursement later for the person who has been robbed by the state but committed no crime. Currently, according to Kopel and Blackman, U.S. and some state laws go like this: whenever a police officer is permitted, with or without judicial approval, to investigate a potential crime, the officer may seize and keep as much property associated with the alleged criminal as the police officer considers appropriate. Although forfeiture is predicated on the property's being used in a crime, there shall be no requirement that the owner be convicted of a crime. It shall be irrelevant that the person was acquitted of the crime on which the seizure was based, or was never charged with any offense. Plainly, Judge Kafka was presiding in 1987 (*United States* v. *Sandini*) when this deranged formula for theft by police was made law: "The innocence of the owner is irrelevant," declared the court. "It is enough that the property was involved in a violation to which forfeiture attaches." Does this mean that someone who has committed no crime, but may yet someday, will be unable to get his property back because *U.S.* v. *Sandini* also states firmly, "The burden of proof rests on the party alleging ownership"?

This sort of situation is particularly exciting for the woof-woof brigade of police since, according to onetime attorney general Richard Thornburgh, over 90 percent of all American paper currency contains drug residue; this means that anyone carrying, let us say, a thousand dollars in cash will be found with "drug money," which must be seized and taken away to be analyzed and, somehow, never returned to its owner if the clever policeman knows his *Sandini*.

All across the country high-school athletes are singled out for drug testing while random searches are carried out in the classroom. On March 8, 1991, according to Bovard, at the Sandburg High School in Chicago, two teachers (their gender is not given so mental pornographers can fill in their own details) spotted a sixteen-year-old boy wearing sweatpants. Their four eyes glitteringly alert, they cased his crotch, which they thought "appeared to be 'too well endowed.' " He was taken to a locker room and stripped bare. No drugs were found, only a nonstandard scrotal sac. He was let go as there is as yet no law penalizing a teenager for being better hung than his teachers. The lad and his family sued. The judge was unsympathetic. The teachers, he ruled, "did all they could to ensure that the plaintiff's privacy was not eroded." Judge Kafka never sleeps.

Although drugs are immoral and must be kept from the young, thousands of schools pressure parents to give the drug Ritalin to any lively child who may, sensibly, show signs of boredom in his classroom. Ritalin renders the child docile if not comatose. Side effects? "Stunted growth, facial tics, agitation and aggression, insomnia, appetite loss, headaches, stomach pains and seizures." Marijuana would be far less harmful.

The bombing of the Alfred P. Murrah Federal Building in Oklahoma City was not unlike Pearl Harbor, a great shock to an entire nation and, one hopes, a sort of wake-up call to the American people that all is not well with us. As usual, the media responded in the only way they know how. Overnight, one Timothy McVeigh became the personification of evil. Of motiveless malice. There was the usual speculation about confederates. Grassy knollsters. But only one other maniac was named, Terry Nichols; he was found guilty of "conspiring" with McVeigh, but he was not in on the slaughter itself.

A journalist, Richard A. Serrano, has just published *One of Ours: Timothy McVeigh and the Oklahoma City Bombing*. Like everyone else, I fear, I was sick of the subject. Nothing could justify the murder of those 168 men, women, and children, none of whom had, as far as we know, anything at all to do with the federal slaughter at Waco, the ostensible reason for McVeigh's fury. So why write such a book? Serrano hardly finds McVeigh sympathetic, but he does manage to make him credible in an ominously fascinating book.

Born in 1968, McVeigh came from a rural family that had been, more or less, dispossessed a generation earlier. Father Bill had been in the U.S. Army. Mother worked. They lived in a western New York blue-collar town called Pendleton. Bill grows vegetables; works at a local GM plant; belongs to the Roman Catholic Church. Of the area, he says, "When I grew up, it was all farms. When Tim grew up, it was half and half."

Tim turns out to be an uncommonly intelligent and curious boy. He does well in high school. He is, as his defense attorney points out, "a political animal." He reads history, the Constitution. He also has a lifelong passion for guns: motivation for joining the army. In Bush's Gulf War he was much decorated as an infantryman, a born soldier. But the war itself was an eye-opener, as wars tend to be for those who must fight them. Later, he wrote a journalist how "we were falsely hyped up." The ritual media demonizing of Saddam, Arabs, Iraqis had been so exaggerated that when McVeigh got to Iraq he was startled to "find out they are normal like me and you. They hype you to take these people out. They told us we were to defend Kuwait where the people had been raped and slaughtered. War woke me up."

As usual, there were stern laws against American troops fraternizing with the enemy. McVeigh writes a friend, "We've got these starving kids and sometimes adults coming up to us begging for food. . . . It's really 'trying' emotionally. It's like the puppy dog at the table; but much worse. The sooner we leave here the better. I can see how the guys in Vietnam were getting killed by children." Serrano notes, "At the close of the war, a very popular war, McVeigh had learned that he did not like the taste of killing innocent people. He spat into the sand at the thought of being forced to hurt others who did not hate him any more than he them."

The army and McVeigh parted once the war was done. He took odd jobs. He got interested in the far right's paranoid theories and in what Joel Dyer calls "The Religion of Conspiracy." An army buddy, Terry Nichols, acted as his guide. Together they obtained a book called *Privacy*, on how to vanish from the government's view, go underground, make weapons. Others had done the same, including the Weaver family, who had moved to remote Ruby Ridge in Idaho. Randy Weaver was a cranky white separatist with Christian Identity beliefs. He wanted to live with his family apart from the rest of America. This was a challenge to the FBI. When Weaver did not show up in court to settle a minor firearms charge, they staked him out August 21, 1992. When the Weaver dog barked, they shot him; when the Weavers' fourteen-year-old son fired in their direction, they shot him in the back and killed him. When Mrs. Weaver, holding a baby, came to the door, FBI sniper Lon Horiuchi shot her head off. The next year the Feds took out the Branch Davidians.

For Timothy McVeigh, the ATF became the symbol of oppression and murder. Since he was now suffering from an exaggerated sense of justice, not a common American trait, he went to war pretty much on his own and ended up slaughtering more innocents than the Feds had at Waco. Did he know what he was doing when he blew up the Alfred P. Murrah Federal Building in Oklahoma City because it contained the hated bureau? McVeigh remained silent throughout his trial. Finally, as he was about to be sentenced, the court asked him if he would like to speak. He did. He rose and said. "I wish to use the words of Justice Brandeis dissenting in *Olmstead* to speak for me. He wrote, 'Our government is the potent, the omnipresent teacher. For good or ill, it teaches the whole people by its example.'" Then McVeigh was sentenced to death by the government.

Those present were deeply confused by McVeigh's quotation. How could the Devil quote so saintly a justice? I suspect that he did it in the same spirit that Iago answered Othello when asked why he had done what he had done: "Demand me nothing: what you know, you know: from this time forth I never will speak word." Now we know, too: or as my grandfather used to say back in Oklahoma, "Every pancake has two sides."

Vanity Fair
November 1998

THE NEW THEOCRATS

June 18, 1997, proved to be yet another day that will live in infamy in the history of *The Wall Street Journal*, or t.w.m.i.p., "the world's most important publication," as it bills itself—blissfully unaware of just how unknown this cheery neofascist paper is to the majority of Americans, not to mention those many billions who dwell in darkness where the sulfurous flashes of Wall Street's little paper are no more than marsh gas from the distant marches of the loony empire. June 18 was the day that t.w.m.i.p. took an ad in *The New York Times*, the paper that prints only the news that will fit its not-dissimilar mindset. The ad reprinted a t.w.m.i.p. editorial titled "Modern Morality," a subject I should have thought alien to the core passions of either paper. But then for Americans morality has nothing at all to do with ethics or right action or who is stealing what money—and liberties—from whom. Morality is SEX. SEX. SEX.

The edit's lead is piping hot. "In the same week that an Army general with 147 Vietnam combat missions" (remember the *Really Good War*, for lots of Dow Jones listings?) "ended his career over an adulterous affair 13 years ago" (t.w.m.i.p. is on strong ground here; neither the general nor the lady nor any other warrior should be punished for adulteries not conducted while on watch during enemy attack) "the news broke"—I love that phrase in a journal of powerful opinion and so little numberless news—"that a New Jersey girl gave birth to a baby in the bathroom at her high school prom, put it in the trash and went out to ask the deejay to play a song by Metallica—for her boyfriend. The baby is dead."

Misled by the word "girl," I visualized a panicky pubescent tot.

But days later, when one Melissa Drexler was indicted for murder, she was correctly identified by the *Times* as a "woman, 18." In a recently published photograph of her alongside her paramour at the prom, the couple look to be in their early thirties. But it suited t.w.m.i.p. to misrepresent Ms. Drexler as yet another innocent child corrupted by laissez-faire American liberal "values," so unlike laissez-faire capitalism, the great good.

All this is "moral chaos," keens the writer. I should say that all this is just plain old-fashioned American stupidity where a religion-besotted majority is cynically egged on by a ruling establishment whose most rabid voice is *The Wall Street Journal.*

"We have no good advice on how the country might extricate itself anytime soon from a swamp of sexual confusion. . . ." You can say that again and, of course, you will. So, rather than give bad advice, cease and desist from taking out ads to blame something called The Liberals. In a country evenly divided between political reactionaries and religious maniacs, I see hardly a liberal like a tree—or even a burning bush—walking. But the writer does make it clear that the proscribed general was treated unfairly while the "girl" with baby is a statistic to be exploited by right-wing journalists, themselves often not too far removed from the odious Metallica-listening orders who drop babies in johns, a bad situation that might have been prevented by the use, let us say, of a rubber when "girl" and "boy" had sex.

But, no. We are assured that the moral chaos is the result of sexual education and "littering," as the ad puts it, "the swamp" with "condoms that for about the past five years have been dispensed by adults running our high schools . . . or by machines located in, by coincidence, the bathroom." Presumably, the confessional would be a better venue, if allowed. So, on the one hand, it is bad, as we all agree, for a woman to give birth and then abandon a baby; but then too, it's wrong, for some metaphysical reason, to help prevent such a birth from taking place. There is no sense of cause/effect when these geese start honking. Of course, t.w.m.i.p. has its own agendum: Outside marriage, no sex of any kind for the lower classes and a policing of everyone, including generals and truly valuable people, thanks to the same liberals who now "forbid nothing and punish anything." This is spaceship-back-of-the-comet reasoning.

The sensible code observed by all the world (except for certain fundamentalist monotheistic Jews, Christians, and Muslims) is that "consensual" relations in sexual matters are no concern of the state. The United States has always been backward in these matters, partly because of its Puritan origins and partly because of the social arrangements arrived at during several millennia of family-intensive agrarian life, rudely challenged a mere century ago by the Industrial Revolution and the rise of the cities and, lately, by the postindustrial work-world of services in which "safe" prostitution should have been, by now, a bright jewel.

Although the "screed" (a favorite right-wing word) in the *Times* ad is mostly rant and not to be taken seriously, the spirit behind all this blather is interestingly hypocritical. T.w.m.i.p. is not interested in morality. In fact, any company that can increase quarterly profits through the poisoning of a river is to be treasured. But the piece does reflect a certain unease that the people at large, most visibly through sex, may be trying to free themselves from their masters, who grow ever more insolent and exigent in their prohibitions—one strike and you're out is their dirty little secret. In mid-screed, the paper almost comes to the point: "Very simply [*sic*], what we're suggesting here is that the code of sexual behavior formerly set down by established religion in the U.S. more or less kept society healthy, unlike the current manifest catastrophe." There it is. Where is Norman Lear, creator of *Mary Hartman, Mary Hartman*, now that we need him? Visualize on the screen gray clapboard, slate-colored sky, om*ni*-ous (as Darryl Zanuck used to say) music. Then a woman's plaintive voice calling "Hester Prynne, Hester Prynne!" as the screen fills with a pulsing scarlet "A."

So arrière-garde that it is often avant-garde, t.w.m.i.p. is actually on to something. Although I shouldn't think anyone on its premises has heard of the eighteenth-century Neapolitan scholar Vico, our readers will recall that Vico, working from Plato, established various organic phases in human society. First, Chaos. Then Theocracy. Then Aristocracy. Then Democracy—but as republics tend to become imperial and tyrannous, they collapse and we're back to Chaos and to its child Theocracy, and a new cycle. Currently, the United States is a mildly chaotic imperial republic headed for the exit, no bad thing unless there is a serious outbreak of Chaos, in which case a new age of religion will be upon us. Anyone who ever cared for our old Republic, no matter how flawed it always was with religious exuberance, cannot *not* prefer Chaos to the harsh rule of Theocrats. Today, one sees them at their savage worst in Israel and in certain Islamic countries, like Afghanistan, etc. Fortunately, thus far their social regimentation is still no match for the universal lust for consumer goods, that brave new world at the edge of democracy. As for Americans, we can still hold the fort against our very own praying mantises—for the most part, fundamentalist Christians abetted by a fierce, decadent capitalism in thrall to totalitarianism as proclaimed so saucily in *The New York Times* of June 18, 1997.

The battle line is now being drawn. Even as the unfortunate "girl" in New Jersey was instructing the deejay, the Christian right was organizing itself to go after permissiveness in entertainment. On June 18 the Southern Baptists at their annual convention denounced the Disney company and its TV network, ABC, for showing a lesbian as a human being, reveling in *Pulp Fiction* violence, flouting Christian family values. I have not seen the entire bill of particulars (a list of more than 100 "properties" to be boycotted was handed out), but it all sounds like a pretrial deposition from Salem's glory days. Although I have criticized in these pages the Disney cartel for its media domination, I must now side with the challenged octopus.

This is the moment for Disney to throw the full weight of its wealth at the Baptists, who need a lesson in constitutional law they will not soon forget. They should be brought to court on the usual chilling-of-First-Amendment grounds as well as for restraint of trade. Further, and now let us for once get to the root of the matter. The tax exemptions for the revenues of all the churches from the Baptists to the equally absurd—and equally mischievous—Scientologists must be removed.

The original gentlemen's agreement between Church and State was that *We the People* (the State) will in no way help or hinder any religion while, absently, observing that as religion is "a good thing," the little church on Elm Street won't have to pay a property tax. No one envisaged that the most valuable real estate at the heart of most of our old cities would be tax-exempt, as churches and temples and orgone boxes increased their holdings and portfolios. The *quo* for this huge *quid* was that religion would stay out of politics and not impose its superstitions on *Us the People*. The agreement broke down years ago. The scandalous career of the Reverend Presidential Candidate Pat Robertson is a paradigm.

As Congress will never act, this must be a grass-roots movement to amend the Constitution, even though nothing in the original First Amendment says a word about tax exemptions or any other special rights to churches, temples, orgone boxes. This is a useful war for Disney to fight, though I realize that the only thing more cowardly than a movie studio or TV network is a conglomerate forced to act in the open. But if you don't, Lord Mouse, it will be your rodentian ass 15.7 million Baptists will get, not to mention the asses of all the rest of us.

The Nation
21 July 1997

Coup de Starr

Like so many observers of the mysterious Starr Ship that President Clinton seemed to sink so gracefully on television, I was mystified by the marauding pirates' inability to go for any loot other than details of his indecorous sex life, a matter of no great interest to anyone but partisans of the far right and a press gone mad with bogus righteousness. But along with mystification over the pirates' obsession with whether or not a blow job is sex (neatly finessed by Clinton because the wise judge in the Paula Jones case had forgotten to include lips in her court's menu of blue-plate delights), I had a sense that I had, somehow, been through something like this once before. Where had I stumbled over the notion that a presidential election could be overthrown because of sexual behavior that is not a crime, at least beyond the city limits of Atlanta, Georgia? Sex as politics. Politics as sex. *Sex Is Politics*. Then I remembered. In January 1979 I had written a piece in *Playboy* with that title, because something new was happening in American politics back then.

The ERA and gay rights were, at that time, under fire. . . . At that time! Clinton's support for women and gays, at the beginning of his first term, was more than enough to launch the Starr Ship. But twenty years ago, the right had already vowed that so-called valence issues would be its principal choice of weapon. Or, as a member of the Conservative Caucus put it then, with engaging candor, "We're going after people on the basis of their hot buttons." In other words, sex, sex, sex. Save the Family and Save Our Children were the slogans of that moment, and one Richard Viguerie was the chief money raiser for the powers of darkness. "Viguerie is not just a hustler," I wrote in *Playboy*. "He is also an ideologue." He was thinking of creating a new political party. "I have raised millions of dollars for the conservative movement over the years," he said, "and I am not happy with the result. I decided to become more concerned with how the money is spent." Viguerie was working with a group called Gun Owners of America.

> Another of Viguerie's clients is Utah's Senator Orrin Hatch, a proud and ignorant man who is often mentioned as a possible candidate for President if the far right should start a new political party. . . . "I want," says Viguerie, "a massive assault on Congress in 1978. I don't want any token efforts. We now have the talent and the resources to move in a bold, massive way. I think we can move against Congress in 1978 in a way that's never been conceived of."

I duly noted that this sounded like revolution.

As it was, the bold, massive move against Congress did not take place until 1994, thanks to the twelve-year Reagan/Bush snooze, capped by Clinton's political ineptitude. But now that the Man from Hope has gained a personal, if temporary, victory against our would-be revolutionaries, I suggest that before the obligatory Capitol Reichstag fire, a charge of treason be brought against Kenneth Starr. Since all sovereignty rests with We the People, Starr's attempt to overthrow the presidential elections of 1992 and 1996 constitutes a bold, massive blow at the American people themselves: a unique attempt in our history and one that must be swiftly addressed in order to discover just who his co-conspirators are and how best to undo their plots. Yes, Hillary, there was—and there is—a right-wing plot with deep roots. Meanwhile, Senator Orrin Hatch, do you solemnly swear to tell the truth, the whole truth, and nothing but the truth, so help you Moroni?

The Nation
26 October 1998

On August 17 the forty-second president of the United States, William Jefferson Clinton, will commit what could be a fatal political error by allowing himself to be questioned under oath by a special prosecutor, Kenneth W. Starr, who has taken over four years and spent 40 million taxpayer dollars in trying to prove that Mr. Clinton must be guilty of something or other and so should be impeached by the House of Representatives and tried and convicted by the Senate (as the Constitution requires) for what the peculiar Mr. Starr will argue is a high crime or misdemeanor, like treason or taking bribes or insufficient racial bigotry.

Foreigners are mystified by the whole business while thoughtful Americans—there are several of us—are equally mystified that the ruling establishment of the country has proved to be so mindlessly vindictive that it is willing, to be blunt, to overthrow the lawful government of the United States—that is, a president elected in 1992 and reelected in 1996 by *We the People*, that sole source of all political legitimacy, which takes precedence over the Constitution and the common law and God himself. This last was a concept highly uncongenial to the enlightened eighteenth-century founders but not, we are told, to a onetime judge of meager intellectual capacity but deep faith in all the superstitions that ruling classes encourage the lower orders to believe so that they will not question authority.

First, what is the president guilty of? Attempts to prove that he did something criminal fifteen years ago in Arkansas in a real estate deal came to nothing. Undeterred, Mr. Starr kept on searching for "high crime and misdemeanors" as the Constitution puts it. Had one of Clinton's associates in the White House been murdered, possibly by Mrs. Clinton, said to be his mistress? This "murder" was found to be a suicide, the result of depression brought on by savage attacks from a fascist newspaper called *The Wall Street Journal*. The restless Starr moved on to other areas. Meanwhile, in 1994, Congress became Republican and political partisans are now reveling in the political paralysis of the Democratic White House. According to Starr, the fate of the Republic now depends upon whether or not Clinton lied under oath when he denied having had sexual relations with a White House intern, Monica Lewinsky, assuming anyone can define, satisfactorily, a sexual relation. Does a blow job performed on a passive president, idly daydreaming of the budget, count as intercourse? Finally, semanticists are stuck with the English word "intercourse." *Inter* means between at least two people. *Intra* would be what we call a gang bang, not practical in the Oval Office unless sturdy Secret Service lads join in. Did they? As I write, the nation awaits the laboratory analysis of what is, according to Monica, a presidential semen stain on her elegant blue dress, carefully preserved so that, when her time comes, she can take her place in history alongside if not Joan of Arc, Charlotte Corday.

A few years ago two pollsters did an elaborate study of a wide spectrum of the American population. Many questions were asked on many subjects. The results were published in a book called *The Day America Told the Truth*, not a confidence-inspiring title when over 90 percent of those polled confessed to being "habitual liars." That the president of such an electorate should lie about sex makes him more sympathetic than not. Certainly, if so irrelevant a question was asked of George Washington, he would have run Mr. Starr through with his sword while Abraham Lincoln would have thrown him out the window. But irrelevance is now the American condition, both as a global empire and incoherent domestic polity. Two thirds of all the world's lawyers are American and they have made a highly profitable, for them, mess of our legal system. They could not prove, in the Fifties, that Alger Hiss had been a spy for the Soviet so they sent him to prison on an unconvincing perjury charge. Al Capone was never convicted of murder or extortion: he was put in jail for income tax evasion. This is law in its decadence.

After four years, Starr has found no crime that Clinton has committed except denying a sexual relationship with Monica which she has already said, under oath, never took place but now says, under oath and with a wink from Starr for her previous perjury, did take place. The president cannot be indicted by a civil grand jury. He need not speak to Starr, who is, ironically, his employee. The president's attorney general, Janet Reno, with the connivance of two right-wing senators (one is Jesse Helms, tobacco's best friend) and a panel of three right-wing judges, came up with Starr as special prosecutor to investigate, originally, Whitewater and then anything else that might undo the results of two presidential elections.

What is behind this vendetta against Clinton, a popular president? First, the most powerful emotion in American political life is the undying hatred of certain whites for all blacks. For American blacks, Clinton is white knight. Arkansas is also a southern state where the Ku Klux Klan is still a force. When the schools were desegregated in the Fifties, a battle line was drawn. A former judge and a member of the White Citizens Council known as "Justice" Jim Johnson waged a war against blacks in general and Clinton in particular. "Justice Jim" is also associated with someone *The Observer* (U.K.) calls "a convicted fraudster," David Hale, in charge of the "Arkansas Project," funded by a conservative billionaire named Richard Mellon Scaife. This brings us to the Clintons' other nemesis: the wealthy conservative ruling class. In order to avoid taxation, they have through their lawyers, both in and out of government, placed their capital in tax-free foundations for "charitable" purposes. But to have such a foundation one must never use it to meddle in politics. But Mr. Scaife does meddle. He gives money to such disreputable papers as *The American Spectator*, which has published numerous wild stories about the Clintons. A year or so ago, Mr. Scaife rewarded Starr with a professorship at Pepperdine University, which Starr accepted and then, as the publicity was bad, he hastily returned to his war on Clinton. Presumably, he will be paid off by Scaife once his holy work is done. Every society gets the Titus Oates it deserves.

Mrs. Clinton is correct when she says that there is a right-wing conspiracy against them. Unfortunately for her, Americans have been trained by media to go into Pavlovian giggles at the mention of the word "conspiracy" because for an American to believe in a conspiracy he must also believe in flying saucers or, craziest of all, that more than one person was involved in the JFK murder. Mrs. Clinton, perhaps, emphasizes too heavily the "right-wing" aspect of her enemies. It is corporate America, quite wingless in political as opposed to money matters, that declared war on the Clintons in 1993 when the innocent couple tried to give the American people a national health service, something every civilized country has but we must never enjoy because the insurance companies now get one third of the money spent on health care and the insurance companies are the piggy banks—the cash cows—of corporate America.

In order to destroy the health service plan, insurance and pharmaceutical companies, in tandem with lively elements of the American Medical Association, conspired to raise a half billion dollars to create and then air a barrage of TV advertisements to convince the electorate that such a service was Communist, not to mention an affront to the Darwinian principle that every American has the right to die unhelped by the state, which collects half his income in life with which to buy, thus far, five and a half trillion dollars worth of military hardware at stupendous—to this day—cost. Then, not content with the political destruction of the Clintons' health plan, corporate America decided to destroy their reputations. Nothing personal in this, by the way. But how else can the ownership of the country send a warning to other feckless politicians that the country and its people exist only to make money for corporations now so internationalized that they cannot be made to pay tax on much—if any—of their profits. Starr is now the most visible agent of corporate America wielding a new weapon under the sun: endless legal harassment of a twice-elected President so that he cannot exercise his office as first magistrate.

All sovereignty in the United States rests, most vividly, on the concept of "We the People of the United States" (with the sometime addition of "in Congress Assembled"). The Constitution, the common law, and even the wealth of corporate America or the rage of lumpen white Americans against the blacks must bow to this great engine which could, through a constitutional convention, sweep into limbo all our current arrangements. President John Adams wanted a republic not of men but of laws. He could not have foreseen the madness of our present condition with everyone at law and expensive prisons filling up while a partisan lawyer, through legal harassment, is busy undoing the presidential elections of 1992 and 1996 because his paymasters did not like the results.

Happily when the collapse begins, there may yet be time for that most feared (Pavlov again) rendezvous with destiny—a constitutional convention. Meanwhile, I should not in the least be surprised if yet another "conspiracy," in the name of We the People, is set in motion against Kenneth W. Starr, who, no matter how meticulously he has observed the rules of the statute creating his monstrous office, did, in effect, attempt to overthrow two lawful elections reflective of the People's will and he is put on trial for—why not?—treason against the United States. If nothing else, such an exercise might reveal all sorts of highly interesting co-conspirators.

International Herald Tribune
11 August 1998

Birds and Bees and Clinton

How time flies! Seven fairly long years have now passed since I explained the Birds and the Bees to *Nation* readers, thus putting the finis to the cold war and, may I boast, more than one case of nervous tic douloureux, which ticked no more ["A Few Words About Sex: The Birds and the Bees," October 28, 1991]. But since that long-ago October day when I explained the mysteries of sex and scales fell from readers' eyes, new hordes have grown up in darkness, among them Kenneth Starr, as well as his numerous investigators and co-conspirators on the House Judiciary Committee, as well as in Pittsburgh's Mellon Patch and Marietta, Georgia, where the nation's Renaissance Man awaits rebirth as commander of the armies of a sinless America, troops whose powder is kept dry as, nervously, they closely shave hairy palms while their minds slowly rattle into madness from abuse of self and others.

It was not until Mr. Starr published his dirty book at public expense that I realized how far off-track I have allowed these sad dummies to get. Simple truths about the birds and the bees have been so distorted by partisanship that blow jobs and hand jobs are now confused with The Real Thing, which can only be classic in-and-out as Anthony Burgess so snappily put it in *A Clockwork Orange*. I take full responsibility for not providing a booster shot of Sex Ed. So, as the old impeachment train leaves the station, let me demonstrate how the President did not commit perjury when he said he did not have sexual intercourse with . . . surely not Abigail Thernstrom . . . I seem to have mislaid my notes. Anyway, you know who I mean.

First, let us quickly—or "briefly" as every question on CNN now begins—review the bidding from our last symposium. "Men and women are *not* alike." That was the first shocker I had for you in 1991. "They have different sexual roles to perform." At this point Andrea Dworkin, with a secret smile, began to load her bazooka. "Despite the best efforts of theologians and philosophers to disguise our condition, there is no point to us, or to any species, except pro-liferation and survival. This is hardly glamorous, and so to give Meaning to Life, we have invented some of the most bizarre religions that . . . alas, we have nothing to compare ourselves to. We are biped mammals filled with red seawater (reminder of our oceanic origin), and we exist to reproduce until we are eventually done in by the planet's changing weather or a stray meteor." Thus, I wrapped up the Big Picture.

Next: Lubricious Details. "The male's function is to shoot se-men as often as possible into as many women (or attractive surro-gates) as possible, while the female's function is to be shot briefly" by Wolf Blitzer . . . no, no, by a male, any male, "in order to fertilize an egg, which she will lay nine months later."

Seven years ago, apropos same-sex versus other-sex, or homo-sexuality versus heterosexuality, two really dumb American sports in-vented by the spiritual heirs of Gen. Abner Doubleday, who gave us baseball, I wrote, "In the prewar Southern town of Washington, D.C., it was common for boys to have sex with one another. It was called 'messing around' and it was no big deal." I went into no more detail because I assumed most readers would get the point.

Recently, the sexologist George Plimpton, a James Moran In-stitute professor emeritus, explained in *The New Yorker* how boys in his youth would go through mating stages with girls, using, sig-nificantly, baseball terminology like "getting to first base," which meant . . . and so on. "Going all the way," however, was used instead of "home run" for full intercourse, the old in-and-out or mature penis-vagina intercourse.

Arguably, Southerners are somewhat different from other resi-dents of that shining city on a hill that has brought so much light and joy to all the world in the past two centuries. In balmy climes, human beings mature early. They also have a lot of chiggery outdoors to play baseball and other games in.

When I was a boy, Fairfax County, Virginia, where I lived, was Li'l Abner country. No glamorous houses. No CIA lords hidden away in Georgian mansions on the Potomac Heights. There was just a Baptist church. A Methodist church. And a lot of Sunday. Also, a whole hierarchy of do's and don'ts when it came to boy-girl sex. What is now harshly called groping was the universal sentimental approach (put down that bazooka, Andrea). All players understood touching. Even without a thong. Endless kissing. First, second, third bases to be got to. Then a boy shootist was allowed, more soon than late, to shoot. Otherwise he might *die*, of dreaded blueballs. Girls tended to be understanding. Even so, all-the-way intercourse was not on offer unless he was "serious." Now add to these age-old rituals of mating cold war Pentagon-CIA terminology, the concept of "plausible deniability," and one starts to understand the truth of the President's denial under oath that he had sexual relations with Miss Monica. From the Testimony: "The President maintained that there can be no sexual relationship without sexual intercourse, regardless of what other sexual activities may transpire. He stated that 'most ordinary Americans' would embrace this distinction." Certainly most lads and lassies in Arkansas or the Fairfax County of sixty years ago would agree.

It is true that in the age of Freud, now drawing to a close, it used to be argued by those who preached the good news in his name that *everything* was sexual. Two men shaking hands. The embrace between baseball players on the diamond. Two women friends weeping in each other's arms, and so on. One can argue that, yes, there is a sexual element to everything if one wants to go digging but even the most avid Freudian detective would have to admit that what might be construed as sexuality by other means falls literally short of plain old in-and-out, which is the name of the game that takes precedence even over General Doubleday's contribution to the boredom of nations.

In reference to Miss Monica's first sworn denial of sexual relations with the President, which Clinton had originally confirmed, he later said, "I believe at the time she filled out this affidavit, if she believed that the definition of sexual relationship was two people having intercourse, then this is accurate." To support Clinton's reading of the matter, one has only to overhear Miss Monica and her false friend/fiend Linda Tripp bemoaning the fact that the President will not perform the absolute, complete, all-the-way act of becoming as one with her in mature heterosexual land forever glimmering somewhere over the rainbow. Without sexual intercourse there can be no sexual relationship. If this sounds like quibbling, it is. But that is the way we have been speaking in lawyerland for quite some time. The honor system at West Point regarded quibbling as worse than lying. So the officer corps became adept at quibbling, even in the ruins of the city of Ben Tre, which "we destroyed in order to save it."

A nation not of men but of laws, intoned John Adams as he, among other lawyers, launched what has easily become the most demented society ever consciously devised by intelligent men. We are now enslaved by laws. We are governed by lawyers. We create little but litigate much. Our monuments are the ever-expanding prisons, where millions languish for having committed victimless crimes or for simply not playing the game of plausible deniability (a.k.a. lying) with a sufficiently good legal team. What began as a sort of Restoration comedy, *The Impeachment of the President*, on a frivolous, irrelevant matter, is suddenly turning very black indeed, and all our political arrangements are at risk as superstitious Christian fundamentalists and their corporate manipulators seem intent on overthrowing two presidential elections in a Senate trial. This is no longer comedy. This is usurpation.

With that warning, I invite the Senate to contemplate Vice President Aaron Burr's farewell to the body over which he himself had so ably presided: "This house is a sanctuary, a citadel of law, of order, and of liberty; and it is here in this exalted refuge; here, if anywhere, will resistance be made to the storm of political frenzy and the silent arts of corruption; and if the Constitution be destined ever to perish by the sacrilegious hands of the demagogue or the usurper, which God avert, its expiring agonies will be witnessed on this floor." Do no harm to this state, Conscript Fathers.

The Nation
28 December 1998

I am writing this note a dozen days before the inauguration of the loser of the year 2000 presidential election. Lost republic as well as last empire. We are now faced with a Japanese seventeenth-century-style arrangement: a powerless Mikado ruled by a shogun vice president and his Pentagon warrior counselors. Do they dream, as did the shoguns of yore, of the conquest of China? We shall know more soon, I should think, than late. Sayonara.

11 January 2001

*Congratulations, Mr. President-Elect. Like everyone else, I'm eagerly looking forward to your inaugural address. As you must know by now, we could never get enough of your speeches during the recent election in which the best man won, as he always does in what Spiro Agnew so famously called "the greatest nation in the country."

Apropos your first speech to us as president. I hope you don't mind if I make a few suggestions, much as I used to do in the Sixties when I gave my regular States of the Union roundups on David Susskind's TV show of blessed memory. Right off, it strikes me that this new beginning may be a good place to admit that for the last fifty years we have been waging what the historian Charles A. Beard so neatly termed "perpetual war for perpetual peace."

* This was written for *Vanity Fair* before the November 7, 2000, presidential election.

It is my impression, Mr. President-Elect, that most Americans want our economy converted from war to peace. Naturally, we still want to stand tall. We also don't want any of our tax money wasted on health care because that would be Communism, which we all abhor. But we would like some of our tax dollars spent on education. Remember what you said in your terminal debate with your opponent, now so much charred and crumbling toast? "Education is the key to the new millennium." (Actually, looking at my notes, all four of you said that.)

In any case, it is time we abandon our generally unappreciated role as world policeman, currently wasting Colombia, source of satanic drugs, while keeping Cuba, Iraq, and, until recently, Serbia "in correction," as policepersons call house arrest. This compulsive interference in the affairs of other states is expensive and pointless. Better we repair our own country with "internal improvements," as Henry Clay used to say. But in order to do this your first big job will be to curb the Pentagon warlords and their fellow conspirators in Congress and the boardrooms of corporate America. Ever since the Soviet Union so unsportingly disbanded in order to pursue protocapitalism and double-entry bookkeeping, our warlords have been anxiously searching for new enemies in order to justify an ever increasing military budget. Obviously, there is Terrorism to be fought. There is also the war on Drugs, to be fought but never won. Even so, in the failed attempt, the coming destruction of Colombia, a once liberal democratic nation, promises to be great fun for warlords and media, if not the residents of a once happy nation. Lately, a new clear and present danger has been unveiled: Rogue States, or "states of concern." Currently, North Korea, Iraq, and Iran have been so fingered, while the world's one billion Muslims have been demonized as crazed fanatics, dedicated to destroying all that is good on earth, which is us.

Since we have literally targeted our enemies, the Pentagon assumes that, sooner or later, Rogues will take out our cities, presumably from spaceships. So to protect ourselves, the Ronald Reagan Memorial Nuclear Space Shield must be set in place at an initial cost of $60 billion even though, as of July, tests of the system, no matter how faked by the Pentagon, continued to fail. The fact that, according to polls, a majority of your constituents believe that we already have such a shield makes it possible for you to say you're updating it and then do nothing. After all, from 1949 to 1999 the U.S. spent $7.1 trillion on "national defense." As a result, the national debt is $5.6 trillion, of which $3.6 trillion is owed to the public, and $2 trillion to the Social Security–Medicare Trust Funds, all due to military spending and to the servicing of the debt thus incurred.

Mr. President-Elect, since Treasury figures are traditionally juggled, it would be nice if you were to see to it that the actual income and outgo of federal money are honestly reported. Last year the government told us, falsely, that its income was just over $1.8 trillion while it spent just under $1.8 trillion; hence, the famous, phantom surplus when there was, of course, our usual homely deficit of around $90 billion. Year after year, the government's official income is inflated by counting as revenue the income of the people's Social Security and Medicare Trust Funds. These funds are not federal revenue. This year Social Security has a healthy surplus of $150 billion. No wonder corporate America and its employees in Congress are eager to privatize this healthy fund, thus far endangered only by them.

Although actual military spending was indeed lower last year than usual, half the budget still went to pay for wars to come as well as to blowing up the odd aspirin factory in the Sudan. Cash outlays for the military were $344 billion while interest on the military-caused national debt was $282 billion: sorry to bore you with these statistics, but they are at the heart of our—what was Jimmy Carter's unfortunate word?—malaise (that's French for broke). The Clinton administration's airy promise of a $1.8 trillion budget surplus over the next decade was, of course, a bold if comforting fiction, based on surreal estimates of future federal income—not to mention expenditures which, if anything like last September's congressional spending spree, will drown us in red ink.

Sir, if you are going to be of any use at all to the nation and to the globe that it holds hostage, you will have to tame the American military. Discipline the out-of-control service chiefs. Last September, the Chairman of the Joint Chiefs of Staff, General H. H. Shelton, declared that more, not less, dollars were needed. Specifically, the Marines want an extra $1.5 billion per year, the Army wants over $30 billion, the Navy $20 billion, the Air Force $30 billion, all in the absence of an enemy (we spend twenty-two times more than our seven potential enemies—Cuba, Iran, Iraq, Libya, North Korea, Sudan, and Syria—combined). You must not grant these ruinous increases.

In August 1961, I visited President Kennedy at Hyannis Port. The Berlin Wall was going up, and he was about to begin a huge military buildup—reluctantly, or so he said, as he puffed on a cigar liberated by a friend from Castro's Cuba. It should be noted that Jack hated liberals more than he did conservatives. "No one can ever be liberal enough for the *New York Post*," he said. "Well, the *Post* should be happy now. Berlin's going to cost us at least three and a half billion dollars. So, with this military buildup, we're going to have a seven-billion-dollar deficit for the year. That's a lot of pump priming." He scowled. "God, I hate the way they throw money around over there at the Pentagon."

"It's not they," I said. "It's you. It's your administration." Briskly, he told me the facts of life, and I repeat them now as advice from the thirty-fifth to the—what are you, Mr. President? Forty-third president? "The only way for a president to control the Pentagon would be if he spent the entire four years of his first term doing nothing else but investigating that mess, which means he really could do nothing else . . ."

"Like getting reelected?"

He grinned. "Something like that."

So I now propose, Mr. President-Elect, while there is still time, that you zero in on the links between corporate America and the military and rationalize as best you can the various procurement policies, particularly the Ronald Reagan Memorial Nuclear Shield. You should also leak to the American people certain Pentagon secrets. In 1995, we still had our missiles trained on 2,500 foreign targets. Today, to celebrate peace in the world, our missiles are trained on 3,000 foreign targets—of which 2,260 are in Russia; the rest are directed at China and the Rogue States. Although President Clinton has spoken eloquently of the need for a reduction in such dangerous nuclear targeting, the Pentagon does as it pleases, making the world unsafe for everyone. But then *USA Today* recently reported that the military enjoys the highest popularity rating (64 percent) of any group in the country—the Congress and Big Business are among the lowest. Of course, the services do spend $265 million annually on advertising.

Jack Kennedy very much enjoyed Fletcher Knebel's thriller *Seven Days in May*, later a film. The story: a jingo based on the real-life Admiral Arthur Radford plans a military coup to take over the White House. Jack found the book riveting. "Only," he chuckled, rather grimly, "it's a lot more likely that this president will one day raise his own army and occupy their damned building." No, I don't agree with Oliver Stone that the generals killed him. But there is, somewhere out there, a watchdog that seems never to bark in the night. Yet the dog that doesn't bark is the one that should be guarding the house from burglars, in this case the military-industrial complex that President Eisenhower so generously warned us against. Although there are many media stories about costly overruns in the defense industries as well as the slow beginning of what may yet turn into an actual debate over the nuclear shield that Reagan envisaged for us after seeing Alfred Hitchcock's *Torn Curtain*, a movie nowhere near as good as *Seven Days in May*, there is, as yet, no debate over the role of the military in the nation's life and its ongoing threat to us all, thanks to the hubris of senior officers grown accustomed to dispensing vast amounts of the people's money for missiles that can't hit targets and bombers that can't fly in the rain. Congress, which should ride herd, does not because too many of its members are financed by those same companies that absorb our tax money, nor is it particularly helpful that senior officers, after placing orders with the defense industries, so often go to work as salesmen for the very same companies they once bought from.

Of all recent presidents, Clinton was expected to behave the most sensibly in economic matters. He understood how the economy works. But because he had used various dodges to stay out of the Vietnam War, he came to office ill at ease with the military. When Clinton tried to live up to his pledge to gay voters that the private life of any military person was no one's business but his own, the warlords howled that morale would be destroyed. Clinton backed down. When Clinton went aboard the aircraft carrier U.S.S. *Theodore Roosevelt* to take the salute, sailors pranced around with mop ends on their heads, doing fag imitations while hooting at the president, who just stood there. These successful insults to civilian authority have made the military ever more truculent and insolent. And now they must be brought to heel.

This summer, the warlords of the Pentagon presented the secretary of defense with their Program Objective Memorandum. Usually, this is a polite wish list of things that they would like to see under the Christmas tree. By September, the wish list sounded like a harsh ultimatum. As one dissenting officer put it, "Instead of a budget based on a top-line budget number, the chiefs are demanding a budget based on military strategy." Although their joint military strategies, as tested in war over the last fifty years, are usually disastrous, military strategy in this context means simply extorting from the government $30 billion a year over and above the 51 percent of the budget that now already goes for war. Mr. President-Elect, I would advise you to move your office from the West Wing of the White House to the Pentagon, across the river. Even though every day that you spend there could prove to be your Ides of March, you will at least have the satisfaction of knowing that you tried to do something for us, the hitherto unrepresented people.

Fifty years ago, Harry Truman replaced the old republic with a national-security state whose sole purpose is to wage perpetual wars, hot, cold, and tepid. Exact date of replacement? February 27, 1947. Place: White House Cabinet Room. Cast: Truman, Undersecretary of State Dean Acheson, a handful of congressional leaders. Republican senator Arthur Vandenberg told Truman that he could have his militarized economy only *if* he first "scared the hell out of the American people" that the Russians were coming. Truman obliged. The perpetual war began. Representative government of, by, and for the people is now a faded memory. Only corporate America enjoys representation by the Congresses and presidents that it pays for in an arrangement where no one is entirely accountable because those who have bought the government also own the media. Now, with the revolt of the Praetorian Guard at the Pentagon, we are entering a new and dangerous phase. Although we regularly stigmatize other societies as rogue states, we ourselves have become the largest rogue state of all. We honor no treaties. We spurn international courts. We strike unilaterally wherever we choose. We give orders to the United Nations but do not pay our dues. We complain of terrorism, yet our empire is now the greatest terrorist of all. We bomb, invade, subvert other states. Although We the People of the United States are the sole source of legitimate authority in this land, we are no longer represented in Congress Assembled. Our Congress has been hijacked by corporate America and its enforcer, the imperial military machine. We the unrepresented People of the United States are as much victims of this militarized government as the Panamanians, Iraqis, or Somalians. We have allowed our institutions to be taken over in the name of a globalized American empire that is totally alien in concept to anything our founders had in mind. I suspect that it is far too late in the day for us to restore the republic that we lost a half-century ago.

Even so, Mr. President-Elect, there is an off chance that you might actually make some difference if you start now to rein in the warlords. Reduce military spending, which will make you popular because you can then legitimately reduce our taxes instead of doing what you have been financed to do, freeing corporate America of its small tax burden. The 1950 taxes on corporate profits accounted for

25 percent of federal revenue; in 1999 only 10.1 percent. Finally, as sure as you were not elected by We the People but by the vast sums of unaccountable corporate money, the day of judgment is approaching. Use your first term to break the Pentagon. Forget about a second term. After all, if you succeed on the other side of the Potomac, you will be a hero to We the People. Should you fail or, worse, do nothing, you may be the last president, by which time history will have ceased to notice the United States and all our proud rhetoric will have been reduced to an ever diminishing echo. Also, brood upon an odd remark made by your canny, if ill-fated, predecessor Clinton. When Gingrich and his Contract on (rather than with) America took control of Congress, Clinton said, "The president is not irrelevant." This was a startling admission that he could become so. Well, sir, be relevant. Preserve, protect, and defend what is left of our ancient liberties, not to mention our heavily mortgaged fortune.*

Vanity Fair
December 2000

* Repeated with the following message to the troops: And so Mr. President, elected by the Supreme Court (5–4), has now, in addition to a vice-president who was a former secretary of defense, appointed another former defense secretary to his old post as well as a general to be secretary of state; thus the pass was sold.

The Vice President to Richard Nixon and bribe-taker to many, Spiro Agnew, was once inspired to say, "The United States, for all its faults, is still the greatest nation in the country." Today, even in the wake of the Supreme Court's purloining of the election for the forty-third President, Spiro must be standing tall among his fellow shades. Have we not come through, yet again? As we did in 1888 when Grover Cleveland's plurality of the popular vote was canceled by the intricacies of the Electoral College, and as we even more famously did in 1876 when the Democrat Samuel Tilden got 264,000 more votes than the Republican Rutherford B. Hayes, whose party then challenged the votes in Oregon, South Carolina, Louisiana and—yes, that slattern Florida. An electoral commission chosen by Congress gave the election to the loser, Hayes, by a single vote, the result of chicanery involving a bent Supreme Court Justice appointed by the sainted Lincoln. Revolution was mooted but Tilden retired to private life and to the pleasures of what old-time New Yorkers used to recall, wistfully, as one of the greatest collections of pornography in the Gramercy Park area of Manhattan.

Until December 12, we enjoyed a number of quietly corrupt elections, decently kept from public view. But the current Supreme Court, in devil-may-care mood, let all sorts of cats out of its bag—such as a total commitment to what the far right euphemistically calls family values. Justice Antonin Scalia—both name and visage reminiscent of a Puccini villain—affirmed family values by not recusing himself from the Bush–Gore case even though his son works for the same law firm that represented Bush before the Court. Meanwhile, Justice Clarence Thomas's wife works for a far-right think tank, the Heritage Foundation, and even as her husband attended gravely to arguments, she was vetting candidates for office in the Bush Administration.

Elsewhere, George W. Bush, son of a failed Republican President, was entrusting his endangered Florida vote to the state's governor, his brother Jeb.

On the other side of family values, the Gore clan has, at times, controlled as many as a half-dozen Southern legislatures. They are also known for their forensic skill, wit, learning—family characteristics the Vice President modestly kept under wraps for fear of frightening the folks at large.

American politics is essentially a family affair, as are most oligarchies. When the father of the Constitution, James Madison, was asked how on earth any business could get done in Congress when the country contained a hundred million people whose representatives would number half a thousand, Madison took the line that oligarchy's iron law always obtains: A few people invariably run the show; and keep it, if they can, in the family.

Finally, those founders, to whom we like to advert, had such a fear and loathing of democracy that they invented the Electoral College so that the popular voice of the people could be throttled, much as the Supreme Court throttled the Floridians on December 12. We were to be neither a democracy, subject to majoritarian tyranny, nor a dictatorship, subject to Caesarean folly.

Another cat let out of the bag is the Supreme Court's dedication to the 1 percent that own the country. Justice Sandra Day O'Connor couldn't for the life of her see why anyone would find the Palm Beach butterfly ballot puzzling. The subtext here was, as it is so often with us, race. More votes were invalidated by aged Votomatic machines in black districts than in white. This made crucial the uncounted 10,000 Miami-Dade ballots that recorded no presidential vote. Hence the speed with which the Bush campaign, loyally aided and abetted by a 5-to-4 majority of the Supreme Court, invented a series of delays to keep those votes from ever being counted because, if they were, Gore would have won the election. Indeed he did win the election until the Court, through ever more brazen stays and remands, with an eye on that clock ever ticking, delayed matters until, practically speaking, in the eyes of the five, if not all of the four, there was no longer time to count, the object of an exercise that had sent trucks filled with a million ballots from one dusty Florida city to the next, to be kept uncounted.

During this slow-paced comedy, there was one riveting moment of truth that will remain with us long after G.W. Bush has joined the lengthening line of twilight Presidents in limbo. On the Wednesday before the Thursday when we gave thanks for being the nation once hailed as the greatest by Agnew, the canvassing board in Dade County was, on the orders of the Florida Supreme Court, again counting ballots when an organized crowd stormed into the county building, intimidating the counters and refusing to give their names to officials. *The Miami Herald*, a respectable paper, after examining various voting trends, etc., concluded that Gore had actually carried Florida by 23,000 votes. The *Herald* plans to examine those much-traveled ballots under Florida's "sunshine" law. I suspect that the ballots and their chads will be found missing.

Thanksgiving came and went. The ballots toured up and down the Florida freeways. Gore was accused of trying to steal an election that he had won. The black population was now aware that, yet again, it had not been taken into account. There had been riots. Under Florida law, anyone with a criminal record—having been convicted of a felony—loses all civil rights. Thousands of blacks were so accused and denied the vote; yet most so listed were not felons or were guilty only of misdemeanors. In any case, the calculated delays persuaded two of the four dissenting judges that there was no time left to count.

Justice John Paul Stevens, a conservative whose principal interest seems to be conserving our constitutional liberties rather than the privileges of corporate America, noted in his dissent: "One thing, however, is certain. Although we may never know with complete certainty the identity of the winner of this year's presidential election, the identity of the loser is perfectly clear. It is the nation's confidence in the judge as an impartial guardian of the rule of law."

What will the next four years bring? With luck, total gridlock. The two houses of Congress are evenly split. Presidential adventurism will be at a minimum. With bad luck (and adventures), Chancellor Cheney will rule. A former Secretary of Defense, he has said that too little money now goes to the Pentagon even though last year it received 51 percent of the discretionary budget. Expect a small war or two in order to keep military appropriations flowing. There will also be tax relief for the very rich. But bad scenario or good scenario, we shall see very little of the charmingly simian George W. Bush. The military—Cheney, Powell, et al.—will be calling the tune, and the whole nation will be on constant alert, for, James Baker has already warned us, Terrorism is everywhere on the march. We cannot be too vigilant. Welcome to Asunción. Yes! We have no bananas.

The Nation
8/15 January 2001

In the end, the American presidential campaign of 2000 ostensibly (pre-fraud) came down to a matter of Character. Specifically, to the characters of two male citizens of hitherto no particular interest to the polity. But then personality is about all that our media can cope with, since the American political system, despite ever more expensive elections, sees to it that nothing of an overtly political nature may be discussed. It is true that one candidate, daringly, if briefly, suggested that since 1 percent of the population owns most of the country, as well as quite a bit of the globe elsewhere, perhaps that 1 percent ought not to pay even less tax than it currently does. This tore it. For a moment, the red flag snapped in CNN's early light, but by twilight's last gleaming, that banner was struck, and no real issue was touched on again.

What then is a real issue? Currently, the United States spends twenty-two times as much as our potential enemies (the seven designated rogue states of concern) spend combined. It used to be that true politics involved an accounting of where the people's tax money goes and why. Since the American military currently gets over half of each year's federal revenue, that should have been the most important subject to chat about. But not this year, and so, dutifully, each candidate pledged himself to ever greater spending for the Great War Machine, as it idly trawls about the globe in search of enemies, leaving us with nothing to chatter about except Character. With *moral* character. Or, as Dr. Elaine May once put it so well: "I like a moral problem so much better than a real problem."

Although one candidate was immediately perceived to be something of a dope—and dyslexic to boot (defense: it's not *his* fault, so why are you picking on him?), there are, we were sternly told, worse things in a President. Like what? *Like lying.* When this bunch of garlic was hoisted high, a shudder went through us peasants in our Transylvanian villages as we heard, across haunted moors, the sound of great leathern wings. The undead were aloft.

One candidate was deemed a liar because he exaggerated. He never actually said that he alone had invented the Internet, but he implied that he might have had more to do with its early inception than he had. Worse, he said that his mother-in-law's medicine cost more than his dog's identical medicine, when he had—I've already forgotten which—either no mother-in-law or no dog. By now the Republic was reeling. The vileness of it all! Could we entrust so false a figure to hold in his hand war's arrows, peace's laurel? All in all, the two to three billion dollars that the election cost the generous 1 percent through its corporate paymasters was, by all reckoning, the most profoundly irrelevant in a political history which seems determined to make a monkey of Darwin while exalting the creationist point of view, Manichaean version.

Today's sermon is from Montaigne: "Lying is an accursed vice. It is only our words which bind us together and make us human. If we realized the horror and weight of lying, we would see that it is more worthy of the stake than other crimes. . . . Once let the tongue acquire the habit of lying and it is astonishing how impossible it is to make it give it up."

But our subject is not the people, those quadrennial spear-carriers, but the two paladins, one of whom will presently be entrusted with the terrible swift nuclear sword, thus becoming the greatest goodest nation that ever was robustly incarnate.

"We are a nation based on Truth," the Republican managers of the impeachment of sex-fibber President Clinton constantly reminded us, unaware that his constituents were, perversely, rallying round him. Pleased, no doubt, by the metaphysics of his "What is *is*?" After all, what is truth, as a Roman bureaucrat once rather absently put it. Yet . . .

"Yet" is the nicest of words in English when logically, non-pregnantly used. The American global empire rests on a number of breathtaking presidential lies that our court historians seldom dare question. It would seem that the Hitler team got it about right when it comes to human credulity: the greater the lie, the more apt it is to be believed. The price of the perhaps nonexistent dog's medicine is not going to go unchallenged, but President Franklin Delano Roosevelt's deliberate provocation of the Japanese, in order to force them into attacking us and thus bring us into the Second World War, is simply not admissible. Contemporary journalism's first law, "What ought not to be true is not true," is swiftly backed up by those who write the "history" stories to be used in schools. Happily, I have lived long enough to indulge in the four most beautiful words in the English language: "I told you so."

In *Burr* (1973), I relit, as it were, the image of that demonized figure, Aaron Burr. In passing, I duly noted that his chief demonizer, the admirable-in-most-things, save a tendency toward hypocrisy, Thomas Jefferson, had lived connubially with a slave girl, Sally Hemings, by whom he had a number of children, kept on as slaves. Dumas Malone, the leading Jefferson biographer of the day, denounced my portrait of Jefferson as "subversive," because, as he put it, no gentleman could have had sexual relations with a slave and, since Mr. Jefferson was the greatest gentleman of that era, he could not have . . . On such false syllogisms are national myths set. Recent testing shows that many of Hemings's descendants contain the golden DNA of Jefferson himself. Loyalists say that it was an idiot nephew who fathered Sally's children. How? Since Jefferson and Sally lived pretty much as man and wife at Monticello, the idea of the nephew, banjo in hand, making his way up the hill to the house, time and again, to get laid by Jefferson's companion boggles the mind. So much for a great lie that court historians and other propagandists insist that Americans believe. Why is it so grimly important? Since the relationship between black and white is still the most delicate of subjects for Americans, Jefferson must be marble-pure and so outside his own great formulation and invitation to the peoples of all the world: the pursuit of happiness.

That was yesterday. Today, any scrutiny of the three powerful myths which Americans and their helpers in other lands are obliged to accept will set off fire alarms. In *The Golden Age* (largely covering the years 1940–50 as viewed from Washington, D.C., by our rulers), I make three cases involving presidential whoppers. One, Franklin Delano Roosevelt (whose domestic policies—the New Deal—I admire) deliberately provoked the Japanese into attacking us at Pearl Harbor. Why? As of 1940, he wanted us in the war against Hitler, but 80 percent of the American people wanted no European war of any kind after the disappointments of 1917. He could do nothing to budge an isolationist electorate. Luckily for him (and perhaps the world), Japan had a military agreement with Germany and Italy. For several years, Japan had been engaged in an imperial mission to conquer China. Secretly, FDR began a series of provocations to goad the Japanese into what turned out to be an attack on our fleet at Pearl Harbor, thus making inevitable our prompt, wholehearted entry into the Second World War. There is a vast literature on this subject, beginning as early as 1941 with Charles A. Beard's *President Roosevelt and the Coming of War* and continuing to the current *Day of Deceit* by Robert B. Stinnett, now being argued about in the U.S. Stinnett gives the most detailed account of the steps toward war initiated by FDR, including the November 26, 1941, ultimatum to Japan, ordering them out of China while insisting they renounce their pact with the Axis powers; this left Japan with no alternative but war, the object of the exercise.

The second great myth was that Harry Truman, FDR's successor, dropped his two atom bombs on Hiroshima and Nagasaki because he feared that a million American lives would be lost in an invasion (that was the lie he told at the time). Admiral Nimitz, on the spot in the Pacific, and General Eisenhower, brooding elsewhere, disagreed: the Japanese had already lost the war, they said. No nuclear bombs, no invasion was needed; besides, the Japanese had been trying to surrender since the May 1945 devastation of Tokyo by U.S. B-29 bombers.

The third great myth was that the Soviets began the Cold War because, driven by the power-mad would-be world conqueror, Stalin, they divided Germany, forcing us to create the West German republic, and then, when Stalin viciously denied us access to our section of Berlin (still under four-power rule as determined at Yalta), we defied him with an airlift. He backed down, foiled in his invasion of France, his crossing of the Atlantic, and so on.

These are three very great myths which most historians of the period knew to be myths but which court historians, particularly those with salaries that are paid by universities with federal grants for research and development, either play down or flatly deny.

David Hume tells us that the Many are kept in order by the Few through Opinion. *The New York Times* in the U.S. is the Opinion-maker of the Few for some of the Many; so when the paper draws the line, as it were, other papers in other lands take heed and toe it. In *The Golden Age*, I revealed, tactfully I thought, life in Washington during the decade from the fall of France to Pearl Harbor to the Cold War and Korea. No one needs to know any history at all to follow the story. Even so, one American reviewer was upset that I did not know how "dumbed-down" (his phrase) Americans were, and how dare I mention people that they had never heard of, such as Harry Hopkins?

But I am a fairly experienced narrator, and each character is, painlessly I hope, explained in context. Unfortunately, the new pop wisdom is that you must only write about what the readers already know about, which, in this case at least, would be an untrue story.

The New York Times hired a British journalist, once associated with *The New Republic*, a far-right paper unfavorable to me (it is a propagandist for Israel's Likudite faction, much as *The Washington Times* supports the line of its proprietor, Korea's Dr. Sun Moon). The hired journalist knew nothing of the period I was writing about. He quotes an aria from Herbert Hoover which he thinks I made up, when, as always with the historical figures that I quote, I only record what they are said to have said.

Hoover regarded, rightly or wrongly, FDR as in the same totalitarian mold as he saw Hitler, Mussolini, and Stalin: "You cannot extend the mastery of the government over the daily working life of a people without at the same time making it the master of the people's souls and thoughts." Our best modern historian, William Appleman Williams, in *Some Presidents: Wilson to Nixon* (1972), noted that it was Hoover's intuition that, in the first third of the twentieth century, the virus of totalitarian government was abroad in the world, and that Hitler in his demonic way and Stalin in his deadly bureaucratic way and FDR in his relatively melioristic way were each responding to a common Zeitgeist.

For a right-wing hired hand this should have been a profound analysis, but the reviewer fails to grasp it. He also ignores Hoover's astonishing aside: "What this country needs is a great poem." Most damaging to the integrity of my narrative (and the historians I relied on), the reviewer declares, without evidence, that . . . But let me quote from a letter by the historian Kai Bird which, to my amazement, *The New York Times* published (usually they suppress anything too critical of themselves or their Opinion-makers):

> Twice the reviewer dismisses as "silly" Vidal's assertion that Harry Truman's use of the atomic bomb on Hiroshima was unnecessary because Japan had been trying for some months to surrender.
>
>   Such assertions are neither silly nor . . . a product of Vidal's "cranky politics." Rather Vidal has cleverly drawn on a rich and scholarly literature published in the last decade to remind his readers that much of what orthodox court historians have written about the Cold War was simply wrong. With regard to Hiroshima, perhaps Vidal had in mind Truman's July 18, 1945, handwritten diary reference to a "telegram from Jap emperor asking for peace."

Or this August 3, 1945, item from the diary of Walter Brown:

> Brown notes a meeting with Secretary of State James F.
> Byrnes, Admiral W. D. Leahy, and Truman at which all
> three agreed, "Japs looking for peace." . . . But Truman
> wanted to drop the bomb; and did. Why? To frighten
> Stalin, a suitable enemy for the U.S. as it was about to
> metamorphose from an untidy republic into a national
> security state at "perpetual war," in Charles A. Beard's
> phrase, "for perpetual peace."

I fear that the *TLS* review of *The Golden Age* battened on the inaccuracies of the *New York Times* review; your reviewer is plainly an
American neoconservative who enjoys crude reversals of categories.
The American hard Right has no known interest in the people
at large, and a reverence for the 1 percent that pays for their journals
and think tanks. He refers to my "universally contemptuous Left-
ism" which involves "sneering in its disregard for 'the lower
orders . . . the rather shadowy American people.' " This is the oldest
trick in bad book-reviewing. A novelist writes: " 'I hate America,'
shrieked the Communist spy." This will become, for the dishonest
book-reviewer, "At one point, the author even confesses that he hates
America." But I know of no "Leftist" (define) who sneers at the
people, while no populist could. Rather I concentrate on what has
been done to the people by the 1 percent through its mastery of the
national wealth and made-in-the-house, as it were, Opinion. Your
reviewer even misunderstands my own sharp conclusion that an era
ended, happily in my view, when the traditional American servant
class ceased to exist, thanks to the 13 million of us in the armed services and the full employment of women in the Second World War.
That some of my sillier grandees mourn this state of affairs is a part
of the social comedy of the narrative, admittedly not of quite so high
an order as the inadvertent comedy of Rightists affecting unrequited
passion for Demos.

The final myth is that Stalin started the Cold War by dividing

Germany into two sections, while trying to drive us out of our sector of Berlin. I'll quote the best authority, thus far, on what Truman was up to after Potsdam when he met Stalin, who, after Yalta, had expected to live in some sort of reasonable balance with the U.S. Here is Carolyn Eisenberg in *Drawing the Line: The American Decision to Divide Germany, 1944–1949* (1996):

> With the inception of the Berlin blockade, President Truman articulated a simple story that featured the Russians trampling the wartime agreements in their ruthless grab for the former German capital. The President did not explain that the United States had [unilaterally—my adverb] abandoned Yalta and Potsdam, that it was pushing the formation of a Western German state against the misgivings of many Europeans and that the Soviets had launched the blockade to prevent partition.

This great lie remains with us today. Please no letters about the horrors of the Gulag, Stalin's mistreatment of the buffer states, and so on. Our subject is the serious distortions of the truth on our side and why, unless they are straightened out, we are forever doomed to thrash about in a permanent uncomprehending fog. Good morning, Vietnam!

The attitude towards truth on the part of Truman's administration was best expressed by his Secretary of State, Dean Acheson, in the memoir *Present at the Creation: My Years in the State Department* (1969). It was Acheson who launched the global empire on February 27, 1947. Place: Cabinet Room of the White House. Present: Truman, Secretary of State Marshall, Under Secretary Acheson, a half-dozen Congressional leaders. The British had, yet again, run out of money. They could not honor their agreements to keep Greece tethered to freedom. Could we take over? Although Stalin had warned the Greek Communists that their country was in the U.S. sphere and they should therefore expect no aid from him, Truman wanted a military buildup. We had to stand tall. But Marshall failed to convince the Congressional leaders. Acheson, a superb corporate lawyer and a most witty man, leaped into the breach. He was impassioned. The free world stood at the brink. Yes, at Armageddon. Should the Russians occupy Greece and then Turkey, three continents would be at risk. He used the evergreen homely metaphor of how one rotten apple in a barrel could . . . Finally, were we not the heirs of the Roman Empire? Was not the Soviet Union our Carthage? Had not our Punic Wars begun? We dared not lose. "America has no choice. We must act now to protect our security . . . to protect freedom itself." It was then agreed that if Truman addressed the country in these terms and scared the hell out of the American people, Congress would finance what has turned out to be a half-century of Cold War, costing, thus far, some $7.1 trillion.

In retrospect, Acheson wrote, cheerfully, "If we did make our points clearer than truth, we did not differ from most other educators and could hardly do otherwise." After all, as he noted, it was the State Department's view that the average American spent no more than ten minutes a day brooding on foreign policy; he spends less now that television advertising can make anything clearer than truth.

Today, we are not so much at the brink as fallen over it. Happily, as of this election, we were not at our old stamping ground, Armageddon. Rather, we were simply fretting about fibs involving drunken driving and the true cost of that mother-in-law's medicine as opposed to the pampered dog's, when, had the candidate been true to his roots, he could have found, in a back alley of Carthage, Tennessee, two pinches of cheap sulphur that would have dewormed both mother-in-law and dog in a jiffy.*

The Times Literary Supplement
10 November 2000

---

* It should be remembered that J. Q. Adams complained of Thomas Jefferson's "large stories." Example? Jefferson claimed to have learned Spanish in nineteen days aboard a transatlantic ship.

JAPANESE INTENTIONS IN THE SECOND WORLD WAR

Sir,—I am in Clive James's debt for the succinct way that he has assembled what must be at least 90 percent of all the Received Opinion having to do with the start and finish of the American–Japanese war of 1941–45 (Letters, November 24). Were it not for occasional Jacobean resonances, one might suspect that Dr. Barry Humphries had been working overtime in his bat-hung lab, assembling yet another Australian monster: a retired Lt. Col. with a powerful worldview fueled by the tabloid press of Oz.

James begins briskly: Vidal has an "admonitory vision" to the effect that the "leadership class" of the American empire thinks "that Washington is the center of the world. Unfortunately, Vidal seems to think the same."

Indeed they do. Indeed I do. Indeed, Washington has been the uncontested global center for most of the twentieth century, which I tend to deplore—Washington's primacy, that is. In a recent book, *The Golden Age,* I concentrate on the decade 1940–50 when the New World gave birth to the global arrangement.

I start with the convergence on Washington of more than 3,000 British agents, propagandists, spies. Yes, I was there. At the heart of an isolationist family that "entertained," as they used to say, everyone, I personally observed the brilliant John Foster in action. Foster was attached to Lord Lothian's British Embassy. He enchanted the Washingtonians while secretly working with Ben Cohen, a White House lawyer, to draft the Lend-Lease agreement which proved to be the first blow that President Roosevelt was able to strike for England. Residents of that other center, Canberra, no doubt have a different tale to tell.

I make the hardly original case that Franklin Roosevelt pro-voked the Japanese into attacking us for reasons that I shall come to presently.

James, armed to the teeth with Received Opinion (henceforth RO), tells us that Japan was provoked into war by the Japanese Army, "which had been in a position to blackmail the Cabinet since 1922 and never ceased to do so until surrender in 1945," brought on, as RO has it, by gallant Harry Truman's decision to drop a pair of atomic bombs. None of this conforms to what we have known for some time about the internal workings of Japan's intricate system of governance, not to mention our own. There was indeed a gung-ho Japanese military war party that was busy trying to conquer as much of China as possible en route to South-East Asia where the oil was. There was also a peace party, headed by Prince Konoye, who was ea-ger, as of August 1941, to meet with FDR, who kept postponing a face-to-face discussion to sort out differences. Had FDR been inter-ested in peace in the Pacific, he could have met with Konoye, much as he was secretly meeting with Churchill on a soon-to-be-related matter.

James correctly notes that we had broken Japan's diplomatic code, Purple, but he seems unaware that, by early October 1940, we had also broken many of the Japanese military codes, specifically parts of the Kaigun Ango: the twenty-nine separate naval codes which gave us a good idea of what their fleet was up to during the entire year before Pearl Harbor. RO assures James that, if FDR wanted war, he would not have sent the Emperor, on December 6, a cable whose only message seemed to be a wistful hope that the Japanese would not try to replace the defeated French in Indo-China. James seems ignorant of the context of that message.

Here it is. On Saturday, November 15, 1941, General Marshall, the U.S. Army Chief of Staff, called in various Washington news-paper bureau chiefs. After swearing them to secrecy, he told them that we had broken Japan's naval codes, and that war with Japan would start sometime during the first ten days of December. On November 26, Cordell Hull, FDR's Secretary of State, presented Japan's two special envoys to Washington with a ten-point proposal, intended, as Hull told Secretary of War Stimson, "to kick the whole thing over." Of FDR's ultimatum, Hull later remarked, "We [had] no serious thought Japan would accept. . . ." What was the proposal? Complete Japanese withdrawal from China and Indo-China, Japan to support China's Nationalist Government and to abandon the tripartite agreement with the Axis. FDR had dropped a shoe. Now he waited for the Japanese to drop the other. They did. RO has it that we were taken by surprise. Certainly, FDR was not. But apparently the unwarned military commanders at Pearl Harbor were, and 3,000 men were killed in a single strike.

RO always had a difficult time with motive. Since FDR could never, ever, have set us up, why would the Japanese want to attack a wealthy continental nation 4,000 miles away? Fortunately, RO can always fall back on the demonic view of history. As a race, the Japanese were prone to suicide. Hardly human, they were a bestial people whose eyes were so configured that they could never handle modern aircraft or bombsights. As a young soldier in the Pacific, I was, along with everyone else, marinated in this racist nonsense. But should this demonic reading of the Japanese character not be true, one must wonder why the Japanese military, with a difficult war of conquest in China that was using up their wealth and energy in every sense, would want to provoke a war with the United States so far away? RO has had sixty years to come up with an answer; and failed to do so.

Today, no one seriously contests that FDR wanted the U.S. in the war against Hitler. But 60 to 80 percent of the American people were solidly against any European war. In November 1940, FDR had been elected to a third term with the pledge that none of America's sons would ever fight in a foreign war "unless attacked." Privately, more than once, he had said to others that the Japs must strike the first blow or, as he put it to Admiral James O. Richardson (October 8, 1940), "as the war continued and the area of operations expanded, sooner or later they would make a mistake and we would enter the war"; hence, FDR's series of provocations culminating not in a Japanese "mistake" but in the ultimatum of November 26 that left the Japanese with no alternative but war, preferably with a "sneak" knockout attack of the sort that had succeeded so well against Russia in 1904, at Port Arthur. Did FDR know that the Japanese would attack Pearl Harbor, where much of our Pacific fleet was at anchor? Or did he think they would strike at some lesser venue like Manila? This matter is, yet again, under scrutiny.

James's RO is correct when he notes that the German-Italian-Japanese tripartite agreement was of a defensive nature. They were not obliged to join in each other's offensive wars. Why Hitler declared war upon the U.S. is still a "puzzle," according to no less a historian than Dr. Henry Kissinger, not a bad historian when not obliged to gaze into a mirror (cf. his *Diplomacy*).

At war at least in the Pacific, how could FDR be so sure that he would get his war in Europe? Well, FDR is easily the most intricate statesman of our time: as Nixon once said admiringly of Eisenhower, "He was a far more sly and devious man than most people suspected, and I mean those words in their very best sense."

Once the U.S. was wholeheartedly at war on December 8, 1941, our artful dodger could, under wartime powers, aid Britain and the Soviets, as he was already doing with Lend-Lease and other virtuous if quasi-legal measures. Also, FDR's problem with his election pledge ceased to exist when the Japanese responded so fiercely to his provocations and ultimatums. As usual, he got what he wanted.

Received Opinion: without Truman's pair of atom bombs, the famous Japanese war party that had seized control of the government would have ordered a million Japanese to jump off cliffs onto the invading Americans had not the Emperor, distressed by the bombs, etc. . . . Let us turn from comfortable RO to Authority, to Ambassador Joseph C. Grew's memoir, *Turbulent Era: A diplomatic record of forty years, 1904–1945*. As U.S. Ambassador to Japan, Grew was dedicated to bringing together FDR and Prince Konoye, little suspecting that, where Konoye was apparently sincere in wanting peace, FDR was not. By autumn 1941, Grew was exasperated by Washington's unrelenting line that the Japanese government was completely dominated by the military war party:

> We in Tokyo were closer to the scene than was the Administration in Washington and we believed, on the basis of the highest possible intelligence, and so reported, that the Japanese government at the time was in a position to control the armed forces of the country. We explained in several of our telegrams to our Government that Germany's attack on Soviet Russia had given those elements in Japan which controlled national policies further and convincing evidence that confidence could not be placed in Germany's promises. . . . No one, I think, would contest the view that the Japanese government was in a far better position to control its forces in the summer of 1941 than it was in December 1938. . . .

The problem with RO, even when served up by so sensitive a writer as Clive James, is that contrary evidence must not be admitted. RO still clings to the myth that Japan would have fought to the end if Truman had not dropped his A-bombs. But Japanese envoys had been making overtures for a year in, variously, Sweden, Switzerland, Portugal, the Vatican, etc. Message: the war is over if the Emperor is retained.

Finally, the most important Japanese player, as I noted in my piece (November 10), the Emperor himself, on July 18, 1945, wrote Truman a letter "looking for peace" (Truman's words). On August 3, 1945, an official's diary notes that Truman, Byrnes, and Leahy were discussing a telegram "from the Emperor asking for peace." Truman, inspired, some believe, by Secretary of State Byrnes, wanted to intimidate the Soviets with our super-weapon. So he had his two big bangs, contrary to the advice of his chief military commanders. Here is Eisenhower: "I had been conscious of a feeling of depression and so I voiced to [Secretary of War Henry L. Stimson] my grave misgivings. . . . I thought that our country should avoid shocking world opinion by the use of a weapon whose employment was, I thought, no longer mandatory as a measure to save American lives."

FDR, like so many Americans of his generation, found irresistible the phrase "unconditional surrender"—General U. S. Grant's adamantine message to the Confederacy. FDR applied it to the Axis powers. Truman inherited this policy. Then, once he had dropped his bombs, he promptly abandoned unconditional surrender and kept the Emperor. For Clive of Canberra, I recommend the latest, if not last, word on the subject, *The Decision To Use the Bomb and the Architecture of an American Myth* by Gar Alperovitz. For the why and what of Pearl Harbor, there is now R. B. Stinnett's *Day of Deceit*, soon to be a subject of strenuous debate in another journal.

Again, how could FDR have known Hitler would declare war on us after Pearl Harbor? James's RO provides him with no sensible motive. So he falls back on the demonic—"megalomania" which drove Hitler to ensure that he would be at war on every side. But this won't do. Hitler was certainly subject to fits of inspiration, but he was usually very cautious in his dealings with the "mongrel" Americans. In his December 11 declaration of war to the Reichstag, he gave a seemingly rational if odd reason. On December 4, at the President's request, General Marshall had presented FDR with a war plan in which he proposed that, as Hitler was the principal enemy of the U.S. and the world, the United States should raise an expeditionary force of 5 million men and send it to invade Germany by July 1, 1943. The plan—one hopes of no more than a contingency nature—was leaked onto the front page of the *Chicago Tribune*, the great trumpet of isolationism. The headline, "F.D.R.'S WAR PLANS!" Three days later, Pearl Harbor erased the story, but Hitler had seen it and mentioned it as "proof" of FDR's predatory designs on the Axis, noting (more in sorrow than in anger?), "Without any attempt at an official denial on the part of the American Government, President Roosevelt's plan has been published under which Germany and Italy are to be attacked with military force in Europe by 1943 at the latest." (This is from *A World to Gain* by Thomas Toughill, an intriguing amateur sleuth.)

Finally, for an analysis of the persisting myth about the dropping of the A-bombs, Mr. Alperovitz is hearteningly shrewd.

The Times Literary Supplement
1 December 2000

Sir,—When Kenneth Tynan came to New York to practice his trade as drama critic, he had only recently become a Marxist. Brecht had had something to do with it, and I think he may have read some of Marx. Certainly he often quoted him, usually at midpoint during one of our late evenings at the Mayfair workers' canteen, Mirabelle. "Money should not breed money," Ken would stammer. Upon arrival in New York, he began to evangelize. I watched him with an ancient *Partisan Review* editor, a former Stalinist, Trotskyite, Reichian. Fiercely, Ken told him what it was that money must never do. When Ken had run out of breath, the weary old class warrior said, "Mr. Tynan, your arguments are so old that I have forgotten all the answers to them."

The estimable Clive James (Letters, December 8) is in a time warp similar to Ken's. Thirty years of incremental information about the American-Japanese war have passed him by. He thinks "the real [Japanese] fleet sent no radio messages" en route to Pearl Harbor: that "was long ago invalidated." No. What has been invalidated is the myth that the Japanese kept complete radio silence. In 1993 and 1995 (under the Freedom of Information Act), all sorts of transcripts came to light, as well as Communication Intelligence Summaries such as this one for December 6, 1941, where an American code-breaker reported: "The Commander in Chief Combined (Japanese) Fleet originated several messages to Carriers, Fourth Fleet and the Major Commanders." Each headed towards Hawaii and interacting. Although there is some evidence that James has kept up with the latest Hirohito books (Chrysanthemum Porn, as we call it in the trade), he has no interest in political revelations. I do. But then I spent five years researching *The Golden Age*, trying to figure out what actually happened at Pearl Harbor, and why the A-bombs were dropped *after* Japan was ready to surrender, and why . . . I shall not repeat myself, but I must note, in passing, the purity of a certain mid-twentieth-century journalistic style that continues to reverberate like the beat beat beat of the tom-tom in Clive of Canberra's burnished prose. Ingredients? High Moral Indignation, no matter how hoked up, linked to *ad hominem* zingers from right field. I referred to the leader of the peace party at the Japanese court, Prince Konoye. I was interested in his proposals. Our period journalist is interested in Konoye as an anti-Semite who faked his own suicide note. Is it possible that I have misjudged Konoye's dedication to peace? Was he also, like so many Japanese princes, an adulterer? If so, was that the reason FDR refused to meet him at Juneau, an Alaskan beauty spot that is, in summer, a breeding ground for the largest mosquitoes in North America? FDR's sense of fun seldom abandoned him. In any case, for whatever reason, after suggesting a comical venue, FDR backed down. Peace in the Pacific was not his dream.

Next, Charles Lindbergh, my "other questionable hero," is dragged in, so that we can be told, with righteous anger, how "his isolationism was *de facto* an instrument of Axis policy." Surely James the Latinist means *ad hoc* in a sentence admittedly quite as meaningless as that tom-tom pounding you you you. He does admit that "Lindbergh did loyal service [in the war] and even shot down a Japanese plane but [one] can't help wondering about the American planes he shot down with his mouth"; moral outrage is now in high gear—pass me the sick bag, Alice, or whatever that splendid gel was called. In real life, Lindbergh was sent by FDR to take a look at the German air force and plane production. Lindbergh was sufficiently alarmed by what he saw to urge increased American production of aircraft for war, particularly the B-17. He was, of course, an isolationist, and so was reflective of a majority of the American people before Pearl Harbor.

Then, alas, we hear that "Ambassador Joseph Grew, alas, won't do for a hero either." Plainly my world contained no heroes. Although Grew was much admired for his brilliance and probity by those of us who had relations with him, the great Canberra moralist tells us that he was worse than an anti-Semite, he was a snob. Could it be that this terrible flaw in his character encouraged the war party in Tokyo to attack the United States? But Mr. James—again alas— never connects his enticing dots. Actually, Grew's problem as a diplomat was that he tried to maintain the peace between Japan and the U.S., when his President had other plans which involved maneuvering the Japanese into striking the first blow so that we could go to war. But then James always dodges the great unanswered question: unless provoked by us, *why did the Japanese attack?* He waffles a bit about their desire for "unopposed expansion." To where? Chicago?

Finally, a rhetorical question to me. If I had been told in 1945 that we had a weapon "so devastating that it could end that . . . war in a week," what would I have said? Well, none of us was consulted. But we were, most of us, highly in favor of using the Bomb. On the other hand, had we been told that the war could have been concluded as of May 1945, I would have gone to work for the impeachment of a President who had wasted so many lives and destroyed so many cities in his power game with the Soviet Union which led, inexorably, to a half-century of unnecessary Cold War. I am also bemused that a witness so all-knowing, if not knowledgeable, as Clive James, still doesn't understand what happened to him, to all of us, for most of our lives.

The Times Literary Supplement
15 December 2000

GORE VIDAL'S AMERICAN CHRONICLE SERIES

BURR

Alternating the story of journalist Charles Schermerhorn Schuyler with the Revolutionary War diaries of Aaron Burr, this novel begins Vidal's history of the United States on a note of intrigue and scandal.

Fiction/Literature/0-375-70873-1

1876

The centennial of the nation's founding is the occasion for Vidal to bring back the narrator of *Burr*, Charlie Schuyler, and reintroduce his family line as a force in the history of the nation.

Fiction/Literature/0-375-70872-3

EMPIRE

The rise of the powerful American press—represented by William Randolph Hearst and Caroline Sanford (Charlie Schuyler's granddaughter)—continue the transformation of the empire.

Fiction/Literature/0-375-70874-X

HOLLYWOOD

The future movie capital of the world and the country's capital begin their long and checkered relationship as Vidal continues his saga into the first decade of the new century.

Fiction/Literature/0-375-70875-8

WASHINGTON, D.C.

Set in the period surrounding World War II and FDR's presidency, *Washington, D.C.* centers around the ambitions of a young John Kennedy-like politician.

Fiction/Literature/0-375-70877-1

THE GOLDEN AGE

The Golden Age is a vibrant tapestry of American political and cultural life from the years 1939 to 1954, when the epochal events of World War II and the Cold War transformed America.

Fiction/Literature/0-375-72481-8

ALSO AVAILABLE: *Lincoln*, 0-375-70876-6

Available at your local bookstore, or call toll-free to order:
1-800-793-2665 (credit cards only).